# PRAISE FOR
## *MOTHERING THE NEW MOTHER*
••••••

"Sally Placksin's book has what needy, weary new mothers need most—generous doses of understanding, sympathy, concrete advice, resources, support and assurance that they're not alone. Best of all, it's infused with the voices of real people negotiating their way through the enormous transition to motherhood. I wish I'd had it to read when I was a new mom."
—Roberta Israeloff, author of
*Coming to Terms* and *In Confidence: Four Years of Psychotherapy*

"A terrific and much needed job focusing on the postpartum needs of new mothers. I see too many of them in tears . . . a bestseller for new families."
—Christine Kealy, founder,
In a Family Way Postpartum Care Service

"This book is an empowering tool for mothers in a society where birth procedures are sometimes disempowering and motherhood is undervalued. This book is very childbearing useful for an expectant mother, partner, grandmother, or any caregiver to the family."
—*Journal of Human Lactation*

"*Mothering the New Mother* addresses a sadly overlooked area of need in the United States—the postpartum period. . . . Sally Placksin tackled this void and filled it admirably with clear information on what to expect; what needs, feelings, and changes may occur; and what to do to meet the needs of this period in a woman's and a family's life. . . . The book explores another important aspect of this period for women: recognition of the continuing adjustment and changes of lifestyle, roles, and relationships, and how to integrate motherhood into the complexity of their lives, their sense of identity, and their work. Women's stories, voices, and struggles are strong, vibrant, poignant, and realistic throughout the book and will touch almost any woman facing motherhood. . . . This event of parenthood has to be honored, validated, and prepared for with this excellent resource book as a guide."
—Phyllis H. Klaus, C.S.W., M.F.C.C., Erickson Institute
*Birth: Issues in Prenatal Care*

"The book everyone should have when they become a mom, especially for the first time. It touches on all aspects of life a woman is called on to handle or confront in the complex transition to motherhood, including the range of postpartum feelings, the first weeks at home, creating a support network, and going back to work. . . . Real women's voices are heard throughout the book talking about how they feel, rather than how they are supposed to feel . . . a wealth of resources."

—*Work and Family Life*

"*Mothering the New Mother* draws from the experiences of more than one hundred new mothers, doctors, and other caregivers, who offer information and encouragement. Each chapter includes suggestions and hands-on solutions from caregivers, policy makers, and new mothers. Checklists and planning sheets let mothers create individualized postpartum plans. Also included is information on newsletters, hotlines, support groups, and services."

—International Childbirth Education Association

"On my required reading list for the postpartum doula training course that I offer. . . . A valuable resource for both the new mothers and the doulas who work with them."

—Betsy Schwartz, C.P.D. (NAPCS), C.D. (DONA), Executive Director, National Association of Postpartum Care Services

"*Mothering* begins with a historical background of, and other cultures' approaches to, caring for mothers while they care for their newborn. Placksin also stresses why breastfeeding (not to mention getting support to do so) is best, and she covers the controversial subject of postpartum depression (PPD). There's a separate chapter for second-time moms. Thorough, well-written, and very much needed."

—Jo Peer-Haas, *Booklist* (American Library Association)

"Despite the myriad guides to pregnancy and birth, not to mention the plethora of books (and opinions) on childcare, few works address the needs of the new mother during the first twelve months of her child's life. *Mothering the New Mother* is designed to fill that gap, offering ideas, resources, and support to help the mother through this exciting, challenging, and often confusing period of increasing isolation in our culture."

—*Ways of Caring*, published by La Leche League International

# MOTHERING

## the NEW MOTHER

*Women's Feelings and Needs*
*After Childbirth*

### A SUPPORT AND RESOURCE GUIDE

......

#### SECOND EDITION

## SALLY PLACKSIN

*wm*

**WILLIAM MORROW**
*An Imprint of HarperCollinsPublishers*

*For my mother,*
*Edith Chochlow Placksin*
*(1905-1993),*
*and for*
*Gabriel and Sarah*

• • • • • •

MOTHERING THE NEW MOTHER (SECOND EDITION). Copyright © 1994, 2000 by Sally Placksin.
All rights reserved. Printed in the United States of America. No part of this book may be used or reproduced in any manner whatsoever without written permission except in the case of brief quotations embodied in critical articles and reviews.
For information, address HarperCollins Publishers,
195 Broadway, New York, NY 10007.

HarperCollins books may be purchased for educational, business, or sales promotional use. For information, please e-mail the Special Markets Department at SPsales@harpercollins.com.

First published by Newmarket Press in 1994
as *Mothering the New Mother: Your Postpartum Resource Companion.*

FIRST WILLIAM MORROW PAPERBACK EDITION PUBLISHED 2012.

Library of Congress Cataloging-in-Publication Data
Placksin, Sally.
Mothering the new mother: women's feelings and needs after childbirth:
a support and resource guide/Sally Placksin.—Rev. and updated ed.
p. cm.
1. Mothers. 2. Infants (Newborn)—Care.
3. Postpartum depression. 4. Mothers—Employment.
I. Title.
HQ759.P56     1998
306.874'3—dc21          98-9194
CIP
ISBN 978-1-55704-317-7 (pbk.)

18  19  RRD  11

# Contents

• • • • • •

Contents • ix

# Acknowledgments

······

When you write a book, as when you have a baby, there are always those people who prove particularly helpful—those who nurture, inform, and care for the writer just as a sensitive doula or support team nurtures the new mother. Some help with the work itself; others help manage the far-ranging, diverse aspects of your life so that the work may continue; some help by bestowing the broader gifts of friendship through good times and bad.

As this work progressed from radio program to finished book, many people played important roles. Thanks to Donna Limerick, Senior Producer of the Horizons series of National Public Radio (NPR), for giving me the opportunity to produce the radio show from which this project grew; to Dale Hardman for helping to steer the book to a proper home; to Peter Elek for overseeing with alacrity and enthusiasm all the details that agents oversee so that writers may write; to Keith Hollaman and Esther Margolis of Newmarket Press for believing in and supporting this work.

What gave the book life, of course, were the voices of the mothers themselves. I had the privilege of talking to or surveying close to a hundred women throughout the United States and Canada. All of them were willing to share their most intimate stories and feelings about new motherhood with me. Some chose to include their real names in the book; others preferred anonymity. I owe a special debt of gratitude to all of these women, who answered questionnaires or gave of their time and truth over the telephone.

My thanks also to the many people who shared information on legislation, work-family issues, in-home doula care, postpartum depression, breastfeeding, and the other subjects covered in this book. It would be impossible to acknowledge them all personally here, but they all have my gratitude.

A number of women generously shared knowledge, encouragement, enthusiasm, and insight with me many times over throughout the years that I worked on this book. They and their work were a source of constant and profound inspiration: Jane Honikman, Joyce A. Venis, Jeanne

Driscoll, Anna Werner, Luz García, Honey Watts, Helen Norton, Joan Singer, Sharon Triolo-Moloney, Kathleen Christensen, Norma Swenson, Jane Arnold, Dana Raphael, Lisa Sementilli-Dann, Debra Pascali, Naima Major, and JoAnne Brundage.

For readings as the work progressed, I am grateful to Cheryl Sternbach, Kathleen Berkowe, Barbara Perry Morgan, Joyce A. Venis, and Anna Werner.

A number of other people who helped in all manner of ways also have my appreciation: Jeri Robinson of the Early Childhood Program at the Children's Museum in Boston, Paul Deane of Family Resource Coalition, Gracemarie Farrell of Newmarket Press, Congressional Aide Susan Mason-Morrisey and others in the offices of Representative Patricia Schroeder, Daniel Goodwin, Bernice R. Berk, Ashraf Tymosz at UNICEF, Beverly Solow, Andrea Geyer, Barbara and Lee Morgan, Dylan Morgan, Kathleen and Marc Berkowe, Kate and Ted Desrosiers, Suzanne and Jack White, Martha and Eric Asendorf, Robin and Rick Kline, Henrietta and Harold Danson, Sidney Placksin, David Madee, and Laurie Kranz. I would also like to acknowledge the New York Public Library's Wertheim Study; the WGBH Fellowship Program; the Conference Board; and the National Writers' Union New York Chapter.

Writing a book is always a consuming process. So is mothering two small children. Trying to do both things simultaneously is often incendiary, like rubbing two sticks together. Like many mothers in this book, I worked in a corner of the bedroom, often around the hours of multiple school pickups and drop-offs. When worlds collided, and the book—which I came to think of as my children's five-years-in-the-making sibling—took me over, one person, Maria Fountoukis, was always available to provide our children with love, laughs, chicken soup (with rice), sprinklers in summer, snow angels in winter, games of every variety, and awesome activities. Our love and gratitude to her are immeasurable.

Also on the home front, a special acknowledgment goes to the staff of three schools which were integral parts of our lives over the past three years: Spuyten Duyvil Preschool (Ingrid, Grazia and Sheila, Carol and Marilyn, Edith and Louise, Anne and Beth), Bank Street School for Children, and Riverside Church Weekday School. All three make children and families their top priority. They nurtured our two children—and, by extension, our family—daily, through good times and hard times, and for this strong and loving foundation, we will always be grateful.

On the health frontiers, I would like to acknowledge our pediatricians, Michael D. Mitchell, M.D., P.C., and Rebecca Fisk, M.D., for always being available, always having the right answers, and finding no question too trivial for their valuable time. I would also like to acknowledge our long-time friend Howard Berk, M.D., for seeing our family through two healthy pregnancies.

Four extraordinary people have offered me many years of friendship, generosity, miscellaneous wisdom, and encouragement both general and specific; thankfully, they continued to do so throughout the writing of this book: Phyllis Gaudia, Donald Bogle, Donna Kramer, and Elizabeth Hirsch.

Finally, I extend my deepest gratitude to four people: my mother, Edith Chochlow Placksin, who believed unfalteringly in this project, and who shared with me more than one session of midnight wisdom over the telephone as we discussed aspects of the book and recollections of her own mothering experience.

My husband, Jim Luce, whose carefully blocked out "Every Second I Have to Give" charts on our refrigerator door chronicled his support and dedication to this work, despite the wild disruptions it brought to all of our lives over many years. Jim took on the role of ten doulas not only with our own two children but also during the seemingly endless pregnancy, labor, and delivery of *Mothering the New Mother*. Without his tireless and gargantuan efforts, this book literally could not have been written.

And finally, my children, Gabriel and Sarah, without whom I would know nothing about mothering. With whom, I know the best of all there is to know.

*New York City*
*December 1993*

Special gratitude to Doris Cross for her care and thoughtfulness in checking the old resources—and researching the new—for this updated edition of *Mothering the New Mother*.

*New York City*
*January 2000*

# Introduction

••••••

One morning in 1989, at my then two-year-old's playgroup, I asked the circle of mothers sitting with me if they would be willing to talk about their postpartum experiences for a book I was thinking of writing. In May 1989 I had produced a documentary for National Public Radio on the need for nurturing, mother-centered supports for new mothers and had received a good number of calls from women around the country wanting more information on a variety of postpartum services and resources—how to find them, how to start them. Given this interest, and the limitations of the thirty-minute radio format, I felt the subject could and should be expanded into book form. I tested out my idea on the mothers assembled at the playgroup.

"Do you have to have been depressed?" was the first question that came back to me.

"No," I answered. "I'm interested in everything you experienced after the baby came. What you needed, what you felt, what you learned. What kind of help you had, what worked, what didn't."

"Help?" joked one. "Who had help?"

"You can never have enough help," said another.

As we talked, their comments became more revealing.

A few women had help—relatives who came to pitch in with the cooking, laundry, night shifts, or shopping. But the pressure these new mothers had felt to entertain their "houseguests," coupled with baby visitors, phone calls, and thank-you notes, added to rather than alleviated the exhaustion.

One hired a baby nurse not for two weeks, but for four. "Then when she left, everything fell apart," she remembered. She was laughing now, but clearly her memory of that transition was a vivid one.

As I brought up specific issues, more frustration surfaced.

"I had trouble with breastfeeding," said one. "Most books make it sound easier than it is."

They enumerated problems with sleep deprivation, weepiness, mood swings, child-care arrangements, separation issues, juggling or renegotiating job leaves, and schedules.

Before we knew it, it was time to wrap up. In closing, I shared the names of several supports and resources I'd discovered to help in different, sometimes even indirect ways with this many-faceted transition to motherhood: an agency that provided nurturing, mother-centered home care for the new mom; a book that shared postpartum traditions in diverse cultures where the new mother was supported as a matter of course; a newsletter written by mothers-at-home for mothers-at-home; an organization that specialized in part-time and alternative work arrangements.

"You're kidding!" "Why didn't I know about that?" "I wish I'd heard about that two years ago." "How do you know about all this?"

Oddly, the image that popped into my head was that of the Wizard of Oz, promising courage, hearts, and brains. But these were not humbug hopes. I was not offering false panaceas. They really did exist, some more prominently, some less so on the landscape. Some were uniquely responsive to new mothers and their particular needs and vulnerability; others were not specifically designed for new mothers, but could still prove helpful to women as they navigated their way through that first year.

Clearly, many potential stressors were involved in becoming a new mother today. If, as so many women had discovered, you cannot nurture your baby unless you are being nurtured as well, who was there to mother the new mother in the 1990s? And how long did her need for this special person or team, this recognition and nurturing, continue? Did it end at the two-week mark, when so many women are told they can resume exercise and get back to "normal"? ("I don't know what normal is," said one mom. "I am forever changed by this experience.") Did it go on for six weeks, as the medical texts delineate in defining the literal physical recovery from childbirth? Or did it go beyond that, as so many women seemed to feel it did?

While many books addressed single, specific issues—working moms and breastfeeding, at-home mothers, or motherhood over thirty-five, for example—no one had looked across that first year postpartum to pull together a creative mix of resources, networks, information, and materials that could nurture, validate, and empower women as they entered into motherhood in 1990s America. No one had attempted, to my knowledge, to offer a power base or a knowledge base that touched on all the various aspects of life the new mom might be called on to handle or confront. Nor was there any cultural model for the kind of support network the new mother should have—nothing that went into action automatically, either family- or society-based. If a postpartum plan or support network existed, it was once again the mother's responsibility to start from scratch and put it all together. For many women, for many reasons, this was daunting. The resources existed—some were obvious, some more obscure—but they certainly weren't common knowledge. Most of the women in the room with me had never heard of them. Not only did many of them believe that they had to do it all alone, but even those who wanted help often did not know where to begin to look.

As I listened to my playgroup mothers that day, they confirmed my growing awareness that the complex transition to motherhood was greatly minimized, to say the least. Many of the women did not even realize that it could or should be any different. Society at large did not acknowledge this, and as a result, neither did the women themselves. There were no archetypes and no paradigms. Many of the new moms felt, for example, that unless you were seriously clinically depressed or in some other kind of deep crisis, there was little or no special interest in the challenges and experiences of the postpartum period. If they were not or had not been in a crisis situation, many of them doubted that they even had anything worthwhile to contribute to the discussion. Nor did they think they needed or deserved any special help or other kind of support. To them, "help" went hand in hand with "problem." Many of them did not have particular or big problems; new motherhood, as they experienced it, was a road of struggle, joy, magic, and isolation, highlighted eventually by the occasional pick-me-up of a playgroup, and made all the more dazzling during those intense, intimate moments of connection with their baby: That was the name of the game. With coaxing, eventually stories and identification flowed more freely and more openly among the moms, interrupted by laughs and groans of recognition. And everyone felt the richer for it.

As we talked that day, I remembered back to my own son's birth two years before. I had felt just as scared, unprepared, isolated, exhausted, hungry for information and emotional support—and just as knowledgeable about where to find it—as all the mothers sitting in that room. The deep, constant, vaguely articulated need I felt to talk to female friends and other mothers who knew more than I did, to drink in their experience, and to bask in their encouragement and reassurance seemed to me my own quirky deficiency. Once I had identified sources that validated those needs for nurturing, companionship, and female role models, just the very knowledge that they existed and were valid outside my own fantasies made me feel better. But some small part of me felt a little distant, as though succumbing to these new, abstract, wordless longings were tantamount to admitting individual defeat. In addition, I felt at some level that too many helpers might be intrusive and overbearing at a very intimate time. How did one orchestrate support that was at once truly useful, but also sensitive to that mother/baby bubble that some moms feel surrounds them, lifting them out of ordinary time and talk in the beginning? At that point I had no idea how to even describe such a network, let alone construct one. So with a few telephone lifelines to friends, my husband and I staggered through our sleepless nights and days pretty much unaided. After all, we thought, we were real men and women. We were grown-ups! We could do it!

But then a lucky thing happened. I discovered the doula. Or the concept of the doula. By month two of new motherhood, I was doing research for a radio program for NPR on the subject closest to my heart at that point—the need for support and recognition of the needs of postpartum women. Jane Arnold, certified nurse midwife and founder of The Mom Service, a mother-centered postpartum home-care service, steered me to a book called *The Tender Gift: Breastfeeding*, by anthropologist Dana Raphael. In it, Raphael used the word "doula," which she borrowed from the ancient Greek word meaning "slave." Raphael used it to denote that supportive person who in many diverse cultures is always on hand to nurture, support, mother, and protect the new mom and free her from other responsibilities so she can rest, take on her new role slowly, and breastfeed her baby successfully. Discovering the doula and all that she revealed and represented was a pivotal event for me: Here, then, was the personification of this special being who mothers the new mother. The archetype. Once I knew about her, this nurturing, supportive doula figure dominated my thoughts and shaped my work over the next five years, in the form of this book. I began to realize that today, given all the pressures women face when they become new mothers, this nurturing, teaching doula may often have to translate into a whole support network to continue to inform and buoy up the new mom as her needs change over the first year. If women could share these needs and believe in their validity, they might be able to take a more active role in determining their postpartum course. Two years later, I tested the theory in my own life. When my daughter was born in 1989, the doors of my kitchen cabinets were plastered with annotated lists and telephone numbers of all possible people, neighbors, stores, and other resources that could be of help, so that anyone could take one look at my kitchen and get with the program without even having to talk to me. I had allowed for the time and space to settle in with my newborn and my older child. We all know about prenatal nesting syndrome. I had feathered my nest the second time out with a cushion of support that really made a difference. Our course still wasn't perfect, but at least there was a floor to every crisis, and someone around to sweep up the pieces.

My talk with the playgroup mothers was helpful not only because it brought us all closer together that day, but also because these women showed me the real need for the book I wanted to write: not a how-to book telling the new mom what she has to do and how to do it best; but rather a book that, like a nurturing, nonjudgmental caregiver, gives us permission to accept and express the full range of feelings and needs we may have as we become new mothers—joy, ambivalence, loss, vulnerability, empowerment; a book that opens up the dialogue among women so they can continue to mirror and reassure and teach and nurture each other around this particular central female life experience; and finally, a book that guides women to other women or resources celebrating, grappling, or struggling with similar issues, and lets them know that they are not alone. In other words, the book I wish I'd had when I became a mother for the first time.

To that end, the resources and materials selected for this book are not the usual works telling women how to mother, but rather a mix of networks, organizations, people, or materials that were chosen because they reflected in some aspect a mother-centered, nurturing philosophy and sensitivity. Some are older and widely known; others are new, innovative, or one-of-a-kind. All are empowering and reflective of what women say they really experience and need, whether it is the Canadian child-centered feminist journal *Homebase*, written by and for mothers-at-home; The Mother's Center, a group designed by each community of women according to its own needs; a nationwide peer support group for mothers experiencing postpartum depression or distress; or a firm that helps women explore alternative work arrangements. I wanted the resources to be inclusive of all mothering experiences. I wanted, to some extent, to erase the dividing lines that separate women as mothers, and seek a common ground while still recognizing and respecting differences and different challenges. I wanted to validate this time in a woman's life by bringing together diverse information, background, and history into one source. Most of all, I wanted to represent the voices of women themselves, sharing their own stories, feelings, experiences, solutions.

In addition to identifying the practical networks, models, programs, images, videos, and books, the other important question I wanted to address in the book was this: How do women today feel as they move through the early days and weeks and months of the first year of new motherhood? Not how do they think they're supposed to feel—although those perceptions are certainly a good departure point for deeper discussion—but how do they *really* feel? And how, in their most open and uncensored moments, do women assess their needs and feelings throughout this year? And what exists—or is needed—to meet those needs?

As I investigated different resources, it became clear to me over time that, in some areas at least, more attention was beginning to focus on the importance of postpartum and early family adjustment—in home-care options, in health-care reform, in awareness about women's mental health both pre- and postpartum, in business and public policy. But there was no companion work to codify relevant information across the board and across that first year. I hope that *Mothering the New Mother* may begin to fill that need.

The book is divided into chapters covering broad categories, although the new mother's life is never as neatly structured or delineated. In reality, every piece seems to affect and bump up against every other piece of the postpartum picture; breastfeeding supports, doula-style home care, and workplace issues merge; postpartum depression and the existence of an overall support network and safe haven for expression bear a direct relationship to each other; mothers doing unpaid work at home and mothers in the paid labor force share concerns about public policy affecting all mothers and families. There are resources as well as testimony that could have gone equally well into several chapters. In reading or looking through this book, it is probably useful to consider the ways in your own life in which all of the pieces come together and affect, support, or detract from each other. Therein may lie another source of stress or strength.

Finally, this is not a comprehensive resource listing in the sense that it will connect you with every local playgroup or mother's group in your area. Rather, it is a sampling of those networks, models, and materials that seemed to me to offer a mother-centered and nurturing philosophy, or to contribute in some other way, either centrally or tangentially, to the new mom's sense of well-being, protectedness, and visibility during the first year postpartum. The support may take the form of a peer group, a center, a person, or even just an awareness or image of something different to hold on to or strive for, other than the isolation and invisibility many women described over and over again.

With her questionnaire, one new mom sent a note to me saying, "I hope this will all be easier for our daughters." It is my hope that this book will help in some small way to make it easier not only for our daughters but for our sons as well.

# A Note on the Resources in This Book
••••••

Recognizing the great diversity of families today, I have attempted to include in this book resources and testimony representative of the general parenting needs of a diverse population of families and new mothers. Clearly there are many special circumstances in which new moms need additional or more specific kinds of support. Attempting to include all or even many of these literally hundreds of specialized groups and associations would be an impossible task for a volume this size. While admittedly touching only the tip of the iceberg, I have tried instead to provide at least a starting place not only for general parenting needs but also for some of the special circumstances, individual needs, or unexpected challenges that might occur for moms and families. (If you do not find your particular needs addressed in these pages, a good starting place in seeking out information or support may be the *Encyclopedia of Associations.* See page 39.)

Although not grouped together in the book by these categories, resource entries were also chosen in part according to the following broad criteria:

1. National organizations that may have chapters or members in your area, or that offer start-up materials if you want to explore starting a chapter where you live (e.g., Formerly Employed Mothers at the Leading Edge; National Black Women's Health Project; Depression After Delivery).

2. Model local projects or programs that might be replicated in your own community, based on your own needs (e.g., Postpartum Education for Parents in Santa Barbara, California; the Doula Project at North Central Bronx Hospital in the Bronx, New York; the Visiting Moms Program of the Jewish Family and Children's Service in Brookline, Massachusetts).

3. Networks or umbrella organizations that also function as clearinghouses or referral services (e.g., the National Association of Postpartum Care Services; Postpartum Support, International; the International Lactation Consultant Association).

4. Books, videotapes, newsletters, and other materials you can acquire directly.

# 1.
# LIFE AFTER CHILDBIRTH

*Asking for Help Doesn't Mean You're Lazy, Crazy, or Bad*

••••••

*It was like there was a bunch of secrets I didn't know—until afterward, and then when I started to get to know more mothers . . . I'd start asking them, and a lot of them had had the same experiences [I had].*

—Diane

*Even though I knew there was nothing wrong with me, I kept thinking, "What's wrong with me? . . . I quit. I can't do this job."*

—Lynn

*It's the postpartum supports that are really most important . . . and it is a very badly neglected subject. . . . Society has not really seen fit to provide postpartum supports for women as a matter of policy . . . we should say we value newborn children, we value new mothers, we are going to give them help, instead of forcing everything on the mother alone.*

—Dorothy C. Wertz

*To put it simply, we must begin to tell the truth, in groups, to one another.*

—Carolyn G. Heilbrun, *Writing a Woman's Life*

## Motherhood by Microwave: Why We Are Overwhelmed

*What I really needed was a full-time mother for myself.*

—Evelyn, a new mother

Joan Bachrach is a childbirth educator and breastfeeding counselor who ran postpartum support groups in the Boston suburb of Newton for six years. During that time, she observed that many of the moms she saw at four weeks, six weeks, or eight weeks postpartum felt unprepared and overwhelmed.

"[Our culture assumes that women], from the moment they deliver," she says, "certainly from the moment they're out of the hospital, can take on all of the emotional and physical responsibilities of caring for a newborn without any kind of training prior to that experience."

While many diverse cultures have given women ample time, nurturing, and encouragement as they grow into the role of new mother, women in 1990s America are often expected to make this transition almost instantly, and largely without much recognition or support. Twenty-four hours, two weeks, six weeks. We even think in small, quick, bursts of time—sound bites, if you will—about our postpartum progress. These time frames correspond to what many consider to be fairly universal pivotal events of new motherhood: discharge from the hospital, baby's first checkup, our last checkup. Yet, the deeper significance of all that happens on our inner landscapes between or on these landmark dates—and even well beyond—is often denied and overlooked, both by others and, consequently, by ourselves. Women are unprepared and may feel overwhelmed because the external circumstances to which they return as new mothers frequently do not address this new internal state and all that comes with it. But indeed, after your baby arrives, you yourself may feel like something of a present, albeit clumsily wrapped in unmatched ribbons and bows, but *new*. Untried. Untested. Unexpected. Longings, memories, anxieties, and competencies may surface and surprise you. But where and to whom will you get the chance to say so? And how, in this sudden, charged, emotional, vulnerable state, will you ever be able to slowly pull the threads of your experience together without a validating map or presence to guide and reassure you?

Basically, your needs as a new mother would seem simple to define: rest so you can heal; gentle education and reassurance as you gain confidence in your mothering skills; nourishing food and drink for yourself; a relinquishing of practical chores to someone else so you can withdraw into yourself and your baby; knowledge about what is going on with your body and spirit; some realistic images and guideposts about the range of feelings other women have experienced postpartum; a place to "debrief" and talk about the birth itself and your emotions; and most especially, some mothering for yourself, so you can feel protected and honored and continually replenished at a time when many women say they feel as if they are forgotten, peripheral, or "running on empty." (It is, by the way, all right to feel the need for this, and absolutely all right to plan or ask for it. It does not make you a weak woman, but rather a wise one.)

Often, though, these needs are difficult to fulfill. Sometimes, women are able to move through this postpartum time in a sharing, protected way, feeling the input and support of people they trust. Perhaps they'll just get flashes of it—from a nurturing female friend or elder; a knowledgeable breastfeeding consultant; a peer group leader who recognizes and respects the feelings they're expressing, whether they speak of doubt or loss or joy. This one person may be sufficient to provide the reassurance and affirmation every new mother needs. More often, though, moms say they feel thrust into new motherhood alone and unprepared, in part because a woman's needs during this rite of passage have not yet been sufficiently identified and met.

In addition to this lack of focus on inner needs, there are tangible and practical reasons why new mothers are easily overwhelmed today: Extended families that might once have helped out are now far-flung; economic demands might keep partners or other relatives from being as available or as flexible as they might like to be; grandmothers are not as young as they used to be; mothers themselves may have to juggle maternal and wage-earner roles earlier and more often—and for great numbers of women, the need to resolve workplace, separation, and childcare issues adds greatly to the stresses of pregnancy and postpartum adjustment. In addition, five years ago, 5 percent of women had a cesarean section; today 25 percent have one, and while they may require greater postpartum support, they rarely get it. Hospitals, driven by insurance companies, increasingly shorten postpartum stays without providing adequate home care to compensate.

Many mothers are also part of the growing number of diverse families that make up the 1990s' American social tapestry and may have their own particular needs postpartum: Professional women between twenty-eight and forty may know many colleagues from work, but may not know the other mothers on their street or in their apartment building. They may also feel conflicted about where they really fit in. Single mothers by choice may need a community to share with and support them—it is most important, says Jane Mattes, psychologist and founder of Single Mothers by Choice, to have at the ready that middle-of-the-night phone number of a friend who has agreed to stand by in an emergency. Teen moms may need special adult mentoring and companionship. Adoptive mothers may feel their own postpartum stress regarding the permanency of their motherhood, though the public at large sees only that they didn't have to go through labor and delivery and so assumes that they don't have the same or equivalent needs as birth or biological mothers. Lesbian birth, biological or adoptive mothers, says Terry Boggis, of Center Kids at New York's Gay and Lesbian Community Services Center, "may experience more intense isolation if they don't have the support of their extended family." Mothers faced with an infant's unexpected illness or another serious challenge postpartum may be operating on an altogether different timetable of adjustment, and may need the special sensitivity and nurturing of respite care or a crisis nursery as part of their overall support.

Still another reason why women are overwhelmed is the absolute newness of it all. "We don't bring pregnant women and women with babies together," notes Liz Koch, founder of *The Doula: A Magazine for Mothers*, and herself the mother of three. "There's no context for that, so there's not a lot of exposure. I wasn't around anyone who had a baby. I had no idea what it was like to have a baby."

"It all starts getting learned once the baby is born," says Raven Lang, California-based direct entry midwife, author of *The Birth Book*, and doctor of Oriental medicine. "Depending upon the confidence of a woman, and her connection to children—how many of them she has held, how many tears she has soothed—that is, it seems to me, directly related to how quickly and comfortably she gets into her mothering. These are some important factors."

Finally, many women today are entering into motherhood in unprecedented states of isolation. Isolation breeds anxiety. "I felt at the beginning, and still feel as a new mother," said Beverly Solow, a New York–based international board-certified lactation consultant (IBCLC), when her first child was five months old, "that the single . . . most difficult aspect is the isolation. To be so alone for hours and hours, in four walls—especially during the winter—you really lose perspective on things, you lose your sense of humor, and the fatigue in being up at night just puts a strain on the whole family."

If you are a new mother, or about to become one, has anyone told you that much of parenting is learned behavior, not—as we have been led to believe—all instinct and motherwit? That nurturers of new infants need nurturing themselves? Does your list of needed and essential things include not only cotton swabs and stretchies, but also someone to guarantee you sleep breaks, someone to sit with you and teach you every day as you learn to nurse your baby and your baby learns to nurse, someone to listen wisely and nonjudgmentally to all your questions and feelings after the baby comes?

Instead of striving for as quick a return as possible to "normal," perhaps you might want to tailor your postpartum wish list more specifically (and by all means, make a wish list!): Ask instead for friends with casseroles, or four hours of sleep at a clip. Ask for a broad-based cushion of support and perspective as you learn to roll with the unpredictable and mercurial. Ask for a loving and listening ear. Ask everyone—friends, family, workplace—for a way to move through this time of new motherhood securely, and openly, and at your own pace.

## Coloring in the Spectrum: A Range of Postpartum Feelings

*It takes your breath away by how it affects your life.*

—Lynn, mother of two

Women cross over into motherhood from every background and situation. And for each woman, the journey is unique, miraculous, unknown, unpredictable. Some fall in love immediately in a way they never imagined. Others are surprised to find that it takes more time. Some are numb. Others are surprised at how emotional they become. Some are proud of how competent they come to feel. Others say their worlds are "topsy-turvy"; and others, still, feel they have to be a Superwoman.

No one can tell better what new motherhood feels like than the new mother herself. Here is how a group of women described their feelings as new mothers—the things that surprised them, the fears, stresses, and joys they felt:

**Rhonda:** "*I feel like I've come into a huge sorority now, having had a child. I can look at other mothers no matter if they've had good experiences or bad experiences, and we wink at each other, as if to say, now we know what you've been through! . . . No one prepares you for it. I missed my mother terribly at that time. I thought, if anyone could take care of me now, my mom could. . . . It's a shock. . . . It's a huge transitional period. It's four weeks now, and I'm not saying by any means I've mastered it. If anything, I look at my baby, and we're feeding, and I think, how can we best provide for him, and, and, and, and . . .*"

**Suzanne,** *adoptive mother:* "*That falling in love—I just didn't realize that I had that kind of love in me. I always knew I would love my child, but I just never knew it would be that intense. I guess I was a little worried about that, because in an adoptive situation you always say in the back of your head, 'Is this really going to be it for me?' As soon as they put him in my arms it was like who cares how he got here, just that fact that he was there . . .*"

**Lynn:** "*I was devastated the first time by this sense of isolation, and the feeling of being overwhelmed by this new job and this whole big change of my role, and being a parent. . . . Just like people experience adolescence differently, it's the same thing. It takes your breath away by how it affects your life, how much it changes your life, and you have to survive it, you have to cope with it.*"

**Gaye,** *single mother by choice:* "*My first few weeks I was numb. I thought I would immediately love her, but I really felt nothing, not even bad things, just nothing. It took a few months till I adored her and each month it grows more. . . . I thought I would love her instantly. I was surprised to find this love had to grow. . . . I was always afraid of sudden infant death syndrome or that something else would hurt her. . . . As a single mother it was stressful worrying about supporting her in a way I would like to. . . . There are too many feelings [to be prepared for], some of which we don't know about until we are mothers.*"

**Tammie:** "*[I was most comfortable] accepting her as my child, loving her instinctively. . . . [I was most stressed about the] baby crying, not knowing right away which of her needs needed to be tended to.*"

**Gay:** "*I was relieved to have a perfect baby and to have the pregnancy over with. I already had two boys, and many people were hoping for a girl, but when I delivered my third boy, it didn't matter what his sex was. . . . It amazed me that I had such strong, loving feelings for the baby. . . . I was happy with the baby, but as the days went by, I began to feel overwhelmed. . . .*"

**Marianne:** "*Once home from the hospital, away from the support of my doctor and the nurses, I felt so frightened and overwhelmed by the responsibility of this fragile boy. Although I was in my home, my familiar environment, nothing looked or felt the same. Suddenly my whole life changed! Initially I don't think anything felt comfortable; however, as time passed, my new role as mother became much more comfortable. . . . Everything [felt stressful]. I wanted to protect, care [for] and love my son as best I could, so I worried that I was doing the "right" thing. . . . Those first few weeks I grieved for my life prior to the birth of my son. I missed the intimacy my husband and I shared and the freedom I had. I suddenly wasn't sure I wanted to be a mother. . . . My greatest fear was knowing that I could protect him only to an extent . . . that something could happen to my son and I would lose him.*"

**Laurie:** "*It was all so unreal. I couldn't believe there was no turning back. I was surprised by my underlying feeling of competence—that I was the one expert over my baby.*"

**Diane:** "*I remember feeling surprised and a bit resentful about how demanding he was, but I was also pleasantly surprised about how confident I was about caring for him. I had pictured myself being neurotic about everything he did, but I was the total opposite. [Most stressful] was the twenty-four-hour-a-day demand of my attention—no break from him, because we don't live near any family or close friends. [Most comfortable] was that he wasn't as much of a mystery as I had expected.*"

*Spalding*: "*I was happy to finally be a mom, but I had the dreaded postpartum blues. I didn't feel sad, but for the first week I cried all the time over nothing! I remember not wanting my mother to return home (only two hours away), and was a little apprehensive about going it alone. I wondered how long it would take for things to be 'normal.' (Is there such a thing?) I was very surprised at my crying spells. I'm such an upbeat person that I skipped all the chapters in my birth books about postpartum depression! The house was a mess! My body was weird. Nursing was demanding at first, and if one more relative came to town to 'help' (ha!) I thought I would scream! [Most wonderful] was the joy of holding my child, knowing that my husband and I 'made' this tiny person, nursing him, and knowing that I was providing for his every need.*"

Other terms women have used to describe what they felt or felt like in the early weeks and months include "overjoyed," "disconnected," "resentful," "unreal," "lacking in self-confidence," "anxious," "overzealous," "self-assured," "accepting," "just a wimp," "despair," "high," "euphoric," "melancholic," "perfectionist," and "sense of loss."

As always, it should be remembered that many of the more negative feelings women experience are exacerbated by the lack of external supports, and the isolation many women feel.

# Talking About
# Our Feelings—All of Them

*It's a catharsis to be able to talk about these things, because the general feeling I get is that people think they're boring to talk about. Nobody really wants to hear it.*

—Elizabeth

"Darling, you must be overjoyed!"

"Enjoy it, these are the best years of your life."

"This time will go by all too fast!"

We all know the high end of the new motherhood spectrum. The joy. The magic. The miraculousness. The relief.

But how many well-wishers have actually said to you, "Honey, you must be exhausted!" or "Wondering what you've gotten yourself into, dearie? I know how you feel, it will get better. . . ."?

While joy and elation are surely present after a new baby has entered our lives, it is also within the realm of possibility that other feelings might crop up: neediness, fear, ambivalence, anger. But often there seems to be no really appropriate time or place to talk about these darker feelings. Because traditionally they have rarely been acknowledged or discussed as part of the new motherhood package, we rarely discuss them widely among ourselves. Often they are unexpected, and when they arise—even to a small degree—we feel unprepared and alarmed—"embarrassed at our own ungratefulness," as one mother put it. "You have a beautiful, healthy baby—how can you feel like crying, or just wanting to crawl under the covers forever?"

Given the strong social pressure to be only happy, or only overjoyed, we may not feel safe enough to admit such intense feelings, even to ourselves. The myths about what we're supposed to feel as new mothers run strong and deep. If we are able to acknowledge our postpartum struggles and mixed feelings privately, we might not always feel comfortable sharing them with other people. We may believe that we are the only ones who have ever had mixed feelings; we may have no awareness that other women have experienced the same thing. If we do feel like talking, we may not know who has the time or interest in listening to us. We may also (and often rightly so) fear speaking out to the wrong person. Or we may feel we have to keep controversial feelings secret and maintain a contented mother image. This feeling that we have to keep it secret only adds to the new mom's sense of isolation. Some of what we can accept within ourselves also has to do with how we were mothered—the role models we had; the messages our own mothers passed along about motherhood; and the roles they want to play as grandmothers.

It is important for women to feel that they can safely air some of these less socially acceptable feelings about new motherhood. It is also helpful to understand some of the reasons why women feel they have to keep silent. Here's what some women said about why it was hard to share their own mixed feelings about new motherhood:

**Charlette:** *"Everyone else seemed so happy with their babies. I 'knew' not to say anything—no one wants to hear about it—or knows what to say or do about it."*

*Tanya:* "I thought [my anxiety] to be a sign of craziness. A new mother has to be strong physically and mentally for her child. Therefore I thought it unacceptable to admit it to others or even myself. . . ."

*Gay:* "I didn't want to talk to anyone because society teaches us that a mother loves her children and wants to take care of them. I didn't want to be seen as a 'bad' mother or see myself as a 'bad' mother."

*Laurie:* "I was, the first time, wrapped up in 'doing it right,' especially compared to other mothers, so it was hard to admit ambivalent feelings."

*Gaye:* "I have never spoken of this as all the new moms I knew seemed elated at the birth of their children. I, of course, acted the same."

*Elizabeth:* "From prior experiences with other issues, I knew in my head that it was all right to talk about these things if I talked to the right people. It's not something you should share with just anybody. But it was still hard."

*Kathy:* "[I talked] only to certain people who I knew wouldn't judge me. All others, I felt almost like an alien around them."

Most of these women did find someone to talk to and share their feelings with, whether it was a partner, friend, relative, support group, or counselor.

*Marianne:* "Although I definitely feel ambivalent about sharing my negative feelings, I have shared them with my husband and friends. I was worried that something was wrong with me so I asked questions of my friends who are/were new parents. . . . If it wasn't for them, my initiation into parenthood would have been much more difficult. They validated my feelings of inadequacy, fear, overwhelming joy, etc."

*Diane:* "I feel comfortable talking about these kinds of feelings [of stress and anxiety] to my husband, because he understands them and shares them, and to a few very close women friends who also admit to them. But to casual friends, I find it difficult because either they don't *feel that way or don't admit it. . . . I feel most comfortable talking with my best woman friend who had a baby soon after I did and has very similar thoughts and feelings."*

**Elizabeth:** *"My sister had her first child the day before I gave birth to mine. Fortunately, we could speak on the phone daily and commiserate/share our happiness."*

One mom, Diane, used journaling as a way to stay in touch with her feelings:

"Most of it was dealing with my anger at how things had changed, the frustration of the way I used to do things not working at all now that I had a baby to care for. It was a real big time of transition for me."

And in contrast, while Spalding felt comfortable talking about her feelings, she noticed "that it often made others uncomfortable. To me, the whole thing was very natural."

Although you cannot talk to "just anyone" about feelings so deep and so intimate, there are people who will listen nonjudgmentally and offer understanding and support. As we begin to hear the voices of other women and realize that we are not alone in our many and varied reactions to new motherhood, we may continue to envision and create a postpartum landscape that will serve and cushion new mothers more responsively.

# What Is This Period Called Postpartum, and How Long Does It Really Last?

The postpartum period. Literally, the word means "after birth"— those minutes, hours, days, and months following the birth of a baby. The word "period" gives us the comforting—but also misleading—illusion that it's neatly finite (though as mothers know, it may feel from time to time, or even constantly, as if it lasts a lifetime—and in the broadest sense, quite literally it does).

In the United States, medical texts have traditionally defined the postpartum or "postpartal" period as lasting six weeks—"that period of time during which the body adjusts, both physically and psychologically, to the process of childbearing."[1] It is described as "the six-week interval between the delivery of the newborn and the return of the reproductive organs to their normal nonpregnant state."[2] (Interestingly, many diverse cultures allot the new mom a forty-day period of rest—the equivalent of these six textbook weeks. But those six weeks are clearly special, often filled with mother-centered care, attention, and recognition automatically showered on the woman, catering to her spirit as well as to her physical state.)

When she first became involved with the childbirth movement in the 1950s, recalls Norma Swenson, coauthor of *Our Bodies, Ourselves* and *The New Our Bodies, Ourselves*, and current president of the board of directors of the Boston Women's Health Book Collective, the term "childbearing year" was very much in vogue. Women recognized that there were other needs besides the physical, and found a way to address them over a longer period of time. "The fact that there were trimesters was borrowed from medicine, but it also gave us the opportunity to talk about the fourth trimester. I remember workshops on the fourth trimester and it was, to be sure, borrowed from the notion that all this involution was going on and there was lactation going on, there were all these physical changes, but it became a basis of discussion of postpartum," and presumably all or some of what went on besides the physical recovery. In the 1991 edition of *The Essentials of Maternity Nursing*, the fourth trimester is defined as the first month postpartum, a time "characterized by intense learning and need for nurturing," coupled with the next two months—"a time of drawing together and uniting the family unit."[3]

Whether we think of six weeks or three months, it is often hard for women to focus on postpartum before their babies are born. Preoccupied with all the changes in our bodies, anticipating labor and delivery, when we are pregnant we often feel as if postpartum is a territory far off in the distance. For many women, the six-week mark is the one that stands out—a prescribed time that, we have been led to believe, will serve as a short bridge back to the plateau of "normal life." Our perceptions are largely shaped and reinforced by a broad and powerful combination of forces: the medical world; the workplace; state and federal legislation regarding family leave policy; insurance carriers who shorten our hospital stays (if we deliver in the hospital) and then fail to allow for or provide adequate home care or psychological and emotional cushioning, whether we deliver in the hospital or at home. As new mothers, we also receive guidelines from sources outside ourselves about when our bodies will be physically ready to resume exercise, sex, work—whether we feel ready to or not when those days arrive. When it will be all right to separate from our children to return to work (if we still have a job waiting for us). How we should be looking and feeling.

The underlying message of all this is simple: Whatever feelings, longings, needs come up during that postpartum period are just self-indulgent, imagined, even "normal"; everyone gets it together in six weeks, and you can, too!

Pulling numbers out of this grab bag of various, sometimes misleading, sometimes contradictory figures, women may pull together a timetable for their postpartum course and come to it with certain expectations, mostly expectations of themselves to meet the deadlines: What time frames stand out in your mind as you contemplate and organize your life postpartum? The twelve weeks of your job leave (if you have job leave)? The six weeks between the birth and your final checkup? The two-day or shorter hospital stay before you're on your own?

Because there is not yet enough of a widespread postpartum map or universal language created by women who have been through it (although the vocabulary is growing), we internalize these guidelines—sometimes the only ones available to us—and then run the risk of feeling guilty and inadequate if we don't adapt—even thrive—as our friends and as women in some magazines seem to do. But if we don't have enough time and compassionate support, enough instruction and information, rest and nourishment, it is likely that we will be less well able to care for our newborns and, over time, our growing children. And, as Adrienne Rich notes in her landmark 1976 book *Of Woman Born: Motherhood as Experience and Institution*, typically for women, "grief at all we cannot do for our children in a society so inadequate to meet human needs becomes translated into guilt and self-laceration."[4] Rather than recognizing that our own deepest needs are not being met or possibly even articulated during this critical transition time in our lives, we run the familiar risk of viewing ourselves as deficient for not being able to "manage it all" better, or well—even though no one has asked us how we would like our postpartum course to go: what we really need, how we really feel, and when we are ready to move on.

Indeed, even those mothers who do realize that the deficiency lies not within them but within the supports (or lack of supports) around them may wish for something different but still find no options available. While we usually get some simple guidelines about when we can resume various kinds of work and physical activity after our babies are born, we may hear less often or less routinely about the other aspects of our postpartum time—these third trimester months of "intense learning" and nurturing. In her book *Reactions to Motherhood: The Role of Post-natal Care*, British midwife Jean A. Ball explains why this is so: "The main focus of post-natal care has traditionally been that of ensuring the physical recovery of the mother from the effects of pregnancy and labour, and establishing infant feeding patterns. . . . The emotional and psychological needs of mothers have not received much attention until recently, and there has been an assumption that these needs will automatically be met if the first two aspects of care are satisfied. The organization of post-natal care has accordingly been based upon this premise."[5]

Some mothers who questioned and redefined the six-week postpartum time frame shared their experiences beyond those six classic weeks:

"I read all the books," said Cheryl, a new mother who is also a pediatric nurse. "The medical books, and the mothering books—they all said six weeks, and I felt aberrant for being in my seventh week and not feeling close to the end of adjusting."

Lynn, a social worker, is the mother of two children—a nine-month-old, and one almost five years old. "If I had thought about [defining a postpartum period] before I had the [second] baby . . . I would have thought six or eight weeks. And it's not. It's still going on. My younger son is nine months, and I feel like now, my feet are just beginning to touch the ground. I was walking, but I was going through the motions. I was almost kind of numb in the process."

Diane was twenty-three when her first son was born. "It seemed like such a dramatic change in my life, I was really shocked by it. . . . I remember feeling overwhelmed and real scared the first day my husband went back to work [after the first week]. I felt real tired for about the first six weeks. I'd feel almost dizzy a lot of the time. I'd feel real strange when I'd go out. I guess by the time he was about six months old, I was feeling a lot more confident, but it really took that long."

"I was one of the first in my peer group to have a baby," said Laurie, "and my mom didn't give me any sense of the emotional tumult" involved in becoming a mother. Laurie felt her first "postpartum adjustment" lasted nine months.

In her book *The Newborn Mother: Stages of Her Growth*, Andrea Boroff Eagan notes that "while we call a woman a mother as soon as she has a child, it will be some time before she herself begins to feel like a mother. . . . A woman first begins to feel like a mother as she develops a profound sense of being completely responsible for her child." In her interviews and studies for the book, Eagan determined that this issue came "to a resting point, if not to a final resolution at nine months after the baby's birth."[6] And in the *Boston Women's Health Book Collective's Our Bodies, Ourselves* (1978), the importance of a role model over the whole first year postpartum was stressed.

Raven Lang recalled that when she first started midwifing in 1968, "some of us considered postpartum two years, and some of us considered postpartum even a little longer. As long as the baby's in diapers, and you're up in the night and your breast is being called upon by that person, you're postpartum."

Looking forward to an upswing after six weeks and then not finding it can hit new mothers very hard, especially if they have not been adequately reassured and supported during those six weeks.

## Getting Real: Expanding the Postpartum Time Frame

In the postpartum support groups she ran in a Boston suburb, breastfeeding counselor/childbirth educator Joan Bachrach saw women who were mostly professionals, between thirty and forty years old, and having their first babies. Despite an intellectual understanding that motherhood would change their lives, they were, for the most part, she says, "completely caught off guard" when confronted with the reality of a newborn. They might have had the changing tables in place and nursery perfectly arranged, but essentially they were totally overwhelmed and "unprepared . . . for the most major part of the continuum, which is becoming a parent."

What women often speak of as they face new motherhood is needing a way to "move through" the experience—evoking the image of a steady, continuous support almost like the handrail on a fast-paced moving walkway that conveys you down an airport terminal. Along with an understanding of your postpartum anatomy, you may also want to be forewarned about some of the more ephemeral mood/fatigue/exhaustion guideposts from others who have gone before. You need to know about the possible subterranean effects of dive-bombing hormones on your emotional state. You may want company and reassurance. Foremothers and nurturers. Even if the facts of your experience don't change, when you add these pieces into the mix, your perspective may. "I found my friends [who were pregnant] were lucky to have me as a friend," said Lynn. When one friend of hers was pregnant, Lynn recalls, "she had a map, a guide. I could say, 'This is what you're going through, this is how it feels, this is how long it lasted for me.' I said to her, 'My world is topsy-turvy.' Nobody ever said that to me. In some ways it was easier for her." Often, such navigational aids are as hard to find as buried treasure.

Childbirth assistant Claudia Lowe is the founder and director of the National Association of Childbirth Assistants. The childbirth assistant, like the birth or labor companion, is specially trained to provide non-medical labor support and educational counseling, as well as comfort care, for the childbearing year. Keenly aware of meeting the postpartum needs of new moms, Lowe also makes three postpartum home visits which, she explains, correspond to the three phases of early postpartum adjustment described in the nursing texts. (These phases include, in part, the mom's need to be nurtured and dependent as the recipient of protective care for several days; the need to talk about the birth; then by day three, "*if [she] has received adequate nurturing in the first few days* [italics mine], the need to begin to strike a balance between her 'need for extensive nurturing and acceptance by others' and the desire 'to take charge' once again,"[7] regaining a sense of independence as she starts to master baby-related tasks; and finally, the potentially stressful phase once the new family system begins to take hold.)[8]

For Lowe, helping women integrate the birth experience, "letting women talk about that . . . is like a completion to that whole process. That's why the postpartum is so important. Letting the mom know that you're available on an ongoing basis, or periodically by phone call." While Lowe is able to respond sensitively to these needs for her clients, often the woman who delivers in the hospital and goes home alone after twelve, twenty-four, or even forty-eight hours may have no opportunity to get that early nurturing and care. (Nor may she have any awareness that this is an important part of her adjustment process.) With increasingly shorter hospital stays, while mom is still feeling dependent, sensitive, focused inward, and needing to talk about the labor and delivery and be nurtured herself, she is already being ushered into the hospital baby basics class, where she must try to learn diapering, bathing, and swabbing of the umbilical cord before she is really ready to take in such information. Suddenly, systems collide. Nursing staff may or may not be engaging and sympathetic. Some may resent the mother's wish to have rooming-in or her temerity in suggesting that she knows what is best for her baby; indeed, others may simply just not have the time to give enough individual attention to every woman on the unit. Uncomfortable with her own unexpected neediness and vulnerability, mom herself might feel she has to hide her real feelings and needs and pull it all together in front of hospital staff. But since the "success" of this adjustment cycle is based on the premise that nurturing and sensitivity will be available to women during these early days, the lack of it can make the days that follow that much more difficult. If a woman moves through this early time without recognizing and fulfilling these needs for "self-absorption," nurturing, and remaining "within herself"[9] and without sharing her total mix of emotions, then these needs may not be resolved, but may linger on, and be incorrectly interpreted by the woman as her own self-indulgence or inadequacy as a mother.

While each woman's experience is personal and uniquely her own, postpartum group leader Joan Bachrach gave her mothers time frames, just to reassure them that nothing, not even the hardest and most discouraging moments, would last forever, which is something new mothers almost universally believe from moment to moment. "Whenever you're in a bad moment," said Lynn, "you think this is going to be bad forever. . . . It was like . . . we can't do anything, this is the way it's going to be forever . . . , that's kind of what happens. You never can really see yourself getting out of it."

For many first-time moms, there is often no sense that it will ever pass, let alone improve; there is just the innate belief that whatever more is to come, for better or for worse, will not replace what is, but will only be heaped on top of it. For Bachrach's moms, even just the intellectual knowledge that stages of infant behavior or parental exhaustion were finite (or at least relatively so) helped them move through the fog of the early weeks and months, if only on a leap of faith. "You totally lose perspective, and that's why I try to give people those guidelines. Otherwise, there's the sense that 'I've made the most major mistake I've ever made in my life, and how am I going to do this forever?'"

Karena Green, a lay midwife in the Philadelphia area and mother of six, also offers the mothers she attends broad time frames for an overall adjustment. "A classic new mother mistake," she says, "is that they think everything is going to be in hand by three weeks, and that's really when it falls apart. . . . Have some realistic expectations . . . especially that you're not going to have it together for quite a while. Minimum, six weeks. You begin to see a lot of progress by three months. By six months, you begin to see the light at the end of the tunnel. I think that's a realistic expectation.

"People who think they're going to get back to normal in two or three weeks," Green continues, "they fall apart. I can usually anticipate when people are going to have that problem, and really work on offsetting it. They're tremendously together, they have pretty unrealistic expectations of themselves and a lot of times of their mates. They don't have a support system. They're not women who are used to being close to other women, or used to being needy or acknowledging their neediness, so they just get hit the hardest with being needy."

Some of the women surveyed prenatally for this book foresaw six weeks or three months as their projected postpartum adjustment time; the women who already were new mothers circled three months minimum, and some chose six and twelve. One new mom noted, "After eight months, I feel like I should have adjusted to this major change— but I am frustrated that it is taking me so long, even though I recognize that it is a major change. I tend to adjust to major changes slowly. I didn't ask for much help, although I would seek out more companionship in the future."

And with great honesty and insight, one mom circled twelve months or more, "depending," she wrote, "on how long you deny your feelings."

In an article for the *Boston Parent's Paper*, Valerie Spain, former midwives' assistant, and cofounder and former co-owner of MotherCare

Services, a postpartum home-care service in Boston, wrote that beyond the fourth trimester, "many experts today say the postpartum period lasts a full twelve months."[10] In her book *The Newborn Mother: Stages of Her Growth*, Andrea Boroff Eagan suggested a way to delineate the nine-month journey of the woman following the birth of her baby to the point at which she "develops a profound sense of being completely responsible for her child" and reclaims her adult self as mother. Eagan begins with the "fog" of the first month, when the woman is still focused inward on herself, and responds more to attention given to her than to the baby; moves through what she calls the symbiosis of the fourth month, when mother and child are still as one; through the fifth month, when the baby begins to "hatch" as child psychologist Margaret S. Mahler, coauthor of *The Psychological Birth of the Human Infant*, called it and the mom starts to reclaim some of her adult life; and through the eighth- and ninth-month "settling point."[11] Claudia Lowe comments, "Personally and professionally, I don't think I would define an end to it. I still get calls from clients a year into it, or a year after the baby's born, and they just need to touch base on something. Or something's come up."

Today adjustments and anxieties for many women are compounded and ongoing throughout that first year, particularly if they face separation issues around returning to work six weeks or six months into it, concerns about trustworthy childcare, or identity issues around suddenly leaving the workplace to be at home. All things considered, it seems more accurate and more realistic to offer women a broad timetable of postpartum cushioning that covers the first twelve months of new motherhood. Some women will feel that they have settled in in a shorter time; others will find it might take longer, depending upon what kind of supports they have to help them.

Expanding this outlook should not frighten us into feeling that the stresses will be never-ending, but rather should give us a sense of relief in the knowledge that we need not feel pressured to conform to an impossible deadline, one that may cause women to compromise or sacrifice altogether important and potentially rich moments in the process of becoming a new mother. Or, as JoAnne Brundage, founder of Formerly Employed Mothers at the Leading Edge put it, "Women need to know that they can feel okay with being a mess for a while, it's part of the job."

# Two into Three . . .

The arrival of a new baby can have an intense and dramatic impact on any relationship. Mothers may need to withdraw deeply into themselves for an extended time, longer than any partner (or mother) ever imagined. And this, just at a time when husbands or partners are needing some extra reassurance that they have not been displaced. Dad or other family members may now subtly or overtly be expecting the new mother to mother them as well, much to her horror. Husbands, equally unprepared for new parenthood, may not understand what their wives are going through. They may feel overburdened, overwhelmed, or left out entirely. They may not be as flexible or as available as they want to be, depending on their work situations and what kind of family leave they have. They may be waiting for someone to ask them how *they* are feeling about transitioning to new fatherhood. Sometimes couples are drawn closer together in a common parental bond, and mutual understanding deepens.

The following women describe aspects of their relationships with mates after the baby was born:

*Spalding:* "*The demanding schedule of a newborn put added stress on our busy schedules. Mostly having my mother staying here for two weeks telling my husband what he 'should' be doing added the extra stress. Other than that our son drew us closer together as we watched him in awe, knowing that we made him together. We were so proud!*"

*Charlette:* "*We were so stressed out the first year, we didn't talk about anything except babies. Sex was totally forgotten. (Who had the time or energy anyway?) I resented my husband because he got to leave and go to work.*"

*Diane:* "*My husband is a very big help in raising our son almost as an equal partner, although because I worry more and anticipate things I tend to feel slightly more responsible. Our relationship has shifted from focusing on each other to focusing on our son's needs. With time and a lot of effort we are trying to get back to focusing a bit on us.*"

**Tanya:** *"Sexual freedom became history. My husband forgot where towels, facecloths, etc., were kept, which made it seem that the responsibility was all my own. We stopped talking about each other and learning about one another. The conversations always revolved around the baby."*

**Claudia:** *"I almost never had time for my husband. He wasn't in first place anymore and he noticed that. I think he felt a little jealous."*

The stresses do not necessarily disappear over time, but couples learn how to work with them, communicate more, and alter their expectations:

**Elizabeth:** *"We worked (and continue to work) well as a team, understanding each other's strengths and weaknesses."*

**Laurie:** *"We have a very solid relationship, so [the] new baby was just generally very stressful. My husband was very disturbed/anxious by the disruption of our sexual activities, but postpartum the second time, he knew what to expect."*

**Lynn:** *"When there's not a lot of time for yourself, sometimes there's not a lot of time for each other. Sometimes [my husband] would feel neglected. He would want attention, he would want affection. Even now, I'm so exhausted that I can't deal with it. Just like I don't take care of myself sometimes, that certainly is not taken care of. . . . When my [first son] was just under two, I felt like I was still on this emotional high, exhausted, but really excited from what I was doing. . . . [My husband] was ready to go on to something else, and I was still excited about my 'mother's class' at the hospital. So we weren't really on the same planet. But hopefully the relationship is strong enough, because it has to be strong to withstand this. This is really quite stressful."*

**Marianne:** *"My husband and I are fortunate in that we have a positive, strong relationship. When my son arrived, we both focused all of our energies on him. We were both so tired each day that we had nothing left over to give to one another. We began to feel distant from one another and tensions arose. Only now that he has been here for three* *months are we working on our relationship again. Fortunately our basis is solid and withstood the strain of being new parents."*

**Carol:** *"It gave us a new patience and appreciation for one another. . . ."*

# I've Got a Feeling We're Not in Kansas Anymore: What Is the State of Matrescence?

*Nothing changes life as dramatically as having a child. And there was no word to describe that. So we invented the word—matrescence—becoming a mother.*
—Dana Raphael

The range of all that happens to the new mom emotionally and psychologically and spiritually as she becomes responsible for another human life over time is frequently perceived as each mother's private, unspoken journey. Or it is minimized. Unqueried. Broadly labeled "normal" and swept beneath the rug. While there may be many common threads among mothers at this time, these common bonds may not yet constitute common knowledge, because so few women feel they have been able to talk about it in a formal or codified way. Many concede that they have barely been able even to acknowledge it to themselves, let alone another person.

Life with an infant unfolds differently for every mother, and gradually we are hearing the deep, inner descriptive language of that process on the lips and pens of women. Some women have used words to describe postpartum life and feelings similar to those they would use to describe natural phenomena or cataclysmic events. "Upheaval." "Numbing." "Primal agony," as Adrienne Rich describes the profound "conflict, between self-preservation and maternal feelings."[12] Often, such powerful feelings inhabit a woman's psyche and spirit only as a subtext to the other stuff of her daily life that she is still called upon to handle and keep going simultaneously.

Given the magnitude of the descriptions coming from the inside, many women find the usual responses of the outside world quite at odds with what they are really experiencing during this female rite of passage. "It is a stage in a woman's development," says Martha Lequerica, Ph.D., assistant professor of psychology at Montclair State College and herself a mother, "that confronts women with many different aspects of self which may have been unidentified or dormant until then. One of them is the 'nurturing self,' which wants to hold, protect, but also deeply wishes to be held and protected, to regress to the early original symbiosis with her own mother. In order for her to nurture, she wants to get some nurturing, which in this society is basically given by the husband. But I think what the mother needs is a much more primitive type of nurturing. We have to acknowledge the wish for this nurturing, and nourish and come to terms with it. In order to protect, we have to feel protected."

Women may also feel in touch with an "out of control" self at this time, she says, because of the "physiological/hormonal changes and the demands of the new task. Because of lack of sleep, exhaustion, disinterest in sex, breast engorgement or dripping if breastfeeding is involved, women often feel out of sync with their own bodies, not 'in control' of their own physiological patterns. It's like you're in a fog or a zombie state. Day becomes night and night becomes day. The circadian rhythms are altered, plus the hormonal aspect really throws you off."

British pediatrician and psychoanalyst D. W. Winnicott observed the heightened sensitivities of new mothers during their earliest weeks postpartum, and gave this state the name of "primary maternal preoccupation." "I suggest that sufficient tribute has not yet been paid in our literature, or perhaps anywhere," he wrote, "to a special psychiatric condition of the mother, of which I would say the following things: It gradually develops and becomes a state of heightened sensitivity during, and especially towards the end of, the pregnancy. It lasts for a few weeks after the birth of the child. It is not easily remembered by mothers once they have recovered from it. I would go further and say that the memory mothers have of this state tends to become repressed. . . .

"Only if a mother is sensitized in the way I am describing can she feel herself into her infant's place, and so meet the infant's needs."[13]

Anthropologist Dana Raphael, author of *The Tender Gift: Breastfeeding*, has called the postpartum stage in a woman's life "matrescence"—the state of becoming a mother. Much like adolescence, it is an intense time that does not last forever, though for each of us as we go through each separate minute's highs and lows, questions and fears, it seems all too much as if it will.

"A woman can get married," says Raphael, "and her life does change. And a man can get married, and his life changes. But nothing changes life as dramatically as having a child. . . . It's a really dramatic and never-to-be-equalled, sudden change. In this country, it is a particular experience, a rite of passage, if you will, that is unsupported for the most part, and rather ignored. Somebody will send you a couple of presents for the baby, but people do not acknowledge the massive experience that it is to the parents involved. And nothing is ever the same after that."

In the book *Making Connections: The Relational Worlds of Adolescent Girls at Emma Willard School*, Carol Gilligan, professor of education at Harvard University, in seeking a greater understanding of what she calls the "underground" of female adolescence, writes that "adolescence is a critical time in girls' lives—a time when girls are in danger of losing their voices, and thus losing connection with others, and also a time when girls, gaining voice and knowledge, are in danger of knowing the unseen and speaking the unspoken and thus losing connection with what is commonly taken to be 'reality.'"[14] To a degree, a comparison might be drawn with women's rite of passage into motherhood, a time when they may feel severely limited in what they are able to explore, pull to the surface, or say aloud; for some, it may be a time when voices that have become strong and bold in other areas of life may need to develop a whole other language and courage to tell these new stories, despite the relative lack of framework or theory to guide and validate them. But in listening to and documenting enough individual voices, perhaps a range and overview of matrescence will suggest itself from the lives of women themselves. Pulling forth and welcoming and celebrating these stories is critical. As poet Sue Silvermarie writes, "The passion of the motherbond demands whole persons."[15] Everything must be acknowledged.

Like female adolescence, the depth and range of all that may occur during this state of matrescence needs to be continually informed by mothers, and made more widely known, so that women and those working with them have a language and framework within which to prepare, guide, and support them. As important as what happens during matrescence is the context within which it happens.

# Who, Me? Needy? Accessing (and Accepting) Support

For many women in the United States today, the image of the nurturing postpartum doula or caregiver described by Dana Raphael in her book *The Tender Gift* is an exotic one, long ago erased from our maternal consciousness. Overtly and covertly, consciously and subconsciously, generations of women have been instructed that they would know how to mother because motherwit and the maternal instinct is a "sacred calling" and birth rite. We all know how to do it; all that we lack is the baby to put our innate talents into practice. But while mothers should be encouraged to trust their instincts, the missing piece of the message is that much of this mothering behavior is learned, not instinctive; and without the educational and emotional support of teachers and nurturers, it is much more difficult and stressful to master.

"No matter what you have to provide," says Philadelphia-based lay midwife Karena Green, "if people don't feel comfortable with accessing it, it's invalid. I think that's something that needs to be done prenatally—create not only a support system, but an awareness of the rightness of [having] a support system."

There are many reasons why women don't feel comfortable asking for or accepting help after they've had a baby:

**Laurie:** "*The first time, I didn't realize I'd need much help.*"

**Spalding:** "*Our society has put women in a position to think they must do it all. Supermoms, in reality, are few and far between.*"

**Carol:** "*. . . motherhood is not appreciated in this society. . . .*"

**Gaye:** "*It's very hard [to ask]. People always seem to think you know how to manage immediately, and especially with a first child you don't.*"

**Tammie:** "*[Asking for help brings up] feelings of failure.*"

**Charlette:** "*You never really know what kind of reaction you will get—*"

*especially from other women. My mom said, 'You just have to deal with it.' This attitude just shuts people down."*

**Gay:** *"Because you see other women who seem to do it all—bounce right back after the birth, never look tired, and seem to handle all the pressures of a new baby. Also, I think husbands expect us to get back to doing what we'd previously done before the birth."*

Other women cite the need for intimacy as opposed to contact with the "outside world," the need to strike a difficult balance, and the wish to remain in a private orbit with their infant. They fear—sometimes rightly so—that outside contact will be too intrusive. Still, a last reason is a simple one: Many women are just afraid everyone will say no.

Sometimes, even when you do want help, it's hard to come by. "[In part it] depends on where you are in the birth order in your own family," says Suzanne, an R.N. and adoptive mother of two. "They'd all been used to me being the oldest one, the caretaker, and the watcher-out for everybody else, so it was weird for them to have me in this role . . . they also think that because I'm a nurse, I've got some kind of edge. I might have a little bit of an edge, but in the end, I was just as exhausted as anybody else. They all thought I would just pick up the ball and run with it, and I did to a certain extent, but it was still not easy. . . . If you're used to doing things for yourself, and people are used to you being independent, then that's how they're going to treat you, even when you wish they wouldn't."

It is not surprising that many women often have no easy way to create a helping, nurturing community. Unless we have extended family close by or relatives who still observe rituals and traditions that nurture the new mother, it just may never have occurred to women that there is any way to move through matrescence other than by biting the bullet and toughing it out alone. The roots of this are deep in our history, our technology, our institutions, and our psyches. The messages come from our own mothers (depending upon who was there to help them when they were new mothers), and from our mates, who, as one woman said, may have their own expectations of us and are just as unprepared as we are for the dramatic changes of new parenthood. As women, we may buy into the myths of perfect mothering without knowing where these images have come from, or who has manipulated them, and to what end. We do know, though, that feeling needy—mistaking vulnerability for weakness—doesn't fit in with our image of what being a mother is all about. If we are needy, how can we care well for a much needier baby? There is a widespread feeling that we have to do it all alone, and if we don't know something, or can't manage it, or, heaven forbid, don't want to, there is something lacking in our makeup. Doctors, busy with medical emergencies, may become impatient with our many questions when often, in fact, we're asking not so much for medical counsel as for some emotional reassurance and contact with someone we perceive to know more than we do. At such times, women often don't know whom to ask. When one mother was having difficulty during her second pregnancy, "somewhere inside of me," she said, "I felt no one was really going to listen. They would just say, 'Well, she's pregnant, she's got to live through it.'" The doctor she approached, she recalls, made her feel as if she "was three years old." Message: If my needs were valid, someone would be there to meet them. Since no one ever talks about this, or listens when I try to, I must be unusually incapable or defective.

Today, many new moms feel isolated, dazed, even defensive, not because they're doing something wrong, but because, often, many of society's institutions—from delivery room to corporate boardroom—fail to meet the needs of the laboring, birthing, and postpartum woman. Sometimes moms are so overwhelmed, they don't know what to ask for first, or what they have a right to ask for. If they can acknowledge their need for a support network, where then do they begin to look? The roles of traditional doctors are not always clear, particularly if you have a nonmedical issue to discuss, or just a sense that things are not going well or as you would like them to. Some doctors or their nursing staff may be able to refer you to other resources, such as local new mothers' groups, breastfeeding supports, or a home-care service suited to your needs.

While some doctors may not involve themselves very much with the emotional and psychological needs of the new mother, some will take a more proactive and positive role in discussing and supporting the ups and downs of postpartum life. Suzanne Rosenfeld is a pediatrician who has had a practice in Manhattan since 1986. She is also the mother of three young children, so understands firsthand the transition to new motherhood and the struggle to balance motherhood, work, and family life. Her practice, she says, has a high percentage of older, first-time moms, in their thirties and forties, many with intense, demanding jobs and strong career focus. She begins to talk to them about their expectations of new motherhood when they come to the prenatal interview that is often part of the parents' process of choosing a pediatrician.

"I spend a lot of time talking about the expectations they have of themselves. Even at the prenatal interview, a lot of women will say something like they are planning [a major trip or event] a month after the baby is born, and I'll say, 'You're having a baby. Are you sure you want to do whatever it is?' These are not very realistic thoughts. . . ."

Perhaps because she herself has been through it, and is a sympathetic listener and support figure, she says that her patients feel comfortable sharing with her the full range of issues they are dealing with—breastfeeding problems, guilt about not going back to work, guilt about going back to work, "some women pushing themselves intensely, trying to do everything, falling apart with it. . . . A lot of them burst into tears on a regular basis in my office—not all but a lot of them do. I know a lot of intimate details about my patients. They talk to me a lot." In part, she says, this is so because different women have different needs from their postpartum caregivers. Her patients, because they are older, tend to have more previous life issues to handle than a practice that sees younger moms in their twenties who may also have more extended family available to help. The older moms she sees don't necessarily have "the support of their mothers, or can't get those relationships back. I'll make suggestions that they'll need some help and talk about different possibilities.

"It's usually after that two-week visit where a lot more things start surfacing. But people call a lot, and in fact we worry more about people we never hear from. Then they show up, completely missing the boat. I think women should be calling. I think they should feel comfortable with their pediatrician." She also adds that if you don't have that comfort level with your doctor, it is appropriate to consider making a change.

Dr. Rosenfeld also observes that despite her gentle warnings about needing supports, many women cannot take them in before the baby arrives. "I often tell people you need someone who's just going to be there for you. Not necessarily to take care of the baby—that's why I have a problem with baby nurses, *per se*, especially since so many women that I see nurse now. I'm always telling people when they have a new baby to really take it easy, and people say, 'Well, you know, I can do this myself,' and then they end up having nobody. The husbands may be home for the first two weeks, but babies wake up after about two weeks and become more needy, and then the mother is alone with them. What I tell people is they have to roll with the punches and try to maintain their perspective and sense of humor. Something else nobody ever listens to is how important it is to find a way to get your rest. Sleep deprivation becomes horrendous."

At times, she sees postpartum women who are more seriously distressed. "I've had a lot of women fall apart at various times, or we may have someone who's having a lot of trouble grappling with the whole thing, and I'll make an appropriate referral. Not that people always follow our referrals. The feeling again is that 'I can do this myself.' A lot of the women I see think they're supposed to be really strong. They're partners in law firms, they're editors of magazines, they think they shouldn't be falling apart because they can't nurse very well."

If feminism taught women that they were entitled to support groups or support people in their lives, "when it comes to parenting," says Norma Swenson, president of the board of directors of the Boston Women's Health Book Collective, "we don't seem to have the same sense of entitlement, and I think it's getting worse. One of the things that makes it worse is that we would be trying to make the support group out of other women like ourselves, meaning [taking] on the role of this Superwoman who's trying to do everything. You certainly couldn't ask a friend who's in the same boat to drop what she's doing and come and take care of your kids. How could you do that?"

Historically, birth in this country was a more social and woman-centered event. Help came more naturally; it automatically congregated around the laboring and postpartum woman. The birth, as Jane Honikman, founder of Postpartum Support, International, said, "elicited the response of the culture." You didn't have to ask. If there was not a community of female neighbors and relatives such as existed in Colonial New England, there were often household help or large extended families and friends ready, willing, and able to help out. It is not difficult to see why a postpartum support network is so important. Yet asking or providing for one nowadays can be very difficult for some women. For one thing, postpartum life is an emotional and physical state that cannot really be imagined until experienced. "[Another] reason," says Liz Koch, founder of the magazine *The Doula*, "is that [many women] have trouble visualizing postpartum . . . because they have trouble being in their pregnancy. If they [could] really honor their pregnancy, they might be able to hear something about postpartum. . . . [If during pregnancy] we began to get in touch with those places of vulnerability and softness, then I think maybe if someone said, 'You're going to need help afterward,' you wouldn't immediately say, 'Oh no, not me. I don't need that!'"

One new mom said she was wary of the response of other women to the fact that she needed help or felt needy. For many women, these close relationships with other women are still uncomfortable. "One of the difficulties of women is sharing," says Dana Raphael, "sharing this [nurturing] role. Because from the early century, we were put into our own rooms, and the door was closed, and we're very isolated in that sense for very intimate things. . . . We were estranged from each other. . . . Margaret Mead used to say that you had to pretend you were niece and aunt, or cousins, or whatever, if you wanted to be together, because there is still so much homophobia, if you will, in this culture. Also, women were ridiculed for getting together, and being together.

"But," she adds, "there is no question that more and more women now are seeing the value of having these [doula] relationships. Now [there begin to be] wonderful relationships . . . between women, and these are doula, supportive relationships." As for why women resist such closeness, "this is something we really have to get into in our own culture, because it certainly is not the best way to keep mothers joyous and comfortable and [give them] enough free time to be themselves, as they have been taught to be."

# When to Prepare for Postpartum: Before the Baby Comes

Most childbirth educators and other experts agree that the best time to prepare a postpartum support network is prenatally. But for reasons already suggested, many women may find it hard to do this. They are so focused on their pregnancy and delivery, they cannot focus on what comes next. Nor should the burden of pulling this network together be all on their shoulders, and yet it very often is. For the most part, many women agree that childbirth classes often fail to focus enough on the postpartum period, not only in terms of their physical needs, sensations, and other care-related issues, but also in terms of the need for rest and support. In designing a postpartum support network, there are no cultural paradigms. It's every mom for herself. This can be onerous for the woman focused on pregnancy and delivery, particularly if she doesn't know where or how to start.

Typical of many women, Diane, who was twenty-three when her first child was born, recalls, "I prepared a lot for the birth. I read almost nothing about childcare or about postpartum. I was even surprised I bled as long as I did. I never even came across that information anywhere, that I would have the lochia for four weeks afterward. The first two months were really difficult and hard for me to adjust to."

Some prenatal classes, like the one Karena Green teaches through Informed Pregnancy and Parenting, have two classes that focus on postpartum: one on baby care and one on the change in the family. Similarly, childbirth assistant Claudia Lowe, founder of NACA, notes that childbirth assistants do an in-depth focus on postpartum before the mom delivers.

"[The childbirth assistant] sets up a transition into the postpartum period. She would provide her client with community resources. She should also be aware of family and friends and job situation, going back to work, maternity and paternity leave. She [does some] troubleshooting: 'How do you see yourself in the postpartum period? What adjustments do you see yourself making? Babies demand a lot of time, have you thought about who will wake up and who won't?' Just introducing a lot of that, so they can start dialoguing about it . . . infant feeding, day care if that's a choice. Also, stressing to the mother the importance of her resting and having some quiet time for herself, whether it be napping with baby or when Dad comes home from work and takes the baby out for a walk. Hopefully [this takes] some of the anxiety or tension out of that first week. Especially if there's a couple who have priorities like 'I have to have a clean house,' or 'I'm not going to let this baby change my life,' those kinds of things."

Direct entry midwife Raven Lang advises "all the women that I look after in any capacity . . . . to try and form some kind of lasting relationships with one or two women, or one or two of the couples within a group. Find someone they like, invite them over to dinner, and really put some energy into a friendship." She also encourages them to join some kind of postpartum group, mother/infant massage class, or "anything that the community has for them to come together and exchange knowledge and babies and stories. . . . even if they feel a little shy, or that they're not really like these women, they're different. I still encourage them to do it." Similarly, she tells them to follow up with bonds the babies make with each other.

While you certainly can and should contact support people after your baby is born, doing some of the legwork, screening, and planning beforehand can serve you well. This may include one person who will be there emotionally for you after you deliver, or a larger network of providers, and it can help give you a sense of security both going into and coming out of the birth. It can also help keep things from escalating unnecessarily to a state of crisis.

# Help in Hindsight

Some moms talked about the kind of help they wished they'd had:

*Laurie:* "*[The] first time, needed help that put ME first—second time, got it.*"

*Elizabeth:* "*I wish I had someone to help me out a few hours a day every day for the first few months, so that I could take better care of myself and the baby.*"

*Carol:* "*I wish I was part of a bigger community. I wish my mother had been there for me. I needed someone to make me a home-cooked meal and help me with breastfeeding problems.*"

*Gaye:* "*The help I really would have liked was to have someone hold the baby for a while so I could nap or shower or just rest. To me, this was more important than laundry or shopping.*"

*Tammie:* "*Someone to assist with household chores, cooking, cleaning.*"

**Gay:** *"Help during the night—to stay up if the baby stayed up."*

**Charlette:** *"[More emotional support] . . . While I was in the hospital (in Montreal), I never was queried about my emotional state. I was looked after physically, but emotionally I was ignored."*

**Carol:** *"I wish there was some kind of compromise between when my mother was having babies and they kept [women] on their backs for ten days, and now when they send you home in two days, especially when a person labors for as long as I labored [forty hours] and was sleep-deprived for that long. I just felt if I could stay in the hospital for five days and if they let me sleep, [brought] me the baby to feed, and fed me meals, that probably would have done me a world of good. Coming home, even though I had help, it's exhausting because I felt like I had to explain what had to be done. I always have to be thinking, and that in itself is exhausting when you're exhausted to begin with."*

---

## SOME MOTHER-CENTERED NEEDS YOU MIGHT HAVE

• the need for someone to talk to—a good role model and listener
• the need to focus inward
• the need to feel dependent
• the need to feel mothered
• the need to talk about the labor and delivery
• the need to talk about the adoption experience
• the need to feel protected
• the need to feel nurtured
• the need to respect your own vulnerability
• the need for private time
• the need for lots of praise and encouragement
• the need to pay attention to your psychological and emotional states, even if others aren't doing so

# Mothering the New Mother: Mother-Centered Help on the Horizon

*[We must] . . . honor how important the sensitivities of the new mother are.*
—Liz Koch

In recent years, while many people feel the postpartum landscape has become more difficult for women and that mothers, fathers, and families are not as relaxed as they once were, some resources and materials to help nurture the new mom in a variety of ways have come into being, many of them started or inspired by women who themselves had difficulty in their own postpartum transition.

"It's a real time of opening," says Liz Koch, who founded *The Doula: A Magazine for Mothers* in 1985 after having her first child in a "healthy, normal home birth" and then finding herself unable to understand why the transition from being a woman without a child to being a mother with a child was so hard. (Today there are close to ten thousand subscribers to *The Doula*.) "[Postpartum] needs to be honored as a very special time, also a time to heal," she says. "The ability to heal and to strengthen by having other people there to help you makes you a much stronger mother." Nurturing, mirroring, role-modeling, and widespread support should be part of the automatic response to a woman who has had a baby.

When Jane Honikman had her first child in 1972, she, too, experienced a difficult transition. Her solution was to join with several other mothers and apply for a grant from an organization to which they all belonged, the American Association of University Women. With the five-hundred-dollar grant they received, they started Postpartum Education for Parents (PEP), a "freestanding independent nonprofit organization that is run with a large number of volunteers providing emotional support to women and families so that they're not alone after the arrival of the baby."

In 1973, just a year after Jane Honikman's son was born in California, a group of women all the way on the other side of the country, on Long Island, embarked upon another project related to motherhood. The project was started by a social worker in one of Family Service Associations of Nassau County's programs. She had noticed that a high proportion of women described pregnancy and the "early years of childrearing as a painful struggle marked by uncertainty and diminished self-confidence." This led to a research project on women's unmet needs during pregnancy, childbirth, and first experience with an infant. Fifty women participated. "They reported the need to share information, ideas, feelings, and experiences to help them to cope with the new adjustments at these critical junctures in their lives. Moreover, they expressed a concern about inadequacies in health services, a strong sense of alienation, and the desire to identify common objectives and develop remedial actions." They found their coming together in this way so educational and therapeutic, they decided to continue the program, and thus the first Mothers' Center was created in Hicksville, Nassau County, New York.

Susan, an adoptive mother, came to the Westbury Mothers' Center's discussion groups when her baby was five months old. (At present, she adds, the center is working on finding a "happy medium" so that biological mothers and adoptive mothers can comfortably be together in a postpartum group.) "I felt very safe there," she recalled. "The main thrust of the center is to provide a safe haven for mothers so they feel safe enough to say how they really feel without being judged by other people. . . . I think I developed a lot of self-confidence as a mother. People were expressing exactly how they felt and nobody was saying to them, 'Oh, that's terrible.' . . . Everybody supported you, validated you as a person, and validated your feelings. That's really what it's about." For Donna, the mother of a three-month-old, the center provided an outlet and catharsis. "I think it has enhanced the transition. . . . Sometimes you're just sitting home pulling your hair out, but so is everyone else. It's nice to know that you're not the only one. It's almost like a cleansing each week."

In Canada, Madeline Dietrich, who teaches pre- and postnatal wellness classes, and had been working with her own issues around mothering, developed a retreat that enables mothers to focus both on nurturing each other as well as on the self-nurturing component because, she says, "It is painful to give from an empty source."

"One of the big issues that I struggled through," says Dietrich, "was really learning that I had a right and a need to take good care of myself when I was a mother. Seeing women struggle around really claiming that—the self-nurturing aspects—I decided that it would be good to have a forum here to do that with them." She developed a weekend retreat called Journey into Mothering, which combines free-form movement/meditation, massage, quiet time, a circle of self-massage, and vegetarian meals prepared and served to the women. She usually has about eleven or twelve women in her groups, a mix of pregnant women, new mothers, and women who have been mothering awhile. The retreat is held on a private lake in Ottawa. "The themes of the weekend depend on who comes," she says. "One [group] was very focused, women wanted to talk about their relationships with their mothers. That was a big issue for them, and being able to mother themselves and their children. At another one, women came just straight wanting to be nurtured, to receive. They were really sweet to each other. We had fun, we played. They were into taking care of themselves, having quiet time sleeping in the afternoon. All those kinds of things mothers never get the time to do."

In part, says Dietrich, women are always working against the larger notion held by the culture that "mothering doesn't really exist, it just somehow magically happens, women just kind of slip it into everything else that they do, it's nothing special, so therefore, it doesn't require any extra support." It also ties in with issues of deserving and worthiness. "For me, it was necessary to mother myself before I could then do it for anybody else."

Deborah came to a retreat when she was pregnant with her third child. (Her other children were four and seven at the time.) She came "to examine her own role as mother, and the concept of mothering she had grown up with, to share with other mothers and find out how they mothered their children, how they mothered themselves. . . . I think we have to mother ourselves in preparing for motherhood." Deborah recalls that she had grown up learning that mothering was "hard and that mothers weren't there." The retreat helped her greatly with her own feelings of abandonment, as she discovered that other women could identify with her, and could also fill that void in a more nurturing way.

"Women felt really sad that their own mothers didn't acknowledge them as mothers, and didn't acknowledge their children now," says Dietrich. "Almost like some sort of rite of passage. We actually did this little ritual for two moms who came who were new moms, that was like a ritual around welcoming them into the circle of mothers. The ones who'd been mothering awhile gave them little phrases to hold with them, to replicate what might have happened in other cultures and other times. To say, 'Ah, now you're a mother, this is special, and you've made this rite of passage.'"

Whatever a specific group's purpose or focus was, a common denominator for most women was the sheer relief in learning "they were not alone," whether it was being a single mother by choice, facing the birth of a second baby when the first was only ten months old, or simply feeling overwhelmed by unpreparedness and isolation.

How will we continue to learn more about this period and what to expect, what to ask for, and what to give each other? In large part, as many women have started to do, by talking—in groups, if possible, no matter how small. By talking honestly and openly to each other and our elders, by sharing our own experiences, by learning to mother ourselves and each other. By developing a language that recognizes and defines the larger phase of matrescence beyond the isolated joy or anxiety of the momentary experience; a language that will let us strengthen our ties with our own instincts, our histories both common and diverse, our bonds with one another and with those who can help and support us on our own terms. We know, of course, that other women have gone before us, but their individual and collective voices may have been largely hidden, diminished, and certainly not honored by society at large. We need to know not only that they have gone before us, but also how they have gone about it. How they have felt. And what solutions they have come up with or would like to come up with.

After the birth of a new baby, some women say that they themselves, for a time, feel close to that vulnerable infant state, if they can permit themselves to experience and admit that. It is a state of being that deserves recognition and respect.

"It's like doing everything again for the first time," said Rhonda de Gier, when her baby was six weeks old. "Everything is new. First time I stepped out of the house, it was like the world had changed. I had been in a cocoon for a week. It had rained and rained, it was dark out every day, everyone else was probably depressed, gloomy from the weather, but I hadn't even noticed. We were in this bubble. We went for a walk and it was Sebastian's maiden voyage in a way. We went up and around the block, picked up a book from a friend . . . and came back. And I felt, Oh! the enormousness of the world! How big and scary everything was, the sounds of things—the train going by, and a car racing past. Some dogs bounded out of their front door and came at us, and I just got the baby in a protective sort of way. You really have to take a lot of time and care with yourself. Everything was so new!"

# Notes

1. S. B. Olds, M. L. London, and P. A. Ladewig, *Maternal-Newborn Nursing: A Family-Centered Approach*, 2nd ed. (Reading, Mass.: Addison-Wesley Publishing Company, 1984), p. 901.

2. I. M. Bobak and M. D. Jensen, *Essentials of Maternity Nursing*, 3rd ed. (St. Louis: Mosby-Year Book, 1991), p. 549.

3. Ibid., p. 566.

4. Adrienne Rich, *Of Woman Born: Motherhood as Experience and Institution*, 10th anniv. ed. (New York: W. W. Norton & Company, 1986), p. 52.

5. Jean A. Ball, *Reactions to Motherhood: The Role of Post-natal Care* (Cambridge, Eng.: Cambridge University Press, 1987), p. 129.

6. Andrea Boroff Eagan, *The Newborn Mother: Stages of Her Growth* (New York: Henry Holt & Company, 1985) p. 5.

7. Bobak and Jensen, p. 568.

8. For a fuller discussion of these phases see Olds, London, and Ladewig, p. 941, and Bobak and Jensen, pp. 566–69.

9. Eagan, pp. 12–13.

10. Valerie Spain, "Growing Into the Mothering Role," in *Boston Parent's Paper*, May 1986.

11. Eagan, p. 3.

12. Rich, p. 161.

13. D. W. Winnicott, *Collected Papers: Through Pediatrics to Psychoanalysis* (New York: Basic Books, 1958), cited in *Babies and Their Mothers*, eds., C. Winnicott, R. Shepherd, and M. Davis (Reading, Mass.: Addison-Wesley Publishing Company, 1987), pp. 36, 93–94.

14. Carol Gilligan, *Making Connections: The Relational Worlds of Adolescent Girls at Emma Willard School*, eds. C. Gilligan, N. P. Lyons, and T. J. Hanmer (Cambridge, Mass.: Harvard University Press, 1990), pp. 24–25.

15. Rich, p. 208.

# Resources

The resources listed here are described in further detail in the following section:

## Model Postpartum Support Programs

UNITED STATES
The National Association of Mothers' Centers
Postpartum Education for Parents
CANADA
PASS-CAN (Postpartum Adjustment Support Services—Canada)

## Family Support Organizations

Family Focus
Family Resource Coalition
National Parenting Association

## Women's Health Organizations

UNITED STATES
The Boston Women's Health Book Collective
International Childbirth Education Association
National Black Women's Health Project
National Women's Health Network
CANADA
Vancouver Women's Health Collective

## Supports for Adoptive Mothers and Families

Adoptive Families of America
Adoptive Parents' Committee

## Support for Single Mothers and Families

Single Mothers by Choice

## Supports for Lesbian Mothers and Families

Center Kids
Family Pride Coalition

## Support for Mothers and Families Who Need Crisis or Respite Care

ARCH National Resource Center for Respite and Crisis Care Services

## Referral Resource for Mothers and Families with Specific Needs Not Covered Elsewhere

*Encyclopedia of Associations*

## Videotapes

*Diapers and Delirium: Care and Comfort for Parents of Newborns*
*Postpartum: A Bittersweet Experience Especially for Fathers:*
*New Fathers, New Lives: A Video to Help Men Make the Transition to Fatherhood*
*Sex, Love, and Babies: How Babies Change Your Marriage*

## Books

*After the Baby's Birth: A Woman's Way to Wellness*
*The Lesbian and Gay Parenting Handbook: Creating and Raising Our Families*
*Loving Hands*
*Of Woman Born: Motherhood as Experience and Institution*
*Pregnancy, Childbirth, and the Newborn*
*Family Wisdom*

# Model Postpartum Support Programs

Some of the following resources may have local chapters you can join, or else may have available start-up materials if you wish to start a similar group in your own community.

## UNITED STATES

**The National Association of Mothers' Centers (NAMC)**
64 Division Avenue
Levittown, NY 11756
Tel.: (516) 520-2929; (800) 645-3828

NAMC can refer moms to mothers' centers in their area, or provide information to women interested in starting a program. There is a national network of centers, and while each center varies according to each community's own interests and needs, the general model offers discussion groups with childcare available. The mothers take part in every aspect of the center's operation and are trained by a social worker to conduct groups, design research, offer childcare, and develop advocacy action plans to make health-care and community institutions more responsive to the needs of families. Some centers maintain a resource library.

**Postpartum Education for Parents (PEP)**
P.O. Box 6154
Santa Barbara, CA 93160
Warmline: (805) 564-3888
www.sbpep.org

PEP is celebrating its twentieth anniversary as a local Santa Barbara program that was started to help ease the adjustment of the family immediately after the arrival of a baby. PEP is an all-volunteer organization that offers discussion groups, classes in baby basics, a baby basics book written by the PEP volunteers, ongoing outreach to postpartum women, and a twenty-four-hour-a-day warmline. Books, materials, and a training manual on how to start a similar program in your own community are available.

## CANADA

**PASS-CAN (Postpartum Adjustment Support Services— Canada)**
P.O. Box 7282, Station Main
Oakville, ON L6J 6L6 Canada
Tel.: (905) 844-9009
New Parents' Information Line
(NPIL): (905) 897-MAMA (6262)

PASS-CAN offers a variety of programs that offer support to new parents. These include Mother's Morning Out, You and Your Baby, Not Just the Blues (a program for parents experiencing a mood disorder related to pregnancy), the New Parents Info Line (provides parent-to-parent support seven days a week from 9 A.M. to 9 P.M.), community education, workshops, training, and referrals.

# Family Support Organizations

**Family Focus (FF)**
310 South Peoria Street, Suite 510
Chicago, IL 60607-3534
Tel.: (312) 421-5200

Founded by Bernice Weissbourd in 1976, this is a nonprofit organization which promotes the optimal development of children by supporting and strengthening families. Community drop-in centers offer new mothers and families the chance to meet other mothers and families, learn about community resources and how to access them, attend new mothers' groups, and learn basic child development principles. FF develops and operates family resource centers in diverse communities by promoting public and private sector policies that support families, through a training division, and by helping others to develop community-based programs. FF can also play a role in helping start similar programs in other communities.

**Family Resource Coalition**
20 N. Wacker Drive, Suite 1100
Chicago, IL 60606
Tel.: (312) 338-0900

Family Resource Coalition is a leader in the field of family support. It provides technical assistance and publications for professionals as well as for parents who are interested in starting their own support groups. Parents can also request a tip sheet, which will guide them in locating family support services in their own community. Membership information is available from the Coalition.

**National Parenting Association (NPA)**
51 W. 74th Street, Suite 1B
New York, NY 10023-2495
Tel.: (212) 362-7575
Fax: (212) 362-1916

A national nonprofit, nonpartisan organization dedicated to building a nationwide parents' movement that supports the critical role of mothers and fathers in shaping their children's futures. With the leadership of a highly distinguished and diverse group of board members and task force participants, NPA offers a way to bridge America's racial and gender divides by uniting a broad spectrum of American families with shared concerns about policies and practices that impact on parents and children. Their mission is to put the needs of America's 62 million parents at the top of the national agenda by making their voices heard in the voting booth, the schools, the workplace, and the media. NPA promotes dialogue with thinkers, policy makers, and business leaders; conducts surveys; organizes task forces; and publishes a series of handbooks on family issues and concerns.

# Women's Health Organizations

UNITED STATES
**The Boston Women's Health Book Collective**
P. O. Box 192
Somerville, MA 02144
Tel.: (617) 625-0271

The Boston Women's Health Book Collective is a nonprofit women's health education advocacy and consulting organization devoted to helping individuals and groups make informed personal and political decisions "about issues affecting health and medical care, especially as they relate to women." They are also the authors of *Our Bodies, Ourselves* and *The New Our Bodies, Ourselves*.

**International Childbirth Education
    Association (ICEA)**
P.O. Box 20048
Minneapolis, MN 55420
Tel.: (612) 854-8660
E-mail: info@icea.org
www.icea.org

Founded in 1960, ICEA unites people who support family-centered maternity care and freedom of choice based on the knowledge of alternatives in childbirth. It offers training and certification for childbirth educators, postnatal educators, and doulas. Of particular interest to new parents is *Bookmarks*, a catalog of books, pamphlets, and audio- and videocassettes, some of which deal with postpartum issues.

**National Black Women's Health
    Project (NBWHP)**
600 Pennsylvania Avenue, SE
Suite 310
Washington DC 20003
Tel.: (202) 543-9311
E-mail: NBWHP@nbwhp.org
www.nbwhp.org

The National Black Women's Health Project has been organizing black women in America to take an active role in maintaining their physical and mental health since 1984. It is an advocacy organization that is committed to improving the overall health status of black women, with a special focus on black women living on low incomes. While not centered specifically around the issue of postpartum, these groups include pregnant and postpartum women and offer them the opportunity to develop support systems for themselves. NBWHP has developed extensive audio-visual and written materials for black women, including *Black Women's Guide to Wellness: Body and Soul*, a book on health information and self-care guidelines, which is available in your local bookstore. NBWHP's most recent publication is *Our Bodies, Our Voices, Our Choices: A Black Woman's Primer on Reproductive Health and Rights.*

**National Women's Health Network**
514 Tenth Street, NW, Suite 400
Washington, DC 20004
Tel.: (202) 347-1140

Established in 1976, the National Women's Health Network is the only national public-interest membership organization devoted solely to women and health. It has for sale information packets on a wide range of topics concerning women's health, including postpartum depression and breastfeeding.

CANADA
**Vancouver Women's Health
    Collective (VWHC)**
1675 West Eighth Avenue, Suite 219
Vancouver, BC V6J 1V2 Canada
Info line: (604) 736-5262
Office: (604) 736-4234

This resource and information center for women was founded in 1971 "on the principle of self-help, to promote women's active participation in and control of their own health care" and to offer adequate and clear information that considered health alternatives. Information is available on subjects including postpartum depression, birthing options, local support groups, nondrug treatments, skills on doing breast self-exams,

PMS, and more. VWHC also does advocacy work within the community, and educational outreach; maintains a library with information on various health issues across the age spectrum, including pregnancy and childbirth; and has a health practitioner and therapist directory with notes from women evaluating the care they've received from individual practitioners.

## Supports for Adoptive Mothers and Families

**Adoptive Families of America (AFA)**
2309 Como Avenue
St. Paul, MN 55108
Tel.: (651) 645-9955

This is a private, nonprofit membership organization and a national umbrella group of twenty thousand families and more than one hundred fifty adoptive parent support groups in the United States and around the world. AFA addresses the full range of needs of adoptive and prospective adoptive parents, providing both assistance and information. It can provide new adoptive or prospective adoptive moms and families with local referrals to experts and support groups nationwide. It has an 88-page full-color magazine, *Adoptive Families,* written by professionals and parents, and has for sale books, tapes, toys, and other materials appropriate for adoptive families. It also advocates for equitable treatment of adoptive mothers and fathers with regard to family leave and insurance coverage.

**Adoptive Parents' Committee (APC)**
P.O. Box 3525, Church Street Station
New York, NY 10008-3525
Tel.: (718) 259-7921

More than forty-five years old, this nonprofit, nonsectarian support group serves the NY/NJ/CT tristate area. Monthly meetings and workshops involve members before, during, and after adoption. Members voice their needs, create the agenda, and follow through. Meetings address a variety of issues of concern to adoptive parents, from legal questions to basic baby care to postadoption syndrome. Smaller groups from within the larger meeting continue to meet on their own (e.g., mothers who want to talk with other adoptive mothers more regularly, the growing number of single parent members of APC, or moms wanting to form playgroups).

## Support for Single Mothers and Families

**Single Mothers by Choice (SMC)**
P.O. Box 1642, Gracie Square Station
New York, NY 10028
Tel.: (212) 988-0993

A national nonprofit organization founded in 1981 by Jane Mattes, a single mother and psychotherapist, SMC provides support and information to single women who have chosen or who are considering single motherhood, and has more than twenty chapters throughout the country and in nearly every state and Canada. Membership entitles women to a membership directory for their area; the name of a local contact person if there is one; an information packet of resources for donor insemination and adoption; a literature packet of articles about single motherhood; and a one-year subscription to the quarterly newsletter. Small groups around specific interests often form within larger meetings. Back issues of the newsletter are available. A free information packet on services is available by writing to SMC.

## Supports for Lesbian Mothers and Families

### Center Kids
The Family Project of the Lesbian and Gay Community Services Center
1 Little West 12th Street
New York, NY 10014
Tel.: (212) 620-7310
E-mail: centerkids@gaycenter.org

This model program offers ongoing support for gay, lesbian, bisexual, and transgender people anticipating children either biologically or by adoption, and it coordinates social events for lgbt families—parties, picnics, and trips that include brand-new mothers. Official and unofficial support groups for new parents are also part of Center Kids services. The group covers the NY/NJ/CT tristate area. No membership fee. Newsletter. Program information available.

### Family Pride Coalition
P.O. Box 34337
San Diego, CA 92163
Tel.: (619) 296-0199
www.familypride.org

Founded in 1979, this is a nonprofit, tax-exempt advocacy and support group for lesbian, gay, bisexual, and transgender parents and those

considering parenthood. It provides referrals to local support groups and helps with the formation of new groups depending upon community needs, or with one-on-one contact if the formation of a local support group is not feasible. FPC also offers bibliographies for both children and parents, a quarterly newsletter including resources, articles, and information for parents and organizations, and another newsletter.

## Support for Mothers and Families Who Need Crisis or Respite Care

### ARCH National Resource Center for Respite and Crisis Care Services
Chapel Hill Training-Outreach Project
800 Eastowne Drive, Suite 105
Chapel Hill, NC 27514
National Respite Locater Service Tel.: (800) 773-5433

ARCH can help new mothers and families in crisis or facing serious challenges, such as a newborn with many medical needs, by directing them to local crisis nurseries or respite care services. These services are intended for parents who need a break from caregiving either due to sudden or significant stress in the family, or to an ongoing situation such as a child who has many medical needs that require that the parents have a break during the week to continue caregiving the rest of the time. The childcare provided might be in-home or out-of-home, depending on the circumstances. ARCH also can direct new mothers and families to local warmlines (telephone numbers to call for information and support), parent support groups, counseling, education classes, and other resources. In addition, ARCH supports service providers through training, technical assistance, evaluation, and research.

## Referral Resource for Mothers and Families with Specific Needs Not Covered Elsewhere

### *Encyclopedia of Associations*
Gale Research
Tel.: (800) 877-Gale (for orders)

This contains detailed information on nearly 23,000 nonprofit associations and organizations, including many of interest to new parents with a wide variety of needs. The three-volume set is available in most public libraries throughout the United States and Canada.

## Videotapes

### *Diapers and Delirium: Care and Comfort for Parents of Newborns*
Distributed by Injoy Productions
Tel.: (800) 326-2082 or fax: (303) 449-8788 (for Visa and MasterCard orders only)

A reassuring tape that focuses not so much on the new baby, but on how life has changed for the new parents. Host Jeanne Driscoll, R.N., M.S., C.S., and cofounder of Injoy Productions, with Nancy Fernandez Mills, offers perspective, advice, humor, and com-

fort in her presentation of the sometimes unexpected stresses of the postpartum period. Driscoll has been teaching postpartum classes in the Boston area since 1979 and is one of the leading experts on women's mental health issues. Her message in this tape is clear: After the baby arrives, make sure you're taking care of yourself! A free catalog of other Injoy videotapes is available from the company.

### *Postpartum: A Bittersweet Experience*
Distributed by Injoy Productions (see telephone ordering information above)

This supportive tape lets Mom know that she is definitely not alone as she listens in on candid discussions with other moms and dads during the early weeks of new parenthood. Topics include mother's postpartum sadness, couples' feelings of estrangement, father's baby blues, sexuality after baby, and adjusting to chaotic lives. Driscoll offers lots of down-to-earth advice and humor.

Especially for Fathers:
### *New Fathers, New Lives: A Video to Help Men Make the Transition to Fatherhood*
Distributed by Injoy Productions (see telephone ordering information above)

A diverse group of fathers share their feelings about fatherhood and strategies for coping. Features a panel of four new fathers and a studio audience of forty men, each with a child under a year old. Issues discussed include: What is the role today's father should play? Is there a paternal instinct? Why can Dad sometimes be jealous of the mother–baby relationship? How can parents cope with a loss of privacy and intimacy? How can Dad juggle work and family responsibilities? Hosted by Dr. Tim Johnson of ABC News and Alvin Poussaint, M.D., of Harvard Medical School.

### Sex, Love, and Babies: How Babies Change Your Marriage

Distributed by Injoy Productions
(see ordering information on page 45)

In this video six couples openly share the challenges they are facing as new parents, and the actions they are taking to improve their marriages. All couples can learn from the participants' candid exchanges on the common, but rarely spoken about, communications problems a new baby can bring to a marriage. There are also creative solutions to emotional and sexual problems, and advice on where to find support.

# Books

While there are many how-tos and books for new parents about parenting skills, the following are included because of their mother-centered perspective. They also share a number of discussions about the feelings of and transition to new motherhood.

### After the Baby's Birth: A Woman's Way to Wellness

Robin Lim
Celestial Arts

A book that honors mothers and motherhood. This covers the physical healing as well as the emotional aspects of the postpartum experience, including sections called "Postpartum Primer: Taking Care of Yourself and Your Baby," "Toning Your Body as You Play with Your Baby," "Herbs for the Postpartum Woman," "Women's Health Wisdom from the East: Internal Massage Exercises," and more.

### The Lesbian and Gay Parenting Handbook: Creating and Raising Our Families

April Martin
Harper Perennial

A guide to parenthood for lesbian and gay people, this includes sections on relationships and communications within the family, extended family members, friends and one's community; options for creating a family; single parenting; emotional resources; families of origin; neighbors and communities; legal considerations; special circumstances; needs of children over time; referrals for information and support; and more.

### Loving Hands

Frederick Leboyer, M.D.
Newmarket Press

In this book, scientist, mystic, and poet Frederick Leboyer uses his deep insight into childcare—as well as knowledge gleaned from traveling in India—to show us how, in the weeks and months following birth, we can use the flowing rhythms of the art of baby massage to communicate our love and strength to our infants.

### Of Woman Born: Motherhood as Experience and Institution

Adrienne Rich

W. W. Norton & Company

This seminal work, first written in 1976 and reissued in a tenth-anniversary edition in 1986, abounds in revelations about women as mothers. History, mythology, primal life experience, and insight fill these pages as Rich examines and redefines women's maternal role in a patriarchal society.

### *Pregnancy, Childbirth, and the Newborn*
Simkin, Whalley, & Keppler
Simon & Schuster

Covers nutrition, prenatal procedures, health care providers, birth places, labor support techniques, medical interventions, exercises, relaxation, and breastfeeding, with strong presentation of parental choices; excellent charts.

### *Family Wisdom*
Susan Ginsberg, Ed.D.
Columbia University Press

Encompassing a remarkably rich spectrum of reflections, inspiration, and advice, this book spans centuries and cultures to offer 2,000 of the most perceptive, exhilarating, helpful, and humorous remarks on the subject of parenting, children, and family life.

# 2.
# ROOTS

*Diverse Cultures, Earlier Times*

......

## Mothering the Mother: Traditions Lost and Found

.............................................................................................

Sara Kunsa is from Uganda, East Africa. Her children were born there in the 1970s. After each birth, her mother was with her. "You have some women relatives who come to knead your body with fresh banana fibers . . . and cook you special soups so you have milk to feed the baby. . . ."

Luz García was born in Colombia, where her father was a doctor and her mother a midwife. There, she says, "The [new mother] becomes a queen for six weeks. Everything is done for her. . . ."

Diosa Summers is a Native American artist, writer, and mother whose children were born in New York State. She recalled that, historically, Native American women entering into motherhood were treated with great respect within their own communities because they had a special gift—the gift of giving life. "Older women have the responsibility of caring for the younger women and helping them in any way. . . ."

All mothers need instruction, nurturing, and an understanding mentor after the birth of a baby, but in this age of fast foods, fast tracks, and fast lanes, it doesn't always happen. While we live in a society that provides recognition for just about every life event—from baptisms to bar mitzvahs, from wedding vows to funeral rites—the entry into parenting seems to be a solo flight, with nothing and no one to mark formally the new mom's entry into motherhood. After day three, we may feel as if we're on our own (which we often are), wondering exactly what to do next and where to turn for help, especially if we haven't been able to orchestrate a support system or delegate the chores fully. Even the responsibility of having to think about the work and who will do it can seem as daunting as the work itself, particularly if there is no one who can be readily called on. The fact that many diverse cultures consciously and consistently gave ample time and support to new moms, freeing them totally from certain kinds of responsibilities, may come as a welcome revelation to some women. For others, the thought of being less than self-sufficient may be so alien to all their images of motherhood that it causes uneasiness instead of relief.

At other times, in diverse places, the "lying-in" period—"the state attending and consequent to childbirth"—has been defined and observed with an infinite variety of customs and traditions. Some practices are based on religious beliefs. Some are based on tribal taboos. Some are believed to be beneficial from a medicinal perspective. Some are practical, protecting the new mom from overexertion, or even too many visitors. Some are more universal—assuring the presence of a close female relative or doula, or a female network to care for the new mom and help ease her transition into motherhood. Some, like *la quarentina*—the forty-day retreat described by Melida Jimenez and Luz García—seclude the mother and baby and treat mom like "a queen." In Southeast Asia, the tradition of "mother roasting" provided for heat or fire treatments for the mother during the lying-in period, and, as direct entry midwife and doctor of Oriental medicine Raven Lang notes, these practices served both practical and ceremonial ends. (In her own practice, Lang has used treatments of moxa, an Oriental herb, with postpartum women, and has found "mothers are spiritually and emotionally filled by the heat and the amount of touch which comes from the person administering the moxa."[1] Still other traditions, even though they do give women the time to rest and recover, are felt to be too restrictive, or based on an image of the female as impure or defective and unfit to return to society until a proscribed amount of time has passed. These taboos that segregate the mother, "not surprisingly, are strictest in the most patriarchal societies."[2]

As varied and as variously motivated as they are, what the most nurturing of these built-in customs provide is a map or "buffer zone" for the woman as she recovers and assumes the role of new mother in the society. They provide the care she will need to recover (e.g., rest, massages, or herbal baths), the nourishment she will need for herself and for successful breastfeeding (e.g., herbal teas, porridges, or soups to stimulate lactation), and the presence and companionship of a wise elder to instruct and encourage her with the unknowns. And in their very predictability—the fact that they will automatically go into motion as soon as the birth takes place—these traditions, like all myth and ritual, provide a way to bring order and control to a chaotic time and event. They offer the reassurance and security and sharing of responsibility the new mom needs to relax and move through this new phase of her life with ample time and acknowledgment of what she has done in creating a new life.

When anthropologist Dana Raphael was seeking an explanation for the frustration she felt as a new mother struggling with breastfeeding and matrescence in the modern American technological setting of the mid-twentieth century, she studied the postpartum traditions of more than two hundred cultures. She found that the common denominator in most of them was the amount and quality of care and energy given to the brand-new mother/baby unit, whether it came in the form of a circle of women relatives, a special soup or ritual, or the presence of a female elder or doula. Raphael observed that, unlike herself, the birthing and postpartum women in these diverse cultures were not burdened with answering the telephone constantly, entertaining visitors, writing thank-you notes for baby gifts, wondering when or if they would have a minute to feed themselves, trying to teach themselves how to nurse in isolation, or trying to find a rocket scientist to help them figure out how to fit the baby into a back sling or baby carrier.

Neither were the silverback gorillas that Raphael studied. In her search for postpartum practices, Raphael also observed the world of animals, from whales and dolphins to her "favorite" social mammal, the silverback gorilla. She extrapolated that in the animal kingdom, too, models of female-centered birthing and postpartum practices existed.

"Of course, men were the ones who did most of the analysis of these animals [silverback gorillas], and what they described was a harem. A magnificent male with all the females and the young. And, of course, my interpretation was, here were a bunch of females with their young, and an unpaid male guarding them against other males, so that they could do what they had to do—lactate, keep their infants alive. And when you look at most of the social mammals, what you find are patterns of female–female interaction and social support."

In the Euro/Anglo-American tradition there is also a legacy of social childbirth—that is, birthing and postpartum customs that were women-centered, neighborly, and reciprocal rather than hired. "This period really lasted through the 1600s and much of the 1700s," says Dorothy C. Wertz, coauthor with Richard W. Wertz of *Lying-In: A History of Childbirth in America.* "Wherever we had a frontier with small communities, it would have lasted probably through much of the nineteenth century. But as soon as you started to have cities and class stratification, some people started buying services, so already you read by the 1770s in Boston, middle-class women [were] hiring nurses and household help. They no longer depended on the neighbors. By the twentieth century, the era of social childbirth was long past. There were still some immigrant communities that did this but as they became Americanized, people bought services." Prior to the start of the childbirth movement in the 1950s, she says, "the only times in America that men were present would have been on the frontier, when families may have been very isolated and there was simply nobody around except the husband. Having the husband present is something very new, really since the 1950s."

One example of social childbirth existed in the New England settlements of Colonial America. There, says Wertz, "childbirth was a woman's event and the woman invited the help of friends and neighbors, and the entire community would pitch in, not only to help with the birth but to help with the postpartum care. Anywhere from six to eight weeks was considered a suitable lying-in period, during which a woman rested, and other people helped for free with the care of her other children and the house, and taking care of a house was really a physically energetic task in those days. Things were heavy and there was a lot of really hard labor. So it was very necessary that other people helped. Some of them were family but a lot were neighbors. At the end of the period, it was custom for the woman to give a party. . . . They called it the groaning party. And we don't know whether it was because the table groaned with food, or whether it refers to the groans of labor . . . she would invite all of the women who had helped her during the birth, and the lying-in period, and they would have really a woman's festival, and there's been nothing like it ever since."

By the turn of the century, says Norma Swenson, president of the board of directors of the Boston Women's Health Book Collective and coauthor of *The New Our Bodies, Ourselves,* most middle-class family arrangements provided the new mother with a female relative to help, whether she was a widowed aunt, or an "emerging adult" who couldn't be supported by her family and was sent along to earn her keep. "There were things wrong with that," says Swenson, "but the net effect [if we see] the female as a center of a childbearing arrangement [was to provide] a sense that she was in some kind of a web, a safety net. Now it may have been lethal . . . but still the sense of isolation, abandonment, and crushing responsibility [women feel today as they become new mothers]—I don't think most women ever had that."

In the 1920s, childbirth for middle- and upper-class women began to move to the hospital, and women (or their household help) started packing that famous suitcase for the ensuing and rather lengthy lying-in. Hospitals came into vogue because doctors found it more convenient to centralize their activities and, following the example of the industrial assembly lines[3] that were in use, set up a system that could move a woman from labor to delivery to postpartum in much the same way that a car moved along from chassis to cushions to paint. Certain kinds of heavier equipment that was being used during childbirth—anesthesia or X-ray machines—could be found only in the hospitals, and the postpartum care offered by hospitals and staff was attractive to many middle-class women who found themselves lying-in in rooms resembling accommodations in luxury hotels.

Some women of the decade were also experiencing a social revolution that influenced the way they viewed childbirth and childrearing. "A lot of middle-class women didn't really want their mother taking care of the new baby," explains Wertz. "They wanted to be independent. They had the generation gap, and the 'new woman' of the 1920s wanted to do things differently from her mother. One way to do things differently was to have the baby in the hospital and have professional nurses take care of it for the first couple of weeks. We think a lot of women regarded the hospital as a hotel with room service, and that's how hospitals advertised themselves—twenty-four-hour room service by licensed nurses. You stayed in there two weeks at least after the birth, to lie-in. Everybody took care of you. You had a room with Oriental rugs and curtains that looked very much like your own bedroom, maybe nicer. It was expensive, yes. Not comparatively as expensive as it is today. And the hospital, once more in its advertisements, told you that it was cleaner than your own home, because around 1920, advertisers discovered the household germ lurking somewhere behind your water faucet or in your kitchen sink—some dangerous germ that was going to get you and the baby."

Hospitals also advertised anesthetics that couldn't be used at home—for example, Twilight Sleep, a combination of morphine and scopolamine, an amnesiac, and which was advocated by feminists in the 1920s. "Complete unconsciousness at birth. This was how they saw equality," says Wertz. Although women did not become addicted to morphine from one-time use, Wertz points out that some decades earlier, medical ideas about women and their postpartum recovery did pose serious threats. "A lot of women did become addicted to morphine in the nineteenth century," she says, "[because it] was prescribed postpartum for recovery from childbirth. Eugene O'Neill's *Long Day's Journey into Night* is about his mother's experience of becoming addicted after his birth."

Until World War II, middle- and upper-class women continued to have long hospital stays, with a vacation from domestic responsibility and a level of postpartum care they often would not find at home. But with the war, hospitals became more efficient, more streamlined, and far less luxurious and leisurely places than they had been in peacetime. The shortage of personnel diminished the length of women's normal postpartum stay, and by the 1950s, the consumer movement toward natural childbirth had begun. The reclaiming of rights with regard to how one's child would be born was, to some extent, further propelled by the women's movement of the 1960s. Women in some—but only some—segments of the society were able to become more aggressive about regaining control over where and how they had their children, and some fathers or partners also became more involved in the birthing process.

With this focus on childbirth education and options regarding the birth itself, more women came into the labor room with a clear idea of what they would or would not accept in the birthing process. But that sense of preparedness did not necessarily extend to the earliest days and weeks of motherhood. Postpartum supports that new mothers automatically fell back on in earlier decades—including social systems such as large extended family, neighbors, and communities—seemed less easy to find or rely on, or possibly—for some women—to accept. Women's lives, choices, and economic responsibilities grew more

## RETAINING OR RECLAIMING POSTPARTUM TRADITIONS

The stories told by individual women who have experienced or observed postpartum practices in diverse contexts tap into a universal, everymother need which women historically recognized and had ways of accommodating. Today some women are able to continue the traditions or find ways to re-create and reclaim them.

• In her research on how the traditions of diverse cultures survive in large "melting pot" cities, Dr. Gerita Ho-Sang, originally from Jamaica, studied women in New York City's East Harlem community. "Among Latina and traditional African-American women," she observed that in many cases the mother or aunt still plays the central, supportive, nurturing role for the new moms. "I found that contrary to what a lot of people feel, some of those traditions still hold true there. The grandmother, the aunt still play that significant role."

• In "Three Generations of Native American Women's Birth Experience,"[5] Native American poet/writer Joy Harjo writes about her own family—her mother, herself, and her daughter. She recalls scenes of alienation, indignity, and disrespect for the customs and peoples in the hospitals where Native American women had to deliver their children. (Particularly for those women who delivered in hospitals near reservations, says Diosa Summers, a Native American artist and mother, such experiences were rampant. For this reason, she notes, many Native American women she knows are opting more and more for childbirth with lay midwives from within their own communities.) Harjo was able to maintain a sense of cultural lineage and heritage through the birth of her grandchild, who, although born with numerous medical interventions in a hospital, was born with Harjo present, and four days later was named by her in a ceremony in the Saguaro forest.

• In the northernmost regions of Canada—"north of [latitude] 60"—a project of cultural survival is under way, documenting the pregnancy and childbirth traditions and stories of the Inuit women of the region for an eventual book to be published in Inuktitut and English. Initiated by Pauktuutit, the Inuit Women's Association of

Canada, this is a participatory research model that rejects the idea that "research can be gathered only by experts and professionals. It is based on the premise that ordinary people, if encouraged and allowed to express themselves, have inherent knowledge about issues that affect their lives."[6] One of the project's goals "is to recognize and legitimize the right of people to identify their own problems and problem-solving mechanisms."[7]

Identifying pregnancy and childbirth traditions as an important element of the culture that could "die with the elders," Pauktuutit traces the shift in childbirth customs from the thousands-of-years-old home birth "in the context of home and family, with the assistance and advice of their elders" to the nursing stations, sometimes with the participation of local Inuit midwives, to the present day, where the vast majority of births take place in hospitals. Those women living too far away are routinely evacuated to larger centers away from family and friends, often to circumstances where their language is not spoken and their customs are not respected. Indeed, in 1988, Inuit women passed a resolution at Pauktuutit's annual meeting addressing "the need for medical personnel to show more respect for traditional Inuit childbirthing practices."[8]

In this project, elders will tell their own stories, and as a way of allowing younger women of the community the chance to learn about traditional practices, each elder will be able, if she chooses, to invite a young woman to be present during the interview. The passing on of skills, knowledge, and traditions in this direct way also imparts to younger generations of women in the community the gift that Dana Raphael called the "sacred supportiveness" of the help-giving circle that buoys up the new mother throughout the centuries and throughout the cultures.

complex throughout the 1980s, and the rituals and community that existed in the distant past were often no longer remembered. Women's support groups did not necessarily extend to motherhood, and as for the right to rites and rituals of matrescence, "We gave it away," says Jane Honikman, "when we said, 'I don't need anything, don't come over, I can do it myself.'"

After so many decades, it seemed that someone had forgotten to tell us that we needed—let alone deserved—a nurturing postpartum experience; we really didn't have to do it all alone.

As women now attempt to define their needs postpartum and integrate motherhood into very different and complex lifestyles, it is interesting to explore how postpartum supports have functioned in diverse cultures and earlier times, so that we can extract and refashion elements to fit or inspire our course for the remainder of the 1990s and beyond. In addition to providing security and a sense of lineage and heritage, an awareness of these traditions can also provide confidence and a sense of collective maternal consciousness—that inner quality and resource that Naomi Ruth Lowinsky has called "the motherline." So often we feel that this valuable lineage is lost. "Women lament the lack of narratives of women's lives, yet women's stories are all around us," she writes in her book *Stories from the Motherline.* "We don't hear them because our perception is shaped by a culture that trivializes 'women's talk' and devalues the passing down of female lore and wisdom. . . . We daughters are left feeling motherless because our mothers have no words to express the depth of their experiences, and no feminine authority with which to value their lives."[4] Yet women still very much feel the need for these stories and this heritage. When her children were born in 1988 and 1990, Canadian filmmaker Helene Klodawsky recalls, "I walked a lot with them as everybody does with strollers, and I would ask people everywhere, 'Do you have children? What do you do for this?' And everybody would give me advice or criticize how I was doing things. I just realized there was this vast world of women's expertise, of knowledge and experience that I just wanted to embrace around me and gobble up and understand."

This sense of sorority and rite of passage is poignantly illustrated in an African story of childbirth and postpartum recalled by Liz Koch:

> There's an African story of birth where the women gather and send you across the river, and as you walk across this log across the river you head out with these women. As you go across on the narrowest part you're alone. No one can be there with you, and as you emerge onto the other side of the river, all the women who have ever given birth are there to greet you. It's that circle of women who are there to greet you. And because we don't have that tribal ability to have those women, the idea of

*a doula, whether it's a circle of women in your community or a woman that you hire to be there for you, to mother the new mother, is really to honor how important the sensitivities of the new mother are. She shouldn't be in the world in the same way. She really needs to be there not only for her infant, but for herself. It's a real time of opening, and a time to also heal.*

A look at some of the diverse traditions as they exist or once did can help us validate the underlying needs they address without perceiving them as weakness or inadequacy, broaden our knowledge base, provide models of mother-centered care and concern that are frequently missing from the postpartum experience today, and ultimately give new moms a chance to broaden their own postpartum options.

The following women represent diverse cultures, but there is a strong universal message in their collective voice.

# Mothers Speak . . .

## LUZ, COLOMBIA

Luz García was born in Bogotá, Colombia, where her father was a physician and her mother a nurse and midwife or *comadrona*. (A *comadrona*, Luz explains, implies someone who has a lot of children; translated literally, it means "along with the mother," and the *a* means "a lot." "So even in the name, it implies that you have helped a lot of women to be mothers.") Her father's ancestors came from Spain, and her mother was of Chibcha Indian ancestry. Luz moved to the United States in 1961, where all three of her children were born. She grew up in Colombia observing her mother's practice, and was herself surrounded by traditions and beliefs that honored, cared for, and nurtured the mother through pregnancy, childbirth, and postpartum. She starts her story before the baby is born.

"My mother practiced not only within a hospital setting, but birth, at that time, was really very homebound. Women did not come to the hospital unless they were diseased. Birth was not seen ever as an illness, but as a sign of health and a sign of beauty and life coming through. . . . If you could bear a child, you were healthy, you were alive, every good thing was coming your way. . . . Regardless of what the family was, that infant was cared for from the moment the mother was found to be in *estado* [pregnant]. The mother got fed better, first portions came to her. . . . [There was no prenatal care.] The mother was recommended often to have long walks, to see flowers, to see baby animals at play, and to hold other babies and to have good thoughts. . . .

"When the mother reached the seventh month, somebody was always with her. That's when her teaching began, and usually it would be a woman who had another child, and they would talk to her about what to expect. 'Mine was like this, don't be worried,' and 'Eat a lot of soups and a lot of liquids.' They made her believe that she was capable of doing this as long as she fed herself well, slept well, rested well, and kept her mind on good things. This was a part of transmitting to her an inner power that she carried. . . . It was positive reinforcement that what was about to happen was a good thing, and that she was perfectly designed to do this and the baby was going to be healthy and do well.

"[When it was time for the baby to be born, the person there to prepare and help the mother was] usually a family member—an aunt or the grandmother, or an elder sister, someone who had gone through it. When the baby was born, of course the baby was put to nurse, which helped with the placenta. [My mother] rarely ever had to use an injection to help stop the bleeding. If the baby is put to the breast, the natural rhythm of the body allows the placenta to go down. Certainly there was no waiting, fingerprinting, or stitching, or attacking the baby at birth. The baby was just wrapped around, the mother was wrapped around. The mother was cleaned up, and that was the last time that she saw water for forty days. Part of it is that Bogotá is a very cold city, and the concern was that this mother might catch a cold or pneumonia or something. . . . Her hair could not be wet for forty days until *la quarentina* was over. What they did do for this woman—I still remember the smell of baby powder—[was sprinkle] scented powder in her hair and her hair got brushed out, so the oils got cleaned that way. Her body was sponge-bathed, always with nice herbs to cleanse the body, to keep it nice. They believed they cleaned her from the inside by giving her good soups, and sometimes if she got constipated—because I guess the pushing does that to you, and you get hemorrhoids—they would give her ruda [an herbal laxative] and oil of ricino, and that was thick and yucky. They gave it to you with oranges, and then afterward the mother was supported and fed constantly by soups.

"No one allowed her to take on any stress of any sort. Everything was done for her. Gifts came to her in many forms—food, time from all the people, family members being with her, and she was really coddled and protected for the whole six weeks. It's a very traditional setting. Even though I grew up in a city, that was the common custom, everybody came to take care of the mother and the baby. It's very different here, mothers have a baby and they get put into an apartment and they have no connections with the neighbors. Even though they have lived there years, they don't know anyone.

"[At home,] people came to visit—the baby was not the center of the whole thing. It was always the mother. The mother was always the center—it was always 'Oh, you did such a wonderful job'—and this is exactly what I tell the mothers here at North Central [Bronx Hospital, where García is the doula or breastfeeding support person]—'Your body did well, how wonderful!' She was praised, she was the center, it was not like here in America, that the baby is everything and the mother is totally discarded and forgotten. It was the mother who did this wonderful, fabulous job: 'Oh, look at your milk, it is abundant,' and it was always positive reinforcement for the mother, and the woman actually did well precisely because her body and her mind and everything were expected to do well, so well she did.

"Her only job was to nurse the baby and learn how to take care of this baby. Women would cook and bring food and whatever she needed, clean house, do laundry. If she didn't have her mother there, someone would always do that work for her, because everybody was concerned that the life of that baby depended on the mommy being able to nurse that baby and keep that relationship going. . . . They took care of the mother so that she could take care of the baby."

## GERITA, JAMAICA

Gerita was born and raised in Jamaica, where her two children were born in the 1970s. She now lives in the United States and has a Ph.D. in nutrition.

"[Postpartum practices] depend on the social structure. For those women who have sort of evolved to the middle and upper class, babies are usually born in the hospital, and they stay three or four days afterward, depending on whether they are okay, and go back home. It's usually a paid housekeeper who is there to help the mom with the baby. Sometimes the mother of the woman, or the mother-in-law, will visit. But not over any extended period. Just for moral support.

"[Among the] lower-income women, childbirth is more like a ritual, and the women, most of them are delivered at home by a midwife or what we call a nanny, and the nannies are not exposed to the new way of thinking, so the tradition carries over from generation to generation. They request that the new moms abide by certain principles. For instance, she shouldn't get out of the house for nine days, she should stay in, and have all her meals. She's catered to, actually, by relatives and friends who come and do all the housekeeping, look after the other kids, and she basically stays in bed and feeds the baby. . . . When the nanny delivers, she's there every day for about a week to check on the new mom to see how everything is going—how the mom is doing, if the baby's feeding.

"Most women are breastfeeding, and that's their role for those nine days. Afterward she begins to go out of bed and do light chores around the house, and then begins to go outside. Even then they tell you she has to be covered up, she might get a cold. We have these taboos, we call them, which are not substantiated by any scientific evidence, but she has to be covered up lest she get a cold. And the baby has to be dressed a certain way if it is taken outdoors; the head has to be covered, because they feel the head is likely to get a cold easiest.

"[The new mom is fed] soups—chicken soup or vegetable soup—and special teas, mainly herbal teas. They have special shrubs and bushes that are good for certain things. For the first two or three days the woman doesn't eat food because they believe that certain foods come out in the breast milk and affect the baby. So for the first few days she is on a very strict diet. The baby is fed on demand and sleeps with the mom. That is very important. They're never separated. In the hospital, yes, unless you specially request. [At home] the child is right in the bed with the mother for a couple of weeks and then she has a cot beside her bed. The baby is always in her room. The mother has to bathe in warm water.

"Middle- and upper-class women are exposed to the usual marketing strategies of milk [formula] companies. When my first child was born, I was studying nutrition at the university, so I knew all about breastfeeding. I decided to breastfeed, and I discussed that with my doctor, and he was very supportive. But I found that the nurses were the ones who couldn't understand that you wanted to feed solely on breast milk, and eventually he had to put up a notice in the nursery saying that baby Ho-Sang should be taken to her mother for all feeds, and they did abide by those rules then.

"When I got home, my mother-in-law spent the first two weeks with me. She helped. I was still quite inexperienced as to what to do with engorgement, because nobody discussed that with me either in the hospital or before, so she was a very good assistant. She had breast-fed her children. She didn't know what a breast pump was, either, so she taught me to apply a hot rag to the breast and squeeze, and it did help. When the baby had gas and it wouldn't burp or something, she would teach me what to do.

"It gives you a sense of security, because everything is so confusing when you leave the hospital, it's overwhelming. The baby is crying, you don't know what to do, your breasts are hurting because they're engorged, it's really confusing, and that person really gives you a sense of confidence. When she left, I didn't want her to go. It was frightening, because here she is going and leaving me all alone with this little baby. It wasn't really very hard after she left, because by then the baby was sucking very well, so I no longer had the problem of engorgement. In general it wasn't bad when she left.

"[She came to help] with both children, because even though you think, 'Well, I've had one before, I know what to do,' each one presents a different challenge."

## SARA, UGANDA

Sara is a Muganda from the Baganda tribe in Uganda. All four of her children were born there in the 1970s, after which time her family moved to New York City.

"I am from Mityana, which is about thirty miles away from Kampala, the capital city of Uganda in East Africa. I had four children in Uganda. . . . They were born in the hospital. If you have a difficult delivery you can stay for a week in the hospital. If you have a normal delivery, you stay overnight. If your mother is alive, your mother can come to look after you, or your aunties, to take care of you and take care of the baby while you rest. Most women will go to the hospital where possible, unless there is no transport and they are deep in the village. . . . Then they get some midwives who help them to deliver babies at home, or all the women who have had babies before and know, as laywomen, how to deliver babies. After the baby is born, the mother has some relatives who come to look after her.

"[The women] take care of you to tone up your body so that it comes back to its normal shape. They use fresh banana fibers, they boil them and then use them to knead and squeeze your body and stomach, to put it back into shape. And they use the big cloth or sash tied around your stomach so that it can go back into normal shape. For the baby, they prepare a special saucepan, and put in special herbs and oil them and use the water to bathe the baby. That is something that has to be done for every baby to bring good luck to them when they grow up. The mother or grandmother prepares it, if you are not able.

"The relatives stay for about a month. In that time you don't do anything. They bathe the baby, they wash the laundry, they cook, and they give you special dishes. They cook special soup so that you can have milk to feed the baby. We feed whenever the baby cries. There's no time schedule.

"My mother was there and even accompanied me to the hospital, because in Africa the men don't play that role the way they take here to be in the maternity room. He can drive you to the hospital, but will stay in the back, especially if the mother is around, because in our culture, the mother and husband are not supposed to be near each other. A sign of respect. They talk, but have to keep at a distance . . . in this case, the mother can come and stay. Usually we have the kitchen outside, and sometimes they have a bedroom added for those people who cannot come near another person through respect, so the mother stays in that place.

"After you give birth, if it is in the village the whole village has to come and visit to see the new baby. A birth is treated like a death—a special thing. Everybody has to come and see the baby, otherwise they think, 'Why don't you come and see the baby? You want to bewitch the baby?' So even the village people when they hear so-and-so gave birth, they have to come and visit and congratulate you. Sometimes they bring food. For the baby, they give money. They have to give money or they say they don't want the baby to grow up a poor person. So they give money and they make the baby hold it. (They did that when my children were born.) It was okay, you feel a special person.

"... My mother stayed for three or four months. They stay until they see that you are strong enough to be able to carry on, or anyway they always make sure that you have somebody to take care of your baby after [your] maternity leave [ends, if you have a job]. The difference [between here and home] is in the amount of help you get from relatives or how easy it is to hire somebody to take care of the baby.

"[When my mother left], of course, I felt terrible! When you start doing all the things she was doing for you—oh, no, no, no, no! They always come. They're always there. I could handle the baby, but usually they leave somebody to help you, someone you pay. That's what people miss here. They have baby-sitters but they're very expensive. There you have somebody who will do the cooking as well as take care of the baby and clean the house. Most homes have somebody like that, especially if you are working."

## IN, KOREA

In was born and raised in Seoul. One of seven children, she recounts that her own mother delivered all but her youngest child by herself. (For the last one, she called the midwife.) In came to the United States in 1970. Her children were born here in 1974 and 1976. She had no extended family here, and was on her own immediately after the births of her daughters. However, she vividly recalls the traditions of home.

"The new mother is not supposed to have visitors until the twenty-first day. After the twenty-first day, visitors can come to see the baby. Until that time, the mother just lies there and sleeps all day and eats and doesn't do anything. [They cook] seaweed soup—it's supposed to clean the blood for the mother, and since we all breastfeed the babies— back then, anyway—it's better for producing more milk. All that time, she has to have that soup at least three or four times a day, including all the other nutritious food. Also, during that time, the new mother is not allowed to touch cold water, and not supposed to go out in cold wind if it's winter. Even if you're not that well off, the neighbors will help you get through the days—I don't know these days [if that still holds true].

"Usually [the helper is] the mother-in-law, since the girl gets married and spends time in the man's house. . . . We never go to have a baby to our own mother. You stay where you get married, at your in-laws'. The mother-in-law has the help, if not relatives, who can pitch in. [A sign goes up outside the house.] It's a rice stalk, and if it's a boy we put a dry red pepper, and if it's a girl, we put a wooden charcoal, so everyone knows if it's a boy or girl. Also that means you're not supposed to go into the house. We don't usually phone the neighbors, we just drop in any time of the day, so if you see those ropes hanging on the front gate, you know you're not supposed to go in. After a little over twenty-one days, then baby can travel to maternal grandparents' house.

"After three months and ten days—what we call a hundred days old—then we have a big celebration for the baby. On that day, the family has a sort of party, all the family, all the distant and the immediate relatives, they all get together, and the house will make all the rice cakes, all different shapes and tastes of rice cakes. And they'll make plenty so they can share with all the neighbors, so we put it on a nice plate and send it out to all the neighbors, and in return they place on the empty plate a long, long white cotton thread, meaning long life for the baby. They don't give you elaborate gifts for the baby, that's just a symbol, the long thread [wound] continuously. It still happens today, even in America, if you have a family. But I didn't have any family [here] so I had to cook my own meals and everything. That's the best time of life, all the ladies get pampered during the birth of their child."

## DIOSA, RHODE ISLAND

Diosa is a Native American artist, writer, educator, and mother. Her father is a Mississippi Band Chocktaw, and her mother grew up in Rhode Island. Her maternal grandmother spoke an Algonquian language and came originally from "somewhere between Maine and Nova Scotia." Her grandfather was an indigenous Indian from Brazil. Diosa herself grew up in Rhode Island in a community where the Native American people were Narragansetts. She was also adopted in her teenage years by a Narragansett family, and later in New York State was an adopted Seneca very much involved with Iroquois ways and traditions.

"Children are very special to Native American people. They're gifts and very precious and every child is to be loved and cared for by everyone. Mothers are special. The first important thing you learn about mothers in the Northeast is they have a gift of reproduction. Histori-

cally, the women farmed the land because they could make things re-
produce, they had that special ability and it was recognized. Women
owned the land, women owned the houses, the children belonged to
the women. All of this has continued in New York State with Iroquois
people, who have a very strong tradition and still practice their histor-
ical-religious traditions and maintain the languages.

"Historically when an Indian woman had a child she had support
from the women in her family. Families lived in a longhouse, which
was just that—it was a long house. And the person who was the leader
of that house was the grandmother because it was a matrilineal, matri-
archal system. All of those women were related. The men were related
only through marriage. They came into the house, and those women
united and formed a major support system. Often, if the mother of the
mother-to-be was not there, maybe she had died, maybe she was away,
there would be a surrogate person who would take over with comfort,
advice. The respect is wonderful. Indian women receive very special
respect and recognition among their own people, particularly as mothers. . . . Older women have the responsibility of caring for younger
women and assisting them in any way. The clan system provides a lot
for that. Clan mothers are very helpful with advice, comfort, there's
just so much that's provided by the community. . . . Everyone feels this
child is their child, and that's how it is with every child. . . . [It] makes
it a real happy situation, which is always what it should be—lots of
holding and talking and singing and always having baby with you. The
cradleboard, which is a Native American tradition that everybody
knows about and learns about in elementary school, is wonderful. It's
good for the child to be in this hard board, and you can bring your
baby with you everywhere. . . .

"In different communities, transitional things have happened over
the years. . . . The support that comes from the family and from the
women in the family is important and it's still part of that longhouse
tradition and that historical tradition. It just happens with telephones
and cars now, rather than everyone living in the same building."

## AMAL, LEBANON

Amal is from a Lebanese Christian family and is the middle of five
daughters born in the 1950s and early 1960s. Although she was born in
a hospital in Lebanon, her family lived in Shreen, a mountainside vil-

lage in Mount Lebanon, about eighteen miles northeast of Beirut. She came to the United States to study in the mid-1970s, married, and stayed here. Her own son was born here in 1987. Amal has a Ph.D. in education of public health, and wrote her dissertation on breastfeeding practices among recent immigrants from southern Lebanon.

"In general, in the villages [the postpartum experience] is going to differ from the cities. When I was growing up, we lived in an extended family setting, at least for the first maybe eight years of my life. When we were born, there were the grandparents present in the house, and also my uncle and his wife and their children. When my mother or my aunt would give birth, either the sister-in-law or mother-in-law or mother of the mother who had given birth would come and help out. It was more preferable for the [woman's own] mother to come and take care of the household and the older siblings, so the mother would have time to spend with the new baby and to nurse herself back to health. Even though my paternal grandmother was already living in the house, my [maternal] grandmother would come and spend the day with us and cook for us and wash. Washing was a major chore then that this woman would assume, and keeping the house together while my mother rested and nursed the baby. Nursing was very important. That allowed her time to nurse on demand and not worry about cooking and cleaning and entertaining guests. The oldest child, too, took care of a lot of the chores and a lot of the work to assist the grandmother and also when the grandmother wasn't present. My older sister really did what a mother would do. She was there for us and helped us and managed the house.

"There were particular foods that were encouraged. The mother was encouraged to eat a lot of stews, particularly soups, like chicken soup, something that's hot, because that was believed to increase the milk supply and make the mother stronger. It was traditional that somebody—maybe a relative—in the village would bring a big rooster over, and that would be a nice gift, and then it was killed and cooked. The soup was very, very good, and was believed to be important to give the mother back her strength, and also help her produce more milk.

"For at least a couple of weeks, the mother would do very little. In the older days, I heard, it used to be at least forty days that the mother would not stay in bed per se but be in seclusion almost, be in bed with the baby, and not have any responsibilities whatsoever in the household other than taking care of the baby and nurturing and nursing. As things progressed and [there were] more demands on the mother and more children around, and perhaps the grandparents [were] not as available or perhaps sick, there was more pressure on the mother to get up earlier and begin doing her chores. But it's not like what it is here—after three days I came home and I was washing floors! And there's no way on earth, even these days, new mothers would do something like that in Lebanon. The mother is much more pampered. She's allowed to sit in bed, stay in bed. Her food is brought to bed. She's literally relieved of all responsibilities of the household except for the new baby for at least a couple of weeks.

"When somebody gives birth, a lot of people come to congratulate you from the village. It's usually after the first two weeks or so, people would come and congratulate you. That involves passing out candy or special sweets, depending, in those days, on the sex of the baby. If you had a baby boy, what you pass out to your guests would be the best that you can find. In those days it used to be baklava, the special kind that you buy in the stores and distribute and are very proud [about]. . . . In the event that it would be a boy, the whole environment would be very happy and festive and cheerful. And the mother would also get a lot more pampering from the in-laws and the husband. In the cities and in modern days, I don't think that's as noticeable, although it's still very important for a family to have a newborn—especially the firstborn—be a male or at least have one male offspring. If she doesn't, she's not as pampered. If the newborn is a girl, then it's less festive, less fancy, a little bit more subdued. In our case, we were five girls, so every time it was almost like people came to pay condolences rather than to congratulate. [For my own mother], even her mother would feel sorry for her, and say, 'So you have another girl, but it's all right, maybe the next time . . .' Emotionally and psychologically, it takes a toll on you, especially after the fifth one!

"The end of the forty-day period in the old days used to signify that the mother was back to normal, back to health. I don't think that having a postpartum checkup like they do here was something that was done often. As long as the mother had healed, and there were no signs of bleeding or infections or any problems, she would probably not see her obstetrician until the next pregnancy.

"[I got married in 1986.] I'd been here for twelve years almost, and when I had [my son] I really had this enormous need to be with my mother or my sisters. Even though my in-laws were here and were supportive it wasn't anything like being with your own. . . . . I had to just pull myself together and get up and do everything. . . . When my sister had her baby, she went and stayed with my mother. These kind of support systems don't exist here. Then you begin to doubt yourself and say, 'Why can't I do it all?'"

## LUFI, CHINA

Lufi was born in 1957 in the city of Hangzhou, close to Shanghai. She was married at home, and her daughter was born there in 1987. While she recalls that the birth itself was difficult and unsupported, the postpartum time was honored. Five months after her daughter arrived, her husband moved to the United States. When her daughter was nearly three, Lufi came to the United States, and three and a half years after that, she and her husband brought their daughter over to join them permanently.

"I was born June first. My name is sort of related to the season. Lu means green. My mother gave me a very pretty name. Hangzhou is a middle-sized city and later became an international tourist city because there is a very beautiful lake there. I was born there, grew up there, finished my high school education. [When I was nineteen] I went to the countryside to get what was called 'reeducation' from workers and peasants. At least one child in a family after high school was obliged to go to the countryside for reeducation. I was there for about a year and half. It was an area where cotton and linen were grown. [Then] the cultural revolution was officially over, Mao died, the college exam system was restored, so I participated in the national college exam and I got accepted in foreign language department, Hangzhou University and majored in English literature. Early in 1982 I graduated and then went to a college to teach English as a second language.

"When we got married, we lived with my parents. My parents don't have a lot of room so they give us one room and they had one room and that's that. When I was pregnant and the whole period of time until my husband left, I was still living with my parents. I delivered the baby in the hospital but the whole experience was three generations under one roof. I got tremendous support, especially from my mother, but that's because my husband wasn't there anymore.

"For a new mother, the first month after the baby was born you're supposed to lie in bed. You're not supposed to go out at all. Not supposed to have a full-scale bath, not supposed to have a hair washing. Very rigid rules, and special food to try to get more milk. I remember one thing—pigeon or pigeon soup. Of course, chicken, older chicken. Chinese hen. There's a lot of other stuff I didn't eat. The other thing is a lot of soup, bone soup, pork soup, marrow, because it has a lot of calcium. And chicken feet is good, too.

"I stayed in the hospital about five days. That's about average. I had a difficult time. The most difficult time compared to here was that no family members are allowed to be with you in the hospital. You just stay by yourself. You cannot have a lot of food quite a few hours before the birth. . . . There was no emotional support, which is not that good, especially compared with the process here.

"My grandmother had fifteen births and they had a midwife. I haven't heard a lot about midwives because I'm not familiar with remote areas. [On the farm where I worked], women were sent to the hospital. The only thing is, in the countryside it is hard to take a pregnant woman from home to the hospital. Literally there was no transportation in most of the areas. Even in Hangzhou, I remember my husband had to find a rickshaw cart, a three-wheel cart and wheel it because I couldn't sit on the bicycle. So a three-wheel cart is popular. I guess now the taxi would be popular. In the countryside they would make sort of a homemade carriage and put the woman on it, and four, five, six men carry it, walk around the mountain area or countryside.

"In China, I would assume there are a lot of traditions. However, after 1949, the Communists took over so a lot of traditions were eliminated. So basically, right before the baby was born, we had sort of a baby shower. The baby shower to me is a little bit different. Probably it is still popular in China. Here we have a baby shower, we have bought all the new clothes and friends coming. My baby shower, my mother-in-law gave to me. They would come to where I live. My mother-in-law and her mother, who is 85, she had kept all the little clothes that my husband and his brother wore when they were young. She had kept everything, and chose quite a few and wrapped them up and came to my house and presented me—it's a good luck sign. It's not new clothes, but clothes that were worn by former generations. A month after the baby is born, we have what in Mandarin dialect is called *man yue jiu*—

the literal translation is 'full month wine'—but it is a party actually, and at a good party you always give wine. You invite the family members or your friends to have a big party to meet the baby, to meet the mother. Because for the first month, you were not allowed to go out, you are very weak, so you're not supposed to have a lot of visitors.

"There really aren't any strict laws about visitors. My friends came. And my mother-in-law, and they'd come once every few days and make some food, and send it to me. Both parents went to the hospital every day or every other day and sent special foods for the new mother. Everybody does that.

"The family is the key in the emotional support. I would not say the husband, I would say the big family. They participate in all the process, and I had to go back to work in eight weeks. Unless there is some special reason, we're allowed about two months' leave from work fully paid and fully insured. Both my mother and mother-in-law, they tried to find a baby-sitter, and my mother doesn't have a big house, but we had to hire a baby-sitter to live with us. So it's very difficult for her, but she just did it for me. The physical presence of the [family members], it just makes you so comfortable.

"Having been surrounded more than the usual time with so many people around me, I never had a feeling of being alone, never ever. I felt lucky that I lived with my parents and my mother-in-law's family in one city. Things would be different if you lived away from them. Usually they would literally come to you for a month but after that you take over alone.

"I guess it can go both ways. To me it is a very positive thing. I'm sure there's a restrictive side which is not reflected in my experience."

## MYINT-MYINT, BURMA (MYANMAR)

Myint-Myint Si, M.D., was born and raised in Rangoon (Yangon) and moved to the United States in 1979. She recalled some of the traditions of the more remote villages at home "where different tribes of Burmese live. In most cities," she says, "the trend is more or less like in Western culture.

"[At home] the word *mie nay the* means 'mother of a newborn.' It has its own meaning, probably came from the ancient tradition when young moms were suggested to stay near the fireplace and warm themselves to avoid sluggish circulation in their system, because *mie nay* simply means 'stay near fire.' *The* means 'a bearer or person.' In most remote places and villages where modern medicine cannot be reached, people still practice those traditional ways.

"When you do something for the mom, that should also have direct benefit for the baby—for example, offering special food, especially soups like oxtail soup. Traditional people believe that it helps for good flow or lactational process, as noted by a very famous old poet in his poem 'Goodness of Oxtail Soup for Lactating Moms.' Also, some people believe in eating a lot of chicken meat to make the bleeding womb heal faster. In old traditional ways, people believe in rubbing turmeric paste all over the body of the young mom to enhance better circulation and expel old unclean blood out of her circulation via bleeding from her womb.

"Usually any older family member who may be helping her throughout her pregnancy takes care of the household. Sometimes, maybe more than one person. The mom or aunt or older or younger sister. Sometimes her in-laws may help her by taking over the house. Traditionally, people would allow the young mother to stay in her own bedroom for five to seven days, and in the house for about forty-five days. They labeled that period as *thie-dwin,* meaning 'postpartum period.' Moms were suggested not to lift heavy objects or even elevate their arms and hands during the first few months because these activities can prevent or delay womb healing and may cause uterine prolapse. Elevating the arms will prevent good circulation to the breast and upper part of the body and thereby lactation will be delayed.

"Except for city dwellers and working mothers, all Burmese moms breastfeed their young ones. Usually, elders like their own mother or aunts will teach them. Even for those who do not have close relatives around, there will always be a good neighbor or local midwives would help them out to learn how to nurture the babies."

## MELIDA, GUATEMALA

Melida Jimenez is a political exile from Guatemala now living with her husband and three children in Toronto, where she is a multicultural health educator at the Women's Health Center at St. Joseph's Health Center. Her first two children were born in Guatemala. Her third was born in Toronto.

"[At home] it's the family system. Everybody's close and traditional, and they provide young women with information and when the baby's born, everybody's close to you, they attend you, they give you soups. We usually give chicken soup, but it's a chicken that is grown in the fields, not with chemicals. So every woman that has a baby has soup. It's a part of the family, everybody's there and everybody's helping. One person bathes the baby, the other person takes care of the baby, the other person takes care of you, they don't let you do exercise, they give you good meals and good rest, and usually when the woman doesn't live with her family, these women go to their mom's home and stay there for forty days. That's *la quarentina*. We call it *la dieta*—the diet—no sex, no exercise, only take care of your new baby and adapt to the new life. After this she goes home.

"More than talking about [adapting to the new role], it's doing. They are helping you, teaching you how to bathe the baby, so they bathe the baby. They are teaching you how to breastfeed, so they are giving you hot drinks and herbs and they rub your back with some herbs. They take care of you because there is a tradition that if you have a cold drink or if you go [out] in cold weather, your milk is gone, so you have to be very warm. They take care of your back, giving you a massage, and hot drinks like chocolate, and herbs. I had the support of all my family, my sister. You never take care of your baby because somebody is taking care of your baby. You're happy with your baby, you're not anxious about what do I do, where do I go. . . . Somebody is there always. You feel good. I was feeling very good. Everybody's visiting you, too. A lot of friends. [At the end of the forty days] you feel more secure about doing all these things.

"I had my third child in Canada [in 1986], which was a very traumatic experience. When I was having my labor pain . . . I was flashing back to the traumatic experience of the kidnapping and the persecution, all the violence that we are suffering back home. . . . I felt very isolated. It was one year after I was living here, so my network of friends was very [small], my knowledge of English was small. I felt very isolated, very alone. . . . It was a sad experience. It was mixed emotions, and there wasn't any support at all. I was feeling very tired. . . . It was the last [child] but I was feeling like the first, without any support at all."

"Many people think that it's only a physical experience, but I think it's not only a physical experience, it's more than that. It's emotional, too. We always focus on the physical, but not on all that is happening emotionally."

At the multicultural Women's Health Center at St. Joseph's Health Center, Jimenez works with Latina mothers. An irony of life for immigrant and indigenous women, she notes, is that sometimes women whose cultures offered the most supportive traditions of all may today be the ones who are most bereft of the nurturing ways of their foremothers. The clinic takes a holistic approach, viewing the whole woman, physically and emotionally. Jimenez remains in contact with the women after they deliver, and sometimes the group will meet after the babies are born.

"This group is working for people who come [prenatally], and then afterward they maintain and make more friendships. This postpartum support is still individual, and it's always ongoing for people who need it. Usually I see women right after they deliver, and when they go home, I still call and they still call me." Some women experience the same sense of isolation that Jimenez did, especially "when women are alone, when they don't have family, only husbands, or sometimes they don't have any husbands. But always when they have family here, when they have their mothers here, I think it's different. They have the same family support, which I think is the best. They don't have any problems after all."

## ZAHAROULA, GREECE

Zaharoula was born and raised in Demonia, a small, closely knit village four hours' drive from Sparta, the closest big city. She moved with her husband to Canada in 1961. Her first two children were born there in 1961 and 1963, and her third child was born in the United States in 1973.

"[At home in Greece] the family members (grandmother, aunts, in-laws) did most of the preparations prior to the birth—cleaning and the washing, mostly linens and cloth diapers. They were also the ones to care for the mother and child afterward, giving them sponge baths, feedings, changing linens. When it came to the cooking, it wasn't uncommon for neighbors to contribute food. Maybe soups the first couple of days. The idea was to have the kitchen well stocked, so that when the mother was up and about, she wouldn't have to spend a lot of time on her feet by the stove. I think part of it was to also prevent the father from preparing his own meals and burning down the house!

"The one tradition that stands out, that had to be followed, was that the mother and child could go out when both were strong enough, but they could not enter into anybody's home. For example, they were allowed to sit on a stoop or in a yard so that the mother could have coffee with friends, and they could coo over the baby, but mother and child were forbidden to go inside [another] house for forty days. At the end of the forty-day period, the mother took the baby to church, where both received Communion and then were free to go where they pleased.

"The mother usually stayed in bed three or four days almost completely. After that she would get up for short periods of time, but resting frequently. Family members were usually still available for chores until the mother was fully recouped. This usually went on until the forty-day waiting period was over.

"Almost all women breastfed. The mother, sister, or aunt of the new mother was on hand to answer any questions, but by the time a woman was married, she had usually helped her own mother or other family member or neighbor assist in the aid of a new mother. It was rare that a woman had never been involved in some way in a birth.

"Babies were born at home with the help of a midwife. That's how I was born, as well as my two older brothers, and how most of the children in the village were born. If the woman had had a very difficult pregnancy or if she had a history of stillbirths, and complications, then a doctor would have been summoned.

"I left Greece in 1961. After the birth of my first child [in 1961], I stayed home a few days and then returned to work. There was no one to stay home with the baby, so my husband and I worked out a schedule where I worked days and he worked nights, so that one of us would always be home. This was different than the 'traditional' Greek way of life. I couldn't be with my daughter as much as I wanted, or for as long as I was taught was proper, although I did follow the forty-day custom strictly with all three of my children. Also my husband was very involved in feedings and changings as well as taking the baby out and bathing her. This was uncommon for a Greek man, but circumstances were the way they were, and we had no choice. Although, circumstances or not, I think it is good for a man to participate in raising his children. We had good friends in Canada, but they all worked full-time, too. As close as you are, it's hard to get as involved in each other's life in the city, compared to a small village or town. Life is just too hectic.

"When my oldest daughter was two, my mother came from Greece, so she was there for the birth of my second daughter. She took care of both girls while my husband and I worked. We moved to New York in 1972. By the time my son was born, my oldest daughter was twelve and was very capable of caring for him during the day, with the help of her sister, who also contributed in his feedings and changings. My brothers lived nearby but they were busy with their own families. I relied much more on my immediate family than I remember women doing in Demonia. There, giving birth and raising small children seemed more of a community affair. Everybody looked out for everybody else. But things are changing in Greece, too. Even in the villages, it's getting more common for doctors to replace midwives. In Athens, of course, everyone gives birth in hospitals now. Women go back to work soon after giving birth, and many no longer follow the forty-day waiting custom."

## Translating for the New Millennium

For most of us, the reinstatement of the supports and networks described above is not possible in today's world. But in these models and stories are the reminders and raw materials we can use to validate the needs of the postpartum period and the importance of a support network for mothers.

Joan Bachrach, who works with postpartum moms in the Boston area, summed up her ideal vision of the early postpartum transition. In its universal elements, it is not so different from the customs described by the women from a wide variety of cultures.

As Bachrach sees it, "Ideally, after women delivered there [would be] a very smooth transition to home, either family or women just literally surrounding her and taking care of her as she steps through these first six weeks. If people were there from day one teaching you how to breastfeed, teaching you about bathing, and all the practical issues, and then women were there to take care of you so that you really felt in the early weeks that there were people to talk to you, people to teach you, and people to feed you. And there would be an opportunity for couples to be more relaxed with each other as they get to know their baby and as they experience the fact that they're parents, and understand how their relationship had changed. Wouldn't that be nice?"

In the final analysis, says Dana Raphael, what matters is that we are supportive of new mothers. "Whether you give ritual baths, or say things over the mothers' heads, or over the babies, the point is that we do it and that there are people around. It's the interaction and the power of that to help the mother, to make her feel that she's done something great, she's protected, and she's raring to go."

# Notes

1. Raven Lang, "Motherroasting/Postpartum," *The Doula*, Vol. 1, No. 4 (Spring/Summer 1986), pp. 13–17.

2. Barbara Ehrenreich and Deirdre English, *Complaints and Disorders: The Sexual Politics of Sickness* (New York: Glass Mountain Pamphlet No. 2/The Feminist Press, 1978), p. 6.

3. Richard W. Wertz and Dorothy C. Wertz, *Lying-In: A History of Childbirth in America* (New York: The Free Press, 1977), p. 165.

4. Naomi Ruth Lowinsky, *Stories from the Motherline: Reclaiming the Mother–Daughter Bond, Finding Our Feminine Souls* (Los Angeles: Jeremy P. Tarcher, 1992), pp. 2, 6.

5. Joy Harjo, "Three Generations of Native American Women's Birth Experience," in *Ms.*, Vol. II, No. 1 (July/August 1991), pp. 28–30.

6. "Documentation of Traditional Inuit Practice Related to Pregnancy and Childbirth, Pauktuutit," Inuit Women's Association of Canada, p. 4. Submitted to: National Health Research and Development Program, Special Initiative on Community Health and Health Service Delivery "North of [latitude] 60" (updated June 1992).

7. Ibid.

8. Ibid., p. 2.

# Resources

The resources listed here are described in further detail in the following section:

## Model Primary Care Programs
Women's Health Center
Women's Health Clinic

## Model Cultural Preservation Project
Pauktuutit, Inuit Women's Association of Canada

**Books for Mothers**
*Culture and Nursing Care: A Pocket Guide*
*Lying-In: A History of Childbirth in America*

**Books for Children**
*A Ride on Mother's Back: A Day of Baby-Carrying Around the World*
*Welcoming Babies*

# Model Primary Care Programs

**Women's Health Center**
St. Joseph's Health Center
30 The Queensway
Toronto, Ontario M6R 1B5
Canada
Tel.: (416) 530-6850

Founded in 1990, this center offers a prenatal screening program, a prenatal support program, maternal support classes, a program for postpartum depression, and a multicultural health education program. It offers classes in Polish, Somali, English, and Spanish as well as an ESL prenatal class.

**Women's Health Clinic**
419 Graham Avenue, 3rd Floor
Winnipeg, Manitoba R3C 0M3
Canada
Tel.: (204) 947-1517

Started in 1981, the Clinic is a feminist, community health center providing a range of health-care and counseling services, community education and resources, support groups, and special programs for women from teens to elders on a variety of issues, including postpartum and motherhood stress. A woman-centered approach emphasizes prevention, education and action and encourages women to learn about their health so they can make informed choices. The Mothers' Program Coordinator would be glad to share ideas and information about the Clinic's outreach programs with women from diverse communities. An information package on motherhood stress is also available.

# Model Cultural Preservation Project

**Pauktuutit, Inuit Women's Association of Canada**
192 Bank Street,
Ottawa, Ontario K2P 1W8
Canada
Tel.: (613) 238-3977
www.pauktuutit.on.ca

Pauktuutit is an organization representing Inuit women of Canada. Pauktuutit is currently conducting a research project aimed at "documenting traditional Inuit practices related to pregnancy and childbirth through a series of interviews with Inuit elders and returning this information to the people in the form of a book published in Inukitut and English." The project has been funded by the National Health Research and Development Program, Special Initiative on Community Health and Health Service Delivery "North of [latitude] 60." While this particular project focuses on pregnancy and childbirth and only the immediate time following birth, it is a model of the kind of participatory research project that could be undertaken to document postpartum practices and experiences of women in diverse cultures, particularly those in which these women-centered traditions are in danger of being lost over time.

# Books for Mothers

### Culture and Nursing Care: A Pocket Guide

Edited by Lipson, Dibble, and
  Minarik
Available from ICEA Bookcenter:
Tel.: (800) 624-4934
Fax: (612) 854-8772

This book provides a general set of guidelines to the similarities as well as differences between and within culturally diverse groups. It outlines issues related to health and illness, symptom expression, self-care, birth, death, religion, and family participation in care among twenty-four cultural groups. Included are Native Americans, Arab Americans, Black/African Americans, Brazilians, Cambodians, Central Americans, Chinese Americans, Colombians, Cuban Americans, Ethiopians, Filipinos, Gypsies, Haitians, Hmong, Iranians, Japanese Americans, Koreans, Mexican Americans, Puerto Ricans, Russians, Samoans, South Asians, Vietnamese, and West Indians.

### Lying In: A History of Childbirth in America

Richard W. Wertz and Dorothy C.
  Wertz
Free Press, Macmillan Publishing

The authors trace more than 350 years of social and medical history and changes in attitudes toward birth rites and practices, including postpartum rituals and routines.

# Books for Children

### A Ride on Mother's Back: A Day of Baby-Carrying Around the World

Emery Bernhard
Illustrated by Durga Bernhard
Harcourt Brace

This full-color book shares baby-carrying traditions in eleven countries around the world, from the rain forest in Brazil to a river in Papua, New Guinea, to a frozen inlet in the Arctic. It shows young children how their counterparts are transported on mom's back and also shows us each culture from a child's point of view. It provides a good jumping-off place for mom and older siblings-to-be to reminisce about babyhood, how the siblings were carried when they were babies, and how mom will carry the new baby.

### Welcoming Babies

Margy Burns Knight
Illustrated by Anne Sibley O'Brien
Tilbury Press

People in diverse cultures have special customs and traditions to welcome a new baby into the world. In this book we see children and their families from different parts of the world welcoming the newcomer. The artwork reflects the ethnic and cultural background of each family, and the text is clear and direct. The book concludes with several pages that describe each tradition in more detail and give additional examples.

# 3.

# YOUR FIRST WEEKS AT HOME WITH BABY

*Who's There with You?*

••••••

*[After my children were born] I needed to be with another woman. I needed breastfeeding support. I needed someone to say to me, "You're doing fine. You're breastfeeding fine." I needed someone to support my choices. I didn't need someone to come in and boss me around or give the baby a bottle while I was out. I needed someone to support and nurture me.*

—Jane Arnold, certified nurse midwife
and founder of The Mom Service

## Improving the Postpartum Scenario

How many of us as new mothers have shared Jane's feelings? At the same time, how many of us have felt those needs were just an indication of our own personal inadequacy as new mothers, a weakness that, if revealed, would prove to the world that we really weren't ready for it, not quite up to the job?

What we need most of all during those fragile, vulnerable days at home with a brand-new baby being integrated into a brand-new family is a honeymoon. Too often, what we get is panic, confusion, self-doubt, anxiety. Well-intentioned relatives may have their own agendas and may prove intrusive, demanding, or judgmental. Mates, equally unprepared to begin with, can also easily become overextended—or overlooked—in the nuclear family structure. Mom has not yet come to really believe in Bruno Bettelheim's concept of good-enough parenting, and with the best of intentions, is increasingly driven to perform as the perfect parent all at once, as she believes she must. She tries to do too much too soon, the baby senses the stress and confusion, and the honeymoon turns quickly into chaos.

Instead of planning ahead and preparing for this time at home, many women often find that they have been led to underestimate it entirely. They may plan on little or no help, not realizing the kind of cushioning they will need as they are suddenly thrust from Eastern Standard, Central, Mountain, or Pacific Time into that twilight zone known as Baby Time. "Getting on a baby's schedule really slows you down," warns Kerry Vincent, cofounder and co-owner with Maureen Berra of Mother's Helper, a postpartum care service that they founded and ran in St. Louis for close to seven years.

After a couple of sessions on the sitz bath, some tender (or too tender) moments trying to get breastfeeding going well, and a few days or weeks alone with baby, it is easy to become totally overwhelmed and exhausted, particularly if food is running low, laundry's piling up, and your mate is spending half his time walking the baby around the house and the other half on the phone frantically trying to make a deal with the local take-out restaurant. Alone as a first-time mother who has never been around babies before, not getting a simple answer to basic questions such as "Am I fastening this diaper right?" or "Is his belly button supposed to look like that?" can send anxiety soaring and insecurity snowballing. You haven't slept, you've forgotten to feed yourself, and suddenly breastfeeding goes totally on the blink.

How many times a day can you call the pediatrician? How about the neighbor down the street who has a toddler? Maybe she would know. (Certainly more than one maternal friendship has been forged here on the front lines; if you know someone with a toddler, by all means give her a call. Mothers love to share their hard-won wisdom.)

So often, the need for home-based support is largely underestimated, especially by first-time mothers who have never been around babies before and have never been told what to expect. If anything, they get a contrary message. The attitudes that childbirth, breastfeeding, and parenting are "natural and instinctive," combined with their daily roles as competent, in-control actors and doers, may give them the misimpression that they won't need postpartum care or help; that help is necessary only if there is a "problem." The push for early hospital discharge following birth also tends to convey and confirm this message tacitly.

In her videotape *Postpartum: A Bittersweet Experience*, Jeanne Driscoll, R.N., M.S., C.S., likens the experience of new motherhood to an initiation "by fire." Those days and first several weeks at home are when that fire is heating up. After a week or so, you may be feeling better physically, depending on how your delivery went, but by then the baby's waking up. And by the second week (if your mate's workplace allowed any parental leave in the first place), you're totally on your own. If you've had a cesarean section, you will very likely need a longer recovery period. (One R.N. pointed out that for other major surgery, visiting nurse service would automatically be provided, whereas for cesarean sections, women are expected, once again, to do it on their own.) Single mothers by choice may be working around the baby clock without a sign of relief; adoptive mothers who had literally only hours of preparation before the arrival of their babies may not even have a bassinet or diaper in the house, let alone the cursory knowledge at hand that many women gain from brief baby basics classes in the hospital.

Suzanne, an adoptive mother on Cape Cod, recalled that friends told her how lucky she was not to have gone through the exhausting experience of labor and delivery. "But what they didn't understand," she said, "was that my nerves were just as frazzled. Physically I was in better shape, but I think mentally just not knowing until the last minute whether or not it was actually all going to happen was as nerve-wracking as going through labor and delivery. What I could have used is someone to let me sleep during the day, because he was up all night. I just got up with him. During the day I would just fall asleep when he napped. But I think it would have been nice if someone had offered to stay for a couple of hours while I slept, and that never happened." Instead, when the "masses" of visitors kept coming, she found herself "running to the store, making sure that I had enough food for everybody, making coffee, and being the hostess, when I should have been relaxing."

Jessica, also an adoptive mother, encountered the same attitude despite the fact that her journey to new motherhood involved a midnight phone call, a cross-country flight to pick up the baby (whose birth mother nearly changed her mind when Jessica and her husband touched down to change planes three-quarters of the way there), and a week in an efficiency cottage and another week in a cousin's home before the flight back home. "I was exhausted," she recalls, just trying to keep up with taking care of a child and trying to . . . get a room ready, doing the things people do in nine months' time."

Although her mother-in-law came to stay with her for a week after the birth of her birth son three years after she adopted, "nobody offered to come and stay when we brought [our first baby] home," she recalled. While there may be differences in how society views the needs of mothers in different circumstances, there are still certain universal everymother longings. "You are more tired after physically giving birth," she says, "but just needing some help or support—the loneliness of being alone all day with a child, you need somebody to talk to and get used to the whole idea. [Someone to] help you understand what you've gotten yourself into! In that sense, I could have used somebody!"

"[Having a child is] so minimized in this culture," says Rhonda de Gier, a thirty-one-year-old musician who has lived in the Netherlands with her Dutch husband but who came home with him to have her first baby in her native St. Louis. She had a home birth three weeks before her interview.

"No one prepares you for it. It's a shock. It's a huge transitional period. . . . This [postpartum] time . . . is much more profound than the time before [the baby was born]. The time before . . . waiting for the baby . . . so much of it is your interaction with your husband, just the two of you before the first baby. . . . Two days afterward—it's like when you're an athlete, and push yourself beyond your limits, burn, no pain, no gain. You feel all the muscle aches and tiredness the second day. And it's really hard to do things. I wished that I'd had someone there that I didn't feel that I was imposing on, because even after a while with my husband, as wonderful and sweet and great as he is— and he was there the whole time with me, after a while it starts to be a drag when you say, 'Honey, can you bring this?' or 'Honey, can you lift my arm?' or 'Honey, can you lift the baby?' And you're asking for these things, which seem so unnecessary to them, because mentally you're fine. . . .

"I did my best to stay in bed for that first twenty-four hours, definitely, take it very easy the first two days. The third day, things started having to be done. My husband went out for an hour or two, the phone would ring, I couldn't get to the phone quick enough, the baby would cry, I would feel like, 'Oh, my gosh, I can't handle it.' It would suddenly blow out of proportion, these little things would become very, very stressy."

Having had a midwife attending her, Rhonda felt as if she had a lot of reassurance. "I had a lot of support, and I really felt well cared for." But negotiating home territory alone was not easy. "It wasn't the first night, but the next night, in a way I wished I'd had a nurse with me. Just someone to pick up after me, hand me things in the bathroom, or set my sitz bath up for me. . . . Having had a home birth, I think that would be the ultimate."

Home-based support and encouragement for all moms during the early postpartum weeks are critical, and can also carry with them long-range implications for the mom and her family's well-being in future times.

Ideally, what mothers should be able to have at this time is a self-styled sanctuary. A suspension of usual activity. A shower. A massage. A comforting grandmother. An extra pair of hands. A stolen moment between cries or feedings for Mom and Dad to remember who they were and to "try on" who they are now (or, in their state of stressed-out euphoria, a secret moment to indulge themselves, lie back, kick their arms and legs, and identify with the baby's vulnerable state—an exercise that can be a great momentary relief, according to one new mother). And the new mom needs time for herself, by herself; she also needs time with her infant, letting everything else outside this special orbit of early matrescence melt away. Rest speeds recovery. Support for Mom and the new family unit reduces the possibility of postpartum depression and child abuse.

The scenario of that home-based support system should be written by each woman according to her own needs and budding parenting style. (Some women feel it takes quite a while to develop any style at all.) But the components are fairly universal: the practical—meals, laundry, baby basics, and your immediate environment; the physical—help with sitz baths, showers, breastfeeding, massage, and rest; and the intangible—all the emotional and psychological factors that might suddenly and unexpectedly erupt on this delicate landscape. "If you haven't experienced it firsthand, you can't understand," says Diana McQuiston, who founded and ran Motherlove, a postpartum home-care service in Indianapolis for close to five years. "If the new mother is sitting there, crying at an M&M's commercial on TV, there should be someone with her who can say, 'That's okay. Here's a Kleenex. I'll be in the kitchen if you need me.'" That person should also be able to remind you that you have just done an extraordinary thing in creating, carrying, and delivering a new life into the world, and that you deserve some special recognition and rest. While you are nurturing your newborn, you need someone to nurture you, whether it is with healthful drinks while you're nursing, or with words of recognition and encouragement as you talk about your feelings. In this state of continual giving to your infant—whether it is nourishment or care or love—you are easily drained, and you need to be replenished from sources outside yourself so that you will have reserves to draw from. Once you are aware of this, paying attention to and respecting these needs of the early postpartum weeks at home do not make you a weak or self-indulgent mother. They don't make you a wimp. Rather, applaud your wisdom in respecting your own most intimate needs and the needs of your family.

## Yelling for Help: Is Anybody Out There?

To a large extent, this kind of help and reassurance used to come automatically from large, extended families, more close-knit communities, and a more leisurely lifestyle. A different kind of help used to come from the traditional baby nurse, who generally took over the baby's care completely. In recent years, as women tried to do it all themselves and take it all in stride, and husbands and partners became more active birth partners, pressure shifted to the new father as sole companion-cum-caregiver in the nuclear family structure. As one new father said, he felt as if he had been called on to replace an entire community of women, grandmothers, and household help that might have supported the new mother in the past.

The reality of life for many women today is that, in fact, extended family and close-knit community are simply not as available as they once were. Or, if families are nearby, it may be sorely disappointing to realize that they are not necessarily the best people to help keep you calm and collected. Our own mothers, who mothered us in the 1940s, '50s, or '60s, may have lifestyles and childrearing philosophies vastly different from our own. In the absence of close family comes the painful reality that there may be no substitute community or person we can turn to. Most of the women we know may still be working in an office—maybe even our own old office—ten hours a day; their own children may be older, or if not, they may be too busy trying to manage their own little ones and overburdened schedules to be of any help. As for neighbors, often we don't even know their names. Changes in attitudes that encourage more direct parental involvement in childbirth and parenting make the idea of the traditional baby nurse seem too intrusive for many new families. And as the real-life difficulties, challenges, and stages of the postpartum period are more openly acknowledged, so is the realization that fathers need their own help adjusting to parenthood. As a result, a new kind of bridge between pregnancy and parenthood has emerged: the postpartum doula or caregiver.

As Dana Raphael explained in her book *The Tender Gift*, the doula is that singular role-model/elder/nurturer who, in traditional cultures, came to help the new mother and be there for her, primarily to help facilitate breastfeeding, since no other methods of infant feeding were available. (Raphael first heard the word when she was describing the function of such a person to a Greek friend whose grandmother asked for a simultaneous translation. "Ah, that's the doula," she exclaimed, "the woman who comes from across the street to do the cooking, put the older children to sleep, and generally care for this little family unit.") In ancient Greek, the word meant literally "slave," but it has today come to have a gentler connotation, that of one who nurtures the new mother by performing those tasks that comfort her and free her to be with her baby. She is nonjudgmental, intuitive, and experienced. She has seen it all before, and she will be there, like the mothers in the African tale, waiting for us with open arms as we cross that river by ourselves. And she will know what to do without our having to tell her.

This one-on-one caregiver may enter the picture in a variety of ways. One way is as a paid postpartum caregiver or doula.

## THE BIRTH OF THE DOULA SERVICE

In 1981, Jane Arnold, now a certified nurse midwife in New York City, was living in New Mexico, feeling very isolated after having had four children in five years. Setting out on a personal quest to see what other women experienced postpartum, Arnold started going into the homes of new mothers in her community.

"I worked with them in any capacity," she recalls. "I did housekeeping, I did cooking, I did errands, and my overwhelming impression at that time was of women following me around the house with their babies in their arms asking me about breastfeeding, about what was happening to their bodies, about older children's reactions to the babies. And I listened. I just listened, because I needed to know. And what I found out was that other women did have the same needs that I did." That need was essentially for someone to support and nurture her. She was also greatly affected by the message of Dana Raphael's book. When Arnold moved to New York City in 1981, she started one of the first postpartum care services, The Mom Service. Although she closed the service in 1991 to concentrate full-time on her new path of midwifery, Arnold remains one of the pioneers in this area.[1]

In 1982, without knowing anything about Arnold's work, Joan Singer and Valerie Spain began to respond to the emotional and physical needs of new mothers in the Boston area (Spain has since retired from doula work). Singer had helped a friend after the arrival of her firstborn, and seeing the need for such a service, she and Spain joined forces to found MotherCare Services (MCS), which is today one of the largest such services in the country. As word of The Mom Service and MotherCare began to spread, other services sprang up around the country, and, as Singer notes, "Professional postpartum care has moved to the forefront as an economical and necessary alternative to traditional support measures."

Sensing that the birth of a new industry was at hand, on April 15, 1989, representatives from fifteen postpartum care services around the country gathered in Montclair, New Jersey, for the first meeting of what would become the National Association of Postpartum Care Services (NAPCS). Some were one-woman operations; others had large staffs. The NAPCS seeks to provide an educational network for doulas, can provide local referrals, and will also help women start their own doula service. They hope, too, that their very existence will begin to validate postpartum care as a profession. They seek to meet all the needs of the families of the 1990s; perhaps the most difficult battle they face is in establishing a viable partnership with insurance carriers and other third-party reimbursers.

The women who work as caregivers are carefully screened and come from a variety of backgrounds. Most are mothers themselves, but they don't have to be. They represent a great range of training: Among founder/supervisors are a cardiology technician, an emergency medical technician, an OB technician, an elementary school teacher, an R.N., nursing and midwifery students, a midwife, childbirth educators, elder caregivers, massage therapists, and even one park ranger.

The NAPCS has grown in a short time to a membership of more than one hundred services throughout the country, with the highest concentration of services in California, New York, and Massachusetts. While there are some large services in other parts of the country, some caregivers have found certain areas slower to accept the concept of nurturing new mothers. "The Midwestern woman," says Ann Schramm, R.N., M.S.N., and vice president of Chicago's Mother's Cradle, "tends to be a definite 'I should be able to do it all' woman, and so such a service has been slow to arise. However, we are being very well received by clients and health-care providers who are having difficulty with the still decreasing length of hospital stays and the lack of postpartum support."

In St. Louis, after a week of struggling, Rhonda de Gier learned about Mother's Helper. Concerned about the cost but not uncomfortable with the concept, she discovered that her Dutch husband's health insurance (still in force through the Netherlands musicians' union) would cover seventy hours of postpartum home care in the United States. The Dutch model under socialized health care, considered by many experts to be "the most exemplary primary maternity care system in the world,"[2] covers a period of up to eight days after delivery of up to eight hours a day of a state-paid, state-trained "home health nurse" who is partially subsidized by either public or private insurance. Her role is to assist the midwife or general practitioner during home delivery, care for the new mother and newborn baby, provide infant health education to the family, perform household chores, recognize deviations from normal in mom and baby, and if necessary contact the midwife or general practitioner. The home health nurse is considered an important member of the overall team.

Courtesy of their Dutch insurance, Rhonda hired Kerry Vincent of Mother's Helper to come in when the baby was six days old. (Of all their clients, Rhonda's claim was the only one to have been honored by an insurer, notes Vincent.) It was a great relief, says Rhonda, "to have someone there to pick up the phone, answer the door, come and ask you not 'Do you need something?' but say, 'Would you like such-and-such, here is your drink, you're breastfeeding, you have to drink while the baby drinks'—things like that. So when Kerry came, then I sat back and said, 'This is what I wanted from day one. This is what I was hoping for. This is what I really needed.' . . . That really got us back on our feet. I must say, literally, it got me back on my feet. I was much more positive. I'd had a big crying spell on the Saturday after Sebastian was born, because I felt so overwhelmed. I think postpartum depression is mainly due to women's worlds being turned upside down after having the baby, especially when it's your first child."

## WHAT THE DOULA DOES

The doula's basic role is to provide nonintrusive, nonjudgmental support according to the family's needs and wishes. She is there to facilitate your time to settle in, relax, and heal, while assuring that the familiar daily underpinnings of your life and household remain

### THE NETHERLANDS MODEL: A CENTURY OF MATERNITY HOME CARE

The Dutch concept of primary maternity care dates back as early as 1902, reports Dr. J. J. Kerssens of the Netherlands Institute of Primary Health Care (NIVEL), when "in several cities and villages organizations were founded to train young girls to take care of a healthy woman and her baby." In 1922, the Dutch Association of Maternity Home Care was founded. When, in the mid-1950s, the government began to subsidize maternity home care on a modest scale, only a minority of women called upon the maternity home-care center for assistance, although a large majority (76 percent) of Dutch women gave birth at home. By the 1960s, as births moved into the hospital, the demand for maternity home care decreased, but at the same time, maternity home care entered into the public health insurance, "which increased the demand considerably." Today in Holland, says Dr. Kerssens, women delivering at home or released within twenty-four hours of hospital birth are eligible for the aid of this skilled caregiver.[3]

anchored as much as possible. She is there to free you up to do nothing but be with your baby and other family members, or to take the baby so that you can sleep, if that's what's needed. She is the peace-of-mind factor. Laurie Aron, a New Yorker who had a doula, noted that for her, of all the wonderful things her doula did, "The best thing that she did was listen!"

The doula may provide help with any or all of the following services: shopping, cooking, emotional and moral support, breastfeeding or bottle-feeding support, massage (for baby and/or Mom), laundry, answering the telephone and taking messages, fielding visitors, teaching or giving help with baby basics (hospital instruction is sometimes eclipsed now by increasing numbers of early releases), errands, pet and plant care, help with older siblings, light housekeeping, help with baby so Mom and Dad can have time together to settle into their new roles, and referrals to other sources the mom may need to contact or know about. Some doulas also provide labor support.[4] And although she is not there in a medical capacity, she should also be able to keep an eye out for anything out of the ordinary in the mother or the baby, and suggest when medical referrals might be in order.

Some doulas specialize in vegetarian cooking, or know the rules of keeping a kosher home. Others come with their own "old pro" wisdom. "I have found that what is common sense to me is not necessarily common knowledge to all mothers," said Maureen Berra of Mother's Helper. Berra recommends (and helps with) setting up multiple changing stations for nighttime feedings for houses with two stories; preparing do-ahead meals; keeping the telephone notepad, a pitcher of water, and a selection of healthy snacks (nuts, cheese, whole grain muffins) on the night table; and storing things such as yogurt or juices in a cooler by the bed. She also keeps ice packs on hand for sore nipples or perineums. And while some moms have the perfectly decorated nursery, she finds that they might not have a diaper pail. "We'll try to get moms thinking along those lines," says Kerry Vincent. They will also show Mom how to prepare for baby needs by putting cotton swabs in a jar half filled with alcohol and cotton balls in water in a covered plastic container. During their prenatal visit, doulas Berra and Vincent make sure to ask the mom where her own resting place is. Typically, while women will have thought about vacuuming and laundry, they haven't thought about creating a comfortable corner for themselves where they can retreat with baby (or without), put their feet up, have a cup of tea, read, zone out, or whatever. "We tell moms, 'Make your atmosphere where you and the baby will be as pleasant as possible, whether that's music, flowers, or snacks by the bed.'"

Another critical role the doula fills is helping moms with breastfeeding and bottle-feeding support. Bottle-feeding moms may have just as many questions as breastfeeding moms, observes Pat McMakin of MotherCare Services and just as much of a need to discuss them with a supportive helper. In general, pediatricians should guide you as to numbers of ounces per feeding, how and when to increase quantity, kind of formula to use (cow milk-based vs. soy milk-based), use of pre-mixed vs. powdered formulas, and styles and shapes of bottles and nipples. But, says McMakin, spitting up, gas, scheduling, sleep patterns, and nipple design are all subjects bottle-feeding moms bring up with their doulas.

For some women, the relationship with their doula becomes an intimate and lasting one. In New York City, Anna Werner, an international board-certified lactation consultant and a doula with The Mom Service, was Beverly Solow's doula when Beverly's son Joel was born. "He was so tiny, and seemed so fragile," recalled Beverly. "We were in the hospital and had all these people helping us, and then all of a sudden we were on our own with this little creature who was totally dependent on us, and it was pretty scary." Beverly's own mother had died approximately two months before Beverly had become pregnant, "so there was that whole loss to be dealing with, and lack of emotional support and sharing that most women really enjoy with their mothers when they become a mother. I think you really appreciate and understand your mother a whole lot more when you have a child. Anna really filled the gap."

"They really needed somebody with whom to share all this on a very nurturing level," says Werner. "The first few days, it was really, look what's happened and isn't this wonderful! Because they didn't have anybody outside of the specialness of the married couple with whom to share it. And that's a very important part of the early postpartum experience, the sharing of what in the Jewish world is called nachas [joy]. If you can't have that, it's a depressing event. So my being there was their opportunity to be elated with an outsider. . . . I [was] the person with whom the couple is elated, with whom the couple first shares the experience of retelling the story of the birth, and retelling the story of the first nursing and—I'm getting chills just saying it!—but that's really what my role was! I was Grandma!"

Liz Koch, who founded *The Doula: A Magazine for Mothers*, did not actually have a doula herself until her third child was born. "And it was funny," she recalled, "after seven years of doing this magazine, I realized what it really was like to have a doula. How extraordinary it was to have this woman who really understood where I was, really honored it, and was really there for me, in any way I needed her to be, from running the dog to putting fresh sheets on my bed to holding the baby while I showered, to just lovingly giving attention to my five-year-old daughter, listening to her, and giving her what she needed, which was just tons of attention because she was losing her place as baby. Even at five that was still very hard for her. It was just so enriching and it made me feel so strong to honor that time . . . and get this help I needed. Then, when I took over, it was like, 'I'm really strong, my baby's really strong, my family's really strong.' It's a beginning that assures us that as we reach those stages where it gets harder and harder, we have a reserve, we don't start out depleted, we have something to pull from that keeps us all strong."

## HOW DO I CHOOSE A DOULA?

Choosing a doula is much like choosing other caregivers/household helpers, but it has a unique dimension as well. The doula is someone who will be intimately involved with you and your family during a very personal, intense, and emotional time in your life. Will she respect your privacy? Will she be nonjudgmental and supportive of your choices? Can she establish a good rapport with the other members of your family?

"Some moms are very spiritual at the time of birth," says Kerry Vincent of Mother's Helper. "If you get someone you can't connect with spiritually, it can be a problem. You must also believe in her overall competence, and in your own instincts about this person." It is perfectly all right to interview two, three, or more providers, compare their cost, and ask about their philosophy or goal as this kind of care provider. Dorothy Harrison of Mother Care, in Edmonds, Washington, suggests using the guidelines on page 93 when choosing a doula.

## WHAT SHOULD THE DOULA ASK ME AND MY FAMILY?

Services may ask you to fill out written questionnaires, or they may take notes as they meet with you, but the doula should make a thorough assessment of your needs and your household's needs. The following client questionnaire from MotherLove, run by Debra Pascali in Ridgewood, New Jersey, is a good example of the things a service should cover, including a section on the father's needs.

1. Will you breastfeed your baby? If so, do you anticipate needing support with this?
2. Do you have any special needs during your pregnancy? If so, what are they?
3. Are you taking or have you taken a childbirth education class? Please specify what type of class it is or was, e.g., Bradley, Lamaze, Cooperative Childbirth Education, etc.? Who is the instructor?
4. Who is your midwife or physician? Where will you be giving birth?
5. Are you working outside the home now? Do you anticipate working outside the home after the baby is born?
6. What do you anticipate will be your emotional needs after the baby is born?
7. Will your partner be at home with you for a time after the baby is born? If so, how long will he be home with you?
8. Does your partner have any special needs that we should know about (e.g., diet restrictions, etc.)?
9. Is this your first baby?
10. If this is not your first baby, what are the names and ages of your other children?
11. Are any of your children being treated for any special conditions or do they have any allergies that would be important for us to know about?
12. What will be your family's needs concerning the care of your home, the laundry, running errands, etc.?

13. Does your family have any particular style of cooking they prefer, or any special needs concerning meals?
14. Do you have any household pets that you want us to help be responsible for?
15. Does anyone in your household smoke cigarettes?
16. How long do you anticipate needing someone?
17. How did you learn about us?
18. Please add anything you feel it is important for us to know about concerning you and your family.

*Guidelines When Choosing a Doula*

• Am I comfortable with this person?
• Am I able to ask her for help?
• Can she cook simple meals that will fit my family's tastes?
• Does she have experience with breastfeeding?
• Will she think of my comfort?
• Is she empathetic and a good listener?
• Has she had experience with babies?
• Can she get things done without being asked?
• Is her presence comforting and calming?[5]

Another doula suggests that you might also want to ask her if she's taken CPR or first aid, if she has an up-to-date tuberculosis test, and if she would submit to having a police check done.

Doulas should have "good knowledge," says Vincent, "and some of that invisible knowledge helps women get through [these early days and weeks]. The more consistent, correct information and physical and emotional support women get—that's the formula for good birth outcome and good postpartum."

## How Do I Hire a Doula?

If you are looking for a service, but don't know of any in your area, the National Association of Postpartum Care Services can give you local referrals. In addition to networking among their membership, the NAPCS also has an accreditation program in place.

Once you know what services, if any, exist in your area, generally your first contact with a service is by telephone. After you've seen pamphlets and spoken to or seen letters from references (usually former clients or medical childbirth professionals) and have decided on a service, a prenatal visit to your home is the next usual step. (It might be the doula herself or the owner-supervisor of the service.) This visit usually runs from forty-five minutes to an hour. Sometimes it is part of the total package cost; sometimes it is free; sometimes there is a separate charge. (The service should let you know that before you decide to have them make the visit.) At the interview or before it, they may provide you with a questionnaire in which you can describe in detail your family's needs and preferences; some services just take notes during the visit.

During the prenatal visit, the doula will probably want to see your kitchen, bedroom, baby's room, laundry room, local shops, and anything else she will need to know about during her time with you. (In this way she can avoid questions later on.) She may also provide referrals or information regarding birth assistance, breastfeeding support, or other issues of concern to you at that time.

Once you have decided on a service, you will probably be asked to sign a contract and make a down payment in order to reserve your place and doula.

## HOW MUCH DOES THE DOULA COST?

Doula services generally charge by the hour, and offer a variety of packages ranging from one to two weeks or sometimes longer, depending on the circumstances. They generally suggest about four hours a day. They may charge from $13 an hour to about $30 an hour, and extra for special services (e.g., infant or mother massage). The service should provide you with a contract (this protects both of you) and should clearly list on their literature exactly what services they will provide. A hint from moms about offsetting costs: When friends or relatives ask what they can get for the baby, suggest that they might wish to contribute to a "doula" fund for you instead. Many services also have gift certificates.

## THE DOULA AND THIRD-PARTY COVERAGE

For many women who cannot afford a doula service, the knowledge that they exist but are unavailable to them may make them feel even more deprived and unsupported during their early weeks at home. As for the doula organizations themselves, despite the fact that their fees may be considered high, many feel they might not be able to survive if they have to depend on the private sector alone. Exploring avenues of third-party reimbursement is high on the agenda of many doula services.

When Debra Pascali started MotherLove in New Jersey in 1987, she recalls, "I couldn't even get any [insurance companies] to talk to me. Now the insurance carriers are actually calling me." While she feels that a real change in terms of insurance coverage for the doula (whom many companies classify as a "homemaker" and therefore ineligible for reimbursement) will still be years down the road, she is hopeful that a change will come. "With the [recent] studies on labor support showing that labor companions in hospitals and birthing centers have helped to cut down on medication and the number of cesareans and other costly interventions, [insurers] see it as very cost-effective."[6] Good postpartum home care could bring women out of the hospital earlier, another measure that would prove cost effective. However, an effective and responsive home-care program has yet to be added to most early-discharge programs.

Many working in the field believe that it will take a large grass-roots consumer movement to secure more third-party coverage for the doula, who is not yet a recognized category of home health aide. "It's going to take a lot of agencies, hospitals, and consumers working together to change that picture," says Margaret Fisher, who ran a doula service in Rochester, New York.

One thing consumers can do is go to their employers, home health care agencies, insurance companies, and hospitals and request postpartum care benefits. "People have a lot of power if they go in and voice their complaints and their needs," says Pascali. "It's only going to change as people get out and say more. I encourage every single one of our clients to submit insurance claims, even if it comes back denied, because the carriers, when I used to call, would say, 'Well, we don't have any requests for this.'"

## SOME AVENUES OF THIRD-PARTY COVERAGE

• One doula service—MotherCare, in Massachusetts—has been associated with an HMO since 1985, and in the consumer-sensitive Harvard Community Health Plan, women choosing the Special Delivery Program—early release within twenty-four hours of delivery—are entitled under the plan to sixteen hours of MotherCare, plus a nurse's visit to the home within forty-eight hours.

• In trying to provide a realistic and appropriate home-care package for moms choosing early discharge in the New York/New Jersey area, MotherLove has combined with Kimberly Quality Care, a nursing service that provides one- to four-hour in-home assessments of new mother and baby in coordination with the services of a doula. "A really important part of an early discharge program," says Debra Pascali, "is to make sure there's some kind of a medical follow-up. Since doulas are totally nonmedical . . . the nurse is able to tell the doula if there is anything to look out for or [anything] out of normal range." (This is reminiscent of the role of the Dutch home health nurse as part of the overall medical team.)

• Corporations might provide doula service as a benefit to employees—mothers as well as fathers. "We've already had small companies pay for us," says Pascali, "because the husband [who was the employee] said, 'I want three weeks off, and if you're not going to give me three weeks off, I need to know someone's at home with my wife while I'm at work.' And the company provided our services so the husband could return to work."

• At the Birthing Inn at the Loudon Hospital Center in Leesburg, Virginia, new moms choosing early discharge are entitled to a certain number of hours of doula care at home as well as an at-home assessment by an R.N. within twenty-four hours of discharge to monitor progress of mother and baby. The Loudon Hospital Center has a contract with Mother's Matters, a local doula service, and pays for the service at no charge to the mothers. The service, says Katherine Cobourn, vice president of Patient Care Services for Loudon Healthcare, "is an important safeguard for the health of our new moms and babies who choose early discharge."

It is the hope of new mothers and services alike that increasing methods of coverage will become available as HMOs and other care providers become more consumer-sensitive and recognize the long-term value of postpartum care, and as increasing numbers of consumers begin demanding it.

On April 8, 1993, Pascali testified before President Clinton's Task Force for Health Care Reform and gave a presentation about the benefits of doulas both prenatally through labor and birth and into the first six weeks postpartum. "It is encouraging to see that doulas and the important role they fill not only as cost-effective helpers but also in the preventative role they fill in decreasing child abuse, PPD, promoting breastfeeding, supporting parent-infant bonding, and contributing to the overall wellness of the family [are] now beginning to be recognized on a national scale as part of health care reform."

## Alternatives to the Hired Doula

Most caregivers believe that their own or equivalent services should be available to help all new families and that new mothers get a better start, regardless of income or risk status. While many services feel that there should be no charge for the tender, loving care they dispense, there is also the feeling that such services are professional, that its providers should be compensated just as other health-care providers are, and that the work they do to help families get off to a good start should be valued by society and the health-care system.

Inspired by the concept of the one-on-one role model to help new mothers adjust, alternatives to the hired doula are being explored:

### NONPROFIT DOULA SERVICES

"I really feel this is something we need to [make] more readily accessible to all parents," says Jane Arnold, founder of the Mom Service, and currently a certified nurse midwife at a birthing center in the South Bronx. Arnold hopes there will come a day when birth centers will be able to offer, through grants and other reimbursements, nonprofit doula services for clients who are discharged from the hospital within four to six hours after delivery. The moms would have the service provided free, with the doulas paid from grants until the program became self-generating. "And the women would be paid, so you'd train women from the community who are jobless." They would have a good skill, could attend women from their community in their own language, and then go out of the community to work.

In St. Louis, in an effort to reach rural communities where services do not exist or are too expensive for most people, Kerry Vincent and Maureen Berra, who founded Mother's Helper, have suggested using doulas to train volunteers and then to function as consultants free of charge. The program would be grant-funded and run through a local university, and the volunteers would then work as doulas within that local community.

## VOLUNTEERS AND MOTHERING MENTORS

Focusing on the special needs of teen moms, a number of programs use the one-to-one support concept and implement it in mentoring programs for teen mothers.

In Boston, the Volunteer Parent Aide Program for Teen Parents is cosponsored by the Alliance for Young Families, a consortium of more than one hundred human service and health-care agencies in the Greater Boston area and the Department of Health and Hospitals of the City of Boston. The focus of this program is not so much on the immediate postpartum period in terms of home care, but rather on an extended relationship over twelve to eighteen months wherein the teen has an ongoing relationship with an adult mentor for some extra support as the teen prepares for and takes on the role of new mother. Often she may also have an extended family, and continue to live with them, and it is explained to them that this adult mentor is a volunteer and is not trying to replace the traditional support of the family. Many of the young women, however, are not connected with an extended family. While all the moms are single, says Joan Tighe, executive director of the Alliance for Young Families, some have partners involved. "If we have an adult couple who is willing to work with that young couple," she says, "we will make that match. . . . A lot of it has to do with just some extra support. Sometimes they just go shopping together. Sometimes they have the young person over for meals. We've also started running some groups for young women who are on the waiting list, more mutual support groups, and some of the teens are now talking about setting up some mutual support groups among themselves. Overall, the dropout rate from the program is very low from the teens' end, so I think that's an indication that the program is of value to them."

The program was started in 1986, explains Betty Holt, director of the volunteer program, "because here at Boston City Hospital doctors and nurses and others saw that one particular area of the city had a high rate of teen pregnancy and infant mortality that far exceeded the rest of the city. Those areas were Roxbury and Dorchester, neighborhoods that are predominantly African-American and Latino." There was a feeling that traditional approaches had failed, and the mentorship idea was developed in an effort to involve the community more by pairing adult volunteers with teen mothers.

"I go to churches in the neighborhoods," says Holt, "predominantly African-American churches, and I talk to congregations about teen pregnancy. Volunteers are trained and sensitized to what it's like to be a teenager today compared to fifteen or twenty years ago." Teen participation is strictly voluntary, and those moms choosing to join become involved with the program during their first trimester. A staff person at each of four health centers is available to talk with the young women during and after prenatal visits, and eventually the moms meet their volunteers, who provide social outings to libraries or museums, a sense of extended family, and a nonjudgmental adult presence who is not their parent to share conversations about baby care, doctor visits, or other questions that might come up prenatally or during the first year postpartum.

One reason for the program's success, suggests Betty Holt, is "because of the way the help is offered. . . . We don't say to them, directly or indirectly, 'You've done something bad or wrong, and we're here to help you get your life together. . . . ' We make sure the teenagers understand that this is a volunteer program: This is what we offer, and if you would like to be part of it, we would love to have you."

The young women in her program all have support, says Holt. "They either live with a parent or a guardian—someone who helps them out generally, who keeps the baby for them to go to school, since one of our goals is to have all the young women go to school and not repeat the pregnancy. It's a little different than if they were on their own, like a lot of women who after they have a baby really have no one to help them. PPD can really become an issue, because they get overwhelmed. I think it's probably less of an issue with our group, because of the support that is available to them."

New York Hospital's Teenage Pregnancy and Parenting Program (TAPP) has also used the one-to-one concept to help teen mothers. Through TAPP, pregnant teens coming in are asked if they would like to be matched with a volunteer mentor. If they agree, the mentor meets with them prenatally, may stay with them through labor and delivery, and can be available to them postpartum if they wish to continue. She does not necessarily visit their home but is available as a continuous stable presence, providing important emotional and psychological support at a critical time.

A volunteer program that serves all new moms regardless of age, income, or need is the Visiting Moms Program of the Jewish Family and Children's Service in Brookline, Massachusetts. Founded in 1989, they provide free trained volunteers to visit the new mom for up to two hours a week both prenatally and then for up to a year after the baby is born. She will confidentially assess your needs with you prenatally, and then be present after the baby is born to listen and nurture, help you network with other new parents, or provide community resource information. The goal of the program, says director Peggy Kaufman, is to help moms gain self-confidence and self-esteem in their own parenting skills, and let them know they deserve some "support and companionship for themselves" during this time. A "primary goal from the very beginning is to teach people that they don't need to do this alone—be super people and super parents—and asking for help is an important and necessary part of the work of parenting."

## MIDWIVES, BIRTH COMPANIONS, AND CHILDBIRTH ASSISTANTS: EXPANDING THE POSTPARTUM ROLE

In her book *Reactions to Motherhood: The Role of Post-Natal Care,* English midwife Jean A. Ball explored the role of the midwife during the first six weeks postpartum. "Most midwifery and obstetrics textbooks," she wrote, "lead one to assume that once the baby is safely born, the mother is instantly able to cope with her new role." Notably absent was material "about how to help a woman cope with the varying demands and expectations which mothering brings."[7] Similarly, she found that while the role of peer and family support was studied in relationship to new moms experiencing postpartum depression, "there was very little about the care and support which midwives give during the postnatal period and the effect which this might have upon the transition to motherhood."[8] In her studies, Ball followed 279 women from the thirty-sixth week of pregnancy till the sixth week postpartum. She explored ways that the midwife, a key member of the continuum team attending the mother prenatally and then postpartum, might help the new mom—for example, by working with her prenatally to let the mom suggest and make choices about her own postpartum plan.

Raven Lang, California-based direct entry midwife, doctor of Oriental medicine, and author of *The Birth Book*, noted in 1986 that while there has been much focus on prenatal care and childbirth itself, "the attention given to the mother in her postpartum state . . . has been negligible. . . . As a midwife, I've felt that the weakness in my profession lay in this postpartum period. . . ." When she gave birth to her first child, Lang, too, "felt an unconscious need for myself to be mothered or nurtured so that I might better be able to meet the demands of my growing infant."[9]

Although it is not always possible, Lang (who stopped practicing midwifery in 1985) feels today that the midwife should be present five, six, or seven times during the postpartum phase, "depending on the need and the relationship." The midwife should know "where [the mom] keeps her towels and her teapot. As long as she's in bed, as long as she's hurting, as long as she's bewildered, she needs that care."

Karena Green, a childbirth educator with Informed Homebirth and Parenting, a lay midwife in the Philadelphia area, and herself the mother of six (including two sets of twins), keeps in close touch with her clients postpartum. "I think health-care providers need to erase some of the lines involved in care, that care is during pregnancy and immediately after birth and after that—what? You don't care anymore? I do home visits the first day after the birth, the third day, a week, and three weeks after the birth. I go to their home and spend time with them. I see them interact with the baby. I see them interact with other people in the family, I watch how the baby's father interacts with the baby. I spend time and attention with them on a one-to-one basis in terms of follow-up care and in the home. The whole concept of assessing anything in an artificial situation doesn't make sense. It's also an incredible hardship for a woman with a new baby to be schlepping herself and her baby out in public very soon after birth. I'm not talking about being physically well or that it's an illness, I just mean within a social context, I think it's hard for a newly postpartum woman to integrate the outside world. Home care is something that's very important. Besides this, I do at least four telephone calls within that first three-week period."

The childbirth assistant, another relatively new figure on the childbirth scene, also plays an important role postpartum. Raven Lang notes that as midwives have become more "heavily put upon," expanded postpartum participation "is a fine role for the childbirth assistant. I consider her part of the midwife team. She's a good one, because she's not going to have to be on call for catching [babies]."

Claudia Lowe, president of the National Association of Childbirth Assistants (founded in 1985), defines the childbirth assistant as "a person who is specially trained to provide nonmedical labor support and educational counseling for the childbearing year." During the prenatal part of their involvement, the assistant helps the woman to focus on the transition to the postpartum period and to set up a postpartum network prenatally. Following the birth, the assistant will then make two or three visits to coincide with the phases of early postpartum as defined by the nursing texts.

"We also encourage our members not only to do those three visits, which are the most intensive part, but then to just touch base at the three-month, six-month, and nine-month period, just kind of a reminder—'What's up for you? Anything you need to talk about?' Because there is no one [else to do this for the moms]."

The birth companion fills the same role as the childbirth assistant. Along these lines, in October 1991, Pam Nessen, a birth companion in the Greater Philadelphia area, founded Birth Companions and Family Care, a program within Valley Family House. Through massage, guided imagery, and general moral support, the birth companion helps the woman to alleviate any fears she may have about the birth, and to tap into her own sources of strength and self-confidence. The organization started out strictly as effective labor support, "meaning that we offered mothers comfort care. Where your midwives and your obstetricians would offer technical and assessment skills, we offered the support from an emotional and physical basis during labor and the birth."

After the birth, says Nessen, the birth companion always stays with the family for at least six hours, whether they're at home or in the hospital (provided the hospital permits their participation), so parents and baby can get settled. She makes sure the baby is nursing well before she leaves, and usually gives Mom a massage "to work out the kinks." In the hospital setting, she can also intercede or advocate for the mom over questions about hospital policy or other problems at a time when the new mom may not be feeling up to taking on hospital administration. Then, over the course of the first few days, she continues to be present through telephone calls to the family. At about the fourth week, the birth companion will make a home visit. "We figure by the fourth week, the honeymoon is over," says Nessen. "Mom's pretty much on her own. . . . Usually there is something set up with all OBs and midwives that you have a six-week postpartum checkup, but I think there's a need in between the two-week postpartum and the six-week postpartum that we kind of fill in there around the four weeks. Just to check in and make sure things are going okay, and helping out [often with local referrals] if they're not."

Although Nessen had initially not included more specific postpartum care, within a week of starting the company she had added the doula or family care component. "It happened from the response of the mothers. We were offering the labor support end of it, but that didn't seem to be enough. There were moms who needed the labor support end of it, but then there were moms who just needed the postpartum care end of it. So we expanded to do both. With health-care reform, I can see that in the future the postpartum doula and labor support person will have increasingly important roles to play." Through the doula service, women could choose a week or two of help. Often the same birth companion from the labor and delivery will also be the postpartum caregiver. "It is nice if you can get the connection all the way through, but I've found that it isn't an absolutely necessary component."

Nessen points out that there is an important distinction between her service and the services that focus primarily on postpartum care. "If you have ever had the privilege of being at a birth, you would . . . know the strength that is in that room. It is amazing, the strength that a mother can project during labor. I think that we did add the postpartum doula end of it only to make us full circle for the needs of mothers. Three-quarters of our circle is truly in the labor support area. That's where the difference is. It's to help mothers realize their own strength. And they all have it, it's just that it has never been brought to the surface. . . . We teach mothers to trust in themselves. . . . That's the major crux of labor [and postpartum] support, to teach the mother that her intuition isn't 90 percent, it isn't 99 percent, it's 100 percent."

For Carol, who delivered her first baby at age forty-three, after a forty-hour labor, the help of a birth companion when her husband went back to work was indispensable. The Monday morning her doula arrived, Carol was totally sleep-deprived and having a lot of difficulty nursing—"I was exhausted to the point of tears." On the brink of giving up breastfeeding altogether, the first thing she did was to send Olivia, her doula, out for formula. When she returned with a six-pack in hand, "[Olivia] encouraged me to take a warm bath and relax, and I did, [the baby] started nursing and everything progressed pretty fine after that." The formula was soon forgotten.

"Olivia was just so calm," Carol recalled when her baby was twelve days old. "That was a good complement for me because I was so totally at my wits' end. She helped me to feel more secure with what I was doing with the baby, because I was just floundering. . . . Knowing that there was somebody here who was competent with babies and could guide me . . . was probably the most important thing for me, the mental comfort and security of knowing that she could answer any questions." In addition to providing education and encouraging her to rest, Olivia also gave Carol another useful lesson of early motherhood. "She taught me to look at things in a different way—everything else can wait, you have to change your priorities. After forty-three years you can get set in your ways, and you feel like you always have to be in control. You can't be in control when you have a newborn baby. He's in control of everything, and basically you have to take it, if need be, one minute at a time. That's something I really have to keep reminding myself."

## A Little Help from Your Friends

The best doula arrangement, says Dana Raphael, is the unpaid reciprocal doula. "Two women in the same reproductive stage, who can help each other, get each other through crises." While nothing beats the rare but wonderful experience of going through pregnancy and birth with a friend—and the telephone can be a remarkably effective doula—suddenly there you are, both at home needing tea, casseroles, and clean laundry, and what can you do? A third or fourth party is still needed to manage the practical. Since some women still feel funny or have trouble asking for help, they may feel that asking a friend to do weeks of cooking, shopping, or laundry is, indeed, too intrusive.

Liz Koch, founder of *The Doula: A Magazine for Mothers*, discovered a solution to the social and psychological discomfort of asking for what may feel like "too much" after the birth of her second child. She gave the job to someone else: Liz enlisted a friend to create her helper's network, taking in hand all the vague offers of help that people made but that often might not get followed up on. The key element for Liz was having her friend act as orchestrator or contractor, so to speak, to coordinate a host of other friends to pitch in. Liz supplied the names of everyone who had made an offer of help, and her friend did the scheduling. "Instead of me calling that person, my friend called. She did a preliminary call to find out what they were interested in doing, whether it was to bring a meal, or take my child to the park if it was someone my child felt comfortable with. . . . And then she created a schedule for me where I had a meal come every single night for at least two weeks." She also incorporated into the schedule outings for her older child, as well as shopping trips, and sensitively suggested to visitors that they not stay too long. "So that's a free way to do it. It's amazing how many people would help if they knew what to do."

Liz also learned that owing people is "okay. It's actually a wonderful thing, a part of the vulnerability and softness we experience as new mothers." In Liz's case, she was later able to act as doula for her friend who served her in that way. This harkens back to the tradition of women-centered, social childbirth customs of Colonial America, and the ensuing "groaning parties" given by the new mother for the circle of women who helped her.

"Hopefully women have friends that they really feel like they can call upon," says Koch. "And if they start doing that, I think that their relationships will deepen. And their community will deepen."

# *Notes*

1. Although it no longer exists, another of the earliest doula services, Doula, was run by Cindy Siegel and Nadine Mendelsohn in southern Rhode Island.

2. "Childbearing Policy Within a National Health Program: An Evolving Consensus for New Directions," p. 14. A collaborative paper from the Women's Institute for Childbearing Policy, National Women's Health Network, National Black Women's Health Project, and the Boston Women's Health Book Collective; a project of the Women's Institute for Child-bearing Policy.

3. J. J. Kerssens, "Patient Satisfaction with Maternity Home Care," in *British Journal of Obstetrics and Gynaecology* (in press).

4. For the most comprehensive coverage of this subject see Marshall H. Klaus, John H. Kennell, and Phyllis H. Klaus, *Mothering the Mother: How a Doula Can Help You Have a Shorter, Easier, and Healthier Birth* (Reading, Mass.: Addison-Wesley Publishing Company, 1993).

5. Dorothy Harrison, "Parent-to-Baby," in *Northwest Baby* (April 1990), p. 2.

6. See Klaus, Kennell, and Klaus, pp. 34–36, 40–41.

7. Jean A. Ball, *Reactions to Motherhood: The Role of Post-natal Care* (Cambridge, Eng.: Cambridge University Press, 1987), p. ix.

8. Ibid.

9. Raven Lang, "The Art of Widwifery," in *The Doula* (Spring/ Summer 1986), pp. 2-13.

# *Resources*

The resources listed here are described in further detail in the following section:

**Postpartum Care Services**

NATIONAL
National Association of Postpartum
    Care Services

INDIVIDUAL IN-HOME POSTPARTUM
    CARE SERVICES
*California*
After the Stork

MotherCare
Tendercare

*Colorado*
Mothercare of America Postpartum
    Care, Inc.

*Illinois*
Birthways, Inc.

*Massachusetts*
MotherCare Services, Inc.

*New York*
Beyond Birth, Inc.
In a Family Way
Mother Nurture
Mothering Mom
New York Nurse

*Ohio*
Birth & Beyond, Inc.

*Oregon*
Postpartum Care
  Services/Kindhearted Women
Sweet Mama Care

*Pennsylvania*
Birth Partners

*Texas*
A Mother's Touch

*Virginia*
Mother's Matters

*Washington*
MotherCare of America Doula
  Service

**Postpartum Doula Training**
MotherLove, Inc.
Online Postpartum Doula Training

**Labor Support Doulas**
Doulas of North America

**Childbirth Assistants**
National Association of Childbirth
  Assistants

**Model Programs Providing
Mothering Mentors and Volunteers**

NATIONAL

Healthy Families America
  National Committee to Prevent
  Child Abuse

*Colorado*
Community Caring Project of
  Denver

*Massachusetts*
Healthy Baby/Healthy Child Program

*New York*
New Mothers Support Group
Teenage Pregnancy and Parenting
  Mentor Program

*Pennsylvania*
Maternity Care Coalition of Greater
  Philadelphia

**Videotapes**
*Special Women—How a Labor
  Assistant Makes Birth Safer, More
  Satisfying, and Less Expensive*
*Taking Care of Mom: A Guide to
  Postpartum*

**Books**
*The Birth Partner: Everything You
  Need to Know to Help a Woman
  Through Childbirth*
*Mothering the Mother: How a Doula
  Can Help You Have a Shorter,
  Easier, and Healthier Birth*
*Nurturing Beginning: MotherLove's
  Guide to Postpartum Care for
  Doulas and Outreach Workers*

# Postpartum Care Services

**National Association of Postpartum Care Services (NAPCS)**
2305 N.W. 37th Avenue
Coconut Creek, FL 33066
General Information:
(800)45 DOULA
www.napcs.org

Founded in May 1989, this is the first national organization of doula postpartum caregivers. As of August 1998, the association had more than 120 members throughout the United States. NAPCS offers training and certification for its members. The NAPCS referral line, 1-800-45-DOULA, acts as a resource for women seeking names of local postpartum care services and certified postpartum doulas.

INDIVIDUAL IN-HOME POSTPARTUM CARE SERVICES

Because many services are small, most prefer to be contacted and contracted before your delivery date so they can save your time slot. If you call after the baby is born, it may be harder to secure a doula. A sampling of individual services follows.

*California*
**After the Stork**
6 San Tomas
Rancho Santa Margarita, CA 92688
Tel.: (949) 589-4311

This service was founded in 1987 by cardiopulmonary specialist Mary Davis after the birth of her own first child. Initially the potential client receives information over the phone, then receives a contract, references, and a flyer. This may be followed by a meeting with the doula to answer any questions. The service, which is also available overnight, offers help with baby care, light housekeeping, meal preparation, and sibling care.

**MotherCare**
1616 N. Ft. Myer Drive, 11th floor
Arlington, VA 22209
Tel.: (703) 528-7474
Fax: (703) 528-7480
E-mail: mothercare_project@jsi.com

Founded by Laurie Dodge in 1990, MotherCare personalizes its service to meet the individual needs of each family. After initial phone contact, a doula makes a home visit. The service offers light housekeeping, care for older children, holding baby while Mom sleeps or showers, errands, and understanding when you're feeling blue. Doulas are mothers from a variety of backgrounds and they work with families experiencing cesarean birth, multiple birth, home birth, adoption, early return to work, having a child later in life, or a new baby when there are children already in the family.

**Tendercare**
26039 Moreno Drive
Valencia, CA 91355
Tel.: (661) 253-2100

This service was started in 1989 by Chris Morley as a "direct result" of her own needs after she gave birth and needed more help than she had available. Tendercare has close to thirty doulas on staff, and in addition to its focus on postpartum, it offers labor assistance, childbirth education classes, and perinatal exercise. Licensed and registered nurses, along with a masseuse, are also on staff. Doulas provide breastfeeding support, meal preparation, one-to-one parenting education, adjustments to parenthood, household organization, and well-mother and baby care. Tendercare also has doulas who work with adoptive moms, postpartum depressed moms, and multiple-birth parents.

*Colorado*
**Mothercare of America Postpartum Care, Inc.**
P.O. Box 61296
Denver, CO 80206
Tel.: (303) 321-3287

This new service was started by Joan Goode to offer postpartum care for new mothers and babies. Doulas who have breastfed for six months and taken a 35-hour training course provide breastfeeding guidance and are trained to detect early warning signs of common problems experienced by postpartum mothers and infants. The service also offers doulas who specialize in caring for multiple newborns and their mothers.

*Illinois*
**Birthways, Inc.**
1484 West Farragut
Chicago, IL 60640
Tel.: (773) 506-0607

Founded in 1997 by the former staff and director of Dana Mothercare, established in 1992, Birthways provides labor support and postpartum doula services, perinatal massage, and childbirth education. Postpartum care services encompass affirming guidance with questions about newborn and postpartum health, breastfeeding support, and help with sibling care and adjustment. Nutritious meal preparation, light household support, and errands help family enjoy time with baby.

Birthways is experienced with supporting adoptive parents, women experiencing postpartum mood disorders, and families with multiple infants. Staff have training in all areas of postpartum care.

*Massachusetts*
**MotherCare Services, Inc. (MCS)**
15 Bayberry Road
Scituate, MA 02066
Tel.: (781) 545-1500; (888) MyDoula

One of the oldest doula services, this was founded in 1982 by Joan Singer and Valerie Spain. They provide "extra hands, a calm and supportive attitude, and any helpful information needed during this time of transition." Services include emotional support, guidance with breastfeeding and newborn care, special attention for siblings, shopping, cooking, light housekeeping and laundry, and referrals to area resources.

*New York*
**Beyond Birth, Inc.**
1992 Commerce Street, Suite 40
Yorktown Heights, NY 10598
Tel.: (914) 245-BABY
Outside Westchester: (800) 907-BABY

Run by president Marguerite Tirelli, Beyond Birth doulas have been working with new moms and their families since 1992. They help families in Westchester, Putnam, Nassau, Suffolk, and Queens, NY, as well as Fairfield County in Connecticut, providing labor doulas and postpartum doulas. Labor doulas assist the mother-to-be during all aspects of her labor. Postpartum doulas assist the new mom with newborn and sibling care and establishing breastfeeding. They provide the extra pair of hands that are so needed in the first few days at home. Beyond Birth's goal is to help women have the birth they envision and to ease the transition from pregnancy to parenthood.

**In a Family Way**
124 West 79th Street
New York, NY 10024
Tel.: (212) 877-8112

This service was started in 1990 by Christine Kealy. In addition to postpartum doula care to nurture and care for the new mother and help her "discover her own intuitive mothering skills," In a Family Way also offers emergency doula care in case of colds, flu, or appointments, as well as pregnancy doula care for "fatigue, Mommy sickness, too much to do, too little time." Packages are customized to meet individual needs.

**Mother Nurture**
P.O. Box 284
Glen Oaks, NY 11004
Tel.: (718) 631-BABY
www.mothernurture.com
doulacomp@aol.com

This service was founded in 1987 by Alice Gilgoff, R.N., certified nurse-midwife, childbirth educator, and La Leche League leader. Clients initially fill out a mother's needs outline. Home visit by the doula to meet client prenatally is available for $25. Care-

givers provide labor support, shopping, cooking, sibling care, breastfeeding support, referrals, laundry, and errand-running.

**Mothering Mom**
P.O. Box 3002
Liverpool, NY 13089
Tel.: (315) 652-9910

Founded in 1991, Mothering Mom offers shopping, sibling care, baby care, mother care, breastfeeding support, laundry, housekeeping, meal preparation, parenting, and emotional support.

**New York Nurse**
130 West 24th Street, #5B
New York, NY 10011
Tel.: (212) 989-3036

Paula Zindler, BSN, RN, IBCLC (also dba N.Y. Nurse) is a pediatric nurse/lactation consultant in private practice since 1986. As a "start-up" specialist, Paula offers a personal prenatal consultation to strengthen the confidence and skills needed by mothers to successfully initiate breastfeeding, followed by postpartum home visits to provide correct, consistent advice in support of continued breastfeeding. She knows that early intervention is crucial in avoiding the mother's discomforts, and infant's slow weight gain, that are all too common among breastfeeding moms.

*Ohio*
**Birth & Beyond, Inc.**
Cleveland, OH
Tel.: (440) 333-4996

Birth & Beyond provides a comprehensive package of professional (DONA-certified) doula and adjunct services. They offer non-medical physical and emotional support to women during the childbearing year, complementing the clinical care provided by physicians and midwives. The services they offer include: antepartum doulas, birth doulas, sibling care during labor and birth, and postpartum doulas, as well as private childbirth education, lactation consultations, and breast pump sales and rentals.

*Oregon*
**Postpartum Care**
**Services/Kindhearted Women**
816 SE 29th Street, Apt. 304
Portland, OR 97214
Tel.: (503) 736-1328

Postpartum Care Services was founded in 1992 by Vicky York. The goal of this service is to give the new mother confidence in her own mothering abilities while offering gentle encouragement, education, and practical help in the areas of breastfeeding, home management, baby care, meal preparation, shopping, postpartum depression, sibling attention, and her own physical and emotional needs. The service extends to accompanying the new mother on her first outing alone with her baby, and connecting her with her community resources. Breast pumps and baby scales are available. Vicky York is a member of the NAPCS and DONA, CPR certified, and a mother and grandmother with newborn nursery experience who has worked with preemies, multiples, and adoptive families. She offers a free one-hour prenatal visit to answer questions and discuss specific needs, and no contract is required for her services.

**Sweet Mama Care**
P. O. Box 6916
Portland, OR 97228-6916
Tel.: (503) 239-4641

Sweet Mama Care (formerly The Doula Circle) is dedicated to in-home care for mother and family before, during, and after childbirth. They are especially inclined to call upon alternative forms of healing, and to nurture the mother's intuitive ability to care for her family. They encourage open, honest communication, and strongly support family-centered community. Services include massage, newborn and nutritional counseling, laundry, wholesome meal preparation, light housekeeping, errands and grocery shopping, sibling care, labor support, community resource referrals, and loving support for the whole family during this most precious, transitional time.

*Pennsylvania*
**Birth Partners**
2591 Corteland Drive
Pittsburgh, PA 15241
Tel.: (412) 833-8116

This service was started in 1994 by childbirth educator, certified doula, and perinatal social worker Kathy McGrath. Birth Partners has well-trained, carefully selected postpartum doulas who provide comforting, hands-on help and support to new mothers and their families. They help mothers get off to a good start by assisting with newborn and sibling care, breastfeeding support and guidance, meals, and housekeeping. In addition, Birth Partners offers childbirth classes, labor support (DONA-certified doulas), and postpartum mothers groups.

*Texas*

**A Mother's Touch**
2031 Rose Hill
Carrollton, TX 75007
Tel.: (972) 492-3122

Based on her own family tradition of mothers and grandmothers nurturing new mothers, Emily Traugott founded A Mother's Touch in 1989. In addition to shopping, light housekeeping, cooking, laundry, errands, breastfeeding support, and referrals, this service also offers light yardwork, dog-walking, accompanying Mom to the doctor, and phone messages.

*Virginia*

**Mother's Matters**
The Reston International Center
11800 Sunrise Valley Drive, Suite 305
Reston, VA 20191
Tel.: (703) 620-3323

Founded in 1991, this maternal-infant care service can provide doulas to help during the prenatal period, with labor and delivery support, and then during the postpartum period with mother and newborn care, care of infants with special needs, guidance in infant nutrition and hygiene, breastfeeding assistance, instruction on infant massage, sibling care and support, light housekeeping, laundry and meals, grocery shopping, and short errands. They also have registered nurses who specialize in maternal–infant care. In addition, a lactation program with certified lactation consultants is available to clients and corporations in the community.

*Washington*

**MotherCare of America Doula**
**Service**

P.O. Box 1012
Edmonds, WA 98206
Tel.: (425) 672-8011

This service was started in March 1988 and offers breastfeeding support, errands, sibling care, laundry, light housekeeping, meal preparation (including vegetarian and kosher cooking), and shopping. Founder and director Dorothy Harrison is mother of six, was a La Leche League leader for ten years, and trained as a natural childbirth instructor. Harrison feels that "Mother-Care fills a need that grandmothers, aunts, and sisters in other times would fill." This is one of the few services in the country that has a hospital contract.

# Postpartum Doula Training

**MotherLove, Inc.**
584 Echo Glen Avenue
River Vale, NJ 07675
Tel.: (201) 358-2703
E-mail:
   Motherlove.doula@prodigy.net

Debra Pascali-Bonaro, C.D. (DONA), president of MotherLove, Inc., provides consulting, training, and design of both labor support and postpartum doula programs throughout North America for both hospital- and community-based doula programs.

**Online Postpartum Doula Training**
Contact: Valerie DiGiovanni
Tel.: (631) 444-3481
E-mail:
   Valerie.DiGiovanni@sunysb.edu
   www.uhmc.sunysb.edu/nursing
The State University of New York

at Stony Brook, School of Nursing, is offering the first online postpartum doula training course. Doula trainers Debra Pascali-Bonaro, C.D. (DONA), and Jane Arnold, C.N.M., have designed and developed the online course and will guide you through the online experience of learning to be a postpartum doula. The course provides extensive knowledge about providing care to women, infants, and their families during the first six weeks postpartum. It also guides you through your community services and helps you integrate doula care into maternity services.

## Labor Support Doulas

**Doulas of North America (DONA)**
Central Office
13513 North Grove Drive
Alpine, UT 84004
Tel.: (801) 756-7331
E-mail: doula@dona.org
www.dona.org

This growing association of over 2,000 labor support doulas was founded by childbirth educator Penny Simkin, P.T., Annie Kennedy, and Marshall H. Klaus in 1992. Its focus is to provide certification for individual labor doulas, act as a central international resource for individual women and families seeking birth or postpartum doulas, train women who would like to be doulas, and seek third-party reimbursement for doula services.

## Childbirth Assistants

**National Association of Childbirth Assistants (NACA)**
P.O. Box 1537 Boyes

Hot Springs, CA 95416
Tel.: (707) 939-0543

Founded in 1985, NACA now has more than 1000 members nationwide. NACA defines "childbirth assistant" as "a person who is specially trained to provide labor support and educational counseling for the childbearing year." This includes postpartum follow-up visits (two to three visits after delivery), and the childbirth assistant remains available to clients on an ongoing basis throughout the first year, or as questions come up. NACA can also give you information on hiring or becoming a childbirth assistant.

## Model Programs Providing Mothering Mentors and Volunteers

NATIONAL
**Healthy Families America (HFA)**
 **National Committee to Prevent Child Abuse**
200 South Michigan Avenue,
Suite 1700
Chicago, IL 60604
Tel.: (312) 663-3520

Based on the premise that the best time to build healthy parent–child relationships is at the time of birth, the HFA initiative was undertaken by the National Committee to Prevent Child Abuse in partnership with Ronald MacDonald Children's Charities based on two decades of research and the successful Hawaiian Healthy Start model. The goal of the initiative is to lay the foundation for voluntary, neonatal, home-visitor programs for new parents through state-level organizations. The home visits, which empower parents to access the resources they need to better care for themselves and their children, and which can last up to five years, focus on parenting skills, child development, child health, and other aspects of family functioning.

*Colorado*

**Community Caring Project of Denver**
Kempe National Center
1205 Oneida Street
Denver, CO 80220
Tel.: (303) 320-1666

This is a home visitor support system for mothers of new babies. The project's trained volunteers offer free support to new moms following the birth of a baby. Recognizing that the new first-time mother may feel overwhelmed as well as overjoyed, volunteers provide personal support, a listening ear, information about babies' individual differences, tips on enjoying your child, resource referrals, specific skills for interacting with your baby, and weekly home visits and telephone calls over a three- to twelve-month period.

*Massachusetts*

**Healthy Baby/Healthy Child Program**
City of Boston Public Health
    Commission
26 Central Avenue
Hyde Park, MA 02136
Tel.: (617) 534-5832

The mission of the Healthy Baby/Healthy Child Program is to increase the ability of infants and young children and their families to thrive, especially in neighborhoods and population groups that are disproportionately impacted by infant mortality. All services are free. The work is done through direct home visiting services and collaborative efforts with other providers of maternal and child health services. Services through home visits and group education are provided within the context of each client's own culture. They include education in parenting skills, health, and advocacy; referral to available community services such as medical care providers, social service agencies and shelters; and a food pantry for emergencies. The Partners in Parenting Project selects and trains volunteers from the community, and Healthy Baby/Healthy Child Program alumni to assist expectant and new parents by serving as role models, advocates, and liaisons with program case manager. Clients are matched with compatible and genuinely concerned peers who address their individual needs while encouraging them to take control of their lives. Fathers in Need of Direction is a project that promotes positive male involvement during the partner's pregnancy, childbirth, and in future parenting. New fathers are taught the importance and practice of pre- and postnatal child care, fulfilling their roles and responsibilities as family members, building stronger relationships with their partners, and playing a prominent role in the life and health of their children.

*New York*

**New Mothers Support Group**
Parent/Family Education Program
Beth Israel Medical Center
First Avenue and 16th Street
New York, NY 10003
Warmline: (212) 420-2999

A hospital-based support group for new mothers and their infants, this meets twice each month. Program includes both informal discussion and guest presentations on topics such as choosing a caregiver, breastfeeding, and infant massage. Program is free, open to the public. Facilitator: Karen Goodman, RNC, MA, ACCE, Coordinator of Parent/ Family Education.

**Teenage Pregnancy and Parenting Mentor Program**
New York Presbyterian Hospital
Department of Social Work
525 East 68th Street, F-134
New York, NY 10021
Tel: (212) 746-1092

This program for teens who wish to participate offers one-to-one volunteer mentors who meet with them prenatally, may stay with them through labor and delivery, and will continue an ongoing supportive relationship postpartum. TAPP also offers a weekly adolescent mothers and infants clinic where mom and baby may be seen together, as well as a weekly obstetrical clinic for teens. Each clinic session is followed by a support and information group and lunch. The sessions are designed to meet the "very specific needs" of the teen population. TAPP also offers continuity of care with the same social workers and a nurse practitioner. Persons interested in volunteering to be a mentor may contact the Volunteer Department at New York Hospital.

*Pennsylvania*
**Maternity Care Coalition of Greater Philadelphia (MCC)**
2000 Hamilton Street, Suite 205
Philadelphia, PA 19130
Tel.: (215) 972-0700

MCC is a nonprofit organization that works to reduce infant mortality and improve maternal and child health through outreach to high-risk communities in Philadelphia. It is guided by a diverse board of health providers, corporate professionals, and neighborhood residents who recruit community members to help improve maternity and infant care in their neighborhoods. They educate pregnant women about the importance of prenatal care, provide postpartum services, and manage health care for newborns until they are two years old. MCC currently operates nine MOMobile sites and a fleet of six outreach vehicles, which enable staff to seek out and offer services to pregnant women in neighborhoods with high infant mortality rates, teenage pregnancy, poverty, and child abuse and neglect. Postnatal services include home visits, follow-up calls, and mentoring of mothers and their families. MOMobile Programs are customized to include such components as HIV prevention and lead education. In addition to its outreach work, MCC is a leader in local, state, and national advocacy of policies that impact on people who live in impoverished and isolated communities.

## Videotapes

*Special Women—How a Labor Assistant Makes Birth Safer, More Satisfying, and Less Expensive*
Distributed by Injoy Productions
Tel.: (800) 326-2082 or fax: (303)449-8788 (for Visa and MasterCard orders only)

In a video hosted by Polly Perez, parents and professionals explain how having a labor assistant present at birth can benefit babies, parents, health care providers and hospitals. Clinical studies are highlighted, documenting how the role of the birth assistant improves birth outcome and decreases maternity costs. Trained labor assistants use labor support techniques and tools such as the birth ball and massage tools. A special section is included for those considering becoming a professional labor assistant.

*Taking Care of Mom: A Guide to Postpartum*
Distributed by Injoy Productions
Tel.: (800) 326-2082 or fax: (303)449-8788 (for Visa and MasterCard orders only)

Hosts are experts Boston obstetrician Beatrice Pitcher (Brigham and Women's Hospital) and Jeanne Driscoll, R.N., M.S., C.S. Topics include how to manage postpartum pain, how to do kegel exercises, how to care for an episiotomy, how to manage nutrition, how to know if it's okay to exercise, and dealing with changing relationships at home. Includes a diverse group of women who talk honestly about the postpartum period. Shot on location in hospital rooms, doctor's office during a six-week checkup, postpartum exercise class, and at home with new moms and their babies.

## Books

*The Birth Partner: Everything You Need to Know to Help a Woman Through Childbirth*
Penny Simkin, P.T.
Harvard Common Press

Used by birth doulas, this book describes the birth process, with special emphasis on the emotional needs of the laboring woman and how to meet those needs. Covering both home and hospital births, it includes information, practical advice, and comfort measures useful to all birth partners and doulas.

*Mothering the Mother: How a Doula Can Help You Have a Shorter, Easier, and Healthier Birth*
Marshall H. Klaus, John H. Kennell, and Phyllis H. Klaus
Addison-Wesley Publishing

This book, by pioneers in the fields of natural, more humane childbirth and the well-being of mothers and babies, confirms the benefit and importance of having a labor support doula and helper during birth and at home after the birth. It also helps women and birthing couples in selecting a doula to work with.

*Nurturing Beginning: MotherLove's Guide to Postpartum Care for Doulas and Outreach Workers*
Debra Pascali-Bonaro and Jane Arnold
State University of New York at Stony Brook

Comprehensive postpartum doula training manual. See pages 115–116 for more information.

# 4.
# YOU'VE CHOSEN TO BREASTFEED

*Who's Showing You How?*

••••••

*One of the common misconceptions about breastfeeding is that it's an instinct. It's not an instinct. It's a learned behavior, just as all aspects of parenting are learned behavior.*

—Laura Best, IBCLC
Beth Israel Lactation Program

*The breastfeeding mom really needs a mothering mother right next to her in order to help her succeed at what she's doing.*

—Luz García, Breastfeeding doula
North Central Bronx Hospital

## The Importance of Having Hands-on Human Help

In times and places where birth and postpartum were women-centered events, and breastfeeding was the only infant feeding method possible, mothers, grandmothers, sisters, aunts, or elders would offer hands-on instruction, companionship, and nurturing care as the new mother established a successful milk supply. Although diverse cultures had different beliefs and traditions surrounding breastfeeding, as Dana Raphael pointed out, many relieved the new mom of all responsibilities and stress, since the infant's very survival depended on the success of breastfeeding. Some of the advice offered was technical and practical: how to prepare the nipple for the baby's mouth, how to express milk, or how long to feed on each side. Some of the support was emotional and psychological: the comforting presence of companions and mentors in whose hands the new mom felt protected and confident.

If you are breastfeeding or are planning to breastfeed your baby, ongoing access to one or several people who can educate, encourage, and continue to advise you throughout your overall breastfeeding relationship is an important part of the support you may need. It may be a friend or relative; it may be a peer group; it may be a staff person at the hospital or birthing center who continues to be available to you after you're home; it may be a lactation consultant visiting you or whom you visit independently. You may find that you and your infant do fine after a few demonstrations at the hospital, and your questions may not surface until you have to go back to work and need to set up an entirely new routine at that point. Or you may find that nursing that went well at the hospital starts to unravel after day four or five at home, especially if support is low, stress is high, and you are getting tired; some immediate help is needed.

Whatever your feelings and needs as you build up a breastfeeding relationship with your baby, remember that a book, a class, and the cheerful admonition that "it's natural, everyone can do it" may be misleading for many mothers. Don't be surprised if it doesn't feel like enough for you. And never minimize or underestimate the value of the helper who may be doing everything from helping you experiment with positioning the baby more comfortably to nonjudgmentally listening to why you are feeling frustrated or exhausted enough to want to throw in the diaper altogether to simply mirroring back to you your own success.

Today, many women who choose to breastfeed come to it with great passion, intention, and desire, and very little practical knowledge, confidence, or broad-based, ongoing support. Some moms may come to it essentially alone, except for one or two hospital staff members who may or may not give adequate or correct information or may even be more aggressively obstructive. How many mothers have memories of sitting in a hospital room or later a bedroom, reading the same pages over and over, wondering if what they're doing is right, feeling uncomfortable, uncertain, sometimes experiencing pain? Mom can only hope that if she doesn't know exactly what to do, at least the baby will. Often the baby needs help, too. Then Mom's really lost. Postpartum anxiety levels rise, and the sense of crisis escalates.

International board-certified lactation consultant (IBCLC) Beverly Solow of the Breastfeeding Assistance Service in New York City stresses the importance of getting help early if you think there is a problem or even if you just have a question or need some encouragement and perspective. She has also observed, however, that "sometimes new mothers see breastfeeding as the problem, when really it is the challenge of life with a new baby. The bottle doesn't solve the problem—nevertheless, it is true that a feeding problem can make a hard time even harder."

Having a breastfeeding support group or individual available to you follows in natural succession the labor companion or doula who may have stayed with you through labor, delivery, and the early postpartum hours, when the early breastfeeding experience is so important. The role played by this supportive female was observed in Guatemala in 1974 when Drs. Marshall H. Klaus and John H. Kennell carried out a pilot study in which an untrained female remained with mothers during labor and birth at a Guatemalan maternity hospital. The positive effects of this for both mother and baby are documented in their book *Parent–Infant Bonding.*

Today, this person who is available to you may take a variety of forms. She may in fact be the same companion or assistant who was with you during labor and delivery, or she may be a postpartum caregiver—hired or free—who comes to help out at home. This is a time when you need steady, informed voices and hands. It is not a time for confusion, conflicting instruction, or piecemeal information. The help or phone availability of this designated person, whether she is paid, a volunteer, or a friend or family member, may feel especially welcome.

Anna Werner is an international board-certified lactation consultant (IBCLC) who, along with Beverly Solow, runs the Breastfeeding Assistance Service. She has also worked as a doula (or postpartum caregiver) for the Mom Service. Interestingly, Werner points out that as much as new moms need food, nourishment, warm drinks, and rest, none of that really affects their ability to nurse well as much as the degree to which they actually feel secure and nurtured themselves.

"There were studies done on women in London during the bombings [in World War II]," she says. "Poor diet, lack of sleep, intense stress, lack of food had absolutely no effect on the mother's ability to produce a high-quality milk. What we do feel is that if the mother doesn't feel nurtured, then she can't nurture her baby. Emotions do affect us physically. If the mom doesn't feel nurtured or sufficiently empowered, that's a problem. If she feels nurtured, she can maintain her child in the face of anything.

"In this country, the preparation for breastfeeding is very poor," says Werner. "It is unusual for a woman upon the birth of her first child not to experience either physical or emotional discomfort that is in some way disorienting or overwhelming. Many women are very lucky and things are uncomplicated and they have no real problems, but when asked to look back, even those women will report that they experienced some intense difficulty because of the lack of support, either in their family or in their community. I don't think it will change unless there is as much attention paid to breastfeeding and early mothering as there was to cholesterol or oat bran."

Sometimes women have one person who helps them start and keep going with their breastfeeding. Very often, women don't. "I had a lot of troubles for the first four to six weeks," said Diane, a Boston-based first-time mom who nursed her baby for four months. "No one really helped solve them. I read *The Nursing Mother's Companion* a lot and wished I had a real person to ask questions. . . . I had a little instruction from nurses in the hospital the first two days and I read a book on breastfeeding the first two weeks for instructions and tips. I naively thought it would happen naturally, and would have found it very helpful to actually see someone do it in person."

The demands of a hungry newborn are considerable, particularly if you are not prepared for it. Often women are taken by surprise at the intensity of the time required to establish a milk supply. "They are surprised by the amount of time per feeding, and the frequency of feedings," says Beverly Solow. They have not planned for this in their postpartum thinking at all, despite their commitment and wish to breastfeed. Marianne, a mom from Boston, was committed to nursing—"I always knew I would breastfeed because I believe that it was the healthiest for my son." She had nurses who taught her in the hospital, she read a book, and she asked questions of her doctor and a lactation consultant. The staff, she says, "was consistent and wonderfully supportive. The routine was supportive. I was able to decide all aspects of my hospital stay." Even so, she says, "Initially I felt overwhelmed by the amount of time my son demanded to be fed, and [I] wanted to switch. But I spoke with my pediatrician and had patience and worked it out." She nursed for fifteen weeks, and was planning to wean over a five-week period.

"There's so much pressure on women now to succeed at [breastfeeding]," says Werner, "and yet there's so little real information of substance given them in order to allow them to successfully breastfeed. They're really being put in a terrible Catch-22 situation. I think that for many women it is extremely difficult and this often causes a lot of distress." If breastfeeding does not go well, new moms often interpret this as personal inadequacy or lack of commitment. Enter guilt and bad feelings. It would be ideal, says Werner, if every new mom could "find somebody who really knows about breastfeeding whom she can have frequent access to before [and after] she gives birth."

In addition to the knowledge and expertise available from a lactation consultant or peer group, the new mom also needs some encouragement and cheering on from within her own family. "If a woman does not have an immediate family member who is supportive," Werner suggests, "and it can be just one immediate family member, her chances of successfully being able to breastfeed her baby are very low. There is research that documents this. We see this all the time. We'll see a woman who has a cousin who supports her very intensely but lives on the other side of the country; nobody who lives in her home area believes that she can do it. The phone calls to her cousin are all that's keeping her going. Many times that's not enough because she may need physical assistance, too, help with positioning, or whatever. She needs hands. There isn't an acknowledgment in our culture of the fact that during the early days following the birth, a woman is physically very vulnerable and very needy, and if she does not have sufficient assistance, she's not going to be able to successfully accomplish her goal. Without help she might breastfeed her baby but she won't enjoy it, and in our mind that's not a success. Breastfeeding is supposed to be pleasurable, as are other aspects of the human experience of creating and supporting the growth of the young."

It is easy to understand why women may feel isolated in this regard. By the mid-twentieth century, breastfeeding in America was considered old-fashioned. At least half of women were no longer breastfeeding. Many of our mothers did not. (And even if they did, this does not necessarily guarantee a smooth course for us if problems arise.) Formula was considered efficient and convenient; properly sterilized bottles represented progress. In addition, the health benefits of breast milk were not yet widely understood. In the face of any kind of breast-feeding problem, Mom would often be advised to wean and switch to the bottle. Since that time, many factors have come into play that have either sabotaged or supported the efforts of breastfeeding mothers. On the sabotage side are, for example, workplaces hostile to nursing women, and formula companies that work to woo women from breast milk to formula. On the support side are peer support groups and lactation professionals who provide answers, companionship, and information for women who choose to breastfeed.

In part because of the access to peer groups such as the La Leche League and the Nursing Mothers' support groups of the Childbirth Education Association of Greater Philadelphia (founded in 1961), more mothers were nursing in the mid-1980s than had done so previously. But today, statistics have dropped from where they were a decade ago, and the goals that former surgeon general C. Everett Koop laid out in 1984—75 percent of women breastfeeding at discharge, and 35 percent at six months by 1990—were far from realized. In 1989, only half of all mothers breastfed after hospital discharge in the United States, with fewer than 20 percent continuing beyond six months. Leaders in the field would like to see better educational efforts, less influence by the formula companies, public policy supportive of breastfeeding mothers who choose or need to work outside the home, and more social support for breastfeeding mothers in general. Suggestions for implementing these changes range from the creation of comfortable and sanitary breastfeeding rooms in offices, malls, and department stores to the dismantling of the attitude that breastfeeding in public is indecent. (The husband of one breastfeeding mother actually called the local police to see if his wife could be arrested for nursing in public after she was challenged by a restaurant owner. He was told she could not.) Writing in *Still More Breastfeeding Myths*, a hospital-based information sheet, Jack Newman, M.D., FRCPC, and director of the Breastfeeding Clinic at the Hospital for Sick Children in Toronto, notes that, "It is the scolding or harassment of mothers who are nursing their babies that is not decent. Women who are trying to do the best for their babies should not be forced by other people's lack of understanding to stay home or feed their babies in public washrooms. Those who are offended need only avert their eyes."[1]

# Getting Started in the Hospital: Possible Obstacles

Many new mothers have stories to share about early breastfeeding and the hospital experience. They range from support to sabotage. Some women were treated with dignity and sensitivity:

**Gaye:** *"I never expected to do anything but breastfeed. I really wanted this. I took a very informative class while I was pregnant. . . . The hospital was wonderful. I had the baby whenever I wanted her except visiting hours, and my wishes were respected. Much to my surprise, my daughter and I took to it immediately. She still nurses twice a day at nine months."*

Some women receive minimal guidance and support, and feel that they are essentially left to map their own course:

**Elizabeth:** *"A lactation nurse was assigned to us in the hospital to help. The hospital staff were not consistent in their instruction or regulations/enforcement. However, I took that as further evidence that different things worked for different people and it made me feel braver about experimenting or asking for help or advice, and about being clear with them about what was and was not okay with me and what I was and was not going to do."*

There may be little hands-on help:

**Elizabeth B.:** *"My mother had no idea how to breastfeed. She was [of] that formula generation and considered this a backward step to breastfeed, so I got no encouragement from her, nor did she know how to do it. I had called [the] La Leche League, and they would tell me, but you have to show the person. Telling a person doesn't help. When I was in the hospital the second time, there was a wonderful night nurse, who was originally from another country, and she actually did it for me, put the nipple in the baby's mouth—'Okay, this is the way you should do it.' [Most] people don't want to touch you for one thing, there's a whole* *thing about you don't touch the person, and if you have to, you wear gloves, so nobody's going to help you do that."*

As with so much else about the birthing and postpartum experience, attitudes that hospitals project about the routine separation of mother and baby are deeply ingrained and internalized by women themselves. "[Having a baby in the hospital] is like an outpatient surgery," says IBCLC Linda Kutner, a former president of the International Lactation Consultants' Association. "You have the baby and they push you out. Even if you have rooming-in in the hospital the implication is that the baby should stay in the bassinet. I had a mother in the hospital. I picked the baby up and the baby wasn't nursing well. One of the first things we do with a [baby who is not nursing well] is have it go skin to skin on the mother's chest, and she just rubs its back. It may take four to five hours, but many times this organizes the baby so that it can then nurse. And she said to me, 'You mean I can hold my baby?'"

Women who experience difficulty with breastfeeding in the hospital in the early hours or days following delivery warn that the following may be among the factors causing problems: routines and attitudes about the separation of mother and infant that still prevail in many hospitals; inconsistent or inadequate breastfeeding instruction; insensitivity among staff; frustration at the failure of hospital staff to respect the mother's requests for demand feeding, rooming-in, or no bottle in the nursery unless discussed with the mother and the pediatrician; failure of nursing staff to assist new moms, especially those who may have had cesarean sections and cannot physically handle their babies in the early days; staff overeagerness to bring in a bottle too readily if they cannot solve a particular clinical problem; easy availability of formula that acts as a deterrent; and the mom's own exhaustion or anxiety and lack of access to supportive family members.

Suzanne Rosenfeld, a pediatrician in New York City, has a high percentage of nursing mothers in her practice—80 to 90 percent—and is sometimes very involved with them before they ever go into the hospital to deliver. Her suggestion to women who are committed to breastfeeding is to speak to their obstetrician/gynecologist and pediatrician ahead of time to see what arrangements can be made in the hospital to support a breastfeeding routine. She also suggests having several options for breastfeeding routines, depending on how the delivery goes.

# The Baby-Friendly Hospital: A New Global Initiative

On February 15, 1991, the World Alliance for Breastfeeding Action (WABA) was formed at a meeting of nongovernmental organizations at UNICEF in New York City. WABA is a consortium of nongovernmental organizations, national-level organizations, and individuals who have decided to work together to protect, support, and promote

---

## THE BABY-FRIENDLY HOSPITAL
### TEN STEPS TO SUCCESSFUL BREASTFEEDING*

Every facility providing maternity services and care for newborn infants should:

1. Have a written breastfeeding policy that is routinely communicated to all health-care staff.
2. Train all health-care staff in skills necessary to implement this policy.
3. Inform all pregnant women about the benefits and management of breastfeeding.
4. Help mothers initiate breastfeeding within a half hour of birth.
5. Show mothers how to breastfeed and how to maintain lactation even if they should be separated from their infants.
6. Give newborn infants no food or drink other than breast milk, unless medically indicated.
7. Practice rooming-in—allow mothers and infants to remain together—twenty-four hours a day.
8. Encourage breastfeeding on demand.
9. Give no artificial teats or pacifiers (also called dummies or soothers) to breastfeeding infants.
10. Foster the establishment of breastfeeding support groups and refer mothers to them on discharge from the hospital or clinic.

*Source: Joint UNICEF/WHO statement, July 1989.

breastfeeding around the world. It is the first such umbrella breastfeeding organization.

In June 1991, WABA launched a global baby-friendly hospital initiative as part of a joint initiative that also involves the elimination of distribution of free or low-cost formula. One specific purpose of the baby-friendly hospital initiative was to establish ten steps of successful breastfeeding as "a systematic way of eliminating obstacles to breastfeeding in hospitals," says Laura Best, IBCLC. "It really is addressing the issue of how can hospitals be more supportive of women and their choice to breastfeed." Its goals are to focus on the needs of mom and baby by treating them with dignity and by providing information and support for breastfeeding.

In the United States as of May 1993, there were no baby-friendly hospitals designated because there was still no mechanism in place to do so. Until such time as one is established, hospitals may apply to the UNICEF/WHO baby-friendly hospital initiative interim program in the United States for a certificate of intent, which demonstrates their commitment toward breastfeeding. (As of April 1993, close to one hundred hospitals had applied.) In the meantime, says Anna Werner, the ten steps (page 125) are a valuable assessment tool for women to use in evaluating what their hospitals have to offer them.

While the results of how your area's hospitals measure up may be discouraging, says Laura Best, "just getting involved in these activities is showing women that they do have a right to expect a certain level of care and there is something they can do as an individual to help bring about change. And we're encouraging women to contact hospitals before they give birth and say, 'Do you use the ten steps? Are you a baby-friendly hospital? If not, when do you plan to become one?' It's this kind of thing we're seeing more and more."

# Choosing a Helper

*Every time I had to have the baby latch on, it was a little trauma.*
—Diana, mother of three

*The fact that [a mom] is into breastfeeding now doesn't mean she is not going to have continuous questions.*
—Linda Kutner, IBCLC

If you know or think that you are going to breastfeed, it is best to start thinking about support people prenatally, if you can. When you sit down for that inventory check that so many mothers-to-be have with a friend or relative—How many undershirts should I buy? Which are better, little sleepers with legs, or layette gowns with strings?—also ask that person whether she breastfed and who helped her with it. What was the experience like? Were there any special problems? Who was the helper? If it was a peer support group, how else did that help in the overall transition in terms of discussions of other mothering or postpartum issues? How was the hospital or birthing center? Can she recommend somebody she liked? If she can, call that person and see if you agree. The person you find may be someone on staff, or someone with a private practice. If she is on staff at the place where you will deliver, she can also answer your questions about rooming-in and other nursing procedures. Ask how much she will be available to see or support you individually postpartum, whether she will be present immediately after the birth, and how much she can help in setting up a hospital nursing routine for you.

But don't forget that one or two or three days later, you come home alone. You're feeling vulnerable. Tired. Consumed and possibly confused by very constant demands of a very hungry baby. You may not have planned for this. Your questions or stress may involve the baby more then yourself, running the gamut from the voracious baby to the screaming baby, to the one who won't latch on at all. Or you may be feeling guilty for wanting to stop it all and get some rest, wondering how to combine meeting your own needs and those of your baby. You may feel shaky just because you don't have the needed support, or even worse, are being criticized by people close to you for wanting to nurse. In fact, says Laura Best, sometimes mates or husbands may be the ones least likely to help, despite their best intentions. "It's not unusual for partners not to understand. The partner may not be able to fill that need at that time, which is something that can be difficult for women to understand when they're in that situation. 'Why isn't my husband or my boyfriend more supportive and able to make me feel better?' And often all they want to do is protect them from the hurt, and don't understand how they could be hurting more by trying to control."

The problem may be physiological, having to do, for example, with the mom's anatomy or the baby's suck, and for which there may be any number of effective solutions if the mom can get to the right helper with the right clinical experience. Or you may just have a general sense that the process is not going well, not going as you wanted it to or thought it would go. The needs of moms in all these scenarios are valid. Like Diane, the Boston-based mom who longed for a person as well as a book to teach her, you, too, may feel that you need a human being to sit with you and show you what to do, let you know you're doing well, or show you what the problem is and how to fix it.

When you think about setting up a support network, or lining up one key support person, there are a variety of routes to take. "There are a lot of different people," says Anna Werner. "Make your first contact before birth. If that's not possible, as soon after birth as possible. Find a person before trouble starts. If you can find an IBCLC in your area, talk to her." The lactation consultant may be on staff at or recommended by your hospital, birthing center, midwife, obstetrician, or pediatrician. You can also contact the International Lactation Consultants' Association (ILCA), a professional organization of board-certified lactation consultants for a local referral. (They currently have a U.S. membership of sixteen hundred.)

Another starting place may be a local volunteer group such as the La Leche League or the Nursing Mothers' support groups of the Childbirth Education Association of Greater Philadelphia.

## PEER VOLUNTEER GROUPS

In 1956, a group of seven mothers outside Chicago were determined to breastfeed their babies against the trend of the times. They gathered in somebody's living room one day to share support and information.

"We just thought we'd have a few support groups within a very small area of people who were interested in breastfeeding and who had learned to breastfeed in a culture that wasn't very friendly [to it]. We all bent in the direction of doing what was natural and what women have done for generations," recalls Viola Lennon, one of the original seven women who got together that fall in 1956.

The new group needed a name: "We were sitting around one evening, the seven of us and friends, and we were playing with everything, you know, and one of the doctors said, 'Did you know about a statue in Florida that's dedicated to Our Lady of Happy Delivery and Plentiful

Milk? And we thought that was an awful tongue twister, so we just short-ened it to La Leche League [LLL] and it worked. . . . When we first ad-vertised for meetings in the local newspaper, we couldn't use the word 'breastfeeding.' It just was not the kind of word that would be acceptable in those times. Now everybody is very comfortable talking about breast-feeding, and there are all kinds of medical statements out about its being the superior food . . . that was unheard of forty years ago."

A little later, in 1961, the Nursing Mothers support groups were started through the Childbirth Education Association of Greater Philadelphia. Nursing Mothers' unique outreach program at one time had five hundred counselors telephoning five thousand mothers to help them with breastfeeding counseling. Its goal was to "provide en-couragement, information, and support to mothers wishing to breast-feed—for whatever period of time they choose to nurse."

When LLL began, recalls Norma Swenson, president of the board of directors of the Boston Women's Health Book Collective, "breastfeed-ing was really in such total eclipse during that period in the late '50s." At meetings, women were able to talk about not only breastfeeding is-sues but [also] a range of parenting issues, giving the group an even larger significance: "The fact that they did that," says Swenson, "re-claimed, in a way, postpartum." Swenson recalls that during her in-volvement with the childbirth movement in the 1950s and early '60s, indeed postpartum was a part of the preparation, but, she says, "The problem was we could never get the mothers to come. That was the dif-ficulty. People were interested, but the only way they would come was around the breastfeeding issue."

Since that time, a number of mother-to-mother support networks have offered a way for breastfeeding mothers to meet and share infor-mation on nursing and other parenting concerns. Today this also in-cludes support for mothers who want to continue breastfeeding after they return to work outside the home. In addition to facilitating group meetings, group leaders may be able to answer some of your questions over the telephone.

## THE LACTATION CONSULTANT

*The philosophy of the lactation consultant is certainly akin to that of the doula. We view the mother and infant as a whole. And we also feel that it's very important that we meet the emotional needs of the mother. When a mother is having difficulty with breastfeeding, she is in a crisis situation, and it's important that she have immediate assistance and that the assistance be accurate and also an emotional support.*

—Laura Best, IBCLC
Beth Israel Lactation Program

*Lactation consultants are health-care professionals who are specially trained in the management of breastfeeding mothers and babies. They are qualified to assist in all routine and special breastfeeding situations. . . . They have as their goal to help you achieve a successful breastfeeding relationship through instruction, encouraging support, and special equipment when needed.*

—Carolina Lactation Consultants

The field of lactation consulting as an allied health field first emerged about fifteen years ago. Trained in all aspects of routine and special-circumstance breastfeeding situations—from an ill or premature infant to a mom with sore nipples, from fussy babies to those with weight-gain problems—a lactation consultant (LC) may be called on as the first person the new mom sees, or she may be someone the mom consults in addition to a peer group or staff person at her hospital or birthing center.

"There are a variety of ways people can prepare for the profession of LC," says Laura Best. "Some may come from a medical background. Others may be trained specifically for the profession of LC. The allied health field of lactation consulting is a relatively new one, and not all LCs will be as proficient or experienced as others."

Those LCs with the letters IBCLC (international board-certified lactation consultant) after their names have passed the licensing exam given by ILCA (International Lactation Consultants Association).

"If she sat for the exam she had to meet certain requirements to sit for it," says Linda Kutner, IBCLC, and a former president of ILCA. "She had to have 2,500 hours of breastfeeding experience before she could sit for the exam." While acknowledging that there may be excellent LCs in the field who have not been certified through the International Board of Lactation Consultant Examiners (IBLCE), ILCA presently recognizes the IBLCE as the only certifying exam and defines the professional LC as one who has passed the exam.

LCs without the letters IBCLC after their names may have taken an educational program that bestows a certificate of completion. These programs may range from twenty-four hours to a comprehensive course of 150 hours or more, and while the person may be excellent, it may be more difficult for the new mother seeking immediate help to evaluate her background and experience.

Anna Werner, IBCLC, and Beverly Solow, IBCLC, run the Breast-feeding Assistance Service in New York City. Werner has also been a doula for the Mom Service, Inc. "LCs generally offer a full spectrum of care to women throughout their nursing experience," she says. "There is usually opportunity for some contact during the late prenatal period, usually sometime in the last trimester. We encourage families to take an in-depth breastfeeding class, just the way they take an in-depth childbirth preparation class. We feel that there is as much a need for focusing on breastfeeding skills during the prenatal period as there is on childbirth, and this is something that generally isn't done. The major focus of our work occurs with women following the birth of their baby. We see women at any point in time following their child's birth, starting from minutes after birth if it is a home birth and we're invited to be there, or if we're in a hospital and they come right up off the delivery floor, to years later at a time when they may be seeking assistance in weaning their child. We deal with the full range of issues that affect mothers and babies, from the simple things like mildly sore nipples due to improper positioning to children that are neurologically impaired, mothers who might be ill—the range is just enormous. Every single possible complication that can be imagined."

LCs who have worked in the field for a long time, and in a variety of circumstances, also talk about the multiplicity of roles they take on. First, there is their clinical role, working as part of the overall team with the other medical personnel involved, as the expert on the physiological aspects of breastfeeding. "The two most common manifestations that breastfeeding is not going well," says Beverly Solow, "are painful nursing and the baby not getting enough to eat and not gaining well. Nursing should be enjoyable. If it's painful, then there's a problem that needs correcting. Sometimes the cause is improper positioning or latch-on technique. Usually this can be corrected simply and quickly. Other times, a mother may be doing everything perfectly, but the problem is the way the baby is sucking. We have lots of techniques for helping both baby and mother to learn the skills they need. Our goal is to help a mother achieve her own personal breastfeeding goals."

Werner and Solow are also called on to provide mothers with information, from the most basic—for example, what to do about an "overstimulated" baby tuning out and turning off—to the most current research in the field—for example, the latest findings on the treatment and storage of breast milk. In addition to this are the emotional and psychological aspects.

Linda Kutner often takes on the role of the protective doula with her moms. "The delivery is medical or intervention, but once the baby's out, there is no thought to the mother anymore. She can go home and be Supermom. She can get dressed. It's nothing to see a newborn baby in the grocery store. Where are our forty days of being taken care of? They make plans for traveling, to have friends in, and friends may come bearing a baby gift, but how many come bearing a casserole? And the mother is expected to look at the baby gift and serve coffee and be chatty. I tell my mothers they're not allowed to wear clothes. They have to wear a nightgown for the first seven to ten days. I want it to be obvious to people that they're not all the way up to snuff. I tell them to take chairs out of their bedroom so when somebody comes to the door they run and jump in their bed and somebody can stand at the foot of the bed, give them the baby gift, hopefully get bored, and leave. And if a mother or an aunt does come, so many of them focus on the baby and don't take care of the mother."

In addition, says Kutner, the act and art of breastfeeding may, as part and parcel of new motherhood itself, bring up deeper, older, potentially painful issues for some women. Some moms she has seen have come in with a breastfeeding problem, and have quickly recalled or revealed a history of sexual and other abuse. If painful memories are jogged, she says, "a good LC is ready to help, listen, and she's also ready to refer." Previous life issues, depression, and later, postpartum depression brought on by too-rapid weaning, may all be part of the overall picture the LC sees and should be ready to support, address, or make appropriate referrals on.

## CHOOSING A LACTATION CONSULTANT

If you are looking for a lactation consultant either prenatally or postpartum, it is likely that your hospital, obstetrician, pediatrician, or friends will have a local referral. If not, ILCA can provide one if there is one in your area.

As with much of postpartum planning, it can be helpful to make this contact before your baby arrives, particularly if you have specific questions or concerns that have not been answered by your primary caregiver or a local support group. "It's actually the very wise mother who gets to us prenatally for a consult," says Chele Marmet, IBCLC, pioneer in the field and cofounder with Ellen Shell of the Lactation Institute in Encino, California. "Here she is shown one-on-one how to latch on, how to position, rather than from a movie or in a class."

Often, though, the new mom's first encounter with an LC may come during a crisis, at a time of high emotion and vulnerability. If your primary caregiver or hospital has not made a recommendation and you are looking on your own, there may be little time for looking at résumés or asking many questions. Certainly, as when choosing a doula, midwife, birth attendant, or doctor, your comfort level with the person is crucial. And unless the individual is known by you or highly recommended in the role of lactation consultant, experience and certification can serve as key criteria, since it is possible for someone to have taken a one-day course and thenceforward call himself or herself a lactation consultant.

"One of the biggest things you want to ask her is did she sit for the IBLCE exam and did she pass it," says Linda Kutner. "If you don't have time for a lot of questions, just start with 'Are you certified by the IBLCE exam?'"

Because it is a new profession, cautions Kutner, "what is happening in some doctors' offices and some hospitals is that they're saying, 'Hey, to be competitive, we need an LC and it's going to be you.' And that person really has her own experiences and her own biases with which to help a new mother. That's not fair, it's not correct, so the consumer needs to know that. Just because a doctor tells a nurse, 'You are our LC,' that does not mean that she is qualified. Nor does it mean that she is not qualified. I just don't think that's the standard by which we would want a new mother to select one."

Another key question, says Kutner, concerns backup in the LC's absence. "If I'm not here, there's always a number on the machine of someone a mom can call. . . . If a new mom is choosing an LC, she needs to say, 'Who's your backup?' If the LC doesn't have a backup, that's not good."

If you have the time and inclination to interview several LCs beforehand, you may ask to see letters of reference from satisfied clients, or résumés, as well. According to Chele Marmet and Ellen Shell, résumés should list the following:

- the courses they have taken
- the number of hours of lactation training
- the number of hours of supervised clinical practice in lactation
- relevant experience in lactation—personal, volunteer, and professional
- certification from lactation consultant training institutions
- academic and professional training outside of lactation
- membership in professional organizations for lactation consultants, such as ILCA[2]

In addition, LCs who are certified by the IBLCE have to be recertified every five years. If one's last certificate was seven years ago, she's no longer certified by the IBLCE. Since new findings are coming to light regularly, it is also important that the helper you choose be current on research and information.

Laura Best also suggests that if someone's been an LC for a good number of years, the new mom might want to ask more specifically, "How many hours a week?" "Some people are very part-time, others are very rigorously full-time. . . . Within the profession there is a wide range of skills that people have that are in practice, so if moms are not getting the answers they need, if things are not improving quickly, they should perhaps get a second opinion. [This could also be true] if they hook up with somebody that they're not really comfortable with. Sometimes if women don't have a success the first place they try, it can be really difficult to seek another alternative, because they feel as if they've tried and it hasn't worked, and it's not going to work. It's hard to get out of that frame of mind when you're in a crisis, and crisis is a normal response to a breastfeeding problem or a difficult postpartum period—[it triggers] the survival mechanism for your baby, that protectiveness."

In their training of staff, Laura Best says one of the strongest messages they give trainees is "trust the woman's perception of things. If she's saying that there's a problem, you can be sure there's a problem. You may not have the expertise to find it right away, but you can be sure there's something going on there. I find that when things are going well there is sort of a physiological mechanism that reassures mothers.

---

## WHAT TO EXPECT DURING A
## BREASTFEEDING CONSULTATION

......................................................

During a breastfeeding consultation, the LC should take a history relevant to the individual mom's and infant's breastfeeding situation. Based on this assessment, the LC should teach the mom and family appropriate techniques to establish successful lactation. If necessary, the LC may recommend equipment and should provide hands-on instruction so the mom can demonstrate back to her during the consultation that she is able to use it correctly, comfortably, safely, and advantageously. The consultation should also give the mom and family members a chance to ask their questions and to feel supported by the lactation consultant.

---

The mothers that need the most reassurance are mothers that need other kinds of help also. Reassurance may not be enough. There's a need for education, resolution of problems, real solutions to problems."

### WHAT DOES THE LACTATION CONSULTANT COST?

If you are seeing a private LC, "some LCs charge by the hour, some LCs charge by the visit," says Linda Kutner. Some also have a sliding scale. It's also a good idea to ask whether and how much the LC will charge for telephone consultations.

One guideline on determining if an LC's fees are appropriate, says Kutner, would be "to compare the fees to a local pediatrician's fee for a comprehensive sick visit, even though that visit is only about twelve minutes, while a consultation may last an hour or more." A follow-up visit is usually less. Fees will usually be higher if the LC comes to your home: She may spend more time, and will have travel time to account for. Kutner also points out that usually all equipment, supplies, and pump rentals are above and beyond the hourly fee.

While not all LC services are reimbursable, if a prescription from the baby's or mom's primary care provider—either pediatrician or obstetrician—accompanies the request for insurance reimbursement, LCs suggest that your chances of reimbursement may be better.

# Other Mother-Centered Messages and Models

From telephone "buddy" systems to programs that involve husbands and grandparents in support networks, efforts have been made to provide the kind of support breastfeeding mothers need. Three approaches to support are highlighted in the following.

## THE DOULA PROJECT

In 1983, North Central Bronx Hospital (NCBH), run by the New York Health and Hospitals Corporation, received funds from a state grant to initiate the Doula Project, whose primary objective, says the project's doula, Luz García, was "to provide information and support for women from the lower socioeconomic levels," where breastfeeding rates tend to fall off sharply after hospital discharge. García, who grew up in Colombia, where her mother was a midwife, was known for her role in helping breastfeeding Latina mothers in this culturally diverse section of the Bronx, and was hired by NCBH to serve as the doula, a role she still held as of October 1993.

Over the course of a year she sees each of the four thousand mothers delivering at the hospital, whether they breastfeed or not. (In 1984, New York State amended New York Hospital Code regulations so that hospitals are now required to provide instruction and assistance to each maternity patient who chooses to breastfeed or who is undecided about her infant's feeding method.) "We have about 60 to 65 percent Latina women—that's twenty-one different cultures within that term. We have African-Americans and Jamaicans and people from the islands, which is another great portion of our patients. We have Cambodians, Vietnamese, Palestinians, Russian mothers, Albanians—we have a very mixed culture. You'd be amazed how sign language works for me and the mothers, and they understand what I'm telling them."

García sees her role as a "mother-to-mother, lay community person. It's really following the tradition of being supportive to the mother postpartum. That's the philosophy, and I still believe that's why it works. I am there to give confidence to the mother. Ideally, I should be with each one six weeks, but I'm spread pretty thin many times." García sees the women both prenatally and postpartum. Before they deliver, she provides education and information so they can make an informed decision about breastfeeding. Many, she says, feel they have tried it in the past and failed. "That's usually because they didn't have the supports," she says. Some will be encouraged to try, but "many of the women have to return to work and school. They give it a chance, and then many of them don't want to give it up and separate. But many wean earlier because they cannot pump where they work. They work in factories where they hardly get a coffee break let alone a pumping break, and they have no facilities, so they make a marriage between the formula and the breast milk, but at least some breast milk is better than none." As for job leaves, "many of them have none. Many of them have quit the job to have the baby, for example, if they're working for the sweatshop on the corner. It depends on where they're working. A lot of the women, once they come here [to the United States], they enter the workforce—and I mean seriously enter the workforce—and breastfeeding gets killed along the way. . . . Maternity leave has not come to be something important in this nation, nor the care of babies at the place of work. So that makes it very difficult for a woman to breastfeed here. But that's all across the board, from the executives to the women who clean the floors in companies."

Following the birth, García will see the mothers again in the hospital. "Postpartum, my job is to tell them exactly what the process is and encourage them and keep them at it for the first two weeks of life. With the beeper, I get calls anytime and I call them. When I hear that it's necessary, I make a home visit." One mother of twins called her to report that one baby had not been eating since the night before and seemed lethargic. "I don't sit on stuff like that. I go. Because the reality is that if the baby has an appointment in two weeks, then the baby is in crisis.

"If I hear over the phone that the mom says, 'Oh, my nipples are bleeding, and I can't take this anymore,' my job is to go and see. And a lot of times, it's not really a breastfeeding problem. It's a family problem. Mommy is exhausted, she's doing so much for others, nobody's backing her up to support the effort, so it becomes a teaching session for whoever is over there as to why it's important that she gets some rest and some care and some food because she is providing life for this baby. It's kind of opening their eyes, because they never see it as that. They feel like well, that's what she wants to do, but they don't really understand that the breastfeeding mom really needs a mothering mother right next to her in order to help her succeed at what she's doing."

García also does proactive outreach with a follow-up phone call. "I don't wait for them to call me, because the majority of them will not call me if they have a problem. Because they feel that they are failing, and that I did all I could, and if they're failing it's their fault. So what I do is call them, and tell them, 'Uh-uh, you're going through this and through this,' and they say, 'Oh, I thought you were going to be upset, because after you said this, and it didn't work, I thought it was me.' And it has nothing to do with them. Part of it is their confidence in their own bodies; part of it is that their ability to mother is undercut by society itself, and certainly their own homes—fathers feel threatened by this because mommy and baby are together all the time, and he's kind of on the side; grandmothers who did not breastfeed feel very threatened because it's one area they have no say over, and they don't know how to help, even the ones who want to help, they don't know what to do. So it remains a teaching, supporting program for women that have delivered and want to breastfeed."

In teaching sessions with various hospital staff—who may include midwives, physicians, obstetricians, or pediatricians—García points out to them that a very important aspect of their interaction with the new mom is "the reinforcement for the mom. Making her feel wonderful about what she's doing is half of the job."

## FRIENDS OF LACTATION: A PARTICIPATORY MODEL

In New York City, at the Beth Israel Lactation Program (BILP)—the largest lactation clinic on the East Coast—previous patients initiated a new community advisory committee, called Friends of Lactation, for the breastfeeding program. "Our previous patients and people in the community are going to be actively involved in determining what kinds of services are needed in the community," says Laura Best, IBCLC and co-coordinator of the program, "and how we can best meet the community needs."

At present the program can conduct appointments in Spanish and Hebrew and can offer printed BILP materials in Chinese, Russian, Spanish, Hebrew, and English. They also have resource materials that were produced elsewhere available in French and in a number of Asian languages.

An important function of this board, says Best, will be "to serve as community advisers. We may have our idea of what people need, but it may not be anything of what people really want, so we wanted to make sure we were consulting with the community about what they wanted to do."

## GETTING TO KNOW YOUR NEIGHBORS

Finally, if you live in an area where there are no LCs or support groups, Anna Werner suggests a slightly more unusual route: looking among the community for supportive women who might help. "There are a lot of people out there who can be found if you just start asking around to find someone who's breastfed a lot of kids. If you live in an area where there are no LCs and no volunteer support groups, if you just start letting it be known, the way you would if you were looking for a job, networking—"I need to find somebody who's breastfed five kids." You just tell everybody and you'll be surprised. Somebody's aunt or the dry cleaner's sister—you have to be willing to have help come from an unexpected direction. But there are a lot of people out there who are very experienced and are thrilled to help someone because they have such fond memories themselves."

Depending on where you deliver, and what kind of help you have at home, hospital-based supports such as the Doula Project or Salvation Army Grace Hospital Breastfeeding Support Service in Calgary, private clinics and services, telephone follow-up, telephone support programs, warmlines or hotlines, printed materials in a range of languages, home-care providers, and volunteer peer group support may all be available as part of a vital and ongoing breastfeeding support network.

# Breastfeeding and Moms Working Outside the Home

*There's a common misconception that breastfeeding and working outside the home are not compatible. . .* —Laura Best, IBCLC

*Breastfeeding requires a new definition of women's work—one that more realistically integrates women's productive and reproductive activities.*
—Penny Van Esterik, *Beyond the Breast-Bottle Controversy*

While going back to work outside the home and continuing to breastfeed once seemed quite impossible for many new mothers who might have weaned at that point—or never have started nursing at all—there is a slowly growing awareness among new mothers, along with new responsiveness from some workplaces, that make this option more feasible today. Attitudes at some worksites are changing; more individual and group supports now address the issue of working and breastfeeding; new research has yielded findings that favor the new mother; and individual nursing mothers are asking for what they need in order to combine breastfeeding and a return to the workplace more successfully.

The World Alliance for Breastfeeding Action has the Task Force on Women and Work, headed by Ontario-based anthropologist Penny Van Esterik, who sets out a definition of the dilemma in WABA's mother-friendly workplace initiative action folder, Women, Work and Breastfeeding. (In 1992 WABA launched a mother-friendly workplace campaign identifying workplaces that support breastfeeding women.) The piece calls for a redefinition of the way in which work is traditionally viewed—that is, from the male perspective. "Can we create a woman-centered approach to work," she asks, "that values women's productive and reproductive work, and reduces the double burdens women carry?" Such an approach would acknowledge pregnancy, breastfeeding, and childcare as socially meaningful and productive work, and recognize the social support necessary for optimal breastfeeding. Men share the responsibility for providing this support in the home and the workplace."[3] The folder also provides suggestions on how to create a mother-friendly workplace:

## TIME*

1. Provide at least four months paid maternity leave (with an ideal of six months) that begins after the baby is born. Offer other options such as longer maternity leave with partial pay.

2. Offer flexible work hours to breastfeeding women such as part-time schedules, longer lunch breaks, and job sharing.

3. Provide breastfeeding breaks of at least an hour a day.

*Source: *Women, Work, and Breastfeeding: The Mother-Friendly Workplace Initiative Action Folder,* World Alliance for Breastfeeding Action, 1993.

## SPACE/PROXIMITY

1. Support infant and childcare at or near the workplace, and provide transportation for mothers to join their babies. For rural worksites and seasonal work, use mobile childcare units.

2. Provide comfortable, private facilities for expressing and storing breast milk.

3. Keep the work environment clean and safe from hazardous wastes and chemicals.

## SUPPORT

1. Inform women workers and unions about maternity benefits and provide information to support women's health.

2. Ensure that mothers have full job security.

3. Encourage coworkers and management to have a positive attitude toward breastfeeding in public.

4. Encourage a network of supportive women in unions or workers' groups who can help women to combine breastfeeding and work.

In reality, few workplaces meet these standards. Options vary. Solutions are individual.

"We have working mothers a great deal," says Anna Werner. "We help women develop back-to-work plans so that they are able to maintain a nursing relationship with their child for as long as they want. Our goal is to make it a nonstress situation. This is supposed to be an enjoyable life experience for mother and baby. There are lots of compromises that can be made, plans are really individually done. No two are even remotely alike."

Linda Kutner has a large population of working mothers.

"What I tell my mothers to do when the baby is born is to find childcare and then they're not to think about going back to work at all until ten days before and then they call me." At that point she can offer them several options. "My goal in doing that is to have them really love and bond with that baby and not to worry about going back to work. It has happened on occasion that they call me at the end of ten days and say, 'I'm going to take another two or three weeks,' or 'I'm not going back to work,' or 'I'm going to work another two weeks and quit.' Most of the moms have six weeks' leave. At ten days before, they call me up, and I will do whatever they want. They have enjoyed that baby, they have not worried about going back to work, because I told them, 'I will be responsible for doing what you want, don't worry about it.' And if I've established that trust with them either through a consult or a class, they trust me and it works out very well."

But the responsibility and responsiveness of the workplace in this nurturing mothering/baby/worksite triad also have to be significant. The woman and her LC may have designed an acceptable plan, but without the cooperation and support of the workplace, it will not work.

Unfortunately, instead of helping new mothers, some worksites, says Anna Werner, have made things even more difficult. With austerity and cutbacks, many moms she sees are reporting that while they can still take leave, they now must do so without pay, compared to several years ago, when they could get possibly up to twelve weeks paid. "We have people going back after two weeks. They really can't, but they convince themselves that they can. We see women going into deep depressions, complications, babies spontaneously weaning at three weeks, and mothers being devastated. It's terrible. It's terrible that women are placed in this position." Given what is now known about the connection between too-rapid weaning as a potential precipitating factor in postpartum depression, this is a particular concern for moms. "Anything less than a month or two [weaning time] I think is too rapid," says Linda Kutner, "but we need research on that. But if you cold-turkey wean over a week, that's not good. Do I see more PPD in mothers forced to wean too rapidly over a week? Oh, yes."

Mothers who choose to continue to breastfeed after a return to work often have to do so under highly unacceptable circumstances. "[One of the things] that I found very difficult where I worked," says Spalding, "was trying to be a nursing mom and work. I worked in the University Hospital, and there were just not very many private offices. I certainly did not have a private office, and where do you go to express milk? I found myself in the supply closet, quite degraded, feeling like I was up to some clandestine activity. That stands out the most in my mind about trying to work with a new baby and trying to continue nursing. I think that's one of the things that sabotaged my nursing so early. I'd beg, borrow, and steal offices and it turned out that the supply closet was the easiest thing—of course, until someone needed a pen, a Post-It note, or something. They'd just have to wait their turn!"

Taking lactating women "out of the closet—literally—is a step forward," says Laura Best. But she also believes that the issue of childcare is equally important. I think women should have options. One should be pumping at work. One should be having the child at the workplace, or near enough to the workplace, with adequate transportation provided by the workplace to have some mother/baby or father/baby contact during the day. And also nursing breaks, which are important—we have coffee breaks! We need nursing breaks."

# Sitting in the Circle: Three Mothers and a Father Share Their Stories

Cultural attitudes, perceptions about what kinds of programs or solutions are possible, and assessments of what is needed to ensure successful nursing all play a role in shaping a woman's and a family's approach to breastfeeding. The mothers and father who tell their stories here are testimony to the enormous commitment of women and men, as well as to the need for dialogue and a great variety of supports for breastfeeding women and their families.

## DIANA: JOINING A CIRCLE OF WOMEN

Diana has three children, all of whom were born in the Bronx, where she now lives. Although she did not breastfeed her oldest child, and struggled on her own nursing her secondborn, the Doula Project helped her to nurse her third child successfully.

Diana was born and raised in Puerto Rico "during a time where bottle-feeding was very much promoted, in the 1950s. I'm sure breastfeeding was antiquated at that point. First time, I had the attitude that the breast was sexual. . . . This was a first child, so naturally I had all the myths that come with breastfeeding, keeping your breast intact, and looking good after the birth and that you're not producing enough milk . . . so that was a deterrent for nursing the first child."

When her second child was born sixteen months later, she "had a little more determination about doing it." She went to visit a friend, and there were three moms there nursing. Diana had a bottle filled with breast milk, but didn't know how to handle actually putting the baby to the breast. She was pumping manually, and giving her baby breast milk in a bottle.

"For me I considered it an art. Some women have such a facility and they put the child up and the child grabs the breast and that's it. Somehow I just didn't have the knack, and I know that I did a lot of things wrong. The baby only got the nipple, so it was excruciating pain; the position wasn't in my favor; [there was] his crying and impatience. I wasn't able to succeed. Then one day I went over to my friend's house, and I felt a certain envy looking at them breastfeeding their children.... Luz was there, and she made me feel terrible, though not intentionally...."

With her third child, Diana still "felt ignorant." I would go through a trauma every time I had to put the baby on the breast," but by this time she had also established a relationship with Luz García and the Doula Project. "I would call Luz. Things that mothers normally had questions about, and there were no answers around—she knew it! She knew exactly what to do, how to make the nipple hard enough so the baby would grab the nipple, what to do if the breast got swollen. She would give me all these logical remedies to soothe my pain in terms of breastfeeding. That myth of five minutes on each side—Luz always said put baby on one side, let him drain you, and then give him the other side...."

For Diana, Luz and her other friends played a crucial role. "I had no one. Absolutely no one. My mother lives in Puerto Rico. My sister lives in Florida. I didn't have anyone except some friends. It was difficult. I constantly called my other friend, and there were a lot of moments when I would say, 'I just feel like giving this up, I can't take it,' and she would reinforce how wonderful it was. It was very frustrating.

"We do need a lot of education on it, we don't get much, and we get such erroneous information that instead of encouraging us, it discourages us—everybody's concept of how long you should do it, how you should do it. I find that the program is helping a lot of women."

## NIKKI: CHANGES IN THE WORKPLACE

With the help of lactation consultant Linda Kutner, Nikki Chadwick of Concord, North Carolina, was able to initiate and implement significant changes at her workplace, the First Union Bank in Charlotte.

When Nikki's son was born in December 1992, the staff LC at her hospital gave her Linda Kutner's name should she need any follow-up once she got home. At nine weeks postpartum, Nikki contacted Linda for help in working out a return-to-work plan.

"When I first went back to work, I was using a manual pump. I stood in a bathroom stall pumping for the first six weeks that I was back at work. Two weeks after I went back, I said, 'I can't handle this hand pump and keep up my milk supply,' plus [I was] frustrated with trying to get back into the swing of work. That's when I went to Linda and got one of the mini-Medela pumps we found for my financial situation. With me not having a place to go and pump, that was the best thing. I borrowed an extension cord from a friend of mine and dragged this extension cord across the bathroom floor and used the mini-Medela, which is either battery-operated or electric. Then a newspaper article was in our Charlotte paper about local businesses helping nursing moms with rooms that they could use. I said, 'First Union needs one of these.'

"I was a real big advocate of nursing. I was determined that my son was not going to use formula and that I was going to nurse him until he was at least a year old. I was going to do anything I could to continue doing that. So I saw the article, and I started talking to my management. One of the managers recommended that I get in touch with the Human Resources Department." They directed her to Joan Hope, the work/family coordinator for First Union. "She is the one who was really encouraged by this and helped me get a room started. She'd been in her position three weeks, and I was her first project. I got with her and I said, 'You know, I'm a nursing mom, and I really could use a place to go and pump rather than standing in a bathroom stall.' She nursed both of her children, and she said, 'That's a great thing, we really need to do that.' She didn't like the idea of women having to stand in the bathroom and provide meals for their children. She found us a small conference room on the floor where she was at the time, not in the way of traffic. We have a log book, we schedule out time. At first it was me and another girlfriend of mine. She came back to work the week it got started. So she had her place where she could go. A lot of moms don't like to share the room and pump with someone else there. . . . The scheduling book got full, so we broke it into two little cubicles inside that room, so we can still talk, and see each other if we want to, but we have a nice little room that we can schedule out. . . . I found it was nice to have someone to talk to who's going through a similar situation. Linda's kind of been in the background guiding us through all of this, telling us the best way to handle things."

One decision that had to be made in setting the room up had to do with refrigeration. "Linda said she would prefer to see the moms handle their own milk, and not trust a refrigerator. Who's going to clean the refrigerator? Handle maintenance on it to see that it stays the proper temperature? What happens if someone comes in and takes the milk? Based on Linda's advice, I bought a cooler, and I keep two ice packs in there. When I get home in the evening, it's cool but it's not cold, but Linda tells me it can stay at room temperature up to eight hours because of the antibodies that are in the milk. I tell everybody that I bring my lunch in the morning and I take my son's home in the afternoon. I just love being able to nurse him."

Nikki has arranged two times a day when she leaves her desk to go and pump. "I would say it takes about twenty minutes—and don't rush! Give yourself a half an hour. It gives you time to get in and relax so that the letdown occurs for you, you pump, and then you get yourself put back together before you get back to work. Don't stand in the bathroom stall! Once I read that article, it grossed me out. There was one piece in there that really hit me, and it said pumping in a bathroom stall is like preparing your child's lunch in the toilet. It really hit me that that's what I was doing, and there had to be a better way of doing things. . . . Linda has been a fabulous support person. Anytime I needed anything, I could call her. We may spend just a few minutes on the telephone talking and I feel a lot better, and I may call her a few weeks later for something else.

"I find it especially wonderful that at the end of a very hectic day, I can sit down in a chair and get fifteen minutes of just cuddle time. And that kind of helps me get adjusted back into that family life, so that I can fix dinner and clean the house, and wash the dishes and give him a bath and then go to bed so that I can be up at two in the morning because he's teething. . . ."

## JESSICA AND WILL: UNFORESEEN PROBLEMS / A TEAMWORK EFFORT

Jessica's son was born in a private hospital in New York City. An unusual number of complications plus inconsistent information at the hospital during her five-day stay sabotaged her early efforts at breastfeeding.

"At the point that we got home, I think I was already on a disaster course, because at that point I hadn't successfully got the baby to latch on properly, in part because my nipples were inverted, and he had a hard time finding out and figuring out where to get his mother's milk. And he was already probably a little spoiled from nursing from a bottle that was designed for a premature baby who was probably half his size. In addition to that, I had been using the nipple shield that had been offered to me at the hospital, which is like a little bottle nipple that you put on top of your own nipple, and the baby was able to get milk through it. But what I didn't realize was that it didn't stimulate the milk production because it made an unnatural juncture between me and the baby, so the breast wasn't getting the correct stimulation. I had this notion I could just build up a milk supply gradually, and as the baby got more used to it and less used to the bottle, the milk supply would gradually build up, but it doesn't really happen that way."

When her baby was three weeks old, Jessica discovered the Beth Israel Lactation Program and made an appointment. Over time, she was given the instruction and support she needed to finally achieve a successful breastfeeding relationship.

"I didn't really have a support network other than that we knew we wanted to breastfeed the baby. My mother was very supportive, although she did not breastfeed myself or my brothers. But that support did not constitute knowledge. Support is one thing and knowledge is something else.

"We used a supplementer. It was hard. It was very hard, but it was worth it. It was disappointing to have to start over again. It's still disappointing. But it worked, and we're still using it.

"One thing that I think we learned from this experience was that the breastfeeding was important enough to us that we wanted to do it even if it wasn't going to be 100 percent. We just had no way of anticipating the number of problems that could evolve. Maybe if only one problem had emerged we would have overcome that without additional help. But with the series of problems that occurred, through no one's fault, and certainly couldn't have been anticipated, it made it harder and harder to breastfeed successfully. The clinic's really turned that around for us."

Like many other parents-to-be, Jessica and Will had attended a breastfeeding seminar before their baby was born. "In fact, at the little seminar we went to, we heard a number of people say this—how could there be a problem, this is what women have always done?—and it certainly seems like that's commonsensical. But there are problems that can occur. Also, I found that even in the reading I had done, the assumptions that were made in describing what to do and how to do it were based on things happening in the right way—that the baby would be born naturally, even if you had a cesarean section you'd be able to nurse the baby in the recovery room, etc. And that doesn't always happen.

"We came [to the clinic] once a week for a period of six weeks and at that point things had settled in and we'd been on our own. It wasn't until we got there that I was able to get the baby to successfully latch on and to work with an inverted nipple. So we learned that skill or ability. And we learned how to start over again to build up the milk supply, which certainly was important because otherwise I wouldn't be able to nurse him now.

"I think women have to know how important it is to have the baby nurse immediately as frequently as possible after the baby is born." They can then make a personal decision about the kind of routine they want, but at least they can do so with correct information. "If there are problems, I think women have to really assert themselves to get knowledgeable answers to their problems. I don't think it's common that women run into quite as many problems in as close sequence as I did, but certainly one or two or three things might crop up that can be unexpected, and they have to be dealt with as quickly as possible in order to assure the nursing works.

"I had a lot of catching up to do. In order to do that we had to revert back to a newborn feeding schedule and feed the baby every three hours at a minimum, even though our baby was sometimes going at night as long as four hours. What that meant was we had to wake him up. . . . This was exhausting, to say the least, and I couldn't have done it without my husband's help. Will did everything around the house, from grocery shopping and food preparation and meals and cleaning—what little cleaning we did—and laundry, diapering the baby, everything that was not directly related to nursing, Will did, for the baby and for me and for the three of us as a family. I could not have done that. It was too exhausting."

Will recalled this transition time in their lives. "Even after going to the prenatal seminar, I had no idea really what was involved and how important it was. Not only in terms of the health benefits for our baby, but also how important it was for Jessica. It was only after we struggled with the breastfeeding and I realized how committed Jessica was, only then did I really begin to get an idea that this wasn't just something where you turn on the switch after the baby is born and it happens. Before we came to the clinic, my attitude was we'd already gotten so much advice from so many different experts, what will one more expert be able to tell us? I really came with a very skeptical attitude, particularly when I'd heard indirectly through my wife that basically we'd been doing it all wrong. I was thinking, we've gotten all this advice and now we're going to be told everything is all wrong. Well, when we got to the clinic, it was handled very well. It was explained to us in very down-to-earth terms exactly what we had been going through, why it wasn't working, what the principles were to make it work, and my skepticism melted away immediately.

"That was really a turning point for me in beginning to understand what breastfeeding is all about, how important it is for the baby, for the mother, and for my role as the father and husband. The next few weeks as we had to go on to fight our way through, it was very difficult but it was worth it. What made us get through it was that we knew finally we were on the right road. It made all the difference for us. We wish we had gotten there long before our baby was born and it would have been easier for us, but even so, having gotten there as late as we did, the clinic made it possible for us to nurse. And I say 'us,' and it really has been a team effort. Nursing mothers just cannot have enough help and support with everything else. I can't emphasize that enough. A nursing mother, particularly if she's had a difficult delivery or a cesarean section that she's recovering from or having any difficulties in getting the nursing established, can't be bothered with any of the other things.

There has to be a significant other person who can handle those other things. She needs to devote her attention to recovering and nursing 100 percent."

# Notes

1. Jack Newman, M.D., *Still More Breastfeeding Myths*, rev. ed. (Toronto: Hospital for Sick Children, 1993).

2. Chele Marmet and Ellen Shell, *Breastfeeding Is Important* (Encino, California: Lactation Institute Publications, 1988), p. 18.

3. World Alliance for Breastfeeding Action, *Women, Work, and Breastfeeding: The Mother-Friendly Workplace Initiative Action Folder* (1993).

# Resources

The resources listed here are described in further detail in the following section:

## Peer Support Groups

INTERNATIONAL
La Leche League International

UNITED STATES
Nursing Mothers' Counsel
Nursing Mothers' Council of the Boston Association for Childbirth Education

CANADA
Centre Local de Services Communautaires de la Haute-Yamaska
Entraide Naturo Lait
Ligue La Leche
New Mothers' Resource Group
Nourri-Source

## Lactation Clinics and Centers

UNITED STATES
Lactation Program, Beth Israel Medical Center
HealthONE Alliance Lactation Program
National Capital Lactation Center
Wellstart International Lactation Clinic

CANADA
Calgary Breastfeeding Center
Toronto Western Hospital
Shinook Health Region Breastfeeding Support Service
Vancouver Breastfeeding Center

## Lactation Consultants

UNITED STATES

*National*
International Lactation Consultants'
   Association
Breastfeeding National Network
*Regional*
Lactation Services of New York
CANADA
*National*
Canadian Lactation Consultant
   Association

**Educational and Other
Organizations**

UNITED STATES
The Lactation Institute and
   Breastfeeding Clinic
Lactation Studies Center
Wellstart International Lactation
   Management Education Program
World Alliance for Breastfeeding
   Action

CANADA
Infant Feeding Action Coalition
   (INFACT) Canada

**Videotapes**

*The Art of Successful Breastfeeding: A
   Mother's Guide*
*Breastfeeding: A Special Relationship*
*Breastfeeding: Better Beginnings*

**Books**

*Bestfeeding: Getting Breastfeeding
   Right For You*
*Breastfeeding Matters: What We Need
   to Know About Infant Feeding*
*The Nursing Mother's Companion*
*The Tender Gift: Breastfeeding*
*The Womanly Art of Breastfeeding*

**Catalog for Nursing Mothers**

*Motherwear*

# Peer Support Groups

INTERNATIONAL
**La Leche League International (LLL)**
P.O. Box 4079
1400 N. Meacham Road
Schaumburg, IL 60173
Tel.: (847) 519-7730;
(800) LA-LECHE
www.lalecheleague.org

The oldest peer support group in the world, LLL is now in 66 countries. It offers pregnant women and new mothers local groups, telephone support, peer group support in inner-city hospitals and clinics, an 800 number for referrals to a local leader, and a catalog of books, pamphlets, and

products. It also runs peer counselor trainings, lactation consultants' and physicians' workshops, and a biannual international breastfeeding conference. In addition, booklets, breast pumps, and information for mothers working outside the home are available in 27 languages. LLL members receive the magazine *New Beginnings*, published six times a year, as well as discounts on catalog shopping.

UNITED STATES
**Nursing Mothers' Counsel (NMC)**
P.O. Box 50063
Palo Alto, CA 94303
Referral line (recorded message):
   (415) 386-2229
   Founded in 1955 by doctors' wives

who gave counsel to new breastfeeding moms, NMC is based in the Bay Area, with additional chapters in Denver, Colorado, and Fort Wayne, Indiana. NMC's goal is to "give information, education, and support to help a mother have a successful and happy breastfeeding experience which is in line with her lifestyle." NMC's trained counselors offer one-to-one phone counseling (which can be one-time or ongoing), and will answer all letters with a personal response. Literature is also available on breastfeeding twins, adoption and nursing, and other subjects. NMC has seven chapters and nearly 400 volunteer members. Trained counselors speak to moms prenatally through hospital classes.

**Nursing Mothers' Council of the Boston Association for Childbirth Education (NMC)**
P.O. Box 29
Newtonville, MA 02460
Tel.: (617) 244-5102

NMC was started in 1962 to provide breastfeeding support for women who took childbirth classes. Today NMC offers support and practical information to all women who wish to breastfeed their babies and it offers professional education for health-care providers who want to learn more about breastfeeding. NMC refers new moms to local volunteer counselors.

CANADA
**Centre Local de Services Communautaires de la Haute-Yamaska**
294 Deragon Street
Granby, Quebec J2G 5J5 Canada
Tel: (450) 375-1442

The breastfeeding clinic is offered through the community-care center, a public health establishment. The service offers a telephone information line, breastfeeding workshops once a month, and medical consultations are available by appointment for breastfeeding problems; the staff works closely with Ligue La Leche, and also attempts to monitor commercial practices of companies that manufacture formula and baby food. All services are offered in French and some of the staff speak other languages as well.

**Entraide Naturo Lait (ENL)**
855 Holland Street, #201
Quebec City, Quebec G0S 3S5
Canada
Tel.: (418) 663-2711

Established in 1982, ENL is one of several French-language support groups in the Quebec area. It offers on-site consultations, referrals, telephone support, prenatal and postpartum breastfeeding classes, equipment rental, and the staff will do home visits under certain circumstances. All of the counselors are mothers who have breastfed their babies for at least six months. Their booklet L'Allaitemant Aujourd'hui is distributed at no charge to mothers taking their courses, and is also available for purchase. The director is Celine Loubier.

**Ligue La Leche**
CP874 St. Laurent
Quebec H4L 4W3 Canada
Tel.: (514) 525-3243

This is the French-language counterpart of La Leche League International.

**New Mothers' Resource Group**
c/o Nancy Harmon
Box 1559
Liverpool, Nova Scotia B0T 1K0
 Canada
Tel.: (902) 354-2238

This local support group made up of successfully breastfeeding moms formed in 1991 at the request of the perinatal committee of the local hospital because Queens County had a low rate of successful breastfeeding mothers. It offers breastfeeding classes, a hotline with the names of available volunteers, special events such as a Baby Fair. Members of the support group try to see every new mother delivering at the hospital several days after the birth (the birth rate is about 100 babies a year).

**Nourri-Source**
C.P. 441 Succ. Montreal-Nord
Montreal Nord H1H 5L5 Canada

Established in 1982, Nourri-Source has French-language support groups in the Montreal area. It offers telephone support, prenatal breast-feeding classes, and group meetings. Its French-language publication, *Le Petit Nourri-Source,* is available for sale. Guylaine Cyr is the president.

# Lactation Clinics and Centers

UNITED STATES

**Lactation Program, Beth Israel Medical Center**
First Avenue and 16th Street
New York, NY 10003
Warmline: (212) 420-2939

Located in downtown Manhattan, this hospital-based program offers prenatal and postpartum breastfeeding classes, in-hospital care, and postpartum follow-up. The program has a Warmline for breastfeeding questions and telephone consultations. Karen Goodman, R.N.C., M.A., ACCE, is Coordinator of Parent/Family Eduction and the Lactation Program.

**HealthONE Alliance Lactation Program**
4500 East 9th Avenue South
Suite 320
Denver, CO 80220
Tel.: (303) 320-7081

Founded in 1985, the Lactation Program is a comprehensive one for breastfeeding services, including consultation with moms and families, parental and professional education, research, and supplies. The program's medical director is Marianne Neifert, M.D. (a.k.a. "Dr. Mom").

**National Capital Lactation Center**
Georgetown University Medical
 Center
3800 Reservoir Road, NW
Washington, DC 20007-2197
Tel.: (202) 784-MILK (6455)

The center was founded in 1986 to serve moms delivering in Georgetown University Hospital, as well as new moms in the general community. LCs see new mothers in the hospital and do telephone follow-up after discharge.

**Wellstart International Lactation Clinic**
4062 First Avenue
San Diego, CA 92103-2045
Tel: (619) 295-5192
Helpline: (619) 295-5193

Provides comprehensive clinical services to support breastfeeding and maternal health and nutrition. Coordinates services with families' primary health care providers and other health care professionals.

CANADA

**Calgary Breastfeeding Center**
Arbour Birth Center
1616 20A Street, N.W.
Calgary, Alberta T2N 2L5 Canada
Tel.: (403) 220-9101

This is a private community-based clinic that operates on a fee basis. The IBCLC-staffed clinic offers postpartum classes and private consultations, as well as ongoing clinical observation and courses for health professionals. Postpartum moms are referred to the community-based La Leche League for ongoing support. Maureen Fjeld, IBCLC and physiotherapist, is director of the clinic. The clinic also offers pump rental, and sells quality breastfeeding products for which it provides instruction.

**Toronto Western Hospital**
399 Bathur Street
Toronto M5T 2S8 Canada
Tel.: (416) 603-5600
E-mail: Newman@globalserve.net

Dr. Jack Newman is the contact person for this and three other programs in the Toronto area. The programs offer one-on-one appointments for new moms having difficulties with breastfeeding, although some women may be seen prenatally as well. Visits are covered by government health insurance; there is no charge for telephone advice.

**Shinook Health Region Breastfeeding Support Service**
Lethbridge Regional Hospital 3C104
960 19th Street
Lethbridge, Alberta T1J 1W5 Canada
Tel.: (403) 382-6283

This program offers inpatient and outpatient services, prenatal breastfeeding classes, a telephone warmline, and in-service for staff. It is an open referral service covered by Alberta Health Care. Jacki Glover is the IBCLC.

**Vancouver Breastfeeding Center**
690 West 11 Avenue
Vancouver, British Columbia V5Z 1M1 Canada
Tel.: (604) 875-4730
www.breastfeeding1.com

This is a referral medical center for families experiencing breastfeeding and lactation difficulties. It is staffed by family physicians and nurses who are all International Board Certified Lactation Consultants, and it is run under the auspices of the University of British Columbia. The center offers prenatal lactation assessments, anticipatory guidance, and early-intervention strategies, as well as a variety of training courses for health professionals. Medical Director Dr. Verity Livingstone, MBBS, FCFP, IBCLC, and associate professor in the department of family practice at the University of British Columbia, is an international master trainer for the baby-friendly hospital initiative.

# Lactation Consultants

UNITED STATES
*National*
**International Lactation
Consultants' Association (ILCA)**
4101 Lake Boone Trail, Suite 201
Raleigh, NC 27607
Tel.: (919) 787-5181
E-mail: ilca@erols.com

Founded in 1985, ILCA is a global association for health professionals who specialize in breastfeeding, including lactation consultants, public health nurses, breastfeeding specialists, midwives, physicians, childbirth educators, nurses, and community-based breastfeeding counselors, among others. ILCA has sixteen hundred members in the United States and can make referrals to women seeking a lactation consultant or other support person locally. Members receive the Journal of Human Lactation. Their "Recommendations and Competencies for Lactation Consultant Practice" offers guidelines for practice that recognize diversity in setting "personnel, style and delivery of lactation support in different cultural contexts" and establishes a foundation for specialty practice as a lactation consultant, as opposed to a standard of care or exclusive rules for practice.

**Breastfeeding National Network**
Medela
4610 Prime Parkway
McHenry, IL 60050
Tel.: (800) TELL YOU

This telephone service, provided by Medela, gives local pump rental information as well as referrals to local LCs. When you punch in your zip code, recorded messages give the telephone numbers, names, and a brief description of the services in your area.

*Regional*
**Lactation Services of New York**
Home Visits
Tel.: (212) 567-1112
(Beverly Solow, IBCLC)

Board certified since 1991, this private practice offers lactation consultations in the home, office, at the hospital or by phone. Beverly Solow offers breastfeeding classes and a bimonthly support group in Manhattan for nursing and expectant mothers. LSNY serves the Greater New York area. Fees are sometimes reimbursed through health insurance plans.

CANADA
*National*
**Canadian Lactation Consultant
Association**
4793 Strathcona Road
N. Vancouver, BC V7G 1G9
Tel.: (604) 929-6751
E-mail: meb@unixg.ubc.ca

This is a network of IBCLCs throughout Canada (membership is over 420). They work to promote, protect, and support breastfeeding throughout Canada.

# Educational and Other Organizations

UNITED STATES
**The Lactation Institute and
Breastfeeding Clinic**
16430 Ventura Boulevard, Suite 303
Encino, CA 91436

Tel.: (818) 995-1913
Fax: (818) 995-0634
E-mail: shells@primenet.com

Founded in 1979 by Chele Marmet and Ellen Shell, this is the first private breastfeeding clinic in the United States. It is a nonprofit, nonsectarian educational organization to help mothers with unusual breastfeeding problems. It also serves as a resource and referral center for moms needing general information and breastfeeding assistance. Nursing aids are available for purchase or rental, including electric and manual breast pumps, supplementer feeding systems, and cotton nursing bras. A wide variety of books and pamphlets on breastfeeding and other parenting issues—from the fussy baby to sibling rivalry—are also for sale at the institute or by mail. In addition, the institute offers complete training for anyone interested in a career in the lactation profession.

**Lactation Studies Center**
University of Rochester
Dr. Ruth Lawrence
and Dr. Linda Friedman
Tel.: (716) 275-0088

The Center has clinical data on 2,000 chemicals that may affect breastfeeding mothers and their babies, and a bibliographical base of papers on the medical aspects of lactation. Since much of the information Dr. Lawrence provides can be quite technical, she prefers to discuss questions with professional health-care providers.

**Wellstart International Lactation Management Education Program**
4062 First Avenue
San Diego, CA 92103

P.O. Box 87549
San Diego, CA 92138
Tel.: (619) 295-5192
Helpline: (619) 295-5193

A private, nonprofit leadership development program for perinatal health-care providers in faculty and policy-making positions. More than 600 Associates are working in multidisciplinary teams to establish and sustain optimal infant feeding practices as well as maternal nutrition and health through comprehensive educational and clinical initiatives in over fifty countries.

**World Alliance for Breastfeeding Action (WABA)**
P.O. Box 1200
10850 Penang, Malaysia
Tel.: 60-4-658-4816
E-mail: secr@waba.po.my
www.waba.org.br

WABA is a global network of organizations and individuals dedicated to advocating for the protection, promotion, and support of breastfeeding. It has literature available, and also sponsors World Breastfeeding Week every August.

CANADA
**Infant Feeding Action Coalition (INFACT) Canada**
6 Trinity Square
Toronto, Ontario M5G 1B1
Canada
Tel.: (416) 595-9819
E-mail: infact@ftn.net

Started in 1979 and incorporated in 1981, this organization works to promote, support, and protect breastfeeding in Canada. It disseminates information on a wide range of breastfeeding issues, as well as on governmental or institutional policies and human rights issues and practices. A free list of publications is available. INFACT publishes a quarterly newsletter for mothers, healthcare workers, institutions, and others, covering in part the politics and economics of infant feeding issues, as well as information on the workplace and other topics which advance the cause of breastfeeding. INFACT can also do local referrals to agencies, lactation consultants, government departments. INFACT is the North American regional coordinator for IBFAN (International Breastfeeding Action Network). The director is Elisabeth Sterken.

## Videotapes

*The Art of Successful Breastfeeding: A Mother's Guide*
The Vancouver Breastfeeding Centre
Tel.: (604) 875-4678
Fax: (604) 875-5017
E-mail: millerb@direct.ca

An award-winning video designed for families who really want to know how to breastfeed successfully. It reviews the benefits of breastfeeding, how to make informed choices about preparation for breastfeeding, prenatal lactation assessment, and how to get off to a good start when the infant arrives. The video also discusses common breastfeeding difficulties and concerns of breastfeeding mothers, and how to overcome them, and covers such topics as the mother's nutrition, breastfeeding and contraception, nursing at work and in public, and weaning. (Also available in Spanish.)

*Breastfeeding: A Special Relationship*
Distributed by Injoy Productions
Tel.: (800) 326-2082 or fax: (303)
    449-8788 (for Visa and
    MasterCard orders only)

In seven logical segments, this encouraging and practical video teaches new mothers how to breastfeed successfully. Very clear shots of positioning, proper latch-on, and breast pumps help with the basics. Fathers are shown being supportive and helpful. Potential problems and issues around going to work and nursing in public are handled positively, and the whole breastfeeding relationship is presented as an attainable, pleasurable experience. (Also available in Spanish.)

*Breastfeeding: Better Beginnings*
Distributed by Injoy Productions
(see ordering information above)

This tape, with host Jeanne Driscoll, R.N., M.S., C.S., focuses on the initial breastfeeding relationship, including correct positioning, latching on, mother's diet, father's role, emotional adjustment, and sexuality. A group of mothers also share their breastfeeding experiences.

## Books

*Bestfeeding: Getting Breastfeeding Right for You*
Mary Renfrew
Contributors: Chloe Fisher and
    Suzanne Arms
Celestial Arts

This book for both moms and their support people is a clear, detailed, well-illustrated step-by-step account of how to breastfeed. Written by two midwives and an author/photographer who has written about childbirth, it focuses on prevention of problems but also discusses management of problems should they occur. Sections include "Starting to Breastfeed: Getting the Basics Right," "The Ten Basic Steps: A Storyboard in English and Spanish," as well as resource listings.

*Breastfeeding Matters: What We Need to Know About Infant Feeding*
Maureen Minchin
Alma Publications and George Allen & Unwin (Australia)

This scholarly work written by a Western woman who breastfed her own children is "a reference text, a practical manual on managing breastfeeding problems, and a political commentary." Simply urging women to breastfeed, says Minchin, is not enough; it is also critically necessary to provide adequate motivation, improve the management of breastfeeding problems, and offer greater support from social structures. Failing this, she maintains, exhortations to breastfeed are only "another stick to beat women with." In one section, "Mothers and Midwives," Dr. Mary Houston, Associate Professor at the School of Nursing, University of Lethbridge, Alberta, Canada, examines the role of midwives postpartum and validates the knowledge base of mothers; she also notes that "our Western culture is the only culture in the world that does not care for its new mothers by giving them the attention and teaching of an experienced older woman."

*The Nursing Mother's Companion*
Kathleen Huggins
Harvard Common Press

A practical, step-by-step guide to make breastfeeding easier, safer, and happier for mothers and their babies. Addresses special needs: working mothers, handicapped, and caesarean mothers as well as mothers of twins and premature babies.

*The Tender Gift: Breastfeeding*
Dana Raphael
Schocken Books

This work on breastfeeding and the need for a supportive figure to mother the new mother includes a look at postpartum practices in diverse cultures.

*The Womanly Art of Breastfeeding*
La Leche League International

This 1958 La Leche League book on breastfeeding was the first published on the subject, and was most recently revised in 2010.

# Catalog for Nursing Mothers

*Motherwear*
Tel.: (413) 584-8291;
(800) 633-0303 for free catalog, publications, and orders

Motherwear is a catalog for the nursing mother. Fashionable nursing clothes are designed with discreet nursing openings for ease in nursing anywhere, anytime. There is a large selection of tops, dresses, nursing bras, breast pads, pumps, pillows, and other items in the 40-page color catalog. Motherwear also publishes and distributes the following free nursing guides: *Motherwear's Guide to Nursing in Public, Motherwear's Guide to Breastfeeding the First Six Weeks,* and *Motherwear's Guide to Successful Nursing.*

# 5.

# POSTPARTUM DEPRESSION

## *You Are Not Alone*

••••••

*If we were going into outer space, we would get all this training and prepara-tion. We're raising the future—and everybody thinks you should just go do it!*
—Chris, a mom who had PPD twice

*I really think that we have to look at this holistically, and the way that we do that is as a biological, psychological, physiological, spiritual problem. I totally believe that we will see less postpartum anxiety and depression if mothers and motherhood are more embraced, if the transition is smoother. . . .*
—Nancy Berchtold, founder, Depression After Delivery

*Our philosophy is that we believe that each woman who calls in has got what it takes to make it. She needs to have somebody there to see and hear her story.*
—Honey Watts executive director, Calgary Post Partum Support Society,
Calgary, Alberta, Canada

---

### FOR IMMEDIATE HELP . . .

If you are or think you are, or if someone close to you is experi-encing postpartum depression (PPD), postpartum anxiety, or panic attacks, postpartum psychosis (PPP), or some other form of post-partum distress or disorder, and you believe the situation is one of crisis requiring immediate help and intervention, the best advice of those in the field is to contact your own caregivers, local crisis hot-line, or emergency room immediately, as there is currently no twenty-four-hour PPD crisis hotline. If you cannot reach one of the PPD telephone lines listed below, bring this book with you for the patient advocate or other hospital or crisis center staff personnel in case they are not experienced or familiar with PPD.

If the situation is not one of crisis, or if in the ensuing days you, family members, or the people who are caring for you seek out local support groups and professionals who specialize or have experience in diagnosing and treating PPD or PPP, the following organizations are good starting places and can direct you to local professionals and volunteers who will be able to listen with knowledge, compassion, and expertise, and direct you and your family to appropriate care.

UNITED STATES
**Postpartum Support, International (California)**
Tel.: (805) 967-7636
Note West Coast hours in phoning.
**Depression After Delivery, National (New Jersey)**
Tel. (during business hours): (908) 575-9121
Information and resource line: (800) 944-4PPD
Note East Coast hours in phoning.

CANADA
**PASS-CAN**
Tel.: (905) 844-9009
**Parent Development Centre (Alberta)**
Tel.: (403) 253-6722
**Pacific Post Partum Support Society (British Columbia)**
Tel.: (604) 255-7999

## SIGNS AND SYMPTOMS

Signs and symptoms of PPD or PPP may range from the weepiness of the mildest form of "baby blues" that may last several hours or days, to the more severe hallucinations, confusion, and agitation of the most severe postpartum psychosis.

Symptoms of "baby blues" may include sadness, lowered self-esteem, mood swings, irritability, decreased sexuality, or feelings of stress. (For a fuller discussion of this subject, see page 170.)

Symptoms of PPD may include anxiety, despondency, insomnia, excessive tearfulness, feelings of being out of control, confusion, eating disorders, panic, an aversion to touching the baby, obsessive thoughts, confusion, disorientation, or fear of harming the baby. (For a fuller discussion of this, see pages 171–173.)

Symptoms of PPP may include agitation, rapid mood swings, irrational thinking, incoherent statements, hallucinations, inability to care for yourself or your baby, loss of touch with reality, or unusual fears. (For a fuller discussion of this, see pages 174–186.)

## TREATMENT

PPD is considered "100 percent treatable."[1]

Professionals and volunteers working in the field of PPD emphasize that each woman's situation is unique and must be thoroughly assessed and referred on an individual basis. The overall plan may include some or all of the following components, depending on the individual woman:

• Warmline for information or hotline for a crisis situation and immediate support or referral.

• Individual sessions with a psychiatrist who is familiar with PPD and who works in unison with the other members of the treatment team.

• Individual support or counseling with a practitioner (e.g., an R.N.C., psychologist, or social worker) who understands PPD and who works interactively with the other caregivers.

• A PPD support group usually made up of lay volunteers—e.g., Depression After Delivery (DAD), Calgary Post Partum Support Society (CPPSS), Pacific Post Partum Support Society (PPPSS), Postpartum Assistance for Mothers (PAM), or Emotional You. The group may offer regular meetings, ongoing telephone support with someone who has recovered from PPD, a crisis hotline, lectures or special events for family members, a fathers' support group or information night, or meetings with guest lecturers. Such a group can be very important because of the sharing involved, and the inspiration of other women who have recovered.

• Education includes articles, books, and other materials on PPD and related issues, as well as on diet and nutrition, relaxation techniques, exercise, and other aspects of a "mentally healthy" life. These materials can also represent what Depression After Delivery founder Nancy Berchtold called "something to hold on to during those first dark days." They will also help the mom and her family to make informed choices about the course of her recovery.

• A support network to help the mom manage her daily chores and routines while she is going through recovery and/or adjustment. (Counselors or support group leaders may work with the mom and family to help her plan this network prenatally, if she is at risk, and implement it later on. Some in-home doula services have some doulas on staff who specialize in working with postpartum depressed moms.)

• Medication in conjunction with the other pieces of the treatment. Careful monitoring and support are imperative, particularly if the medication is psychopharmacological.

• Careful consideration of weaning because it may exacerbate the condition, particularly if it is done precipitously.

• Hospitalization if a controlled environment is required for a time.

• Support and information meetings or groups for partners, grandparents, older siblings, and other family members who are involved in and/or affected by the mom's recovery process.

# Making Up for Lost Time:
## The Growing Awareness

By now, most women have heard the term "postpartum depression." You may have read an article on the self-limiting and self-resolving "baby blues," so common that many people consider it a normal part of postpartum adjustment for all women. You may have seen a TV program about the most severe and very much rarer cases of postpartum psychosis, which affects one to three in a thousand postpartum women worldwide and requires immediate treatment and intervention, but which, like all other forms of postpartum depression, is also, according to obstetrician and psychiatrist Dr. Joanne Woodle, medical director of Cass House Women's Center, "100 percent treatable." You may know something about the depression that falls between these two ends of the range and that itself can be considered mild, moderate, or severe. You may know someone who has experienced some form of postpartum depression; you may have had it yourself and resolved it; you may feel, as most women do, that "it will never happen to me"; you may have felt it yourself and not known what it was—or, like many women, you may have been afraid to admit it.

While the public's awareness of PPD has increased considerably since 1980 (particularly since the founding of the self-help group Depression After Delivery and the publication of Nancy Dix's book *The New Mother Syndrome* in 1985), official controversy, questions, and obstacles still surround this aspect of women's mental health. Official nomenclature is cloudy; more research is needed; and ignorance, denial, and stigma still exist. However, despite this backdrop that has obscured and ignored the postpartum needs and experiences of so many women over so many decades, breakthroughs and mobilization in the past ten years have provided women with new sympathy, awareness, and avenues of help. While the causes are now believed by those leading the research and treatment to be biological—based upon the dramatic drop in hormones and other endocrine levels within the first twenty-four to forty-eight hours after birth—it is also believed that psychological, sociological, and cultural components as well as supports, or the lack thereof, all influence the new mom's overall state. Stress is universally believed to exacerbate things considerably. The role of stress in contributing to postpartum depression is borne out further by the fact that adoptive mothers and even biological fathers may suffer from postpartum depression.

"A woman is never more vulnerable than when she's had a baby," says Jane Honikman, founder of Postpartum Support, International, a network that brings together worldwide lay and scientific people working on postpartum depression. Your body is going through "overwhelming physical changes," your sleep pattern has been shattered, and your emotional and developmental adjustments to the new baby and your new role are just beginning, often in a nonsupportive, nonvalidating, highly judgmental atmosphere. You may feel all alone and be trying to live up to an impossible dream—a perfectionist's standard of mothering—without getting the underpinning of a support network of your own. Your goal may also be to take it all in stride, play out the cultural myth that motherhood is nothing but joyous, and resume your old life as quickly and as smoothly as possible.

"It should be natural to say, 'My life will change, my body will change, my health will change,' and not make it a bad thing," says Honikman. "We are part of nature. . . . We've had a tremendous biological, psychological, environmental, cultural experience [with] pregnancy and birth. Why are we so afraid to say, 'I'm different'? Sometimes it's good feelings, sometimes it's bad feelings. It doesn't matter. Let's not judge them, let's just go with them. Let's be there for one another. . . . In terms of the milder part [of PPD] . . . this culture has alienated the process [of childbirth and postpartum] and made it a foreign experience. [It's told women], 'It's no big deal to have a baby.' It is a big deal and you're never the same again. You have to have rites of passage and ritual and traditions and taboos. We need to re-create those." This is particularly true today.

All women—and all parents—go through an adjustment after the birth of a baby. For some the adjustment is harder; for some it is easier. "It's a form of culture shock," says Joyce A. Venis, an R.N.C. certified in psychiatry, and support group leader and counselor at the Princeton-based Center for Postpartum Depression. "Whether it means you can't change the color of your rug because of finances, or can't fly to Paris for the weekend anymore, or can't even go to the bathroom or take a shower when you want to." Stress and anxiety are not unusual, yet if our stressed-out reality doesn't match our idealized expectations, how many of us still feel the fault lies in us?

In part, the extent to which a new mom is permitted to express her real feelings in a nonjudgmental atmosphere may affect the ease or difficulty of her adjustment. While some women might be genetically predisposed to a chemical depression no matter how much help or support they have, other women may find that a support network and plan will help them minimize stress and reduce depression. As professionals in the field are quick to note, the earlier proper treatment or support is obtained, the quicker the recovery may be.

Some women are surprised to learn that postpartum depression and psychosis have been in and out of medical texts and social history for centuries, even millennia, reflecting the controversy that still surrounds them. Hippocrates observed postpartum psychosis in the fourth century B.C. As early as 1838, the first systematic studies of postpartum depression took place in France, where Jean Etienne Dominique Esquirol studied ninety postpartum women and suggested that many others "suffered silently at home." By 1858, in France, Dr. Louis Victor Marcé observed postpartum women and published a comprehensive study of postpartum psychosis, in which he was convinced that postpartum psychiatric illnesses were physical illnesses and that they were unique to the postpartum period. But in the mid-1950s in the United States, Marcé's findings were widely misquoted in the literature to present a position exactly the opposite of what he had found, and as the nineteenth century expert on PPD, his "alleged denial" of the unique qualities of postpartum illness paved the way for most psychiatrists in the United States to follow suit and deny the unique nature of postpartum depression. The word "postpartum" and its synonyms were removed from the official diagnostic terminology.

Social, cultural, and other factors affecting the lives of women worldwide have also influenced the prominence or invisibility of PPD. At different times in history, attitudes, philosophies, and treatments may have had little to do with the actual experience of women going through PPD or its causes. (Sara Kunsa shares one example of this when she talks about her tribe at home in Uganda. "When a woman at home suffers from postpartum depression," she says, "it is said to be because she had relations with another man during her pregnancy. It becomes a moral and ethical issue," she explains, rather than one of postpartum mental health.)

Throughout the years there have been many opposing schools of thought concerning PPD, and as Norma Swenson, coauthor of *Our Bodies, Ourselves*, and *The New Our Bodies, Ourselves*, and president of the board of directors of the Boston Women's Health Book Collective, notes, when schools of scientific thought gain ascendancy, they often have little to do with those individuals most affected. Traditionally, as "medical ideas" about women—about what was wrong with them and what should be done about it—prevailed throughout history, the voices of the women themselves were often never heard. Feelings, symptoms, and dilemmas were ignored, minimized, or patronized, and women were told to "shape up," "buck up," "get with the program," or "buy a new dress." Or they were labeled mentally ill (with the implication being that it was chronic), and possibly dismissed with an inappropriate or insufficient treatment.

Today it is encouraging to know that the questions and answers of women themselves are increasingly being woven into the tapestry of prevention, treatment, education, and resolution. Through the dedication of members of the scientific and self-help communities, as well as thousands of women who have themselves experienced PPD or PPP, silence is being replaced by the voices of women talking, learning, caring, healing, and by those professionals and volunteers offering education, effective collaborative care, crisis and ongoing support, plans for prevention, and empowerment.

# Some Words of Reassurance: It Is Important to Know . . .

It is crucial that all new parents be aware that there is caring, competent help available if you are, or if you think you are, experiencing postpartum depression or distress.

It is important to know that the rapid and dramatic physiological changes your body is going through in returning to its prepregnancy state, compounded by any other number of stressors of the postpartum period (including the lack of attention that has been paid until recently to PPD), may be causing or exacerbating a very real and treatable problem.

It is important to know that having any of these feelings, whether mild or extreme, and admitting the need for treatment and care for yourself at a time when you feel you should be functioning at your peak, do not mean that you are a "failure" as a mother. They do not mean you are rejecting your "female role," as psychiatrist/obstetrician Joanne Woodle's obstetrics text taught when she was in school. They do not mean that you are a weak or defective human being. "[Women] haven't just suddenly been 'found out,'" says Dr. Woodle. "The shell broke, and this person underneath they never knew was there emerged—and that's really them. . . . That's just not true." Nor do they mean that a woman's effective, functioning, joyous life with her child and family is over, as many women feel it is when they experience the threat of PPD. They may, in fact, mean that at the end of this seemingly endless dark tunnel you may be able to enjoy a strengthened relationship with your child after you yourself have been nurtured and treated and your depression has been resolved.

It is important to know that other women have been there before—and recovered fully, and even been strengthened by their recovery. From their struggles, lessons have been learned which may now help to make the recovery process for other new mothers with PPD less lengthy and less painful, if they are directed to the right sources of treatment and information. Today—particularly with early disclosure, diagnosis, and proper treatment—the prospect for full recovery is excellent. In fact, the earlier it is reported, diagnosed, and treated, the shorter the recovery time may be.

Finally, it is important for a woman and her family to know where to turn with questions and how to get sensitive, up-to-date, informed answers—sometimes needed in a hurry in cases where onset is abrupt—from the relatively small group of professionals and support groups breaking ground in this area. For women experiencing postpartum depression or psychosis, there is caring help available from the first moment they or their family members feel that something "isn't right." That help may come through a Depression After Delivery hotline, a call to Postpartum Support, International, or another health-care provider or center known to be sensitive and multidisciplinary in its approach to PPD and PPP.

If women are to be educated health-care consumers, it is as necessary to include some preliminary information on postpartum depression in a mainstream postpartum plan as it is to include information on breastfeeding or home-care options, perhaps nothing more than a simple brochure and telephone number to be tucked away in a drawer for future reference. "Unfortunately," says Jeanne Driscoll, R.N., M.S., C.S., "there are too many people around who think that by informing women you frighten them. And I think that speaks to how we devalue women. The one way not to handle [PPD]," she says, "is by not talking about it at all. Because then you scare the hell out of [women] when they get it. And they don't know where they're going."

Jan Taylor, a leader of Postpartum Adjustment for Mothers, a PPD self-help support group in California, concurs. "What I have heard so many times is [doctors] don't want to talk about it, because they think women will get it if they talk about it." In addition, says Dr. Woodle, "You're dealing with a whole industry—the medical industry, the insurance industry—it's just not cost-effective to look at it. And unfortunately pregnant women tend to fall by the wayside."

If postpartum depression is a "picture puzzle"[2] with so many pieces falling together and others still missing, then the first postpartum year may be seen as a tapestry into which the threads of adjustment and mental health issues and information need to be more fully and more openly woven so that women can speak out, learn from each other and from sensitive professionals, seek proper help early, perhaps prevent PPD altogether, and make informed choices about their caregivers and treatment.

## Postpartum Depression: Evolving Definitions

*I didn't know what it was, so I never got help.*

—Gaye

*Once I knew what it was, I could go in the direction I wanted it to go.*

—Jan

All new mothers need a language and vocabulary of matrescence to help orient them to the new range of feelings they experience and to guide them as they grow into motherhood.

Nowhere is the need for an expanded, consistent vocabulary more apparent or more poignant than in the areas of postpartum depression and emotional distress that women experience as new mothers. Often, with information still so scarce and language still so obscure, women experiencing postpartum distress do not know what is happening to them. Sometimes they don't even feel comfortable describing it because they don't know that anyone else has ever felt the same way.

While the public knows the term PPD, the terms in the clinical and scientific literature are many: postpartum depression; postpartum panic attacks; postpartum distress; postpartum anxiety and stress;

postpartum emotional syndrome; postpartum emotional difficulty; baby blues; maternity blues; major postpartum depression; postpartum psychosis; postpartum psychotic depression; puerperal psychotic depression.

Even those within the field do not always agree on what to call it. Research is contradictory, and to some degree scientific data have been ignored, obscured, or slow in coming over the years. In addition to the lack of definitive, standardized names, there is information regarding PPD that is only now coming to light, and there is still more to come.

In addition to imprecise language, philosophies differ, and questions remain a part of the current discussions: Is PPD mental illness, or is it emotional difficulty? Are women mentally ill, physically ill with psychiatric symptoms, or are they just struggling in a society that doesn't support them? Or do all three work in combination? (As one Canadian mother put it, "It is a real illness in a society not trained to recognize its own problems.")[3] Is it unique and specific to the postpartum period (as Dr. James A. Hamilton, psychiatrist and associate clinical professor emeritus at Stanford University, and others at the vanguard of the work in the field, believe), or is it not unique, and just the same as an episode from any other time in a woman's life? Why will it occur after the birth of a second or third child when it hasn't occurred with previous children? Why will it occur in one woman and not in another?

As definitions are being hammered out and details brought to light, postpartum depression is an umbrella term used widely by both the lay and professional communities to refer to a variety of postpartum psychiatric disorders. They are "disorders that occur in the postpartum period," says Dr. Ricardo J. Fernandez, a psychiatrist who specializes in the fields of PPD and PMS. In his view, whether they are "only confined to postpartum and will never occur any other time in the woman's life," while important, is of secondary importance compared to the treatment, which he believes must take into account the fact that it is occurring in the postpartum period and take a biopsychosocial approach.

The Pacific Post Partum Support Society in Vancouver, British Columbia, defines PPD as "more than a depressed mood, it continues for an extended period of time, and women definitely feel disabled by the experience."[4] The "baby blues" and the much more rare postpartum psychosis, they say, are often "confused" with PPD.

Even though specific names are not recognized officially, Jeanne Driscoll and psychiatrist Deborah Sichel, who work with pregnant and postpartum women in the Boston area, say that they use and encourage staff to use them, since they believe them to be specific to the postpartum period. They have also observed that once the illness is diagnosed as "postpartum depression, postpartum psychosis, or postpartum panic attacks, patients are markedly relieved to have their distressing set of symptoms given a name."[5]

While research is current and to some degree contradictory, and theories and knowledge relating to PPD are likely to remain in a state of rapid change and/or transition for some time, it is useful to summarize some of the terms that are in use and some of the feelings that go along with them. In the final analysis, if you are or think you are experiencing the kinds of postpartum distress described in the following pages—if things don't feel "right" and don't begin to improve—don't be afraid to acknowledge your feelings and seek the informed help you need and deserve.

## BABY BLUES OR MATERNITY BLUES

*My baby was born Saturday morning before Mother's Day. Sunday, I was ecstatic and felt great all day. Monday, my first day at home, I found myself lying on the floor at the foot of his crib racked with tears and sobbing. I cried much of Tuesday and Wednesday, much the same way—for no apparent reason! When my in-laws arrived on Thursday, I burst into tears the moment they arrived . . . and cried off and on through Saturday. The weird (and reassuring) thing was I knew it was PPD, and it was normal, so I laughed at myself. My main fear was wondering how long it would last. I talked to friends—especially new moms, a pediatrician/neighbor, a nurse, and a special friend who's a former midwife and now specializes in women's psychology. Talking to friends helped me to get through the immediate issues, and later to feel positive toward those early days. It's important to be able to look back and remember the tender moments and not get "hung up" on the wild ones!*

—Spalding\*

\*All of the women who shared their experiences in this section have fully recovered from PPD, and many feel themselves strengthened by the experience.

As with much research and statistics on PPD, numbers vary and may be quickly dated. In the book *Postpartum Psychiatric Illness*, Dr. Hamilton, Patricia Neel Harberger, and Barbara L. Parry, M.D., report that maternity blues occur in "30 to 80 percent of all new mothers, usually three to ten days after childbearing. It lasts from a few hours to a few days. Because of its high incidence it is regarded by many as a normal event" postpartum.[6] Dawn Gruen, ACSW, reports that the baby blues "usually begin early between the third and fourteenth day after birth."[7] The Calgary Post Partum Support Society has extended this time frame to twenty-one days. Jane Honikman notes that she likes to think it affects 100 percent of all new moms, because we all go through adjustments. Maternity blues have also been associated with the onset of lactation on the third day (also the time when many women have just been discharged from the hospital). It is "thought to be benign," writes Jan L. Campbell, M.D., "and self-limiting, resolving spontaneously within two weeks."[8] In her groups, Jane Honikman expands the time frame for self-resolution to six weeks, the time of the mother's obstetric checkup. If you're experiencing maternity or baby blues, symptoms may include weepiness, sleep difficulties, anxiety, exhaustion, oversensitivity, irritability, lack of feeling for the baby, or lack of confidence. The symptoms "will pass more quickly," writes Dawn Gruen, "if you can get good physical care (rest, nourishment, medical care); help with chores and baby care; and someone to nurture and care for you."[9]

## POSTPARTUM DEPRESSION
### (OR MAJOR POSTPARTUM DEPRESSION)

*Eight years later I can still remember and almost feel what the depression was like. It was terrifying in the sense that I felt nothing. I felt absolutely nothing toward the baby, nothing toward my husband, nothing. I had an agitated depression, so I couldn't sit still. . . . The simplest tasks [were] all too much for me.*

*And [there was] also the fear that it would never go away, it would always be like this, and I'll never be the person I was before. It is a hole. You have to struggle to pull yourself out of it. It takes such perseverance, I feel, to get over a depression.*

—Nancy Berchtold, founder, Depression After Delivery

Dr. Hamilton, Patricia Neel Harberger, and Barbara L. Parry, M.D., define PPD as "a slowly increasing depression of mood that begins after the third week postpartum."[10] Dawn Gruen writes that it "can begin anytime from the second week through the first year after birth. However, if the parent does not acknowledge his/her depression, the diagnosis may be delayed well beyond the first year."[11] The Pacific Post Partum Support Society in Vancouver, British Columbia, defines PPD as "tearfulness, despondency, feelings of inadequacy and inability to cope."[12] Dr. Joanne Woodle feels that it is important for women to know that the three times when they are most vulnerable to the onset of PPD are in the first two weeks postpartum; in the two weeks preceding a woman's first menstrual period postpartum; and in the first two weeks following weaning, particularly if it is done precipitously. (If the mom breastfeeds for longer than twelve months, she says, her vulnerability to PPD may still exist during the two weeks after she weans, even if her child is two or three years old.) Joyce A. Venis, R.N.C., of the Princeton-based Center for Postpartum Depression, notes that for bottle-feeding moms, if lactation is suppressed chemically, there may be a higher risk for PPD at that time.

Postpartum depression may be characterized as mild, moderate, or severe (chronic), which is disabling. Symptoms may include feelings of hopelessness, irritability, loss of normal interests, insomnia, agitation, inability to relax or concentrate, confusion, memory impairment, difficulty functioning, tingling in the limbs, chest pains, numbness, inability to cope, overconcern about the baby's well-being despite assurances that all is well, thoughts of suicide or frightening thoughts about harm to the baby or oneself, new fears, or feelings of shame or guilt. Depending on severity, simply identifying the problem and talking about it may help women and families with milder depressions. It is useful for women to know, says Dr. Ricardo Fernandez, when the line is crossed from being "generally miserable" to being "clinically depressed." That occurs, he explains, when a certain number of symptoms have been present for a certain number of consecutive days. In more severe cases, interdisciplinary care models, the design of which should include the input of the woman and her family, may include counseling, a support system, a support group, medication, or in severe cases, hospitalization. "Like depression in general," writes Polly Kornblith, cofounder of Massachusetts DAD, "the duration of PPD depends on the timeliness and appropriateness of the treatment received and usually resolves within six months to one year."[13]

## POSTPARTUM PANIC ATTACKS

*It was awful. Rapid heartbeat, I couldn't sleep, I couldn't eat, all I did was cry. I had some depression but the majority of it was the anxiety. I really truly thought I was going to die, and that's why I was pushed to find help so fast.*

—Jan, leader, Postpartum Assistance for Mothers (PAM)

Although it is not yet definitively known whether panic attacks, like obsessive thinking, exist on their own independent of depression, it has come to light in the past several years that many women experience postpartum panic attacks. "It helps to know what one is," says Dr. Fernandez. "Labeling it helps." During a postpartum panic attack, you may feel numbness in your chest (some women describe it as feeling as if they're having a heart attack), tingling of the limbs, difficulty breathing, the feeling of being "out of control," and great fatigue when it's over. The Pacific Post Partum Support Society handbook, *Post Partum Depression and Anxiety,* notes that a panic or anxiety attack is "a physiological reaction to stress. It is harmless and will pass."[14] They suggest reducing your stress level and nurturing yourself more, and learning how to manage the attack when it is occurring. Some women have used breathing, talking about it, or imagining a pleasant experience. For the sake of treatment, Dr. James Hamilton and others suggest treating this as a separate entity.

## OBSESSIVE-COMPULSIVE DISORDER

*I'd leave my house every morning at eight-thirty and not come home till two-thirty, three, then my husband would be home, and I would go out after he got home because now I could relax. . . . It's horrible, it's like living in hell. Because you want your baby so much and you want to be the best mother there is and all of a sudden you look at them and think that you could hurt them. I got afraid if anybody was going to give them a cold, they'd get sick and die. Here's the normal protective side of the mother that gets shorted out. . . . I used to think, "If I could just get in the car and never come back, because who wants me?"*

—Kate

As with postpartum anxiety attacks, more information about obses-sive-compulsive disorder is beginning to emerge. According to Jeanne Driscoll, women may "start to get afraid that something's going to hap-pen to their baby and they just can't shut off the thoughts." Thoughts might involve harm coming to the baby through sharp objects in the house, or falling down the stairs, for example. "These anxious thoughts are very ego alien—which means they don't belong—and so many women will then develop behavior to cope with the anxious thoughts." Behaviors to avoid the obsession may mean that mothers will not be alone in the house with the baby. "So someone might go stay at her mother's all day and then as long as her husband's home, she feels safe. She won't act on her thoughts. . . . You spend a lot of time trying to get rid of these thoughts, so women will be busy."

Symptoms may include obsessive thoughts, anxiety, and behavior patterns to help avoid the feared activities. Treatment that Driscoll has found successful includes medication coupled with supportive ther-apy, thought stoppage techniques, visualization meditation, and sup-port groups. "If you catch this early," says Driscoll, "I don't think you get the depressive part. That's why it's really important that people as-sess well, and learn to ask questions gently, so women don't feel intim-idated or at risk. That's a critical piece."

## POSTPARTUM PSYCHOTIC DEPRESSION

*There were two weeks from my discharge from the hospital [with the new baby] to readmission to the psychiatric unit. In the two weeks that I was home I became very manic, very speedy, very elated. I was the complete opposite of what you would think when we talk about this being PPD. It was not PPD, it wasn't depression at all. For me it was elation, exuberance, I was so happy. What was not being noticed even by my husband, because I was nursing, was that I was not sleeping, and I was not eating. So I was really just spinning into this breakdown, which happened when the baby was sixteen days old. . . . For a couple of days my parents started noticing something was wrong and showed their concern, but everybody thought they were just reacting to a tired new mother. But they were pretty astute. They were seeing confusion, I was not thinking clearly. . . . Eventually total nightmare fears took over. At that point my husband called the obstetrician, who listened over the phone to hear me and said, "Get her to the hospital as soon as you can." . . . Breastfeeding was abruptly stopped, I had to be separated from my baby. My recovery was swift. I bounced back fairly fast once they got the medications right. I was released from the hospital in two weeks, a real short stay. I got hit with the double whammy of depression, which often happens with PPP . . . which was just as bad if not worse than the psychosis.*

*I was then put on antidepressants, [which] was really a lifesaver for me in my recovery. . . . I stayed at my parents' house for about five weeks because I really was released early from the hospital because I had full care. I came back to my home and rejoined the family, so to speak, took over my responsibilities when the baby was three months old. And from there a steady, slow, uphill battle from the depression. When I was nine months postpartum I was off all medication. And I was blessed with having her first birthday be one of joy. Most women do not even feel any joy at all on the first birthday. They're not even completely on their feet yet. And mine was the typical—they say it takes approximately a year for a full recovery. Even for PPD, they say six months to a year. I was lucky in that I had a psychiatrist who was older, he called it what it was—PPP.*

—Nancy Berchtold, founder, Depression After Delivery

Postpartum psychosis is the most rare form of postpartum psychiatric illness, and it affects only one to three of every thousand new mothers. PPP "often begins between the third and fourteenth day,"[15] writes Dawn Gruen. Polly Kornblith, cofounder of Massachusetts DAD, reports that it "usually sets in during the first or second week postpartum but can occur later in the first year after childbirth," which may imply weaning time for some women, a time when they may be particularly vulnerable to onset.[16] It is "hormonal, biological and genetic in nature," notes Joyce A. Venis.[17] Dawn Gruen points out that "70 percent of all people who experience postpartum psychosis have never had any prior serious psychiatric illness."[18] Symptoms may include confusion, extreme agitation, severe withdrawal, seeing and hearing things that really aren't there, mercurial mood changes, loss of memory, loss of touch with reality, paranoia, irrational fears or fantasies, incoherence, refusal to eat, insomnia, frantic excessive energy, suicidal thoughts, or thoughts of harming one's baby. It is considered a medical emergency or crisis condition that poses a serious threat to the mother's and infant's well-being and requires immediate treatment in a controlled environment for a time. Kornblith notes that "with proper treatment, PPP can often be resolved within several weeks but may develop into PPD unless precautions are taken."[19]

If a woman does suffer a postpartum psychosis, her chances of suffering one again during a subsequent pregnancy increase from one to three in one thousand to one in three or four, so all methods and plans for contingencies and prevention should be explored if the mom is considering another pregnancy. Although mother/baby units where moms and their infants can stay together have been found to be helpful to new moms in England, they do not exist widely in the United States. One of the only mother/baby inpatient units in the United States opened in January 1993 at the Center for Women's Development at HRI Hospital in Brookline, Massachussetts. Elsewhere—for example, at Duke University—while there is no formal mother/baby unit, according to William S. Meyer, M.S.W., B.C.D., and director of the Duke Postpartum Support Program, there is sympathy and sensitivity to the mother-infant relationship at this time, and they will facilitate as much time together as the mom can handle.

Responding to the need women feel to understand precisely and concretely the full range of what is happening to them during the early and extended postpartum period, the Calgary Post Partum Support Society includes two other definitions on their list along with baby blues, postpartum depression, and postpartum psychosis:

## POSTPARTUM EXHAUSTION

*My experience with exhaustion was that it's intense, it almost took me by surprise. I just didn't think that far ahead into having a baby that I would become exhausted from it. I was tired all day, I was tired all night, I was tired all weekend. It was a twenty-four-hour-a-day exhaustion that never ended. . . . It was like a deep physical and emotional exhaustion.*

—Pat

This shows all the same symptoms as depression, including loss of coping skills. The Calgary Post Partum Support Society says that it affects everyone to some degree, and suggest that sleep is the cure. CPPSS helps moms figure out ways to restore some of the sleep cycle, if not in number of hours, at least in terms of getting the deep REM sleep they need.

## POSTPARTUM ADJUSTMENT

*I found the adjustment to be one of the biggest parts of [my overall experience]—in terms of having a third member in our family, in terms of having a new little person around that was totally dependent on me for survival. In terms of loss of career, job, finances, lots of losses that came about and that all is related to adjustment. The adjustment within our marriage, with friends . . . most of my friends are single with no kids. In terms of socialization, spontaneity, mobility, all that stuff got wildly affected, again, coming as a bit of a surprise to me, not really having thought through what the consequences of having a new baby would be, other than the fantasy world.*

—Pat

This is the adjustment to the new baby in terms of marriage, older children, social life, scheduling, establishing routines, and overall coping. It will affect everyone to some degree.

# Why Does It Happen?

The causes or etiology of PPD are not definitively known. Research is contradictory, depending on the criteria used. And as Terra Ziporyn, Ph.D., points out in the *Harvard Health Letter,* research is also hampered by the "small number of severe cases that any individual physician sees over a career."[20] It is also hampered by the minimal amounts of money available for research on something that does not officially exist.

While a variety of theories have been offered, the most useful view, particularly in terms of treatment, seems to encompass a combination of biological, sociological, psychological, cultural, personality, and environmental factors, all in varying proportions, depending on the individual woman. "I've seen women where I think it's 100 percent hormonal, and then I've seen patients where I don't think it's at all hormonal," says Dr. Valerie Raskin, a Chicago-based psychiatrist specializing in PPD. "But in that sense, depression is a real illness, and in that sense, yes, it's a real illness. But it's probably not one disease."

For over thirty years, Dr. James Alexander Hamilton has been a pioneer in exploring and putting forth the biological cause as the primary organic cause of PPD, reflecting "deficits and imbalances in the endocrine system, as this system moves rapidly from the hyperactivity of pregnancy down to, and sometimes beyond, the levels of the nonpregnant state."[21] Biologically, the mother's system is slowing down after pregnancy, perhaps too quickly, perhaps too much. Understanding this biological process and vulnerability, especially when compounded by stress and lack of support, is crucial for women, who otherwise perceive their disability to "mother well" as a personal failure of monumental proportions. With the loss of the placenta, which has generated the higher levels of hormones needed during the pregnancy, after delivery a woman's hormone levels drop dramatically in twenty-four to forty-eight hours. Dr. Ziporyn writes that "at least in some women . . . the fall in estrogen initiated by delivery may spark a cascade of events that curtails the function of the pituitary. This powerful gland nestled at the base of the brain secretes hormones that control numerous other glands. In turn, some of these glands (such as the thyroid and the adrenals) produce substances that affect mental states."[22]

Although they have not experienced the same kind of hormonal drop, fathers and adoptive mothers can suffer from postpartum depression. According to Jeanne Driscoll, the adoptive mom may be "hypervigilant, anxious, up every two hours, same as everybody. . . . She hasn't had the placental drop, but she's having a stress response." Depending on her genetic characteristics, stress combined with the fact that she may already have hormonal difficulties if she wasn't able to conceive can lead to depression. "Unfortunately," says Driscoll, "it is often viewed as an adjustment disorder and it doesn't get the value." Practitioners look at the fact that she's just adopted the baby, and "treat her by helping her to do mothering better, rather than focusing on her. [But] this is more of a crisis rather than an adjustment disorder. [She] didn't have nine months to plan. [No one says to her], 'Your life has changed. Twenty-four hours ago, you got a phone call, now you have a baby. How does it feel?' If you tell people how you feel, they're turned off."

Another factor often minimized is sleep deprivation. Maternity nursing texts acknowledge that the fatigue a woman experiences postpartum is one of the most underestimated problems of this process. One recent study shows that after a normal delivery, fatigue peaks at two weeks, with "a marked decrease in energy related to loss of sleep,"[23] according to Diane Gardner, assistant professor of nursing at the University of Iowa. If a woman is not able to arrange help that will accommodate her need for sleep—particularly at the point at which her helpers may be leaving, and her partner returning to work—she may run into more serious exhaustion or depression than she would otherwise. Gardner suggests that prenatal classes include counseling for postpartum fatigue. In her book *Women and Fatigue*, Dr. Holly Atkinson also addresses the issue of chronic fatigue, which is a cause of PPD. A plan for extra nap or sleep time while a friend or family member watches the baby can help ward off exhaustion.

At the Pacific Post Partum Support Society (PPPSS), a feminist, nonmedical model program in Vancouver, British Columbia, Canada, Penny Handford, one of the society's founders, still believes that environmental and social factors play the greatest roles in causing PPD. Dr. Sandra Knight of the PPPSS surveyed five women who had participated in the program, and cited other nonbiological causes for depression that these women themselves had reported. They included the lack of a support network, lack of structure to the day, pregnancy experiences and labor and delivery fears, personality type (e.g., factors such as how much they were inclined to worry, or how "perfect" they felt they had to be), and "unfinished business" from earlier in their lives. Such unfinished business may include a past experience of incest, child abuse, or living in an alcoholic family. Jane Honikman confirms that on a worldwide basis, counselors report that women with postpartum depression do frequently have such "secrets," which they need to talk about and resolve as they move from being a daughter to being a mother as well. Frequently, the energy they once had to keep such issues hidden is gone during the vulnerable postpartum period, and they may feel suddenly confronted with these realities from earlier times in their lives. This may be particularly true if the issues relate to family and how they were mothered themselves.

In England, Ann Oakley identified another group of factors influencing PPD in the women she studied in London for her 1980 book *Women Confined*. She found that each woman was also influenced by how much her partner participated in having and caring for the child; how realistic her picture of motherhood was; whether she had and could hang on to interests outside of childcare; whether she could call on a network of friends and relations for help and advice; whether she lived in housing that cut her off from other adults; and how much control she had over what happened during pregnancy and birth.[24] Another stressor may be the helplessness, fear, or other feelings that are triggered in new parents when their baby is crying or inconsolable.

Today, daily stress loads, the pressure of trying to rearrange and balance the demands of work, family, finances, and the frequent lack of adequate support in the form of parental leave, postpartum home care, job security, and childcare also affect the difficulty or ease of the new mother and the new family's course. It is an interesting and ironic coincidence that the number of women suffering each year from postpartum depression is said to be 400,000 (though some in the field feel it is higher) and that, as Kay Johnson, senior health policy adviser for the March of Dimes, reported at congressional hearings, "despite recent expansions in Medicaid, an estimated 443,000 pregnant women have no health insurance."[25] Others who do have insurance are not covered for maternity care. This is not to imply that those women without health coverage are the ones who will suffer from PPD, but the similarity in statistics is striking.

However, as Dr. Fernandez says, "when there is a fire raging, you don't stop to look for the cause of the fire. First you put the fire out and then you sift through the ashes." Until there are more definitive criteria, more money for research, and more responsive solutions to the problems all new mothers face, it is important that all of these causal factors be given appropriate weight and validity in guiding women and families to correct treatment of postpartum depression in all of its forms.

## What Does It Feel Like?

For many women, it has taken great courage and the passage of time to be able to talk about what they are going through, or have gone through in the past. "We got a letter from a woman who is seventy," says Nancy Berchtold, "who told us she was sure she had experienced PPD fifty years ago." Whatever their ages, for all of them, the chance finally to speak and be heard is a relief.

One positive thing professionals notice now is that women are speaking out and coming in to see them sooner than they were before.

Joyce A. Venis says, "We are now getting women saying, 'Hey, I just had a baby two weeks ago, I don't think I'm doing so great. What's the story?'" More women will come in at six weeks now, as opposed to waiting twelve or eighteen months, as many women did just several years ago. (In part, they had no choice but to wait, because there was simply no place to go.) Coming in and disclosing such feelings earlier may make the recovery easier, because the woman has had considerably less time to incorporate "self-defeating behavior patterns" or poor coping behaviors.

The women whose comments follow had experiences that ranged from the mildest form of maternity blues (lasting only a couple of hours) to month-long periods of depression that sometimes included panic attacks, anxiety, or obsessive thoughts. Some hooked into programs that helped them; others did not feel informed enough to seek assistance, or felt they had to "hide" what they were feeling and struggle through the experience on their own. Since some women may still do this, it is useful to include descriptions from women who were in treatment, as well as from women who were not in treatment. These moms talked about how they felt, and in some cases, why they did not feel they could disclose what they were going through:

**Tammie:** "*When my baby was one-and-a-half weeks old, one day I just 'didn't feel good.' I felt bad, started crying. It only lasted a couple of hours.*"

**Pam:** "*With my second child, I felt very tired. I didn't really want anything to do with her. I felt I was the only one feeling this way. I became aware of PPD through my husband, who had seen it on a talk show. . . . [I felt] anxiety, exhaustion, fear of harming myself or the baby. My baby was two months old when it started, and it lasted for one-and-a-half years. I didn't receive help. . . . I didn't feel it was okay to talk about being frightened. I grew up in a town where those feelings were never shared. . . . [My sister] was always available. She responded with love and encouragement.*"

**Gaye, single mother by choice:** "*I felt PPD almost immediately. I was constantly afraid something would happen to her [my child] and I could envision all kinds of macabre scenes. It was awful. I told no one*" *and around six months it went away. . . . I knew I had postpartum feelings, but I did not know what to do with them. I had heard about it for years on talk shows, read articles, only I never expected to have it so never talked about it."*

**Tanya:** *"'Baby blues' hit me when my first child was three days old. All I did was cry. I never really changed until after my second child was born [twenty months later], and I swore I was not going to go through that again. I got help. I was very sad. I did not know why. I also felt very tired all the time. There were times when I hated the world and everyone in it, including God. Looking back, I can honestly say I was not happy. I would tell myself that I should be happy and I would even act happy but I never felt happy. I was also scared that I might hurt my baby, like I sometimes thought of doing. . . . After my second child, I discussed with the health nurse my feelings and how often I cried. She then referred me to the CPPSS in our city. She also admitted to me that she went through it and she told me some of her feelings. It felt so good to hear that I was not alone."*

**Lynn:** *"I felt very disconnected the second time. . . . It sort of scared me a little. Something jelled that made life easier for me . . . when we came back from summer [vacation]. My younger son was eight months old. I felt like things were finally starting to fall into place. But what I finally acknowledged at that point was that this time I really felt like I had a postpartum depression to some extent. Not the first time. The first time there was this positive emotional high that was coloring the whole thing. And I feel guilty in some ways saying it because someone might think that would color how I feel about my child. It doesn't. It's two separate things. [It was] strange to have it the second time around and not the first. I didn't have it right away. I had this six-week time block in my mind and for the first six weeks I really handled life well. I felt like I had it all together. . . . [At six weeks], I crashed. . . . I got depressed. I was tired. Also, I had a child that didn't sleep, so what happened was the accumulation of sleep deprivation—six weeks of not sleeping can do that to you. And it continually got worse and worse. I couldn't stand the way I looked, my self-image. All of a sudden, instead of thinking I was skinny and lost my weight, I was fat, I was ugly. I didn't have clothes—all the things that you go through. And that* stayed. I was overwhelmed and exhausted and feeling very isolated with my feelings. Even though I was talking and felt like I was connecting, nobody could make me feel better. I had to wait until that happened in myself. It's a horrible time in a sense. It's bittersweet. You've got this wonderful little baby, and everybody is saying how adorable he is, and you're sitting there feeling all these ambivalent feelings."

**Gay:** "I became tired of everything and didn't want to do anything anymore. I became very angry and directed that toward my husband. I could be fine one minute and the next become very angry, sad, emotional. I had no control over this and literally felt it come over me. I went to my counselor and told her about it. My baby was approximately one-and-a-half months old. . . . I did not know the full range of feelings [women could experience postpartum]. I've had depression before but there were ways these feelings were different. I felt I was the only mother who felt angry when her baby didn't sleep at night, and was so tired herself."

**Karena:** "I had a lot of postpartum depression with my twins and I didn't think I had a right to, so I dragged it out for six months because I was trying to evade it. I was thinking, 'Well, I have no reason to be depressed. I didn't have a C-section. I have two healthy babies,' and that kind of thing. Postpartum depression does not mean that you have to have had a problem with your birth to be depressed. You have a right to experience these feelings. It's a time of upheaval."

**Elizabeth:** "While certain aspects of my experience—the crying, the insomnia, the anxiety, the despair—are classic PPD symptoms, I do have some extenuating circumstances. Two years ago I found out I was an incest survivor but decided against the recovery process because I was afraid of what I would discover. Having a new baby in the house triggered memories and emotional responses to the incest that have been frighteningly intense. While I have had postpartum depression and still feel some of those symptoms at least twice a week, my psychiatrist believes that a good deal of my problem is posttraumatic stress. While that presents an entirely different set of circumstances, I believe that they are connected and it is often hard to say where one ends and the other begins. . . . I have noticed that the majority of women [in my

*support group] have 'extenuating circumstances' similar to mine (gen-
erally it is that they come from alcoholic homes, but there are also incest
survivors and women with chemical or clinical depressions)."*

# Silence Isn't Golden: Getting
## the Words Out

It is important for a new mom to have a safe, nonjudgmental haven
where she can "debrief" and talk honestly, express her emotions, garner
some reassurance, or work through whatever guilt the feelings might
bring up. This is a key element when it comes to the prevention and
treatment of postpartum depression. Women need a supportive and
sympathetic setting within which to express any feelings of loss, doubt,
sadness, or anger, and a reliable source to answer their questions immediately. This is especially important because both lay and professional people working with prenatal women agree that it is often hard
for many women during their pregnancies to hear about any negative
aspects of the postpartum period. If any of these feelings hit you all of
a sudden after your baby arrives, an appropriate telephone number for
support should be at the ready on your general postpartum list.

One common thread women expressed, regardless of how mild or
severe their anxiety or depression was, was the sense that, before they
found help and understood what was going on, they were certain they
were the only mothers who had ever felt the anger, confusion, fear, isolation, resentment, bewilderment, shame, panic, anxiety, depression,
and whatever else was part of their experience. No one had ever even
suggested that such feelings could arise with such intensity after their
babies were born. If they did reach out for information and help, often
professionals and caregivers, despite their best efforts, simply did not
always have a handle on how to treat them.

Fortunately, today there are more places where women can be heard
and helped. But there are still obstacles, for example, stigma, invisible
models, fantasies of maternal emotions, and insensitive or inexperienced listeners.

**Stigma.** There is still great stigma attached to the label "mentally ill."
There is also controversy over whether PPD is mental illness, physical

illness with psychiatric symptoms, or just the exacerbated struggle to mother without adequate support. Women who don't know what is happening to them—and don't know that it has happened to other women as well—fear that if they seek treatment and are judged to be "crazy," their babies may be taken from them. And if women are hardly comfortable asking for help with changing a diaper, how easily can they admit to the darker, unexpected thoughts, feelings, and fantasies they may have in a state of postpartum distress? Sensitive and experienced caregivers should be able to offer the reassurance and perspective that women need at this time.

**Invisible Models.** In addition to the social taboos on negative maternal emotions, Jeanne Driscoll explains that another reason women "have never really been able to share their stories is because they had to fit into the medical model diagnostic category" that does not acknowledge a separate category for postpartum illnesses. Cases of PPD may therefore never have been recorded or reported as such. Women who had PPD may never have known it, and would therefore not have been able to seek each other out to share their common ground or support. (Unresolved PPD can remain a problem for women later, and more and more women are coming forth to question or explore what may have happened to them years ago.)

**Fantasies of Maternal Emotions.** In an article titled "The Mother Myth: A Feminist Analysis of Postpartum Depression," from the Canadian magazine *Health-sharing*, Debbie Field addresses the limitations of the "social definition of what acceptable feelings are in motherhood"[26] and argues, in essence, that the range of these feelings be expanded to include things that new mothers really do feel.

"I think if we could make a social changeover" in terms of what it is acceptable to feel and admit as new mothers, says Joyce A. Venis, "we would have fewer women who suffer as much as they do. Social pressures are very, very significant."

While negative feelings of any kind conflict bitterly with our expectations of unadulterated joy, for many women—even those who aren't suffering from severe PPD or distress—new motherhood may trigger a range of unexpected and difficult feelings. Accepting and sharing these emotions and thoughts might help to prevent or alleviate a more serious depression.

Loss and anger are two of the strong and surprising feelings that women may experience after the longed-for blessed event. These feelings may shock and alarm you. They may seem incongruous against the gentle pastel tones of the layette and crib blanket or the bright primary colors of the baby bears dancing along the borders of your nursery walls. They may feel unnatural and shameful. But even though you may not know it, they are not uncommon. Your life has changed; there have been losses, and there have been gains.

For some women, these feelings may stem from the loss of the birth experience they had hoped and planned and worked for. Months of Lamaze breathing may end in an emergency cesarean section; a long and difficult labor may require medical interventions you hadn't planned on and didn't want; a premature delivery may bring complications of its own.

Other feelings may revolve around the loss of intimacy or sexual relations with a mate. As the twosome becomes a threesome, you may feel melancholy and wistful as you say good-bye to the old one-on-one intimacy with your partner.

Feelings of loss may center around the sudden ending of a relationship with a caregiver you've formed a close bond with. This seems to be less so for women who are tended by midwives, labor companions, childbirth assistants, or doulas who see them prenatally and continue to see them through the early postpartum period, and is felt more acutely by women whose doctors dismiss them after the second or third day and then don't see or talk to them again until the six-week checkup. Jan, who had a complicated pregnancy culminating in an emergency cesarean section, was so anxious in the hospital, she was ready to put her daughter up for adoption. "When I cried all night in the hospital and my eyes were swollen shut, and I looked awful, my obstetrician [who had seen me every other day for three months] came in the morning and she never said a word about anything. All of a sudden after the baby is born, there's nothing there. No support, no understanding. That was real hard for me. And I did call her a couple of times to talk to her, but it is very hard to express yourself and how bad you are when you are in that kind of state. I was very angry about that."

For women without extended family around to help and celebrate, the birth of a baby may evoke those particular feelings of loss and mourning. Evelyn, a new mother, noted, "There's been a working through of the disappointment of not having that, and I don't know if that happens for everyone or not. You kind of mourn the loss of not having supports available to you, like your family."

Sometimes, for women suffering from PPD, anger and loss have to do with specific and deep issues surrounding ineffective treatment or lack of information. When women and their families are hit out of the blue with an episode of postpartum depression, there is often anger that no one warned them such a thing could occur. "I was very angry," said Chris, a nurse and mother of two, who suffered severe PPD twice. "I'm an educated person . . . how come no one told me this could happen? And when I asked how to prevent it, all I got were drugs and a wait-and-see attitude—until I got to Princeton [the Center for Postpartum Depression]. . . . I feel a lot of loss and very angry. I lost the delivery of my second child—I had been attempting to do V-BAC [vaginal birth after cesarean] and lost that whole potential. [She had a second cesarean section.] I lost time with my child. While I was never hospitalized, I certainly wasn't emotionally with her the way I could have been." When Chris was put on medication, she was told to stop nursing immediately. (Some medications do not require weaning, and options should be discussed with the caregiver.) "I cried that entire day. I felt like [my daughter] had been wrenched from me. I couldn't even sit in the room while somebody gave her a bottle. I felt that had been robbed from me. And then there's this joy that you hear so much about. I felt that was stolen from me. Then you feel really angry, like why did you have to go through this experience?"

If women mourn their losses as depression, then the early days and weeks and months postpartum may potentially be a time of double-layered loss. Not only are women possibly feeling the loss of an old life, of their pregnancy, of intimacy with a mate, but the social limitations on what they feel they can admit as new mothers also ban the expression of those losses. So not only have moms experienced some real losses in their lives, they have also lost the ability to say so—more of the lost or silenced female voice. Surely this overlay of postpartum silence must contribute to the upheaval and depression that may be an inherent part of what the new mom is already feeling.

At the Calgary Post Partum Support Society, distressed moms are gently encouraged to accept and talk about their feelings of loss and anger. They need to be able to look at what they've lost before they can appreciate and embrace all that they've gained in becoming a new mother. "In just looking at all the losses that we incur," says executive director Honey Watts, "if somebody would just give us permission to grieve all those losses, then we'd all be well on our way. We're as straight and honest as we can be. We say, 'Hey, you've had a baby, your life isn't going to be the way it was before.' And that will allow us to lead into saying, 'You've had this fantasy.' We always talk about what the fantasy is first. And the fantasy is, 'My life is going to be wonderful and complete, and have this wonderful family where there's never any arguing, and everybody will just be happy and perfect.' We can talk about the fantasy and then say, 'Well, what's it really like?' And the woman is starting to acknowledge right away that reality and fantasy aren't meeting. Once we can get that understanding and be talking on that common ground, then we can go into a whole lot of the other stuff. A simple question here is 'Well, this is a really hard time for you. What are all the losses that you're experiencing right now?'"

In her groups, women listed the following losses: freedom, being irresponsible, body image, spontaneity, time for self and spouse, being the focus, being pregnant, self as an individual, self in relationship to world, income/financial independence, sense of accomplishing tasks, ability to think/concentrate, immunity to early issues, professional identity, being organized, dream of baby and parenting, being in control, active friendships, feeling competent, trust in self, confidence, people contact, vocabulary, privacy, health, energy, sleep, eating habits, appetite, and respect.

Some feelings of anger and loss may be experienced by many new moms. What may differ is the degree to which they are felt, and the point at which women feel they have permission to admit them.

Diane, one new mother who did not have postpartum depression but struggled through a difficult six months nevertheless, used a journal to keep in touch with her feelings. She often started her entries with the words "I am feeling." To her, feelings are what her journal was about. She recalled that one of the strongest and most consistent feelings recorded in her journal was anger—because "nothing worked as it did in my old life."

Marianne, a new mom who felt "frightened and overwhelmed" after leaving the support of the doctors and nurses in the hospital, still had a strong support system of friends and family and was able to address her feelings openly and early: "Yes, those first few weeks I grieved for my life prior to the birth of my son. I missed the intimacy my husband

and I shared and the freedom I had. I suddenly wasn't sure I wanted to be a mother. . . . I felt depressed, sad, dependent emotionally on others, overwhelmed, unable to do anything other than care for my son. He was two to five weeks old when I went through this. I joined a new mothers' support group and called my friends and sister and talked and cried. . . . Although I definitely feel ambivalent about sharing my negative feelings, I have shared them with my husband and friends. I was worried that something was wrong with me so I asked questions of my friends who are/were new parents. . . . I didn't realize that the transition to motherhood would be gradual, difficult, and exhausting. When I felt depressed it took courage and effort to ask for emotional support as well as physical."

Diane is the new mother of an eight-and-a-half-month-old and was also able to accept and share her feelings early: "I was surprised to feel that I yearned for my premother lifestyle. We are in our thirties and we really were looking forward to starting a family, and I thought I was ready for the change, but even now I feel like if we had known, I would have waited a few more years."

In her pamphlet *The New Parent: A Spectrum of Postpartum Adjustment*, Dawn Gruen, ACSW, reassures women that feelings of loss for your "spontaneous free lifestyle" are "very natural feelings,"[27] and urges new moms to allow themselves to grieve and release those emotions.

Again, it is important to recognize that mixed feelings are a valid part of the transition to new motherhood. "The isolation, the uncertainty, the anxiety—they're all there," says Martha Lequerica, Ph.D., an assistant professor of psychology at Montclair College in New Jersey. "And they're all legitimate. The feelings of being down and depressed . . . it's part of what happens when you become totally responsible for a new life. . . . The sisterhood bond becomes very important at that time."

**Who Is Listening?** Even if women do speak out, they may not get a helpful response if they are speaking to the wrong person. The professionals and practitioners who have taken care of you up to the hour of birth may not have seen many cases of postpartum depression and may not recognize or respond to your needs, even if your cries are clear and direct. As was the case for Jan, it is often the obstetrician or his or her staff who has an early opportunity to observe or hear many of your early concerns about how you are feeling in the early postpartum phase. If the mom knows nothing about Depression After Delivery or another local support group, or has never heard of PPD, the advice of her obstetrician or midwife at this point is critical.

If this checkpoint fails, the pediatrician may be the woman's next port of call. But this person is really there for the baby, and often represents a totally new relationship for Mom and Dad. A new mother may feel especially uncomfortable letting the baby's doctor know that she has mixed feelings or doubts about motherhood, isn't sleeping well, can't manage nursing, feels insecure, is exhausted, is feeling very anxious, or worse. She may imagine it will reflect on her baby and her feelings about her infant.

Depending on what these professionals know or believe about the nature of postpartum depression, they may refer you correctly, or may dismiss you with some reassurance that it's not serious, it's normal, and advise you to get some extra sleep or a new haircut. The woman may feel devalued and discredited. Message to Mom: It must be you. Or they may be genuinely trying to make you feel better without understanding the cause of the problem.

While silence isn't golden, in some cases if a woman feels she's talking to the wrong caregiver, then withdrawing, and seeking help from a more sympathetic and informed source, can be the smartest actions she can take.

Chris, a nurse and mother of two in New York City, had PPD twice. Despite the good intentions of her doctors, it took her a very long time to find the help she needed. She is adamant that women must be told that the feelings they have when they are in a state of extreme distress are not "normal." In all the baby and mothering books she read, she says, "very little was written that dealt concretely with the idea of postpartum disorders. If you are having these symptoms, they are not normal. You should not be suffering this way. You need to get in contact with someone. Even just who to get in contact with [can be a problem]. Where do you start?"

Chris's first child was born in a traumatic, emergency cesarean section, from which she seemed to rebound miraculously. "I had a real stiff upper lip, really minimized it. Everybody thought that was wonderful." Yet she started to feel great anxiety in the hospital after the delivery. When she questioned the doctors, they said, 'You've had a lot of pain medication, it was a very traumatic experience, your hormones are changing, ride it out." After a couple of days, it subsided. Added to the trauma and hormonal vulnerability were the social expectations that Chris, like so many other women, placed on herself without question. After she got home, she says, "I remember thinking, 'I should be up!' I can remember pushing myself to walk down the street, and I'm only ten days from a cesarean. Then staggering around all night with a baby that wasn't going to go to sleep, with a husband that had to get up at 5:30 A.M., so what could he do for me because he's got to go to his job. And thinking, 'I must be really inferior, I can't do it!'"

When her baby was nine months old, Chris, who was still breast-feeding, caught a bad case of the flu, and her pediatrician recommended a rapid weaning because mother and baby were losing weight. Although Chris was never told this at the time, experts in the field of postpartum disorders now warn that weaning is another key time when women are most vulnerable to PPD episodes, particularly if the weaning is precipitous. "No one said anything [about that to me]," says Chris, "and I didn't connect that it would create a hormonal imbalance again. I tapered her from breastfeeding over the course of a week and a half, and then things got very strange." Chris's many symptoms included anxiety, insomnia, weepiness, and the inability to be alone. Her obstetrician diagnosed it as PMS and put her on natural progesterone suppositories. She got better in three days, stayed on them for three months, and did not have another problem.

In the meantime, she had seen a television program on PPD, and felt that the symptoms these women were describing resembled her experience more closely than did the symptoms that indicated PMS. When she questioned her doctor, she recalls, his response was, "Well, it's possible, but we don't like to make those kinds of diagnoses, plus it went away, it'll probably never happen again." But she had also read that PPD would be likely to recur with a second child, and since she wanted a second pregnancy, she asked her doctor about this also. His response then was, "It's treatable, and we're not even sure that's what you had." A psychiatrist, recommended because she had some interest and experience with postpartum cases, told her essentially the same thing: "She said, 'You have a one-in-three chance of it happening, and it won't be that bad, we'll give you medication, and don't worry about it.'"

At thirty-three weeks into her second pregnancy, Chris began developing the same symptoms again. (Joyce A. Venis notes that it is important for women to be aware of prepartum as well as postpartum disorders.) "I didn't know at the time that postpartum disorders, especially if you've had them before, can occur at the end stages of pregnancy," says Chris.* With a combination of antipsychotic medication, relaxation tapes, and the constant presence of a family member, she "got through" the rest of the pregnancy, but although she was trying for a vaginal birth after a cesarean section, she wound up having a second cesarean section because the doctors were concerned that it would be "too dangerous" to deliver the baby vaginally. Again, she and her new daughter did well nursing for three and a half months, but when she began to cut down on the number of nursings as the baby slept through the night, immediately with the onset of her first menstrual period postpartum, symptoms came back. (This, warns Dr. Woodle, is the second of the most vulnerable times for onset—the two weeks prior to the return of your period.) For Chris, symptoms came back very rapidly over the course of a day or two. Her psychiatrist, she recalls, "had a hard time getting a handle on which way to treat me." She was given progesterone suppositories again, in the same amount as the first time. "It helped, some, but not enough." She had gone, she recalls, "from being someone with no prescription medications in the house to someone who suddenly had multiple, very powerful drugs in the house. Three kinds of sleeping pills, an antipsychotic drug, lithium, hormones, and all I was getting was very grogged out, and still having all the symptoms. I kept saying to the doctors, 'I have two small children, I can't function like this,' and my family was here, because essentially I couldn't be by myself. I found that very distressing and humiliating. I saw myself very rapidly moving to having to go into a hospital because I was getting worse and worse."

Chris had attended a DAD group where she lived, and at this point a woman from DAD heard about her and called her, because Chris was one of the few women who had gone on to have a second child after having had a bad experience with PPD the first time around. Like

---

*When these disorders occur before birth, they are called prepartum disorders. Joyce Venis notes that it is important for women to be aware that prepartum do exist and that they require the same expertise and experience from caregivers as do postpartum disorders.

Chris, this woman had also developed PPD after weaning her baby. And this woman wanted to help. She mentioned to Chris that there was a doctor in Princeton, New Jersey, who had experience treating women who were planning second pregnancies and who did preventative as well as postpartum work with them. He was Dr. Ricardo J. Fernandez, a psychiatrist specializing in postpartum disorders. Joyce A. Venis, an R.N.C. certified in psychiatry, worked in conjunction with him at the Center for Postpartum Depression in Princeton.

# The Light at the End of the Tunnel: Finding Multifaceted, Sympathetic Treatment and Support

When Joyce A. Venis experienced postpartum depression in 1967, she went to twenty-two doctors before she found one who diagnosed her correctly and set her on the path to recovery. Today she is dedicated to helping other women avoid that frustration and despair.

With the growing public awareness and the growing number of PPD self-help support groups in the United States and Canada, it is much easier for women everywhere to call in for educational materials, referrals, or support—if they know where to call. For many women, a support group such as Depression After Delivery, Postpartum Adjustment for Mothers, or The Emotional You at the Santa Barbara Birth Resource Center are logical starting places.

Although Chris did not start by contacting DAD, it was through DAD that she reached a critical turning point, and she says she will be eternally grateful to the woman from DAD for giving her the name of the Princeton office, where, Dr. Fernandez says, "the approach we take is very biopsychosocial. A lot of biological intervention at first with a lot of support and education."

When Chris called late on a Friday afternoon, she was expecting to leave a message and struggle through the weekend on her own. "When Joyce called me back [that same afternoon], she had never seen me, never talked to me before, she spent easily thirty minutes on the phone with me, and gave me a number that I could call them at over the weekend. And this was before I had even gotten to their office. And that feeling that there was somebody there a phone call away really made the difference. They said, 'If you want to bring your children in, bring your children in,' and they were very receptive to the baby. You felt like this was a place for mothers, and that made a big difference to me."

When she went to see Dr. Fernandez, she recalls, "he disagreed as tactfully as he could with the treatment plan that had been put together for me in New York, and said that he would try a totally different approach." Feeling that she was just going from bad to worse, she decided to follow his plan. "First we have to see how much of this is depression, and how much is sleep deprivation," he told her. With the new medication, she was immediately able to sleep, and her symptoms improved. When he saw her a week later, he recommended that she remain on a small dose of this drug. Dr. Fernandez, she says, did not feel she was becoming psychotic, but was a classic PPD, fluctuating between the very agitated state and the more withdrawn depressed state. He recommended certain medication, and within two weeks she saw marked improvement. She was able to read, write, sleep normally, and about a month and a half later, was able to be alone again.

"As you start to get better," says Chris, "it's like, 'Hey, I feel a little better today, I actually had a good time out in the playground for a little while!' It doesn't happen all of a sudden, you just start to see these little glimmers of hope, and the good hours get longer and the bad hours get shorter and shorter."

But she was very traumatized by her experience.

"I felt like I had gone to the brink of hell and was just pulled back in the nick of time. My entire concept of myself, my self-esteem, was just destroyed. And then I was very angry and upset—why aren't more psychiatrists more informed? When you talk with Dr. Fernandez and Joyce, you look at the profile of people who are at risk for developing this, I had every one of the risk factors. My risk of developing this was so great, yet even when I sought out help, saying this had happened to me before, it was sort of pooh-poohed, and I don't think treated as openly and seriously as if I was, let's say, diabetic. If a woman wants to become pregnant with a history of diabetes, she would be counseled and followed, and really this would be considered a serious risk. One of the first things Dr. Fernandez said is for each successive pregnancy, you have to use a larger amount of the hormones. Progesterone in particular. I had felt that the progesterone had helped but not enough. I had actually gone and asked for more progesterone, and they were afraid to use it. When you look at the information from England you find they're using two and three and four times the amount with much better results. So I felt like I had tried to put together a team to prevent this from happening to me, and I think through general overall ignorance about this subject, I ended up having to go through this horrific experience not once, but twice. That's sort of where I'm at to date, and committed to trying to make as many people as knowledgeable about this as possible."

At Cass House Women's Center (Long Island), Mother Matters (South Bend), the Pregnancy and Postpartum Treatment Program (Chicago), the Duke Postpartum Depression Program (Durham), and the Postpartum Mood Disorders Clinic (Santa Barbara), the approach is also multifaceted. A treatment plan might include education; a local support group; individual therapy; medication; and in some cases, if a controlled environment is determined to be necessary, hospitalization. Women may also learn about diet, vitamin supplements, exercise, and relaxation techniques to relieve stress.

Jeanne Driscoll and psychiatrist Deborah Sichel work with pregnant and postpartum women in the Boston area. Dr. Sichel does the medical consultations and Driscoll does the therapy. "I'm very much in favor of empowering women," says Driscoll. "In a crisis you may have to intervene, but ultimately she has to decide and plan the care with you. It has to be a collaborative care model. First of all, it's her life, her body, her experience, and who am I to tell her what she feels?" Family members should also be involved in creating and implementing the plan.

Dr. Valerie Raskin and Dr. Laura Miller are psychiatrists who work with women at the University of Chicago's Pregnancy and Postpartum Treatment Program. "Some women find the idea of medication, for example, completely intolerable," says Dr. Raskin. "And that's someone who is going to be working probably in a support group and with a therapist who is not an M.D. Not always, but that may be the case. In my case, I coordinate the [treatment plan] and so does the patient."

On Long Island, New York, Dr. Joanne Woodle, obstetrician and psychiatrist, is medical director of Cass House Women's Center, an outpatient psychiatric practice specifically designed for women and for any hormonal-related emotional disorders related to pregnancy, postpartum, PMS, or menopausal problems. "I know about seven [programs like this in the country]. Postpartum depressions are something that occur in up to 20 percent of all women—not to the point where they will all need psychiatric intervention, but there's some significant degree of lack of functioning at a time when they really need to be at their peak. And yet, this is totally ignored."

Dr. Woodle has discovered that setting plays a crucial role in getting women to come in and/or remain in treatment. For a number of years, she had tried to run a postpartum unit out of a major university center. But "most medical settings," she found, were logistically too difficult for the women to handle: "Parking. What do you do about toddlers? What do you do about changing babies? These women didn't know what was the matter with them. If they did go to their doctors, the doctors for the most part would tell them to go out for dinner, get a babysitter, buy a new dress, and everything will be fine. They are not women with prior psychiatric histories. The idea of going to a mental health professional was absolutely appalling. Admitting that there was something wrong when you should be at your happiest, that you're totally out of control—if you're lucky enough to get them to the point where they're willing to seek help, then they're confronted with the mechanics of the system, and the vast majority of them wouldn't come back."

Dr. Woodle set about creating a setting in which the women felt more comfortable. "We've got a big old house, with an enormous playroom, and places for bottles and places for babies, and places for toddlers where they can just come in as if they were going to somebody's house next door. We try to reduce the stresses that surround seeking treatment for themselves. We also try to get them away from the stigma."

An important part of the treatment is encouraging the women to achieve a sense of "mastery of self." She teaches them that their PPD is hormonally mediated, that it will fluctuate, and that "probably one of the hardest things is knowing that when they start to feel better, all of a sudden they start to feel worse. They'll feel again reinforced in their sense of being a failure, and yet this is absolutely normal. They're going to cycle with their period. Sometimes it can be intense, much more short-lived, but it is intense." She has her patients do a lot of charting.

"Daily rating forms, weekly rating forms, so that they know exactly how they are responding to medication, to hormones. They respond markedly differently, even to food. They can't tolerate caffeine. Caffeine is an absolute killer in this.

"They come in feeling out of control, and even if I can completely remove the symptoms, they still feel out of control because it's now a pill that's controlling them, or a therapist or psychiatrist, and yet there are so many things that they can do themselves which make a major difference. And just putting the responsibility on them helps them tremendously."

In Salt Lake City, Utah, in the DAD support group Lynn Neff, C.S.W., runs out of St. Mark's Hospital, the hospital itself provides a grant for a free postpartum evaluation for new moms who could not otherwise afford one. "For some women," says Neff, "all they need is the evaluation, and off they go." Having the name and an understanding of what is happening to them physically relieves their fear and gives them the answers they need to carry on.

For cases where hospitalization is required, a mother/baby model opened in 1993 at the Center for Women's Development, a seventeen-bed inpatient unit at HRI Hospital in Brookline, Massachusetts. In the unit, staff can work with the mother/baby unit on bonding, breastfeeding, and self-esteem. Says Denise Elliott, Psy.D., the director of the center, "There's nothing more crucial than the mother being able to bond with the baby. If they're not together you can't possibly work on the bonding. If the mother doesn't bond, she's never going to feel good about her baby. And the baby's development is hampered without it. . . . One thing that they know very well in England is that it's devastating for the mother with postpartum psychiatric illness to be separated from an infant right at the moment when she's feeling her worst about her ability to parent, and she may even be phobic toward the baby. Her ability to parent-bond with the baby is at a real low point. To be separated from the infant carries the message to the woman that she's so poorly off, or she's in such bad shape that she really can't do it at all, and the baby's better off with somebody else, and that's the worst thing to have happen."

In the past, separation of mother and baby occurred routinely, in part because of attitudes about women's competency to mother when they were experiencing postpartum depression, and in part, says Dr.

Elliott, because of practical considerations. "People didn't want the liability, the noise, the hassle. They had their setup, it wasn't particularly geared toward women, as many institutions are not. I don't think anyone took it that seriously to go out of their way to make some provisions for this. Women's needs haven't really been that delineated and honored and served." At HRI, she says, this mother/baby unit represents their "political commitment to provide quality specialty services for women."

# Some Caveats in Choosing or Assessing Your Caregivers

*Ignorance and denial are the two greatest barriers to this problem.*
—Jane Honikman, Postpartum Support, International

As Chris learned, despite her numerous direct questions and cries for help, and the best efforts of her initial caregivers, the answers she got were not the ones she ultimately needed. "I think it's kind of an area that nobody wants to talk about. I think the obstetricians find it as frightening as the patient. And I think there's so little information and treatment and research." However, Dr. Valerie Raskin points out that as more women who are also mothers become doctors and psychiatrists, PPD becomes "more legitimate."

While more doctors may know about PPD now, or have heard the term, many still may not know exactly how to treat it. One reason is that the number of cases any individual doctor sees may be very small. Another is the stringent research requirements necessary before attitudes and official beliefs about the nature and treatment of PPD change. Still another is the fact that many practitioners fail to recognize it at all, or may treat only one aspect of it, depending on their own particular discipline.

When Joyce A. Venis and Dr. Fernandez lectured on the subject at one Pennsylvania hospital in 1990, one psychiatrist was present in the audience. One year later, when they lectured at a hospital in North Carolina with William S. Meyer, M.S.W., B.C.D., director of the postpartum support program at Duke University Medical Center, ninety to one hundred medical personnel were in attendance. "There is progress, but it is very slow," says Venis. "We get women a lot more quickly than we did before, and a lot less sick. I give credit to the women, because they are the ones who are more educated. I teach the women in both of my support groups to be educated consumers."

As educated consumers, it is important to understand why treatment may not be working for you if you feel it isn't, as well as why it is working when it is.

One of the problems women face in obtaining correct treatment is that the disciplines often take individual approaches and are not always coordinated, or the caregivers may not believe in the kind of multifaceted care model women really need. Ricardo Fernandez believes that "psychiatric disorders, whether they have recurrence at another time or not is not the point, but psychiatric disorders in the postpartum period require a certain type of attention that you wouldn't give a psychiatric disorder at some other point. . . . I see PPD as a biopsychosocial phenomenon. Biological, because definitely, it's hormonal. It's in the postpartum period, and we have to attend to that. Psychological, because most women—even more general human beings, adults—deal with parenting, deal with their own experience in life psychologically, in terms of their own childhoods and where they're going and where they've been when they have the child. . . . It's human nature. Whether it occurs within a year of having that child or within three months, it's different for different people. It's a psychological phenomenon in that we tend to deal with our baggage at those points in time. It's a socio-cultural phenomenon because of all the perceptions in the Western world and American society of how we see women, how we see motherhood, how we see parenting, the feminist movement, and all those other things."

If women don't receive the kind of treatment that takes all this into account, they may have a longer recovery, or may even drop out of treatment they know isn't working. Often, says Dr. Fernandez, when he sees failures in treatment referred to him by other clinicians, it is because they have failed to take a multifaceted approach.

Others in the field echo these concerns. Jeanne Driscoll estimates that 70 percent of the mental health community still does not consider PPD different from any other mental disorder. Seeking psychiatric help in a state of extreme postpartum distress, a woman may find herself talking about her childhood or being overmedicated without being monitored. Another danger with a strictly biochemical theory, *The New Our Bodies, Ourselves,* points out, is that "it may imply to the uninformed caregiver that PPD can be completely cured chemically with the help of mood altering drugs."[28]

If this is the only aspect being addressed in treatment, says Dr. Fernandez, that treatment may be incomplete and possibly ineffective. "[A woman] will go to a psychiatrist who prescribes medication for a major depression, refuses to recognize that it is occurring in the postpartum period, and really doesn't take in hormonal issues and doesn't take in the psychosocial piece. The patient takes the medication and basically the doctor says, 'Come back in a month,' and a month in a baby's life is an eternity. The changes that a child goes through in the first two months of life are enormous. So a lot of psychosocial stuff has occurred in that month that's not being attended to. Patients drop out of treatment."

In Utah, Lynn Neff makes a similar observation: "What I find now is that doctors are more aware, they are validating the problem, but women will call up their doctors and say what's going on, the doctor will . . . give them [a drug], but they're not monitored in any way. I think that's a real concern. The women don't really understand what's going on and I think the understanding is key. Understanding that it's organic, that it's not something they [brought on themselves by being a bad or inadequate mother]. Even if they have risk factors present [such as previous depressions, manic-depression, history of abuse, or others] it does not say that they themselves did anything wrong."

Dr. Joanne Woodle explains the roots of this attitude in the psychiatric community. When she was in medical school, she recalls that "in the psychiatric texts, they basically looked at pregnancy and the postpartum period as a time of major developmental stress in a woman's life that uncovered preexisting psychiatric illness. So if something shows up in the postpartum, [the belief was that] it was always there. And I think that's what we're dealing with. I think fortunately, at least for women with major psychiatric illness in the postpartum, their treatment by and large is appropriate, since they would be treated with the same medications. However, the message that they get is that you've got a chronic psychiatric illness. Now this may be true for some, but it's really not true for the vast majority."

For women seeking a psychologist to work with, Dr. Fernandez warns that psychologists who have not worked with PPD may have "a tendency to see it as only psychosocial. So you have a woman who's dealing with a major depression which implies a biological disorder that needs attention with medication, who is being asked to feel better by dealing with her psychological issues" at a time when she is really not able to do so. "These women drop out of treatment because as sick as they are—sick physically—they don't want to be told that this is all deeply rooted with their mothers."

Again, Lynn Neff concurs. "I think it's also hard for people to do their therapy, get in touch with their 'inner child' when they're very symptomatic. That's one of the things that happens when they go to a therapist who doesn't understand PPD, they start looking for the cause, or childhood issues, and they superimpose more trauma. They cause more trauma than they help."

William S. Meyer feels that "the things that are destructive are to begin making deep inquiries into a woman's childhood while she's in this condition, to suggest to somebody that these troubling thoughts have anything to do with her true or real feelings. [It's important] to not be investigative about trying to uncover some particular dynamic. What's needed is reassurance, support. We've found medications to be very helpful in many of these situations, because if a woman is having these kinds of thoughts, you're in a crisis situation. What you need is crisis intervention, not uncovering psychotherapy. If somebody's in distress for whatever reasons, this is the time to really shore things up and be there in a very supportive, helpful way."

# The Self-Help Movement

*If that woman from Depression After Delivery had not called me, I probably would have ended up in a psychiatric hospital. . . . . I'm eternally grateful to this woman, because she was well [by that time] and had just come to the group to see if she could offer anything to someone.*

—Chris

*One of the most effective and surely the safest way of combating PPD is through contact with other women who have experienced it or are at least*

*sympathetic to it. Getting in touch with other mothers is wonderfully thera-*
*peutic because it solves so many of the problems associated with PPD.*

—Martha Leathe, *Mothering*, Fall 1987

In 1985, anger motivated one mother who had experienced PPD to take action to help other mothers. Nancy Berchtold recalls that her own recovery had been a lonely one in which she did some "here and now" therapy, and felt very isolated from friends and former colleagues in the school where she had taught before her child was born. "There was one piece of paper," she remembers, "one article that the obstetrician gave my husband when I was just hospitalized, and it was written by James Hamilton and I held on to that piece of paper to legitimize what I was going through."

In addition to putting her depression and recovery into perspective, Berchtold says that she, like all new moms, whether they have PPD or not, also had to deal with new motherhood, adjustment to a different lifestyle, and the challenge of making new friends. She joined a local parent support group where she still did not feel entirely comfortable talking about her depression, but considered the group itself "really a godsend. I guess in my own way I started to see this group support was really important."

Then she learned of another woman nearby who was going through postpartum psychosis, having just returned to work after a three-month maternity leave, only to be out again one week later and back in the hospital with PPP. After a phone conversation with the woman's distraught husband and a visit to the woman herself, she says her "anger started bubbling up. . . . I don't think I really was quite in touch with what you might say would be the negative feelings, a sense of betrayal and anger. But that came. It came up probably when I was fully recovered. . . . I thought, 'I'm an educated person, I read a whole lot about babies before I had this baby, I never knew that anything like this could happen to anybody. Why did it happen, and why didn't the childbirth educators tell me, and why didn't the obstetrician talk about it?' I tried to get information on PPD, and there wasn't very much out there."

Galvanized by the lack of support, information, and recourse for herself and her friends, she set about starting her own PPD self-help/mutual aid group "so that other women don't have to suffer alone, so they don't have to be terrified, and other husbands don't have to be thinking that their wife will never be the same." In 1985 she started Depression After Delivery.

Berchtold's action, says Jeanne Driscoll, "gave women permission to scream and yell and share their agitation. And it's been that agitation of women that has changed [the PPD landscape and support]—unfortunately not fast enough or in large enough numbers."

Women had cause to be agitated. The medical research that might have helped them prepare for or cope better with PPD had been stifled or ignored. The changes women had made in their lifestyles during the 1980s had been done without any parallel changes in the social structure to support or accommodate their choices once children entered the picture. Within seven years, DAD had grown from one to more than eighty chapters throughout the United States and Canada.

The warmlines provided by the DAD chapters, the Pacific Post Partum Support Society, and other PPD self-help support groups throughout the world are key in helping women get immediate attention, understanding, and referrals to the right professionals, and should be one of the first means of recourse for a woman, or for her family if she is not able to call herself. The women you reach on the other end of the line have usually been through the experience themselves, and will help you get through the moment, allay your anxiety, assess your need, match you with a telephone volunteer, invite you to a meeting if you can wait, or get you immediate help if you need it.

In California, Jane Honikman runs a group called The Emotional You at the Santa Barbara Birth Resource Center. The group is "strictly self-help, drop-in, and free." Honikman does all the telephoning, and offers her name and phone number for any time a woman needs moral support. "They know they can always reach me in a time of crisis, and they do." The group is confidential and open to whatever they want to say. "I'm not a therapist. We're doing this strictly as moms to moms. . . . Getting support is also learning to accept support, and [acknowledging] that we are worthy of support. But at least some of the women come to my group because it's someplace to come to. They come and feel so great just once a week. And we laugh, we carry on, we moan and groan, whatever you want to do. It's good."

Andrea called Honikman when Andrea was pregnant with her second child. She had just moved into the area, and her first child was only ten months old. "It made me feel 100 percent better," she says, "because it seemed like somebody felt like listening, and they were women and they understood what was going on, and I wasn't the only one out there. Everybody's going through changes. The postpartum blues hit me real late, because I was pregnant, and I just fell in the dumps. Jane helped me out over the phone initially, and I went to the meeting, and felt so much better. I didn't have to be sitting home imagining all this stuff when I could be talking to someone to get out of these blues. I think that's what the culture is, that you have to carry this on your shoulders, the woman is the one who has to carry this, and you have to take it without rebuttal."

In Canada, the seeds for the Pacific Post Partum Support Society (PPPSS), the first postpartum self-help group, were sown in Vancouver in the early 1970s. In 1972, the Vancouver Crisis Center noticed they were getting a lot of calls from new moms in distress. They set up a project and advertised for new moms with postpartum distress. With the help of a graduate student, the Postpartum Counseling Service, a feminist, woman-centered, nonmedical model, was set up in which recovered women were helping those who were "really feeling down." Social worker Penny Handford came to work at the program, knowing very little about postpartum depression. Before long she recognized some common threads from her own life. "I realized that what I had been through with my kids was PPD, and I didn't know that. . . . It was an incredible growth experience for me. . . . I did a lot of reinterpreting of my experience, a lot of reunderstanding of what had happened to me." At PPPSS, says Handford, "Women are the experts in their depression. They're the experts in their recovery. A woman needs a safe, healing place where she can be supported by other women to explore her issues so she can negotiate her own healing and take up her own journey."

A second Canadian support service was founded in 1981, in Calgary. At the Calgary Post Partum Support Society, the philosophy is that every woman who comes in to the program has "what it takes to make it," says executive director Honey Watts. The program has three components: a telephone call for intake, the assignment of a volunteer who has herself resolved a depression, and weekly group meetings. There is also a monthly meeting for dads. CPPSS also follows a nonmedical model, and like PPPSS, defines the time frame in which postpartum distress may occur as the first three years of motherhood. "What we've found," says Watts, "is that the majority of women in our program are all perfectionists. They've got to be perfect, so they run themselves down." Working against the conditioning most women have of putting the needs of everyone else before their own, CPPSS encourages women to respect and focus on their own needs along with those of their infant and other family members. Weekly projects in which Mom does something just for herself, positive instead of negative feedback from group members, and the theory of "recycling" from Jean Illsley Clarke's and Connie Dawson's book *Growing Up Again*, which helps women to understand that their needs as new mothers parallel the developmental needs of their firstborn, are all part of the program at CPPSS.

## The Importance of a Support Network: Moms, Dads, Partners, Siblings, Families, and Friends

Despite the varying theories that exist about PPD, it seems fairly widely agreed that stress is a factor that exacerbates everything, and strong social supports and networks for the mother can be a key component of prevention and recovery. "I think that the model for nurturing and caring for our childbearing women would do a lot for the mental health of the family," says Jeanne Driscoll, while also warning that if a woman is predisposed to a chemical depression, it will happen anyway, regardless of how much support she has. If a woman is known to be at high risk, Driscoll will work with her prenatally to set up a support network based on what she can afford and how she can make it work, either as a preventive measure or to help her if she is distressed postpartum.

Chris, who had family support but not the essential education or treatment she needed during her crisis, feels that for borderline moms—"women who might have a little difficulty postpartum—having a good support network going may be all they need." For Chris, there was also the challenge to find the friendship and support of other women in her community. "Your feelings are so intensified while you're ill," she says, "but it still brings up a lot of issues that all women who are mothers in our society experience. Like isolation. Here I was, so ill, home with these children. I live in a community where I'd say a good 60 percent of the women choose to return to their careers. So the women who choose to stay home are very isolated. Women [who] go back to their careers are very pressured. I think that [making friends is] very important to being a parent today. Finding other women who are either working mothers, going through that stress, or women who have chosen to stay home and are experiencing that. You need that bond with women."

Medical anthropologist Dr. Laurence Kruckman has studied postpartum traditions in diverse cultures and concluded that where there was support for the new mom, including rites of passage and healing ceremonies, there was also what he called a "cushioning" effect that helped ease her adjustment through this transitional time in her life.[29] By comparison, in contemporary American culture, says Dana Raphael, "you're suddenly isolated from everything that was ever yours and you're a twenty-four-hour mama. And it is a frightening experience. Much of the depression I have seen has been the fear that goes with 'Can I handle it? What's it doing to me? Where am I going? What have I done?' No question that the introduction of a doula would be extremely useful, and has been, as have most support groups when that kind of thing happens."

When an episode of PPD or PPP hits, it is not just the mother who suffers. The entire family is affected. "We bring in everyone," says Jane Honikman, who leads The Emotional You groups. "Mother, siblings, fathers. This is not just a woman's issue." At the Postpartum Mood Disorders Clinic in California, Dr. Robert Hickman runs support groups for husbands of women suffering from postpartum depression or anxiety. They, too, need support, education, and information as they are called upon to take on additional anchoring roles in the family. "It's very hard for your spouse," says Chris. "They're frightened for you, they don't know how to help you, and it's more stress for your husband, who's calling home four or five times a day to check on you and is expected to go back to the outside world and function."

# Best of All Possible Worlds: Working Toward Prevention and Early Detection

*I certainly think PPD is stress-related and that just proves itself out over and over again. When I get a mom in my office who is two or three weeks postpartum and feeling really emotional and out of control, her recovery—with edu-*

*cation, support, and educating the spouse and if possible the family—is much greater than someone who is seven months postpartum and has kept it in and created a self-defeating behavior pattern. They're much harder to get through, and the threat of not knowing is tremendous.*

—Lynn Neff, DAD, Utah

"Every birth should elicit the response of the culture," says Jane Honikman. In the best of circumstances, she says, "we would be contacting and following up on a very regular basis every single birth in the United States. Don't go home to isolation and close the door and only emerge when you take this kid to the doctor. That's really what happens now. And who gets the present? It's the baby, it's not the mom. It's all part of that."

Education, outreach, and early recognition on a wide scale are needed for the public and for professionals and staff working with new mothers. Hospitals and birthing centers need only include a simple brochure on PPD in their dismissal packets, explaining the signs and symptoms of postpartum distress and offering a local or national support group telephone number. More in-depth materials, often requested by families at risk of or going through PPD, may be obtained through some of the centers specializing in PPD.

Ideally, screening for high risk for PPD should begin early, either during obstetrician/gynecologist or midwife visits, or during prenatal classes. Dr. Eugene Aron is an obstetrician in private practice at Newton-Wellesley Hospital in Newton, Massachusetts. His practice delivers fifty to seventy babies a month, and Dr. Aron has assumed a role as part of a team effort to screen his patients and identify and help prevent or treat PPD. His screening for women who may be at high risk for PPD begins with a woman's first obstetric visit. "When you identify those people at risk, the incidence of significant PPD drops dramatically," he says. If a woman has had a history of previous PPD, Dr. Aron asks if she is interested in obtaining a consult. "My main source of consults for that is Deborah Sichel [a psychiatrist specializing in PPD]. If [people have] had a problem in the past, we take those issues very, very seriously. We don't tell them that this is common. I don't say, 'Well, don't worry about it, it's just postpartum blues and you'll cry a little bit. Forget about it, you'll be okay.' We really try to tell people that it's a very, very real problem."

During the assessment interview at the first obstetric interview, Dr. Aron asks "specific questions related to emotional well-being, rather than just indirect questions. I will often just specifically ask, 'Are you feeling depressed? Are you feeling anxious?'" He will also ask general, nonspecific questions, and will repeat this inquiry once or twice during the course of the pregnancy. "If you identify somebody who you do think is at high risk, then I think it's absolutely essential to get an early consult with a psychiatrist who knows how to work with pregnant women. I don't think you can just call up any psychiatrist." An early consult allows the woman to establish a relationship with the psychiatrist, who, says Dr. Aron, is the primary contact for the new mom postpartum. Although he is available by telephone if a new mother needs him, he will not generally see the new mom for six weeks, so it is critical to have the psychiatrist playing the major role at that time.

When he discharges new moms from the hospital Dr. Aron also talks to the women "about how it's going to be. Potentially there are going to be some difficult times, some mood swings, and if there are periods of time when depression or sad feelings or bad feelings of any kind feel like they're more often than feeling in control, they should call me and talk about it. I reassure them that most people don't have a difficult time by far, but if they just have that option to call, I think it helps them to feel better. They know they can call if they're not feeling even and stable emotionally." In addition, nursing staff telephone each new mom a week after delivery to see how things are going.

At the six-week visit, Dr. Aron tries to "get a sense of what their sleep deprivation status is, how their relationship with their husband is, how they are doing with their one child or with their other children, how they are managing to get through the day, if they're back at work—just to get a sense of where they're at."

Along with some discussion of the postpartum period in general, PPD should also be addressed in prenatal classes. In the classes he runs at Duke University Medical Center, William S. Meyer respects the fact that many pregnant women do not want to hear in great detail about what they perceive to be negative pregnancy or postpartum experiences. He gives women a simple brochure on PPD to keep, so they will not feel that "no one ever told them" and they will have a reliable phone contact if they need help. He also stresses the positive aspects of having support during the upcoming transition. If a move can be postponed till after the baby is born, for example, he recommends that it be put off. "If not, [I tell them] how important it is to maintain ties to family and friends. I really try to speak very directly to the dads about how critical their support is. I talk with them about who's going to be there with them when they first get home from the hospital. It's a very personal decision and they've got to be honest with themselves about who they want to be there and for how long. I raise the possibility that if Dad can only be off for two weeks and if they're going to have somebody else, maybe he should take off the third and fourth week so that they have a full month's worth of support. I try to give them some practical things to think about, but also prepare them for the fact that it's a very big change."

If a woman is not or has not been identified as being at high risk for PPD, she may begin looking for help after her baby is born, when something seems to be going wrong. Self-help support groups like DAD are excellent starting places, as are the clinics and practices specializing in PPD, if there is one nearby.

In St. Louis, Dr. Christa Hines, a psychiatrist who works with postpartum depressed women, has written a model "New Mother's History" questionnaire, which includes important questions that often are not asked of new mothers. The questions address the woman's concept of what motherhood should be, her relationship with her own mother, her role models for mothering, her prior experience caring for children, and her own feelings about her child and being a mother. The very nature of such questions automatically gives the mom permission to admit a range of feelings no one may have asked her about before. The questions themselves validate what she's feeling, and in her responses may lie some key to early detection of her specific distress, as well as to her quicker recovery.

When women come in to the Center for Postpartum Depression in Princeton, "we look at that person holistically," says Joyce A. Venis. "It's not easy to follow a set pattern." They often check thyroid levels, depending on symptoms; they take a complete history, including history of PMS, and a family history. "The bottom line is you need to do a complete and total initial assessment, inclusive of everything from head to foot," says Venis.

The importance of asking the right questions is borne out in the Canadian experience as well. In Calgary, Honey Watts is working in several ways to promote early recognition of postpartum distress. She gives three-hour workshops with public health units in the city to help them understand "how to get beneath the [women's] smile, and understand their answers about how they are doing." These units have another chance to pick up problems when women come in for the baby's five- or six-month immunizations. This is also a time when many women are weaning, which can precipitate PPD. Watts has also been working in a midwifery pilot program connected to a local hospital, teaching midwives and other staff about postpartum depression.

Finally, for second-time moms: If you have had a history of PPD with a previous birth, it should be seriously addressed by your doctors if you are pregnant again, or want to become pregnant again. If they do not take it seriously, you might want to contact someone known to specialize in PPD for a second opinion or a referral. "Obstetricians need to seriously counsel women who come in who have a history of postpartum disorders and want to have a second child," says Chris. "Just like you would counsel a severe diabetic, or someone who had a heart attack in her first pregnancy. I don't think that was done with me."

# Resolution and Empowerment

*The perfect outcome of this is that it becomes a growth experience . . . it becomes another opportunity like a window to explore unresolved issues that you haven't looked at in your life until that point. If you get the support that you need, it's a real opportunity to do some real growing and come out of it as a fuller person . . . and get back in touch with your joy and love of life.*

—Penny Handford, PPPSS

As women resolve their postpartum depression, they may feel at times that they are having unexpected setbacks. That is part of the process. Jan Taylor felt this way as she recovered. "There were a few times that I questioned it, because I thought I was well, and then I'd have some more bouts with anxiety. My doctor explained that you go forward and then maybe take one step back, and then go forward again." In part, these fluctuations are hormonally mediated. "I guess when the panic attacks slowed down, and I knew that even though I was having them I was still going to survive them, then I began to know that I was okay. It was that realization that I didn't have to panic every time I was having an attack, that I knew I was getting well."

At the Pacific Post Partum Support Society, the list of criteria for recovery includes: subsiding of symptoms; more good days than bad days; no physical or mental abuse with the children; the woman's feeling that it's time to leave the group; agreement of the volunteer telephone match and group leader that it's time for her to go; and, if possible, the termination of any medication she was on.

Many women who have had and resolved a postpartum depression have gone on to become group facilitators or volunteers in PPD support groups, or to work in some other capacity helping women with PPD. Their words are probably the greatest source of reassurance and inspiration for other mothers going through a similar experience:

*Joyce A. Venis: "I have been so empowered by this experience. I feel that it's kind of a gift, that I can help other women. They can relate to me, and I can say, 'I understand your pain, but look what I did. Look what you can do—and I can help you.'"*

*Chris: "In taking care of myself, at first I felt very guilty—I'm at the doctor, and I can't really function that well—but it made me realize that if you're not well and you're not taking good care of yourself, you can't take care of anybody else. So now I have this urge to go around and tell people, 'Are you taking good care of yourself? Because you need to. It's okay to do that! You'll actually be happier if you do that.'"*

*Jane Honikman: "Mainly, I'm a mom who's been there, felt the pain, and can still empathize, and that you don't get in any book. . . . Mainly, it was supposed to be so wonderful, and it wasn't, and it was supposed to be easy and it wasn't, and everybody else seemed to be doing it better, and I wasn't, and all of that. But it was a personal experience. . . . [Now] we can really turn people around, and they go on and call us up again and say, 'Just want to let you know, you saved my life.' That's wonderful!"*

# *Notes*

1. Dr. Joanne Woodle, interview with the author.

2. James Alexander Hamilton, M.D., and Patricia Neel Harberger, eds., *Postpartum Psychiatric Illness: A Picture Puzzle* (Philadelphia: University of Pennsylvania Press, 1992), p. 5.

3. Cited in Jo Ann Robertson, "Sharing the Post-Partum Blues," in *Makara*, Vol. II, No. 2 (February-March 1977), p. 47.

4. Pacific Post Partum Support Society, *Post Partum Depression and Anxiety: A Self-Help Guide for Mothers* (1987), p. 3.

5. Deborah A. Sichel and Jeanne W. Driscoll, "Integrated Care of Hospitalized Women," in Hamilton and Harberger, p. 117.

6. James Alexander Hamilton, Patrica Neel Harberger, and Barbara L. Parry, "The Problem of Terminology," in Hamilton and Harberger, p. 38.

7. Dawn Gruen, *The New Parent: A Spectrum of Postpartum Adjustment* (Minneapolis: International Childbirth Education Association), p. 4.

8. Jan L. Campbell, "Maternity Blues: A Model for Biological Research," in Hamilton and Harberger, p. 90.

9. Gruen, p. 4.

10. Hamilton and Harberger, p. 36.

11. Gruen, p. 4.

12. Cited in *Post Partum Depression and Anxiety*, p. 3. (From B. Pitt, "Atypical Depression Following Childbirth," in *British Journal of Psychiatry*, Vol. 144 (November 1968), p. 1325–35.)

13. Polly Kornblith, "Postpartum Disorders," in *The Midwife Advocate*, Vol. VII, No. 1 (Winter-Spring 1990), p. 2.

14. *Post Partum Depression and Anxiety*, p. 28.

15. Gruen, p. 4.

16. Kornblith, p. 2.

17. Joyce A. Venis, "The Reality: Postpartum Disorders Exist," in *Connections*, Vol. I, No. 1 (April 1993), p. 2.

18. Gruen, p. 4.

19. Kornblith, p. 2.

20. Terra Ziporyn, "True Blue?" in *Harvard Health Letter*, Vol. 17, No. 4 (February 1992), p. 3.

21. Hamilton and Harberger, p. 18.

22. Ziporyn, p. 3.

23. Gardner, cited in "When Postpartum Fatigue Peaks," in *baby talk* (October 1990).

24. Boston Women's Health Book Collective, *The New Our Bodies, Ourselves* (New York: Simon & Schuster, 1984), p. 407.

25. *Update* (February 28, 1992), p. 5.

26. Debbie Field, "The Mother Myth: A Feminist Analysis of Post Partum Depression," in *Healthsharing: A Canadian Women's Health Quarterly* (Winter 1989), p. 17.

27. Gruen, p. 2.

28. *The New Our Bodies, Ourselves*, p. 407.

29. Laurence Kruckman, "Rituals and Support: An Anthropological View of Postpartum Depression," in Hamilton and Harberger, p. 138.

# *Resources*

The following resources are described in further detail in the following section:

## Self-Help Groups

Depression After Delivery
Postpartum Assistance for Mothers
PEP (Postpartum Education for Parents)

## Postpartum Care Services

UNITED STATES
Postpartum Health Alliance, Inc.

CANADA
Parent Development Centre
MOMS (Mothers Offering Mothers Support)
Pacific Post Partum Support Society

## Clinics/Treatment Centers Specializing in PPD/PPP

Cass House Women's Center
Princeton Family Care Associates
Center for Ante- and Postpartum Depression Disorders
Duke Postpartum Support Program
Mother Matters
Postpartum Stress Center
Women's Mental Health Services

## Inpatient Unit

The Center for Women's Development

## International Networking Organizations Specializing in PPD

Marcé Society
PASS-CAN (Postpartum Adjustment Support Services—Canada)
Postpartum Support International

## Videotapes

*Fragile Beginnings: Postpartum Mood and Anxiety Disorders*
*Heartache and Hope: Living Through Postpartum Depression*
*Postpartum Emotions: The Blues and Beyond*

## Books

*Overcoming Postpartum Depression and Anxiety*
*Postpartum Depression and Anxiety: A Self-Help Guide for Mothers*
*Postpartum Psychiatric Illness: A Picture Puzzle*
*Postpartum Survival Guide*
*This Isn't What I Expected*
*Women's Moods: What Every Woman Must Know About Hormones, the Brain, and Emotional Health*

## Pamphlets/Newsletters

*Connections*
*The New Parent: A Spectrum of Postpartum Adjustment*
*Postpartum Depression*

## Self-Help Groups

### Depression After Delivery (DAD, Inc.)

91 East Somerset Street
Raritan, NJ 08869
Information Request Line:
 (800) 944-4PPD
www.behavenet.com/dadinc

This is a nationwide nonprofit organization founded in 1985 to provide support and information for women with ante- and postpartum disorders and their families, and to promote nationwide awareness of mood and anxiety disorders surrounding childbearing. Their services include education, information, and referral to local DAD support groups and people who can be contacted by phone. DAD offers free information to the general public, professionals, and people who would like to become volunteers and start support groups. Membership in DAD includes newsletters on various themes, and current information.

### Postpartum Assistance for Mothers (PAM)

PAM East Bay
P.O. Box 20513
Castro Valley, CA 94546
Tel.: (510) 727-4610 (Shoshana
 Bennett, Ph.D.)

This group was started in 1987 by a woman who had PPD with her second child and had no support. PAM has monthly meetings, couples meetings, and a quarterly newsletter available to anyone who writes and asks to be on the mailing list. Leaders try to refer a mom to someone in the group who is experiencing the same symptoms she is. Latina women can be referred to Spanish-speaking women in the group. PAM volunteers will contact doctors if a woman finds it difficult to do so for herself. They will intervene if necessary, but their philosophy is that women make their own choices. Their goal is to help moms make informed decisions about medication, homeopathic remedies, childcare, and whatever else they might need. There are two support groups for mothers, which husbands, significant others, and mental health professionals are always welcome to attend. Support is available regardless of one's ability to pay.

### PEP (Postpartum Education for Parents)

P.O. Box 6154
Santa Barbara, CA 93160
Warmline: (805) 564-3888
www.sbpep.org

Weekly postpartum distress support groups for mothers, and groups for new parents are held by Jane Honikman, founder of Postpartum Support International. There is a 24-hour Warmline for one-to-one support and information about basic infant care and postpartum adjustment. Brochure available.

## Postpartum Care Services

UNITED STATES
**Postpartum Health Alliance, Inc.**
1193 Piedra Morada Drive
Pacific Palisades, CA 90272
Tel. (Northern CA): (408) 774-1464
Tel. (Southern CA): (310) 915-7028

A statewide nonprofit, all-volunteer organization that promotes awareness and understanding of mood and anxiety disorders experienced by postpartum women. Membership includes a warmline for information and support, and referrals. PHA also publishes the *California Postpartum Depression Resource Guide*.

CANADA

**Parent Development Centre**
Postpartum Support
2749 Sinai Avenue, SW
Calgary, Alberta T3E 7A9
Canada
Tel.: (403) 253-6722

PDC is a not-for-profit agency that provides emotional support to women experiencing a range of postpartum difficulties including depression, anxiety, and adjustment problems. Support is provided by volunteers who have lived the experience and who are trained and supervised by professional staff. Services include a facilitated weekly support group, telephone support, couples group, and educational presentations.

**MOMS (Mothers Offering Mothers Support)**
Parent Resource Centre
300 Goulburn Private
Ottawa, Ontario K1N 1C9
Canada
Tel.: (613) 565-2467
E-mail: prc@storm.ca

Run by the Ottawa/Carleton Health Department, this program offers weekly support groups as well as regular telephone contact for women experiencing PPD.

**Pacific Post Partum Support Society (PPPSS)**
Suite 104-1416 Commercial Drive
Vancouver, B.C. V5L 3X9 Canada
Tel.: (604) 255-7999
www.postpartum.org

The PPPSS is a pioneer organization working in the field of postpartum depression and adjustment. The society was founded over twenty-five years ago and uses a nonmedical, feminist model which considers the women themselves the experts on their depression and recovery. The PPPSS provides telephone assessments, referrals to community resources, weekly support groups, men's information nights, and free information packages for both the layperson and the professional.

The society has written and published a practical self-help guide entitled *Postpartum Depression and Anxiety: A Self-Help Guide for Mothers*, which is now in its fourth printing and is available in both English and French. Community training workshops in group facilitation and telephone support skills are also available through the PPPSS.

# Clinics/Treatment Centers Specializing in PPD/PPP

**Cass House Women's Center**
133 Quaker Path Road
East Setauket, NY 11733
Tel.: (516) 689-5664
Joanne Woodle, M.D.

Cass House was founded in 1989 by Joanne Woodle, M.D. The program saw more than five hundred new moms in 1992. ("For those who question the prevalence of these disorders," wrote Dr. Woodle in a PSI newsletter, "just provide services and watch what happens.") Cass House offers individual psychotherapy as well as a weekly new-mother group for moms experiencing PPD; they have a social worker on staff to do family counseling with spouses or siblings, and a nurse on staff who does lab work on the premises and also teaches Lamaze classes. Children are welcome, and a playroom and baby-sitting are available. They also have a hotline, telephone support, and a library of literature on PPD.

**Princeton Family Care Associates**
33 Witherspoon Street
Princeton, NJ 08542
Tel.: (609) 497-1144
Ricardo J. Fernandez, M.D.
Joyce A. Venis, R.N.C.
**Center for Ante- and Postpartum Depression Disorders**
2400 Chestnut Street, Suite 2203
Philadelphia, PA 19103
Ricardo J. Fernandez, M.D.
Barbara Lewin, M.D.

This outpatient practice specializing in PMS, menopause, and pre- and postpartum disorders takes a holistic approach to every mom and family member they see, and offers a multi-faceted treatment plan depending on her needs. The center offers individual counseling and therapy, telephone support, planning for a pregnancy following an episode of PPD, information about and support with medication, an extensive library of articles and materials on PPD, and Venis runs both a DAD support group and a PMS support group for women and their family members or significant others. Dr. Fernandez and Venis also offer in-services, lectures, and seminars on PPD to hospitals, parenting centers, and corporations concerned with employee education, as well as to a varied range of other interested facilities. Joyce A. Venis, RNC, is also vice-president of DAD (Depression After Delivery).

**Duke Postpartum Support Program**
Duke University Medical Center
P.O. Box 3812
Durham, NC 27710
Tel.: (919) 681-6840
William S. Meyer, M.S.W, B.C.D.

This program was founded by William Meyer in 1990. It offers evaluations, treatment, counseling, and no-fee support groups and has pediatric and obstetric/gynecological liaisons on staff. It has a full range of services for the mom who may just need some words of reassurance over the telephone and referral to a local support group and for moms who are experiencing a more serious depression. It also provides monthly talks on prevention of PPD to midpregnancy classes.

**Mother Matters**
Regional Center for Mother and
    Child Care at Memorial Hospital
615 North Michigan Street
South Bend, IN 46607
Tel.: (219) 284-3243
Jeanette O'Dell, R.N.C., M.S.

Mother Matters offers support to new mothers dealing with postpartum depression. The program was started in 1990 at Memorial Hospital's Regional Center for Mother and Child Care. Jeanette O'Dell is the coordinator and Deborah Allen the assistant coordinator. At Mother Matters new mothers suffering from depression learn that they are not alone, and that it is something that they can get through. The program offers telephone support, education about postpartum depression, assistance in planning for prevention of recurrences in future pregnancies, and referrals to appropriate counseling services if needed. They hold twice-monthly meetings to discuss such topics as what postpartum depression is, types of support that help, parenting techniques, relaxation and massage, and to talk informally about themselves and what they are experiencing. Because the goal of Mother Matters is to offer support to new mothers in order to promote family wellness, some meetings include others who are helping the mothers get through a difficult time.

**Postpartum Stress Center**
Rosemont Plaza
1062 Lancaster Avenue
Rosemont, PA 19010
Tel.: (610) 525-7527
Karen Kleiman, M.S.W.

This support and counseling service specializing in postpartum adjustment disorders was started in 1987 by Karen Kleiman, M.S.W. After an initial consultation, assessment, and psychiatric evaluation if necessary, the center offers a course of therapy aimed at helping the individual mom feel nurtured and strengthened, and regain the feeling of having "private time" for herself and her feelings. As stated in its brochure, "allowing yourself to take care of your needs, too, is a vital first step in your effort to put things back in place." Couples therapy is also available, and a deci-

sion for partners to participate in this process may be made at any point in the program. The service also offers referrals to local support groups, and a pregnancy support program to identify and support women at risk for PPD or stress.

**Women's Mental Health Services**
University of Illinois
912 South Wood Street
Chicago, IL 60612
Tel.: (312) 355-1223
Linda Grossman, Ph.D.
Laura Miller, M.D.
Katherine Tracy, M.D.

A woman goes through many changes during her lifetime. Changes such as pregnancy, having a family, getting a new job, and menopause can affect her both physically and mentally. To meet the unique mental health needs of women, UIC Medical Center's Department of Psychiatry has developed a national award-winning program specifically for women. Because women and men do not respond to medication in the same way due to hormonal differences and other factors, the interdisciplinary team of professionals specializes in considering these factors when prescribing medication and therapy. The staff includes psychiatrists, psychologists, social workers, nurses, occupational therapists, and mental health counselors who actively conduct research and publish articles on women's health issues. The Women's Services program recently won the Gold Achievement Award of the American Psychiatric Association.

# Inpatient Unit

## The Center for Women's Development
HRI Hospital
227 Babcock Street
Brookline, MA 02446
Tel.: (617) 731-3200
Hotline: (800) 828-3934
Denise Elliott, Psy.D., director

In January 1993 this women's inpatient unit opened a mother/baby specialty wing with a nursery for women suffering from PPD or PPP. Services are provided by specially trained mother/baby nursing staff who work with the mother/baby couple. The program also offers groups for individual moms, groups for mother/baby pairs, plus individual and family therapy. The unit can accommodate up to four mother/baby pairs at a time.

# International Networking Organizations Specializing in PPD

## Marcé Society
c/o Dr. Vivette Glover-Treasurer
Division of Paediatrics, Obstetrics, and Gynaecology
Imperial College School of Medicine
Queen Charlotte's and Chelsea Hospital
Goldhawk Road
London W6 0XG
United Kingdom
Tel.: 44 (0) 181-741-7407
E-mail: info@marcesoc.fsnet.co.uk
www.marcesoc.org

Founded in England in 1980 and named for Dr. Louis Victor Marcé, this is a society of professionals dedicated to improving the understanding, prevention, and treatment of mental illness related to childbearing. The society sponsors international conferences, and members receive the *Marcé Bulletin*, which features news, articles, and reviews of recent scientific research.

## PASS-CAN (Postpartum Adjustment Support Services—Canada)
P.O. Box 7282, Station Main
Oakville, ON L6J 6L6
Canada
Tel.: (705) 844-9009
Rita Van Dooren, C.S.W.
Christine Long, Executive Director

Postpartum Adjustment Support Services–Canada (PASS–CAN) links Canadian support services to ensure that families experiencing the challenges of new parenthood will get up-to-date information, education, support, and services. Through PASS–CAN, people can be linked with other support resources throughout the country. Another goal is to end the silence and ignorance surrounding PPD by addressing the stigma, shame, and lack of resources. Services include counseling, phone buddies, individual mother-and-infant bonding; couple counseling, support groups for moms, information nights for dads, educational packages, referrals, public speaking, public education, and workshops.

## Postpartum Support International (PSI)
927 North Kellogg Avenue
Santa Barbara, CA 93111
Tel.: (805) 967-7636

E-mail: jhonikman@earthlink.net
Jane Honikman, Founding Director
For resources, referrals, and research:
www.postpartum.net

PSI is a worldwide networking
group whose goal is to provide education and information about mental
health issues of childbearing. The
group focuses on postpartum mental
health and social supports and attempts to increase awareness about
the emotional changes often experienced by mothers during pregnancy
and after the arrival of a baby. They
advocate for women and families,
promote research, and welcome as
members individuals and organizations worldwide "who are interested
in promoting healthy postpartum development." PSI offers a free
brochure, a newsletter, a library of
materials available on loan to members, and notification of its annual
conference. It also serves as a clearinghouse for women seeking help elsewhere in the world.

## Videotapes

*Fragile Beginnings: Postpartum Mood
and Anxiety Disorders*
Distributed by Injoy Productions
Tel.: (800) 362-2082 or fax: (303)449-
8788 (for Visa and MasterCard
orders only)

Jeanne Driscoll, R.N., M.S., C.S.,
and Deborah Sichel, M.D., are fea-
tured on this tape, which covers the
four postpartum psychiatric illnesses:
postpartum depression, postpartum
obsessive-compulsive disorder, postpartum panic disorder, and postpartum psychosis. Topics include
symptoms and how they can be correctly identified and treated, breast-

feeding, and family support. The goal
of the tape, says Driscoll, "is to educate and promote hope" as women
share stories and identification and
treatment strategies.

*Heartache and Hope: Living Through
Postpartum Depression*
Parent Development Centre
Tel.: (403) 253-6722

This hopeful video profiles families who share their experiences of
heartache and hope as they lived
through postpartum depressions. The
goal of this video is to heighten
awareness of postpartum depression,
encourage families to speak out about
their difficult transitions to parenting,
and provide strategies for recovery.
The original music for this video was
written by one of the fathers as part of
his journey to hope.

*Postpartum Emotions: The Blues and
Beyond*
Family Experiences Productions, Inc.
Tel.: (512) 338-1318
Fax: (512) 338-1564

Author Ann Dunnewold, Ph.D.,
brings her years of experience in the
treatment of postpartum disorders to
this recent video that helps new
mothers understand what is happening to them when they face difficulties
in adjusting to life with a newborn.

## Books

*Overcoming Postpartum Depression
and Anxiety*
Linda Sebastian
Addicus Books

Linda Sebastian, a psychiatric nurse
with twenty-five years of experience,
provides a comprehensive guide to

recognizing and treating the mood and anxiety problems that can be an unexpected part of giving birth.

## *Postpartum Depression and Anxiety: A Self-Help Guide for Mothers*
Pacific Post Partum Support Society

Prepared by women from one of the oldest self-help PPD groups in North America, this is a practical, comforting guide for women who are or think they are experiencing PPD. It is based on the experience of thousands of women sharing their thoughts and feelings about what helps get through this difficult time. The book includes sections "What Is PPD?"; "Why Me?"; "What Helps Get Through It?"; "Getting Help from Professionals"; "Recovery Process"; and "Resources."

## *Postpartum Psychiatric Illness: A Picture Puzzle*
Edited by James Alexander Hamilton and Patricia Neel Harberger
University of Pennsylvania Press

Published in 1991, this book brings together contributions from thirty-one leading experts in the field and should be of interest to professionals as well as to women or families suffering from postpartum emotional difficulties.

## *Postpartum Survival Guide*
Anne Dunnewold, Ph.D.
Diane G. Sanford, Ph.D.
New Harbinger Publications

Written by two psychologists, this book offers practical information and coping strategies for new moms and families. Topics covered include types of postpartum adjustment problems;

risk factors; and help for single moms, older moms, adoptive moms, moms with special needs, and fathers and other caregivers.

## *This Isn't What I Expected*
Karen Kleiman and Valerie Raskin
Bantam Books

A mother's guide to understanding postpartum emotional distress, with useful advice on how to alleviate it, and where to find support and help.

## *Women's Moods: What Every Woman Must Know About Hormones, the Brain, and Emotional Health*
Deborah Sichel, M.D.
Jeanne Watson Driscoll, M.S., R.N., C.S.
William Morrow and Company

This book by two experts in the field of PPD offers a new understanding of the female brain-body connection, explaining why a woman's unique brain and hormone chemistry make her vulnerable to mood problems at critical times in her life, including after she's had a new baby. The authors also share their unique self-care program and give women tools to support healthy moods and get help if they need it.

# Pamphlets/Newsletters

## *Connections*
Women's Health Connection
P.O. Box 6338
Madison, WI 53716-0338

*Connections* is a publication "dedicated to the education and management of PMS, menopause, infertility, postpartum depression, and other hormone-related disorders."

*The New Parent: A Spectrum of Postpartum Adjustment*
Dawn Gruen, ACSW
International Childbirth Education Association

This eight-page pamphlet helps new parents prepare for some of the adjustments of new parenthood, from the new demands on your time, feelings of loss, and changes in the couple's relationship, to the more distressing emotional difficulties. Gruen defines the stages of emotional difficulty, from "baby blues" to the most severe postpartum psychosis; looks at theories about causes; outlines symptoms, risk factors, and barriers to treatment; and gives thirteen very helpful suggestions for those who may be or think they may be suffering from PPD.

*Postpartum Depression*
American College of Obstetricians and Gynecologists (ACOG)
Patient pamphlet AP 091
Tel.: (800) 673-8444

This is a long, informative patient education pamphlet written and published by the Committee on Patient Education of the ACOG. Sample copies are available free by phoning the 800 number above.

# 6.

# GOING BACK TO WORK FOR PAY

*What Does the Workplace Offer You?*

••••••

*I don't think there's much public understanding of what it's like to have a new baby and go back to work. It's a really tough process.*

—Linda Tarr-Whelan, B.S.N., M.S.
president/executive director, Center for Policy Alternatives

*We compel working women to pretend that maternity is not a big issue, whereas it is central to life.*

—Felice Schwartz, *Breaking with Tradition:*
*Women and Work, The New Facts of Life*

*Women don't want to talk about flextime, they want to talk about the deeper issues.*

—Helene Klodawsky, mother and filmmaker, Toronto

## Motherwork/Otherwork

You're having a baby. Maybe it's your first. Maybe it's your second. In any case, there's already a lot on your mind. Labor and delivery. Breast-feeding. Doulas. Casseroles. Too many relatives. Too few relatives. Birth plans. Hormones. If a return to work outside the home is part of your plan, throw a few more items into the mix: Adequate leave time. Job security. Wage replacement. Professional image. On-site infant care. Infant care referrals. Worksite support groups. Flexibility. Managers. Sticky floors. Glass ceilings. Phase-in return.

In 1990 in the United States, 51 percent of mothers of infants under twelve months of age were in the paid labor force,[1] either full-time or part-time, by choice or of necessity. Some of these brand-new mothers had two weeks' leave; some had six; some had twelve; some had none. And some had more—six months or, in some instances, up to a year or longer, depending on the employer. Some came back to raises and reduced schedules. Some came back to no job at all and to canceled insurance benefits. Many came back to a position between these two extremes.

If you are, or are about to become one of these moms, not only are you adjusting to new motherhood, but you may also be simultaneously trying to define a new relationship with work—or, in some cases, struggling to maintain the guise of the old, despite a whole new set of ground rules that the workplace often may not acknowledge or respect.*

As you integrate motherhood into your life, are you doing so within the context of a workplace that seems to be with you, or against you? Hearing you, or ignoring you? Respecting your prebaby talents, ambitions, and abilities, or assuming that they went down the drain with the newborn's bathwater? Are they acting as if you haven't really had a baby at all, or are they offering you support and understanding during this vulnerable time in your life?

"It's only been very recently that employers were willing to talk about breaking down the walls between work and the rest of your life, particularly family," says Barney Olmstead, cofounder of New Ways to Work, a San Francisco nonprofit organization that explores alternative work arrangements. "You were not supposed to bring any of that into

---

*Until the passage of the Family and Medical Leave Act of 1993, the United States did not have even minimal family or parental leave guaranteed at the federal level. At the federal level in Canada, "a new mother with at least twenty weeks of insurable employment may take seventeen weeks of maternity leave paid at 60% of her previous earnings until a ceiling payment is reached. The start date of this leave is flexible and many women remain at their paid jobs until just before the baby is due to maximize time at home with their infants. An additional ten weeks of parental leave is available to either parent, natural or adoptive, again paid at 60% of previous earnings until the ceiling payment is reached."[2] Robert Glossop, director of programs at the Vanier Institute of the Family in Ottawa, notes that variations on this leave have been introduced "either by provincial governments or private employers with negotiated contracts. Quebec is the only jurisdiction in Canada that provides an enriched set of leave benefits to new parents as a matter of statute." On the European front, in September 1992, the European Community Commission issued a directive "requiring that all member countries provide a standard minimum of fourteen weeks paid maternity leave."[3]

the workplace. As more and more dual-paycheck, dual-careers became the norm, that became impossible. Then you began to get the sandwich generation issue and it became even more impossible. Employers have finally realized it is a bottom-line issue, they're beginning to attach cost to things like turnover and recruitment and feel that retention is a positive bottom-line issue."

While half a dozen years ago, the concerns and needs of mothers of infants in the workplace were still seen largely as a "woman's issue," today they are gradually being recognized—in some quarters, at least—as a family and societal issue. But the old patterns are changing slowly. Even in the best of companies, women say the messages can be mixed: Some companies may offer progressive family-friendly policies, but still publicly praise the woman who is on a business trip halfway around the world ten days after giving birth; even when the policies are in place, they may not always translate in practice as well as they read on paper. "We are just at the beginning," says one mom who had a very generous full year of family leave, including flexible hours on her return, but came back to an unacknowledged demotion in her duties. Sometimes, even after all the logistics of the postpartum leave are in place, what often still seems to be missing from this overall picture is the individual woman herself, her needs, and her feelings.

Cheryl left a job she loved at one of the largest cosmetics companies in the world after her child was born. Her comments may sound familiar: During her unsuccessful four-month prenatal attempt to establish a satisfactory leave-and-return arrangement for herself, she says that she hadn't "run into very many organizations that offer help for the individual mother—seminars, lectures, groups that you can join to help new mothers with this working/caring situation that we're all in. All I seem to sense from the women that I speak with is this sense of dilemma."

On the positive side are companies that offer enough flexibility and range of options for women to make or alter their final decision even after their baby is born; organizations that help women find part-time and alternate work arrangements and are working to integrate these options into the standard practice of the workplace; some new and innovative workshops that do help individual women through the changes of motherhood in the workplace; and family-friendly legislative advances on local, state, and federal levels.

If you are going back to work after the birth or adoption of a new-born, a great number of work-related (and potentially stressful) issues may concern you, in addition to all the other adjustments of new motherhood. Some may concern you before your baby is born; some may not occur to you until after the baby arrives.

Some questions may be practical: What kind of parental leave policy does your workplace offer, and what will you be eligible for? Is the policy clearly spelled out? Will you have to create a patchwork leave of disability and vacation time (in some extreme circumstances, even having to borrow time from a coworker), or is reasonable family leave provided? How will passage of the Family and Medical Leave Act of 1993 affect your leave time? How much time will be paid? How much unpaid? Will you have job security—that is, are you guaranteed your same or a comparable job and salary when you come back to work? How long will your leave be, and what if you need more time? Will your benefits continue while you're on leave? How about your seniority—will that be protected, or will it be lost? How will you arrange child care for your new baby? If you are nursing, how will you continue to nurse your baby once you go back to work? Will your office have accommodations for pumping milk? Will you have a flexible or phase-in schedule available to you on your return? What arrangements will you or your workplace make for days when your child or her caregiver is sick?

If you are adopting, how much leave time will you be entitled to? Are biological mothers at your worksite covered by disability insurance for pregnancy and childbirth, and if so, will there be any wage replacement available for you when you adopt? Will your employer's health insurance cover your new child, or will you have to seek out other coverage?

Some questions may be more abstract, unknowable, and unanswerable until the moment arrives, but still worth pondering nonetheless: Will your leave be long enough for you to build up confidence in your parenting skills, so that you know what you want in a caregiver, and can face a return to work feeling secure and ready? Where, in your best-case-scenario visions, do you want to be emotionally, psychologically, and practically at the end of your leave so you can ensure as much as possible a successful transition back to work? What will help you to accomplish this? How might you feel about separating from your infant, especially if your leave is short? How have other women felt about work after the birth of a first baby? How might your personal goals or definition of success change?

Finally, if you need legal, emotional, or practical help with any of these work-related issues, who can you turn to for answers and support?

As you plan your postpartum network, if work for pay outside the home is part of the picture, the answers to some of your work-related questions should become part of your postpartum plan; the names of people who helped you with these questions prenatally and can continue to help you after the baby arrives should be part of your postpartum support network.

# To Return or Not to Return

*The first thing you have to understand is that nobody knows what she's going to really want to do until after the child is born. That's the one thing you should try not to hold anybody to.*

—Joan Hoskins, dean, Division of Continuing Education, Community College of Denver

Experts and new mothers alike will be the first to tell you that despite all your planning, you may not really know how you feel about going back to work until after your baby has arrived. Fitting yourself into that new identity before you actually experience it may turn out to be a far cry from the real thing. Hard-won work arrangements that seemed satisfactory three months earlier may go out the window once the baby comes, and the difference between what you thought you'd feel postpartum and what you actually do feel may surprise you. Whether a change in plan is a realistic option at that point or not, it is not uncommon for new mothers to change their minds about work—either for or against return—once their children are born.

Your feelings about how you want to handle mothering and work outside the home are as personal and unpredictable as everything else about new motherhood. Many factors affect the decision-making process. Some you know about and try to consider sensibly: economic necessity, childcare arrangements, workplace options. Others cannot be imagined beforehand and may defy sensible solutions. There is what one mom called "that incredible falling in love" with the baby. There is fatigue and exhaustion, particularly if you have a short leave and an inflexible workplace. There may be concern over who will be able to care for the baby as well as you do. There may be ambivalence—both about baby and about work. There are altered priorities. There is the cabin fever that makes some moms want to reconnect to the adult world as soon as they can. For some, especially women who are able to go back to phase-in work after a leave that has been adequate in length, work may offer a structure and familiar adult identity that is a relief amid the feelings and demands of new motherhood. Work also offers that very welcome paycheck.

While many new moms still face all-or-nothing options when it comes to a return to work, some women are finding that new flexibility at the workplace enhances their ability to make a satisfactory long-term decision, even though it may, in some cases, mean changing their job status. It also enables the workplace to retain valued employees. Regina works for Stride Rite Corporation, one of the highest-rated companies in the annual *Working Mother Magazine* survey that ranks the top hundred companies nationwide. Her contemplation of work-life after baby began months before her baby was born. The questions she grappled with during her third trimester may sound familiar to you, especially if you have a workplace that offers some leeway.

"In approaching motherhood," she recalls, "I really didn't know what to expect. I was kind of tenuous. I thought, 'Will I be coming back to a full-time position? Should I? What about all the work that I've done—do you just switch gears?'" She knew of only one other woman in the company who had taken a family leave. "I had lunch with this individual around my sixth, seventh month. Even though it's a policy that's on the books and available to employees, there was still an apprehensiveness for her just to speak openly, to say, 'This was what I did and this was how I did it.' It was almost like, 'This is so different from the norm, I don't know how well accepted it is to do this, but this is how I approached it.'"

During their talk, Regina's colleague gave her some sense of the adjustment involved in balancing her personal and professional time when there was also a new baby in the picture.

"[My colleague] took the maternity leave time and took her vaca-

tion so that she would just have time, not knowing what she was expecting [postpartum to be like]. I felt the same way. After the maternity
leave, I had vacation time. If I chose not to use the vacation, I could
have come back earlier. But if I needed it, it was there, and I had that
cushion of time."

Regina knew that she wanted to come back, but wasn't sure about
the time commitment she would be ready or able to make. Up until the
birth of her son, she had worked full-time in the human resources office (where, she notes, she was frequently queried by women from
other companies who felt torn by the lack of flexibility at their own
worksites and were calling Stride Rite for advice).

"As it turned out for me personally, I had an emergency C-section,
and it took me just a little bit longer to get out of the starting gate and
get into the new role." She took her leave and vacation time, and then
had the option of tacking on up to eighteen weeks of family leave time
or coming back to a part-time position. "I just felt like I enjoyed taking
the slower time to get back to how I used to approach things, because I
really did fully absorb myself 110 percent when I was here. I just had to
see what balance would be right. I wasn't quite sure whether or not I
wanted to work in a full-time capacity, and I maintained the part-time
schedule of two days and then gradually increased it up to three days a
week." She moved up to five days for three months, and "at that point
decided that it was in my best interest to do a different work and family balance, and elected to seek a part-time position if it was available. I
have now plateaued into a narrower focus as a compensation manager,
which is basically more do-able in a part-time capacity."

One word of warning comes from work and family experts, management, and mothers themselves: If you know for sure from the beginning that you won't be coming back to work, they suggest that it is
best to be honest with your employer and say so up front. "When
women stall and stall and then don't come back," says one new mother,
"that makes it hard for all mothers." If companies have some lead time
in preparing for your departure, and know how to plan accordingly,
suggests Judsen Culbreth, editor in chief of *Working Mother Magazine*,
some may actually offer an amicable separation, continuing your benefits for a period even after you leave.

Finally, Barney Olmstead of New Ways to Work reiterates that "if it's
a first child, I keep hearing again and again that after they've had the

baby, women are sort of surprised that they don't want to go back to work that fast. They didn't expect that. It's worth talking with some of your friends who have had babies about that so that you understand what a powerful feeling it is. So you expect it in yourself a little bit more when it hits you, and you begin contingency planning, and keeping your options open, and seeing what might be available if you really work toward it. [It's also important] to feel that you can work toward it—that [other] people have negotiated it, they are continuing to, more and more of them."

## Giving Your Workplace the News

*I told them right away, I was so ecstatic. . . . When the news became public in the company, I was immediately treated as a liability.*

—Cheryl

*I didn't want anyone to know I was pregnant. . . . I didn't feel people would take me seriously as wanting to stay on the job.*

—Elizabeth

Strategies about how to tell your workplace, how to plan or negotiate a return, and how to do it successfully against all odds may occupy you long before your baby is born, particularly if there are no flexible options or clear policies. Along with doing your regular job, taking good care of yourself, practicing Lamaze breathing, and preparing for the baby, you may also find yourself somewhere around the fifth or sixth month suddenly doing full-scale research projects on your legal rights, or turning yourself into a work/family expert, penning proposal after proposal in a harrowing and stressful effort to sell an inflexible employer on a flextime schedule for your return. If you are planning to adopt, you may need to let your workplace know that you plan to adopt at some point, and start exploring leave options and health-care coverage, and start negotiating with them as soon as your paperwork is signed, even though you may not know whether your ultimate time frame for getting the baby will be a month or a year or more from the day you start.

In *Breaking with Tradition*, Felice Schwartz writes about the "conspiracy of silence" that still shrouds motherhood in the workplace. She notes that many working women conceal the fact that they are pregnant because they will be perceived to be in a weakened position, and they will have less leverage in negotiations. For the mother-to-be, regardless of her intentions to return and ability to work, the physical and emotional changes of pregnancy are still largely "inadmissible" in the workplace, writes Schwartz, whether it be joy, anxiety, or just plain fatigue.

Several women talked about how they felt as they gave their workplace the news:

**Elizabeth:** *Elizabeth, a New York–based corporate lawyer, postponed announcing her pregnancy as long as she could. "I didn't want anybody to know I was pregnant. I didn't feel that people would take me seriously as wanting to stay on the job. I had just gotten a promotion and considered myself sort of on the way up in the company. I was the only woman in the legal department and truly the second-highest woman executive in the company. The company has about four hundred people, and the executives are probably about sixty people, including all of the management. I was one of two women executives—which doesn't say much for the company. I was very afraid that I would not be taken seriously, that once I had the child and was out for a while, somebody else would jump in my place, that people would figure that I was going to stay home and take care of the child, and I was very worried about that. There was no policy in my company because it had never happened—to anyone in the executive ranks—because there weren't any execs who were women. . . . Finally, when I got up to four months and couldn't fit in any of my clothes, I had to tell my boss, and I really worried about how I was going to tell him. I had talked with a couple of outside lawyers whom I work with and they were of the old school that had their child, went back in three weeks, worked all the way through the time they were in the hospital, or at least told everybody they did, and pretended like there was no difference. So that's what I proposed to do."*

*Although Elizabeth continued to work up through her last day before delivery, determined to "outmacho the men," ironically, her boss, a man who had himself had a family, recognized her need for recovery time, and told her she would not be ready to come back in three weeks.*

He suggested that she take two months and that the company plan on working around her absence during that two-month period. "I felt very relieved that he said, 'You physically won't be able to do it.'"

**Jill:** In some cases, even in larger companies with policies that look exemplary on paper, responses might be subtle or unspoken. Policy may say one thing; reality may be a horse of a different color. Jill, a magazine editor in New York, worked for a company that offered a very generous family leave policy. However, despite the full year she was able to take off and the flexible way she was able to arrange her return, working part-time at home and part-time in the office, she noticed that "from the instant that I started to show, things changed. I was passed over for stock options for the first time in years. . . . When it came time for my raise, I got not a horrible raise—what [my boss] termed an 'average raise.' It was the lowest raise I'd ever gotten. Things like that all along the line."

**Cheryl:** Cheryl had been working for six years for one of the largest cosmetics companies in the world when she became pregnant in 1989. The company was inflexible in its family leave policy, offering just the six or eight weeks' disability plus vacation time.* She told her manager immediately. "I basically didn't wait to tell people because I had a job where I had to travel a lot, there was carrying of large cases . . . and I wanted people to know that I was pregnant because I didn't know how I would react physically with the job and pregnancy. I wanted people to know also because I was so excited, I couldn't keep it to myself. I was really ecstatic about it. I still don't know how people manage to wait three months. I did notice that there was just a difference in the way I was treated after people did find out that I was pregnant. . . . When the news became public in the company, I was immediately treated as a li-

*For many women, maternity/parental leave falls under the disability mantle, explains Helen Norton, deputy director of the Work and Families Program at the Women's Legal Defense Fund, because "a lot of employers had medical leaves or health insurance policies that covered all sorts of conditions except pregnancy, so Congress and women's rights advocates were trying to find a way to make sure that pregnancy—to the extent that it is—is clearly a medical condition that received coverage on an equal basis. The net result is that some women are now legally entitled to be treated in the same way as other workers with a temporary disability. So if the employer chooses to provide disability leave, then women in that workforce are entitled to disability leave just like everybody else." Adoptive mothers, however, are not covered by disability coverage.

*ability. It's difficult to specify why I felt that way, it wasn't that any-thing specific was said or done. People wanted to know if I would be coming back."*

**Spalding:** *Spalding worked at a university medical center in South Carolina. She knew she would be entitled to six weeks' leave and told her boss immediately. "Right off the bat! The day I found out, really. I wasn't really concerned. It wasn't as much of an issue. I had read in magazines about timing it just right. I worked for the state and they had defined policies on all this and it wasn't as if it was going to cause some sort of problem. . . . You got six weeks off; however, you could put it together. Some of mine was sick leave and some was vacation time. If you had enough sick leave to take it all as sick leave, then you could do that. If not, you had to take vacation time. You only got as much time as you had accrued, but there is something within the state system where if someone needs to, you may borrow sick leave from another person. I've never run across anybody that's had to do that for mater-nity leave. I called the human resources department and said, 'What if at the end of six weeks I decide I'm really not ready to come back, and need a couple of weeks?' She said, 'Well, we really discourage that. Six weeks is all we allow for maternity leave, but if there is a problem, it can be worked out but without pay.'"*

# Defining and Negotiating Your Leave and Return Schedules

Along with making the announcement at your workplace may go the working out of your leave and return schedules.

In Denver, Joan Hoskins is former executive director of the Work and Family Resource Center, a program of the Community College of Denver where Hoskins is now dean of continuing education. The center contracts with local corporations and national resource and referral contractors to provide enhanced resource and referral information to parents and families.

"Women begin calling [the center] certainly by the third trimester," says Hoskins, "and they say, 'I really want to think this through.' They really want to talk to somebody. Then once they've had their children, I think the stress is really there, because even if they've had absolutely no intention or desire to stay home, once they have that child, that very often changes. We counsel employers all the time. They're very frustrated and saying, 'This woman was going to come back to work, we had all that set up, and then all that changed.' If you've never had a baby before, you don't know what you're going to feel and want to do. Of course, the great majority of women have to go back to work, it's not a choice, it's a necessity, and they feel extremely anxious. They want to be at home with this baby. And they feel bad about leaving the child. They really did want and enjoy that child, and now they're feeling very conflicted about what they should do. I think that's the main thing we hear from parents all the time."

Five months into her pregnancy, Cheryl was already feeling that six weeks with her new baby would be "nothing, absolutely nothing," although she had "every intention of going back to work." When she made several proposals to her employer for flexible or part-time return, she was turned down. While she enjoyed her six years and two promotions there enormously, she says, "Ultimately, I would not go back because it is simply not something that works out with motherhood. There is not the flexibility, there is not the understanding." The lack of room for negotiations and flexibility was a key factor in her decision to leave the company. "I made a couple of different proposals to them for something part-time, and there was one other woman who was doing part-time. This was kind of a big deep dark secret that nobody was supposed to know about, and they really didn't want to set a precedent with her, and they certainly were not going to do it for me."

If there is some leeway at your worksite, Barney Olmstead counsels women who are broaching the subject of family or maternity leave at the office that hard-line negotiations may not always be the answer. "You have to understand where you're at, both on a personal basis and within an organization. If you have some specialized skills that you know they need, you're obviously in a much better negotiating position. For a long time all of these issues were driven by people negotiating for themselves. The big trend for employers was to look at these things as a way to retain good employees. That's beginning to broaden out a little bit now, and they're beginning to think of it as a competitive strategy and those companies are moving in this direction so they know they better start thinking about it and moving in that direction, too. But it's still a very difficult thing to try to say to somebody, 'Yes, you have to go out and take a hard-line negotiating position.' You really have to feel your way, check around, and see whether there are some people in your firm who have negotiated, and build on that. Find out what your company's policy is."

Kathleen Christensen, Ph.D., is a professor of environmental psychology at the City University of New York, author of *Women and Home-Based Work*, and director of the National Project on Home-Based Work. She advises women who are arranging for leave to negotiate for the most generous terms they can get, and then come back earlier or get some part-time work to do at home if they find they want to after the baby has actually arrived. It's far better to err on the side of too long a leave, she reasons, than to overcommit yourself beforehand and have to ask for additional time away. "Most women don't know what they want on a maternity leave until they have a baby, so it's always very difficult to plan that ahead of time," she says. "It really comes down to a personal choice, but if a woman can hold off making that decision until her child is a month old or three weeks old, I think she'll be able to make a better decision."

Finally, Karen, a mom who was notified one week before her scheduled return to work that she had been laid off, counsels women where policy is not clear or written to "negotiate and put it in writing. . . . Pay attention to what's happening to other people in both pregnancy and medical illness situations. Come to an understanding and take into account that you may not be able to work up until the due date." If some of your leave time is used up prenatally, try to make arrangements for additional leave time postpartum.

# Family Leave/Job Security: Who's Providing It? Who's Getting It?

In planning for a leave, there is often a lot of information-gathering and strategizing women have to do, sometimes just to be clear on what their rights are. The state you live in, the company you work for, or the union you belong to will have a lot of bearing on how smooth or stressful your course may be. You may want to consider some of the following questions:

What laws have your federal, state, or county governments enacted to protect your job and salary? Do the laws cover only federal or state employees, or the federal, state, and private sectors? Do you work in a state that provides temporary disability insurance? If so, what about job security—will your employer provide that? (They do not necessarily go hand in hand.) What policy does your company have regarding parental or family leave? Is it clear and supportive? Is there a written vs. an unwritten policy? (Even in the most family-friendly companies, reports Ellen Galinsky of the Families and Work Institute in New York, in one of their studies 52 percent of women who worked in one company with family-friendly policies felt they "would pay a high career price for using flextime or family leave."[4]) If you belong to a union, what does your specific contract provide, and how active is your union in supporting you and fighting for family-friendly initiatives, or defending you if you are treated unfairly? How does the Family and Medical Leave Act on the federal level impact on your state's or employer's policy?

For many women, trying to get the answers to these questions is overwhelming, particularly if they are in the middle of a first pregnancy and feeling overwhelmed already. Needing to ask for help—or even troubling over where to go for answers—may make many new parents or parents-to-be feel that, once again, the failure is theirs—that they should somehow be able to manage it all better. In addition, the highly technical nature of the details and the relative lack of consistency nationwide, and even from workplace to workplace, can make the job of fact-gathering and broad public understanding of these family leave issues difficult at times.

Helen Norton is deputy director of the Work and Families Program at the Women's Legal Defense Fund in Washington, D.C. Before the enactment of the Family and Medical Leave Act of 1993, she says, "I got several hundred calls a year from people who had lost their jobs, men and women, when they needed time for a family or medical crisis, and they could not believe that there was no legal protection for them in place, that there was not a law against it. Unless they lived in one of those states that has a good leave law, they had no legal protection."

With passage of the Family and Medical Leave Act of 1993, says Norton, 57 percent of all workers will be covered, and as the workplace adjusts to implementing the new law, women and families may need extra information and guidance. The next step, says Norton, is to explore options for wage replacement, because even though twelve weeks are now available, there are still women and families who cannot afford to take the time off and forfeit their salaries.

## KNOWING WHAT YOUR RIGHTS ARE

Women and families can check at the federal, state, and local levels to know what laws protect them after the birth or adoption of a baby. Legislation will vary from state to state, even from county to county, because as the FMLA languished under the federal government, between 1983 and May 1993, twenty states and the District of Columbia took matters into their own hands, providing for gender-neutral leave laws. In 1983, Illinois became the first state to take independent action regarding parental and family leave when it allowed its own employees to take family leave. In 1992, impatient with federal government and state legislators, Dade County, Florida, became the first county in the country to pass legislation granting maternity and family leave. Commissioner Larry Hawkins, "tired of waiting" for the federal protection to come through, introduced and got the measure passed, giving both state and private-sector workers a "psychological cushion"[5] they did not have before. In addition, some states may offer maternity leave or temporary disability coverage.

As for women and men working for companies of fewer than fifty employees, they are not covered under the FMLA, and still enjoy no protection other than what their employer is willing to offer or what their state or county may provide. According to Adoptive Families of America, adoptive parents and prospective adoptive parents also face great inequities compared to birth parents when it comes to family leave arrangements, wage replacement, health-care insurance, tax code, and other issues.

To ascertain your rights at the federal, state, and local levels, women and men in all fifty states can call the Women's Legal Defense Fund (WLDF) or the Center for Policy Alternatives (CPA) to find out what laws are in place where they live and how these impact on each other. (For example, if your state law entitles you to four weeks of disability leave with pay after the birth or adoption of a new baby, the FMLA

## THE FAMILY AND MEDICAL LEAVE ACT OF 1993 (FMLA)

In 1987, as it became clear that more and more mothers of young children were entering the workforce and that the demographics of the postmanufacturing economy were changing, Representatives Patricia Schroeder (D., Colo.) and William L. Clay (D., Mo.) introduced the Family and Medical Leave Act of 1987, and Senators Christopher Dodd (D., Conn.) and Arlen Specter (R., Pa.) introduced the Parental and Temporary Medical Leave Act of 1987, in an effort to provide federal legislation that would guarantee family leave and job protection for increased numbers of American workers. (Representative Schroeder had already begun efforts toward this end in 1985, when she introduced the Parental and Disability Leave Act of 1985.) Versions of the bills were introduced in both houses of Congress in 1987 and again in 1991, but despite passage both times, two presidential vetoes kept the bills from becoming law. On January 5, 1993, the House introduced the Family and Medical Leave Act of 1993, which was virtually identical to the bill vetoed by President Bush during the 102nd Congress; on January 21, it was introduced in the Senate. On February 5, 1993, the law was enacted and signed by President Clinton and took effect on August 5, 1993.

states that you must receive your four weeks with pay, and can then tag on an additional eight weeks without pay to make the full twelve-week leave.)

Through the WLDF and the CPA you can also find out what legislation is pending, which lawmakers are working for the legislation, how you can work for progressive legislation, and what federal or state regulations govern posting and enforcement of the law. If you need legal assistance, you can also get local referrals. Adoptive Families of America can provide comparable information for adoptive or prospective adoptive parents.

## SOME HIGHLIGHTS OF THE FAMILY AND MEDICAL LEAVE ACT OF 1993*

### What the Family and Medical Leave Act Does

Allows an employee to take up to twelve weeks of unpaid leave per year:
• to care for a newborn child or for a child newly placed for adoption or foster care
• to care for an employee's child, parent, or spouse with a serious health condition
• to care for an employee's own serious health condition

### Who Is Eligible

• To be eligible, an employee must have worked for his or her employer for at least twelve months and for at least 1,250 hours during the twelve-month period immediately preceding the commencement of the leave.
• When an employee returns from leave, he or she must be given his or her previous position, or an equivalent position with equivalent employment benefits, pay, and other terms and conditions of employment.

### What Employees Are Covered

• all private employers with fifty or more employees within a seventy-five-mile radius
• employees of state and local governments
• employees of the federal government
• the Congress

For husbands and wives employed by the same company, total leave is limited to twelve weeks between the two of them.

### Additional Provisions

The FMLA also establishes the federal Commission on Leave, whose mandate is to evaluate how the law is working and how it can be improved, including a study of various options of how wage replacement might be included ultimately with family leave.

*Excerpted and adapted from Women's Legal Defense Fund Information Sheet "The Family and Medical Leave Act of 1993."

# Taking Your Leave: The View from Within (or, How I Spent My Parental Leave)

*I think increasingly we're going to recognize that parents—the mother or the father—need and want to be with the baby for a lot longer than our policies now allow. No matter how wonderful the outside care is, there ought to be some way, without putting their careers at risk, for parents to care for their baby themselves for longer than a few weeks.*

—Linda Tarr-Whelan, B.S.N., M.S.
president/executive director, Center for Policy Alternatives

Regardless of where you live, what your job is, or what kind of job protection and leave you have, there will come that day when your baby is born, and after months of strategizing, negotiating, and planning with other adults, suddenly there is a tiny new rookie in the game who is not going to strategize, negotiate, or function as a team player, accommodating whatever schedule you may have preplanned. All the rules have changed. In addition to giving you a vital, incomparable new human connection that cannot be described until experienced, this baby has also, in effect, given you a new job. As you apprentice at your motherwork, there is a whole new set of feelings, hours, statistics, and demands you may not have anticipated. Who is there to help you? How are you feeling? Do the arrangements you made at work still seem adequate and realistic? Do they make any sense at all? Is your leave time enough to give you confidence in your own parenting skills, and if not, how will you know what to look for in an outside caregiver? What is your partner's role in all this? And how important does flexibility at your partner's workplace become?

Although many women do not want to think about postpartum while they are pregnant, many women returning to work outside the home may have an additional set of questions they may not want to think about: How can I separate from my baby so soon? Who can I trust to take care of him or her? What are my options for extended family leave time? How much can my spouse or partner do?

While there are companies with helpful human resources departments, if women find that they cannot talk easily and openly about such things at their workplace, perhaps they can talk individually and confidentially with other mothers who work there, or to a local work and family resource center. Another good resource may be an already established mothers' group, whose leader or members may be able to help you network with other moms who have already gone through the transition and share specific interests.

In the Boston area, MotherCare provides home-care service that nurtures and focuses on the brand-new mother. Many of the working moms whom founder Joan Singer and her staff see go back to work two to six months after their babies are born. Like many new mothers, they do not necessarily know what to expect.

"When I see them prenatally," says Singer, "and ask them if they're going back to work right away, they'll say, 'Oh, no, I'm taking a lot of time off—two or three months!' In their context, they think that's a long time. They just can't conceive that it's not a vacation—that's almost what they're thinking. . . . For them it's two months of not working, but they don't realize that the other kind of work is work! It's very unrealistic or romanticized."

Why? Because, says Singer, in planning for this leave, there are a significant number of factors that can't necessarily be planned for in advance. Legitimate and important needs may arise: If the mom has had a cesarean section, recovery may take longer; getting breastfeeding well established may take weeks; the search for childcare—that perfect caregiver to come into your home—may take far longer than you imagined it would, and in fact your search may not be going well at all. Suddenly your leave is half over, you're still tired and feeling engulfed by what D. W. Winnicott called that "primary maternal preoccupation," but now you have to get ready to return to work. At this point, before they are really ready to, some moms start thinking about weaning or nursing at the worksite, getting the infant on a schedule so the grown-ups can get more sleep, and facing separation from their baby.

"If she's really enjoying herself and she realizes this is really wonderful," says Singer, "then she starts feeling, 'Oh, my gosh, I have to go back to work!' And then just the idea of the psychological separation—when they're just learning how to be together, they have to start thinking about separation.

"If she had a job," adds Singer, "especially [one] that has more professional responsibilities, that, too, is overwhelming. Just another demand,

and that takes away from being with the baby." The same responsibilities you could handle well, prebaby, are suddenly too much. They may be intellectual, while your physical self is experiencing sleep deprivation, exhaustion, stitches, and recovery. "You have this body, and it's not your body anymore. Women think their bodies are just going to go right back into shape, and that's another thing they deal with."

Singer gives her moms who work for pay outside the home a tip sheet, "Making the Most of Your Maternity Leave." Before the baby is born, Singer advises that you, among other things, interview and choose a pediatrician, not plan to use your leave to redecorate or renovate the house, and that you discuss your company's policy on parental leave for parents of sick children who may not be able to go to day care with a fever or infection. After the baby is born and while you are on leave, she advises that you contact your company to check on exactly what day they expect you to return, find a few trustworthy baby-sitters for evenings and weekends, and try on all the baby's gifts of clothes, even the six-month and older sizes, as babies quickly outgrow their newborn-size outfits.

Singer also suggests that one useful program for worksites might be prenatal seminars focusing on family or maternity leave, and then picking up with the same women and families when they do return to work. "A lot of them are just not prepared when they actually have to say good-bye to their baby for eight hours a day in two months. It's devastating. Unless it's just so absolute, the best thing would be to start going back to work part-time, even if they can go back earlier, so they can do more part-time for a longer period of time."

Judsen Culbreth advises women that even if they don't want to think about things postpartum while they are pregnant, they should try to make some plans before the baby is born so it doesn't hit them all at once later. "It's very hard to get it organized," she says. "It's such a life-changing experience. Think about these decisions. The problem I find is that many women don't want to think about postmaternity when they're pregnant. You're so involved with the amazing changes in your body that you don't think about the other side. And then when you get to the other side, you're so busy that it's hard to organize."

On the following pages, eight mothers share some recollections of their leave time:

**Jill,** magazine editor,* New York City: Jill had eight weeks' paid leave, then opted for an additional ten-and-a-half months to make a full year leave, during which time she did some freelance work at home for her company. After returning to work at the one-year mark, she soon left to work freelance, and made the decision, she says, for purely business reasons.

*"I think in the first three months of my daughter's life I really needed to be just with my daughter, both to recover physically and to get used to being a parent. It would have been very difficult for me to do anything professionally. Somewhere around three months, when I found that I was walking around my house humming the themes from daytime TV shows, I knew I was in serious trouble. And I really did begin to feel like I needed to work. But at that time . . . I couldn't have put in a full day, so it was an ideal blend. I got back into some sort of work just at the point where I might have been feeling, 'Oh, God, all I do now is watch daytime TV and change diapers and have some problems with self-esteem and what my conversations would be about, and all of that business.' I started working just when I was beginning to feel odd about things. But I didn't have to work so much that I felt that I was losing the time with my child. I think that you have a period of time when you can devote yourself to the business of becoming a parent, and then if you can ease back into the workplace rather than jump in with both feet, it works really well. I needed that time to get to know my baby."*

**Elizabeth,** corporate lawyer, New York City, twelve weeks' leave: Elizabeth had a difficult pregnancy and delivery but still worked full-time until the day before she gave birth.

*"I was completely exhausted afterward. It was weeks before I even felt that I was able to not sleep all day. After I had the baby, I completely dropped out of work. They would call and ask me questions and I would say 'I'm sorry I can't even answer.' I was taking pain medication, and I would just sleep the entire day. My parents came up on the weekend after the baby was born and they stayed at a hotel close by. They would come at lunchtime to help me out, and I would greet them in my nightie, maybe having had breakfast and maybe not. I was completely*

*Jobs mentioned were at the time they were on leave.

overwhelmed. I couldn't do anything. You ask whether I knew how to care for the baby. NO! They gave us a little, very short course in the two days I was in the hospital. I was barely even able to concentrate on it, and my baby was like a breakable doll as far as I was concerned. I didn't know what to do with her. At the hospital they said, 'Oh, just do it, and you'll be all right,' and I wasn't. Basically I spent most of my time with her lying down beside me. I was reluctant about sitting up with her.

"I stayed out for eight weeks, I couldn't really do anything for the first four weeks. . . . [My parents] did absolutely everything. [Each day when they arrived] I went in and took a shower for the first time that day and they would fix a meal, and would do everything. My father is great with kids, he loves kids, they would trade off between them. They would bathe the baby and get her dressed, and then give her to me and they'd stick around till my husband came back. They did all the shopping. I had organized before I had the baby, labeling all the shelves, so it was pretty easy for somebody to come in and fit in. At about six weeks, I was able to walk out with the baby and stop feeling totally exhausted. I was out for twelve weeks. The last month was fun because by that time I had enough strength to walk around. We went on vacation with [my husband's] parents, and I was able to do everything for myself."

During her leave, she also found a full-time baby-sitter she felt very comfortable with as she prepared to go back to work after a twelve-week absence. Both her mother and mother-in-law had met and "approved of" the baby-sitter as well, so Elizabeth had the input of female family elders in evaluating what she wanted in a caregiver.

When Elizabeth's second child was born four years later, she again had complications during her pregnancy and this time again had to have bedrest. She set up her terminal, modem, and fax and worked from home, and was also able to continue with some of that work after her baby was born. This time she took a four-month leave. This worked well, she said, because she had taken charge of her work situation, invited colleagues up to see how efficiently it was set up, and showed them that she was really "in control."

**Cheryl**, trainer, cosmetics industry, New Jersey, six weeks' paid leave: Cheryl got an extension on her disability leave because she developed mastitis. She went back after three months, freelancing three days a week for nearly a year.

*"That was fine, it was flexible. But after that I just decided that the corporate structure was not for me anymore. . . . I would not go back because it is simply not something that works out with motherhood. There is not a flexibility there, there is not the understanding. I would rather try to stretch every dollar and deal with making things a little tighter financially than having to deal with that. [During my leave time] I was worried about my disability running out and I was worried about money, because that was the very beginning of letting go of the corporate structure. But the early time with [my son] was just wonderful, and such an exploration of this new little person. Because I was a first-time mother, too, everything was new. The first rolling over, the first little movements toward crawling, and watching him fall asleep, it's just magical, it's absolutely miraculous. The first step, the first word, that first year is just monumental with what they accomplish. It's incredible to see. And I'm totally grateful that I had the option to freelance three days a week during that period. . . . And I'm still not working full-time."*

**Tammie,** field manager, New York City: Tammie had six weeks' paid leave, with an option of three years of family leave with benefits continued and a guarantee of the same or a similar job. Tammie planned to take off nine months after her baby was born. After six months, she found out that because of the poor overall economy, her company would not necessarily be able to guarantee that she would have a job when she was ready to return in three months.

*"So now it's stressful, it's very stressful, it really is at this point. But I'm not going to worry about it because there's nothing I can do. I have a lot of confidence in myself, in my own skills and abilities, and if I do have to leave, which I don't want to do, because it's a very good company, especially benefits-wise. . . . [But] even with the economy being what it is and the job market, I feel that I'll eventually find something if I have to. But I don't want to. I want to stay there."*

**Spalding,** part-time administrative position, twenty hours a week, South Carolina, six weeks' paid leave: Spalding worked up until the day she delivered, which was five days past her due date.

*"The first week I stayed in touch with the people at the office and they would call and ask me questions, which was wonderful because I still felt like they needed me, and then at the end, I guess they figured*

out everything they needed to know because they never called me, which was wonderful because they didn't bother me at home, but in a way I almost wanted them to bother me just so I didn't feel like I was so removed when I got back. . . .

"[The terms of the leave were] not adequate or fair. A woman should not have to use her sick and annual leave for maternity leave. . . . I just think that's unfair that we have to use up our vacation time to take care of our children, which is just a basic need of life. It's not like we're taking a vacation, by any stretch of the imagination. That was one thing I could not get over, to save my life. . . ."

**Regina**, compensation manager, Boston: Regina took her full eight weeks of disability plus three weeks of vacation, and then started back on a phase-in schedule of two days a week.

"The vision I had was to take the time plan or anticipate an eight-week maternity leave, then a three-week cushion of vacation time to do whatever I wanted, maybe get away with my husband and the baby, and use it as a vacation. And then [during the extended phase-in family leave period], just see how it was to adjust to a part-time work schedule. I went one day at a time, and I think it worked very well. There was no pressure on either end to feel like, well, I'm not holding up what I should be doing on this end because I'm not there enough. It really was a little smattering of both, enough to keep an equilibrium of stress level and guilt level and responsibility level. I think it was terrific." At home, Regina had two sisters who were great sources of support and role-modeling as she became a new mother, and she also maintained contact with the office. "Different people . . . called and talked, and [I could] tie into the different things that were going on either professionally or personally. That was part of it, too, that I was available to be contacted if the need arose for a work project."

**Gay**, administrative assistant, Utah: Gay had a six-week leave before she went back to working forty hours a week.

"My employer has no maternity policy at the present. I was only able to use what vacation and sick leave I had available to use. If a supervisor allows for leave without pay, an employee had to pay for their benefits, so this results in 'going in the hole' financially. I didn't feel this was adequate time off, nor are the terms of my employer for maternity leave."

*Wesley,* manager, New York City: Wesley took eleven months off after the birth of her first child (disability plus unpaid family leave with benefits and job guarantee). When her second child was six weeks old, she learned that the extended leave she had just started taking was in jeopardy. Nevertheless, her priorities are to be with her children as long as she can.

Contemplating her leave is still hard for Wesley.

*"When I first had my baby, I wasn't sure how long I would be able to stay off. My brother sent me some money so I was able to take off. [My company] had an arrangement where you could take off a year without pay but with benefits.*

*"[It was] unbelievably stressful. I can remember, with my daughter, any time you mentioned work to me, I just burst into tears, because I couldn't imagine leaving her. It was terrible, terrible, terrible. I was extremely depressed. None of my baby-sitters worked out. . . . Being able to be there for them [is so important], the bonding period that takes place between you and your child in the beginning—you can't replace that."*

Once you know definitely the terms of your leave, you can try to tailor a support network within that framework, as much as possible leaving time for yourself, your recovery, and your other needs. If keeping in touch with work will be necessary or important to you during that time, set up a work connection that will be supportive. Husbands or partners who have no leave might also want to check with their benefits or human resources department to see if their employer might provide a week or two of home-care service as a benefit, so that a nurturing caregiver can be on hand in their absence.

## Returning to Work: Your Emotions

*My first day back at work, of course I missed her, but I felt so relieved!*
—JoAnne

*The first day, I dropped him at day care and cried all the way to work.*
—Spalding

Returning to work outside the home brings up different feelings for every woman. Moms have spoken of separation anxiety, guilt, sadness, relief, anger, devastation, personal satisfaction at being able to strike an appropriate balance, the need to phone home often during the day. You may feel cheated of time with your baby, or relieved to have some time in the adult world. Often your feelings may depend on when you come back and how ready you feel, how much control you have had over your situation, how you felt about your work before you left, how you feel about the caregiver or childcare arrangement you have for your child, how your priorities about work and family might have changed or remained the same, and how you are treated when you do get back to the workplace.

Many women may experience tacit but clear limits on how much of their new life they can bring into the office. Some women feel the unspoken pressure to disassociate from motherhood and keep that deep connection hidden, hanging their new raiment of motherhood at the door like a cloak when they come in, and putting it back on when they go home. For many, this charade of disinterest in maternity is a burden, making their time in the office possibly distracted and less productive.

Some women come back to face negative experiences: the unfriendly attitudes of coworkers who had to cover for them, the deliberate silence that says they have too many pictures of the baby on the wall, an office move to a corner closet, or an unexpected proliferation of work they're overqualified for and underinterested in. Others come back to more positive arrangements: coworkers and management ready to support their needs, even raises and promotions.

When her first child was born, Judsen Culbreth returned to her job after a three-month leave, but soon after, wound up taking off a year and a half. "It's a stressful time. It's very hard. I still remember the shock of my first day back with my first child. On that day back, when I was just reeling from being away from my baby—[wondering], 'Am I doing the right thing?'—I got to work where I had had an office, and I was out in this cubicle. I was told that they didn't like the arrangement they had made with me while I was pregnant, they were paying me too much money, and they redefined my duties. It was almost like I suddenly came back with a handicap. I just remember being so shocked and hurt, and amazed that my company, which had really liked me, would do this. Suddenly I was a different person. And I think that happens a lot, and is one of the reasons women have trouble adjusting. Women lose their jobs while they're on their leaves. They're fired, demoted, transferred. It happens quite a bit."

Linda Tarr-Whelan, B.S.N., M.S., executive director of the Center for Policy Alternatives and also an adoptive mother, recalls that when her children arrived, her employer allowed her to work three days a week at the office and two days a week at home. "It was wonderful. I was, I think, as productive as I had been before, but it was an entirely different process compared to having to go five days a week."

Still, assumptions about the "rightness" of the old work patterns are hard to shake. Jill also came back after a twelve-month leave that included some freelance work at home to a full-time workweek that was divided between home and office. Her daughter was in day care full-time, so she was also available to come in anytime she was needed, and at her boss's suggestion she came in earlier and left earlier each day so she could do the day-care pickups. She never took a lunch break, she recalls, and was always available by fax or modem or telephone. "With all of that effort, it became increasingly clear to me that there were people in positions of authority, people higher than me in the hierarchy who felt that I was working part-time because they couldn't physically see me. The same person who would comment to me about the great and successful effort I was making to show that these sort of flexible efforts worked, and would say that to me on a variety of occasions, that same person would say in conversation something about, 'Well, when you come back to work full-time,' and not realize what she was doing. There was no question that I was taken less seriously as a professional, despite all my running to show how committed I was to the job and how much work I was producing, and the quality of the work I was producing. I didn't come back to my same job."

In some ways, Jill says, her sensibilities and feelings about work did change. She no longer wanted to work twelve- or fourteen-hour days and be away from her daughter for days on end. But did her work suffer? "I really tried to think hard about it, and the answer is no. And that is the answer of the people who worked with me on a daily basis and would be able to see it. It is true that the hours weren't as long, but I was much more efficient. Yes, sure [my sensibility] about work changed, I think for the better. I think when you have a little bit more balance in your life, you have a little more energy and passion to give to both. But I turn off at a certain time. I happen to be truly captivated by my daughter. I really find her a charming and very enchanting little person. And I have what I consider to be relatively little time with her, so I really did have a shutoff valve where I could stop thinking about the work most of the time."

Then there is the daily caretaking. And the arrangements. The endless arrangements and logistics. When your baby's ride home from day care cancels at four o'clock, your world still comes to a halt until an alternate plan has been made. As Helen Levine, Canadian feminist counselor, and adjunct professor of women's studies at Ottawa's Carleton College, puts it, often Mom may not have the support system; rather, she is expected to be the support system for the family.

"Sometimes," says Sharon, a mother of two, "you get a sense when you're at work and you're sitting there worrying about all the logistical problems that have come up . . . that maybe you're just by yourself and that somehow your life just hasn't worked out properly. . . . Once you start to talk to other working moms, you realize that's definitely not the case, that our problems are very similar."

Hewitt Associates has legitimized the concerns of new moms and families by offering "Juggling Work and Family" sessions for their new parents. "Just knowing that you're not the only one in that situation is a tremendous help. Knowing there are others to talk to," says Dawn, who has been working as a secretary at Hewitt for six years, and has two children, ages two and four.

Twelve mothers shared their feelings about returning to work for pay outside the home:

*Spalding (baby's age at Mom's return to work, six weeks):* "I guess I had real ambivalent feelings, but I pretty much was ready. It was just always sort of in the back of my mind that I was going back. It took me about a week to get back into it. What I wasn't prepared for was leaving my child in day care, and walking out of the room and feeling okay until I got in the car and drove off and then it was just tears. That was just to me the hardest thing, just picturing him there in that tiny little room with all those other babies. . . . My coworkers were very understanding—most of them are parents. There was no formal support. [After one week] we changed to a woman who kept him in her home with her girls who were of the baby-sitting age. It worked out very well."

*Although South Carolina had no maternity leave policy at the time, Spalding said her boss did make things very easy for her, and even said she could do as much of her work at home as possible, "but I found I needed to be there most of the time anyway. However, just knowing that he was supportive and understanding made it easier."*

After four months, Spalding was offered her position full-time, and she turned it down, opting for home-based work instead. "When [my boss] offered it to me, I anguished over it for about two hours, because my work was such a part of me, I couldn't imagine not doing it anymore. But then I thought about it. My child is so much more a part of me, I probably don't realize the full impact of that yet because he's only a few months old, but it didn't take me long to make the decision."

**Lynn** (baby's age, nine months): Lynn, a social worker, had a nine-month leave, and then hired a full-time baby-sitter while she went back to work full-time for four months.

"I didn't last longer than that. I knew that I wouldn't. I was devastated by the separation, and I was on such an emotional high being a parent, I felt like the baby-sitter got all the good stuff. I didn't want to be missing that piece. I didn't have a child so that somebody else could raise him. I left when he was about a year, and I was home until he was a little over three. I went back to work part-time."

**Sharon** (baby's age, six weeks): "When [my first] was born, I didn't even think twice about it—you just go back to work after six weeks. That's what everybody does, and it's really no big deal, you just go back to work and everybody seems to live through it, and how naive I was! So I did that, and I was a wreck. Emotionally and physically, I was just nowhere ready to leave that baby. So it was very difficult. When I look back on it now, I realize that I was pretty useless in the workplace for a while. It was a hard thing to live through, but I think again, many people are under the impression that this is the way it's done. I was real fortunate. I had family members that could do childcare for me with an infant. . . . I didn't have to go out and look for a spot for an infant, which not only is tremendously expensive, but there are very few of them." (When her second child was born, she took off three months.)

**Gay** (baby's age, six weeks): During her six-week leave, Gay applied for a transfer and promotion and was hired for a new job.

"My new supervisor worked with me really well and allowed me to work flextime (part-time) for approximately four weeks. This helped me ease back to work. It was very hard for me to leave my baby. I did not want to return to work so soon. The fact that I was starting a new job was exciting to me, but the guilt I felt for leaving such a fairly new baby was hard on me. I just had to accept that this was what I had to do."

**Elizabeth** (baby's age, three months): Elizabeth was paid for four weeks of time off and had a sitter coming to her home when she returned to work on a part-time schedule of two days a week.

"I knew that it was important for me to have constructed time outside the home."

**Marianne** (baby's age, five-and-a-half months): "My supervisor is extremely supportive and flexible. She gave me five-and-a-half months' leave (partly paid), created a new part-time position to come back to, gave me a raise, and once I return to work will allow me to work at home. . . . I will be returning to work in four weeks. Even though family and a neighbor, people I know and trust, will be caring for my son, I am still having separation anxiety. I will miss him tremendously, will worry that he misses me and needs me. My workplace is very supportive. Most of my coworkers are parents themselves."

**Jill** (baby's age, twelve months): When Jill returned to a full-time schedule, she divided her time, working three days at home, two days in the office.

"The mornings were a very stressful time, having to get everyone out of the house at a certain time—see, it's even that use of language—my husband got himself ready, it was just my daughter and myself—it felt like a whole crowd."

**JoAnne** (baby's age, three months): JoAnne Brundage founded FE-MALE (Formerly Employed Mothers At Loose Ends, now Formerly Employed Mothers At the Leading Edge) after the birth of her second child.

"My parents were available to take care of her at that time, so I felt very confident that she was left in loving hands. To tell you the truth—and maybe this is hard for a lot of women to say—but my first day back *at work, of course I missed her, but I felt so relieved! I remember sitting during a coffee break and, you know how when you have a newborn, your ears are just perked all the time to hear the baby crying—and I realized I didn't have to do that. I could actually sit down for ten minutes and relax. And that was such a huge relief, to get my life back at that point, that it helped me a great deal."*

**Wesley** (baby's age, eleven months): Wesley returned to work full-time, but was dissatisfied with the childcare she had found and went through several caregivers before finding one she was pleased with.

*"I was devastated. It was terrible, terrible, terrible. I didn't want to leave that girl for nothing. God bless moms going back after six weeks . . . but today I'm glad I did it."*

*When her second baby was six weeks old, she was hoping to be able to take the full six-month leave her company offered employees. Unexpected problems with her job security, however, made her only sure option a return to work when the baby was six weeks old. She declined and decided to wait the six months to see if a job was still available. "She's only six weeks old, I look at her, and I can't imagine leaving her. I can't do it. It kills me. . . . I'm trying not to think about it because it is a stressor, but I have my priorities right here. I'll just have to do what I have to do."*

**Melody** (baby's age, fourteen months): Melody works at the Black Women's Wellness Center in Atlanta. She left her teaching job when she was eight months pregnant, and waited until her son was three months old before she took a new job at the center. Because of the priorities of the Black Women's Wellness Center, women working there are greatly supported in the maternity/matrescence process. They are offered flexibility, generous leave, and support from the self-help groups and other staff at the center. Melody had family nearby to help out, and also found a highly recommended local childcare provider with whom she was very happy.

*"I really missed working and I wanted to get out of the house. Working is very rewarding and fulfilling for me because of the nature of this work. We work with women and I could identify with them—mothers and their children. But the adjustment came in a long day, nine to five. The first week I worked half days, and then full-time. Now that I reflect*

*back on it, it wasn't difficult, because for a time I did let [my daughter] spend some time with my mother. I did some part-time work for my church so I wasn't with her all the time. I wanted her to be used to other people, and she was, she was very friendly and would go to others. My husband would leave the house earlier in the morning than I did. I would get up and dress her and let him take her. So I had a few moments to collect myself before the day began. That was very helpful."* (When her son was born, she took off seven weeks and then returned to work.)

**Regina** (baby's age, eleven weeks): Regina works as a compensation manager at Stride Rite Corporation and had an option of taking up to eighteen weeks off, including her disability and vacation time. She chose to start back two days a week after her eleven weeks of leave and vacation.

*"I don't know if I ever would have felt ready. If I hadn't had a timetable to work against, I probably would have taken longer than I did, because at the time I was breastfeeding, just trying to acclimate myself to what kind of developmental things are going on with the baby that I have to stay in tune with. Now looking back, I say to myself that was the easy part, when they're that small, but you don't know it while you're going through it.*

*"Coming back [to work], I was very apprehensive. I would look at memos that I had written and think, 'I can't even believe I thought that through.' I had worked before I left on summary plan descriptions for benefit programs—they are very legalese in terms and so forth—and I was somewhat surprised, and said, 'How did I do this?' I think a lot of pressure you put on yourself—'Can I ever strive for this level of performance again? Am I going to be so fragmented that I won't be able to focus as I did then, because I need to put so much time into it?' It's a rocky road, but I'd have to say personally a lot depends on your work group, your peers, and the support you get. Even coming back after eleven weeks, it was different, to come back in through the doors, okay, now sit at a desk, not worry about what time is it, what feeding is it, but what meeting to go to, what deadlines have to be met, what is this project that we have to heighten our interest. . . .*

*"I think one of the key things was the constant questioning of myself about what role do I play after being single-minded about things, being*

on a career track. When you're steady Eddie on a career track with one focus, and you always feel in control—one thing, I always have the need to feel in control—you have to give out some rope and give yourself a little leeway to say, 'Live with imperfection, it's not the worst thing. Just go with the flow to some extent, and if things aren't going the way you think they should, just give in a little and be flexible.' One day I thought, 'Gee, is this the right thing, am I doing right by walking into work and wondering what he's doing all day long?'—I had somebody come into the house when I came back here, instead of doing a child-care/day-care setting. That made me personally feel better than making the adjustment to a day-care setting. Even when I came back full-time I had somebody in the house. That kind of alleviated the guilt of leaving him often."

**Deborah** (baby's age, seven weeks): Deborah is a physician's assistant at the Black Women's Wellness Center in Atlanta. When she returned to work, she held two jobs and worked for a total of forty to fifty hours a week. When her son was seven months old, she opted to work only at the center, cutting down to two days a week so she could be with him. She left the baby at home with her parents, while her husband, a physician, was on a fellowship in Chicago. She also had a babysitter come into the home for several months. Deborah realizes that not having those supports in place can add additional, even incapacitating stress levels for new mothers who don't know where to turn for help. She articulated the deep feelings many mothers have about separating from new babies, as well as feelings about the rigors of working at a job and also mothering an infant. She understands the pull on the new mom returning to work:

"The problem is not having support networks and not having someplace that they feel comfortable with leaving the child in the first year, first few weeks. It was hard for me—and I left him at home! You have that desire to be there for the child, but you can't be there twenty-four hours a day. And then when you come home, you're tired, but you still have the need to spend time with the baby, so you spend time with the baby and you don't get any sleep, and you're constantly going. You're still going to work, you come home, and you have that full-time job with the baby, and the first six months a lot of times the baby's still getting up at night, so that's the hard part. Then there's the emotional *drain where you don't want to leave your child. Here at the Wellness Center we have staff meetings and we could talk about things and they were supportive. We have self-help development groups, so that's a time when you can all get together or even in smaller groups, and talk about the things that are happening, and with myself, there was another lady in the office who was pregnant so we could sit down and talk about some of the things we were experiencing. That helped a lot."*

# A Sampling of Family-Friendly Programs and Resources

In Denver, any citizen with work/family questions can call the Work and Family Resource Center's new parents' helpline. . . . Stride Rite maintains a family resource library providing access to printed materials, videotapes, and regular workshops on family issues such as prenatal care, as well as the internationally acclaimed Intergenerational Center for child care and elder care. . . . At the Royal Bank of Canada, a large network for work/family issues is in place to help employees. . . . At Hewitt Associates, an Expectant Parents' Registry offers parents an information kit on child-care options, benefits, and leaves, an Expectant Parents' Session, and postpartum follow-up, as well as a gift and card when their child is born. . . . Time Warner offers its seventy-seven hundred New York employees a Manhattan-based emergency drop-in childcare center also available to nursing mothers who don't yet have childcare in place and are still transitioning back to work. . . . At the National Black Women's Health Project in Atlanta, nursing mothers are allowed a longer midday break to nurse their babies, and in some instances space has been made to keep infants in the office during the day. . . . Employees whose companies contract with the Partnership Group can call its 800 line for help with any number of work/family issues. . . . Apple Computer gives new parents a birth or adoption gift of five hundred dollars. . . . Hanna Andersson, an Oregon-based company of close to two hundred employees (the majority of whom are female), gives parents a very generous leave policy as well as a 30 to 50 percent discount on their high-quality children's clothing. . . . And at Ben & Jerry's Homemade, Ben Cohen and Jerry Greenfield are two of the few CEOs who took a public stand in favor of the Family and Medical Leave Act of 1993.

In addition to these family-friendly models, there are also newsletters, policy initiatives, workshops, seminars, on-site resource rooms, and other support models and materials that exist toward a mother-friendly, family-friendly end. Some help women to plan and implement for the long term; others exist to help them on those days when, says Karol Rose, former director of Work-Family Initiatives and Training at Time Warner and currently a principal with Kwasha Lipton, a consulting firm specializing in employee benefits, "they're struggling with really the most difficult thing, and that's when everything falls apart."

Companies that have been successful at expanding along these lines cite as benefits the attraction and retention of good employees, bottom-line costs, employee morale, public relations, and image among clients or consumers. Those at the forefront of change are usually only too happy to share their knowledge and experience, both with individuals from other companies trying to advocate for improvement and change, and with management seeking advice about how to implement change themselves.

## Solutions at Work: Striking the Balance

More and more, women are cast in the dual roles of caregiver and wage earner outside the home. Dialogue, options, and flexibility are some elements that have enabled new mothers to make a more successful transition back to work.

At New Ways to Work, Barney Olmstead has been interviewing new parents and doing research "trying to get some keys about what allows people to feel good about the choices they make." One woman, she recalls, who had no choice and had to return six weeks after the birth of her first child and three months after the birth of her second to a firm she herself had helped to start, is still, seven years later, "feeling pain and grief about leaving her child that young. . . . One of the interesting things that has come out of our interviews here with married couples that have arranged some flexibility, often with both of them able to arrange a little bit, has been the real joy of the men who have gotten more into the nurturing side, and how little it takes if both partners are able to be even a little bit flexible. It doesn't take a whole lot to put together something that really works in terms of having parents able to parent."

Art Strohmer, executive director, Human Resources Policies and Strategies, at Merck Pharmaceuticals, one of the top-rated companies in the Working Mother Magazine survey, echoes this endorsement for flexibility. "Support mechanisms have to be available if you want both parties in the marriage to work. Whether you provide those kinds of mechanisms directly, or provide the flexibility for the employee to use them on their own [doesn't matter. If a company can't afford to build a day-care center], what they can do, which doesn't cost them much, is recognize that flexibility is probably one of the biggest needs, and not having people tied to what is supposedly the only way to work—the eight-to-five syndrome."

Below, several moms talk about some of the factors that have combined to help them make what they consider to be a successful transition back to the workplace after having a baby.

Deborah, who works at the Black Women's Wellness Center in Atlanta, reiterates the need for women to talk about their common needs and emotions as new mothers returning to the workplace, often with strong feelings about the separation from their baby. For her, on-site, work-sponsored support groups provided the necessary outlet for this. Especially if women are in an unsupportive workplace, she says, they have to know "that they need to find some type of outlet, or some type of network, some one individual that they can talk to about it, express those feelings, let them know that they're not alone in those feelings. It's something that the average woman has to deal with and go through and it does pass. You just do the best you can with what you have. A new mother should seek some type of outlet so she can talk about it and get the support she needs."

For Regina, Stride Rite and her husband's employer together provided the degree of flexibility that made her successful return possible. Of the three days a week that she works, her son spends two days a week with a neighbor, and one day a week with Regina's husband, whose boss allowed him to build that flexibility into his schedule. Her workplace allowed her to work different schedules until hitting upon one that worked best for her, and her colleagues were supportive. "I've broadened myself by passing a hurdle, if you will. I did get back into the workforce and managed myself." In addition, she adjusted her old standards of perfection to a more realistic level as she managed both pieces of her life. "The house didn't have to be perfect. [At work] I was a little bit anxious about getting home when it was fiveish, and previously, five o'clock came and went and oftentimes I didn't leave here till six, but now that's not practical, because there are other things that have to get moving by the time I get home. I had to say, 'That's okay, you get done what you have to get done, but you do it in eight hours.' I think it's great because had I not come back and had the opportunity to do the work-family balance, I think you just never know if you can do it. I'm very happy that I didn't have to make a commitment one way or the other, and I've had this interim gray period that I feel very comfortable in. . . . It's been very satisfying personally and professionally."

Dawn is a secretary at Hewitt Associates. She has worked there for six years and has two children, ages two and three-and-a-half. She returned to work about eight weeks after the birth of her first son, and about seven weeks after the birth of her second. For about a week-and-a-half she was on a phase-in schedule, coming in only several days during the week, and then she came back full-time. "I was ready, I'd had both of them home with me, and being only eighteen months apart, I was kind of ready to get back into the organization of my life." Her workplace took a hands-on, "family-sharing" role and responsibility in many ways. When she was looking for baby-sitters, Dawn brought in newspaper ads, and Work and Family staff members screened candidates so she wouldn't have to do it at night or on her lunch hour. Their database helped her to find in one day the baby-sitter she's used for two years. Their Mother's Room made it possible for her to return to work when she needed to, and when she was having problems with nursing they provided a lactation consultant for her to call for answers to all her questions. When she had to have medical tests done and couldn't give her son her milk, the office provided a breast pump for her to use at home so she could pump to keep her supply up and continue to nurse afterward.

When her second child was a year-and-a-half old, Dawn requested flexhours. "Instead of working eight-thirty to five, I work seven-thirty to four. And that one hour has made a tremendous difference in our home life. It's unbelievable. I actually get to play with my kids after we have dinner, instead of putting them in the bathtub and putting them to bed. We actually have some time there. Everyone is so understanding. They know I have primary responsibility to pick up my sons. I have to leave on time. [Sometimes] I have to leave to take them to doctors' appointments, and when they're sick, I'm usually the one that stays home. My husband works construction and he doesn't get paid if he doesn't work. Everyone's always willing to pitch in. The hours are the big thing for me. It's working out great. My boss even said not long ago he couldn't believe how well things were working out as far as me working these hours. I get here earlier, and get twice as much done in that first hour, it's so quiet. I do feel very fortunate."

For Harriet, the feeling of overall support she felt at her worksite was critical. Harriet, twenty-nine, is a volunteer who works as receptionist at the Black Women's Wellness Center. She lives in the McDaniel Glenn Public Housing in Atlanta, has two older children, and planned to come back to work two months after the birth of her third child. For Harriet, the center has provided more than just a place to work. The caring and supportive attitude of her workplace has helped to enhance her experience of motherhood and turn her life around in general. As she prepared for the imminent birth of her third child (she was in early labor during her telephone interview), the center had become not only her worksite but also her extended support system. "My mom passed, my father's not here, and I don't have any brothers or sisters. Only the ladies at the center." Through the center, she says that she has also gained knowledge she did not have before—knowledge about the work she wants to do; knowledge about pregnancy, childbirth, children, and families; and the ability to say no if she is faced with a situation that is unacceptable to her. She says she has gained the ability to "talk differently" to her children and companion, "to give hugs where there were no hugs. . . . Since I've been here, I've been motivated. I know that my time is valuable."

When her first two children were born, she did not feel as empowered as she does this third time, thanks in large measure to the support of the circle of women who see her every day. "I've also planned for when my body heals, coming back to work. I've already set up plans for who's going to keep the baby. This is real different and I feel real good about it. I love the difference. A lot of times we just don't have the knowledge, the information. Information is so important. . . . It's real fun this time, and I've been doing a lot of laughing, so it's going to be a giggly little baby."

# *Notes*

Jessie Bernard, *The Future of Motherhood* (New York: Dial Press, 1974), p. 111. (Bernard defines the emotional and physical components of "motherwork" or the work that relates to women's role as mother.)

1. House of Representatives Report 103-8, Part 1, on the Family and Medical Leave Act of 1993, p. 23.

2. Shelley A. Phipps, "International Perspectives on Income Support for Families with Children," paper presented to the Canadian Employment Research Forum Workshop on Income Support (Ottawa, 1993), p. 21.

3. House of Representatives Report 103-8, Part 1, pp. 31–32.

4. Cited in Sue Shellenbarger, "Work & Family," in *The Wall Street Journal* (April 22, 1992), p. B1.

5. Barbara Presley Noble, "Making Family Leave a Local Issue," in *The New York Times* (March 22, 1992), p. 25.

# *Resources*

The resources listed here are described in further detail in the following section:

## Help for Moms

*Workshop*
"Managing Career and Family"
*Legal Help and Advocacy*
Center for Policy Alternatives
National Partnership for Women and Families
9 to 5, National Association of Working Women
Women's Bureau Clearinghouse
*Organizations Specializing in Part-Time or Alternative Work Arrangements*
M2
Pickwick Group

## Help for Corporations

*Help in Structuring and Supporting Alternative Work Schedules and Family-Friendly Initiatives and Policy*
Catalyst
Ceridian Performance Partners
The Conference Board
Dependent Care Connection
New Ways to Work
WFD
Work and Family Connection
Work and Family Resource Center

## Pamphlets/Newsletters

*The National Report on Work & Family*
*Update on Women and Family Issues in Congress*
*Work and Family Life: Balancing Job and Personal Responsibilities*

# Help for Mom

*Workshop*
"Managing Career and Family"
Boxtree Communications
Tel.: (212) 496-5600

Lisa Buksbaum, president of Boxtree Communications, a full-service advertising and public relations agency and marketing consultancy, offers workshops for women on making the transition to parenthood with a return to the workplace "as painless and professional as possible." Her workshop covers such topics as creating balance, activating and building a support network, learning how to say no, and the psychological aspects and rewards of managing work and family. Corporations are welcome to bring the seminar to their employees, or send individual employees to the Boxtree seminars.

*Legal Help and Advocacy*
**Center for Policy Alternatives (CPA)**
1875 Connecticut Avenue, NW
Suite 710
Washington, D.C. 20009
Tel.: (202) 387-6030

Founded in 1977, the Center for Policy Alternatives is a nonprofit, nonpartisan, progressive organization that helps to shape progressive public policy. The Women's Economic Justice Program monitors progressive legislation on the state and local levels and can help individual women and families by providing information on family and medical leave in their area. CPA also offers legislators advice, support, and information on shaping progressive public policy. In addition, CPA is developing for release a paid leave model that states can implement and that individual families and women can access and support in their local areas.

**National Partnership for Women and Families**
1875 Connecticut Avenue, NW
Suite 710
Washington, D.C. 20009
Tel.: (202) 986-2600

WLDF's mission is to make the world a better place for women and their families.

Founded in 1971, WLDF aims to improve the economic status and health of women and their families, and to eliminate discrimination in all its forms. WLDF works with all branches of government, the courts, and the grassroots for equal opportunity for every American. WLDF develops and fights for policies that help women meet the dual demands of work and family, achieve economic security, and gain access to affordable, quality health care for themselves and their families.

**9 to 5, National Association of Working Women**
231 W. Wisconsin Avenue, Suite 900
Milwaukee, WI 53203
Tel.: (414) 274-0925
9 to 5 Job Survival Hotline: (800) 522-0925
E-mail: naww9to5@execpc.com
www.9to5.org

This membership organization helps employed women handle job rights, work and family balance, and job discrimination including pregnancy discrimination, and more. It also has available a free brochure, "Work and Family Shouldn't Have to Be a Balancing Act: Your Rights Under the Family and Medical Leave Act of 1993."

**Women's Bureau Clearinghouse**
Room South 3305
U.S. Department of Labor
Washington, D.C. 20210
Tel.: (800) 827-5335

Established in 1920 to improve women's opportunities for profitable employment, the Women's Bureau offers free publications and fact sheets, including a working woman's guide, a fact sheet summarizing each state's maternity and parental leave policy, and an information sheet on the history of the bureau. In addition, it provides information to employees regarding dependent care policy at the worksite. The bureau has ten regional offices to help women on the local level.

*Organizations Specializing in Part-
    Time or Alternative Work
    Arrangements*
**M2**
235 Montgomery Street, Suite 760
San Francisco, CA 94104
Tel.: (415) 391-1038
www.m2net.com

This San Francisco–based company is a value-added broker of independent consultants. M2 helps its clients structure projects, then provides a choice of professionals who could complete those projects. Projects can be full- or part-time and usually average 3 to 6 months. Projects can also include interim and leave assignments. M2 serves all industries but

targets mid-senior-level projects in marketing, human resources, finance, operations, information technology, and top management. Five to eight years' experience in a particular field is preferred. M2 is a women-owned business.

**Pickwick Group**
36 Washington Street, Suite 240
Wellesley, MA 02481
Tel.: (781) 235-6222

This is a matching service that focuses on providing companies with flexible staffing solutions, including interim executives, contract professionals, project people, and permanent part-time. It matches skills of registered candidates with the needs of clients or companies, including workers to fill in for management women on family leave. Pickwick Group can sometimes provide referrals to similar services in other locations.

## Help for Corporations

While the organizations that follow do not work directly with individual moms, it is important for women in the workplace to know that such services do exist to work with corporations large and small, as well as with other employers, to bring about more family-friendly policies and initiatives. Resources are available to women who may be trying to strategize about implementing change at their own worksite, gathering information about other companies, or seeking ideas about how to proceed. If a woman cannot consult directly with a service, their materials may be available to her through a library or work/family program; she may also wish to suggest that her company contact any of the services listed below in its effort to tailor a more family-friendly work environment.

*Help in Structuring and Supporting Alternative Work Schedules and Family-Friendly Initiatives and Policy*

**Catalyst**
120 Wall Street, 5th Floor
New York, NY 10005
Tel.: (212) 514-7600
Fax: (212) 514-8470
info@catalystwomen.org

Founded in 1962, Catalyst is the nonprofit research and business advisory organization that works with business and the professions to advance women. Their dual mission: to enable women to achieve their full professional potential and to help employers capitalize fully on women's talents and abilities through research, advisory services, and communication. Catalyst's research department formulates, conducts, and publishes cutting-edge studies and practical guides to the retention, development, and advancement of women. Advisory services works with leading companies and firms to create custom-tailored, practical solutions to recruit, retain, and advance women. With working mothers and dual-career couples on the rise, Catalyst has published several studies on corporate childcare, parental leave, and flexible work arrangements, culminating in 1998 in *Managing the Work/Time Equation: A New Approach to Flexibility,* a report that focuses on making part-time arrangments work for the organization and the employee.

**Ceridian Performance Partners**
1400 Union Meeting Road
Blue Bell, PA 19422
Tel.: (800) 847-5437

Founded in 1982, Ceridian Performance Partners consults with companies on the full range of WorkLife strategies, including such topics of concern to new mothers and parents as parental leave, flexible work options, and lactation services. It also has a nationwide childcare and elder care Resource and Referral service called the Family Resource Service. Once a company has contracted with Ceridian Performance Partners, its services are also available to employees; it can, for example, help them to access other programs already in place in their company (such as a prenatal wellness program), or answer questions about entitlements under the new FMLA. It can provide information to companies that want perspective on what other companies are doing in terms of WorkLife strategies, and can provide information to employees who are making a grass-roots effort to initiate change in their own workplace.

**The Conference Board**
845 Third Avenue
New York, NY 10022-6601
Tel.: (212) 759-0900
www.conference-board.org

Founded in 1916, The Conference Board is a membership global network of senior executives. Its mission is to improve the business enterprise and to enhance the contribution of business to society. It provides a variety of forums and a professionally managed research program that identifies and reports objectively on key areas of "changing management concern, opportunity and action," including the Board's Work and Family Group, which "examines how employers are responding to the challenge of diversity in the workforce and reports on employers' initiatives through case studies, surveys, and seminars."

**Dependent Care Connection (DCC)**
P.O. Box 2783
Westport, CT 06880
Tel.: (203) 226-2680
www.dcclifecare.com

Founded in 1984, DCC/The Dependent Care Connection, Inc. is the nation's leading provider of dependent care counseling, education, and referral services to employees and their families across America. Widely recognized for the breadth, depth, and quality of its services, and for its innovative use of technology, DCC currently works with hundreds of corporations and governmental agencies representing over 1.5 million covered employees. DCC's LifeCare services help employees locate childcare options, prenatal resources, public and private schools, and summer care for their children. DCC also finds care and resources for adoptive parents, children with special needs, college-bound students, and adult dependents. Along with referrals, DCC provides employees with educational materials filled with helpful tips, checklists, and other important information tailored to their care needs. More information about DCC's services is available on their website.

**New Ways to Work (NWW)**
785 Market Street, Suite 950
San Francisco, CA 94103
Tel.: (415) 995-9860

Based in San Francisco, this innovative nonprofit group, founded in 1972, studies general worktime alternatives and promotes a wide range of alternative work schedules. While not specifically for postpartum women, many of NWW's questions come from new mothers and women. NWW offers materials to both corporations and individuals, and it sponsors a variety of workshops in the Bay Area. Although this is not its primary focus, if you send a stamped, self-addressed envelope with your request, NWW will send a free list of resources for people interested in telecommuting and other work-at-home arrangements, as well as a publications list. Membership entitles you to a subscription to its newsletter, *Work Times,* as well as a 10 percent discount on all its publications, including the definitive, newly revised *Job-Sharing Handbook* by founders Barney Olmstead and Suzanne Smith.

**WFD**
(Formerly Work/Family Directions)
928 Commonwealth Avenue
Boston, MA 02215-1212
Tel.: (617) 278-4000

WFD is a consulting firm specializing in workforce commitment, and the leading provider of corporate work-life services. They have helped over 300 organizations conduct research, set strategies, and implement programs dealing with issues such as manager and employee support, workplace flexibility, career mobility/glass ceiling, and linking community dependent care and educational programs with business and employee needs.

Through their LifeWorks employee resource program they help over 2.6 million employees at more than 150 companies manage their work and personal responsibilities with practical advice, useful materials, and referrals to local and national resources.

## Work and Family Connection
5197 Beachside Drive
Minnetonka, MN 55343
Tel.: (612) 936-7898; (800) 487-7898
www.workfamily.com

This company offers a menu of items to help management monitor and implement work and family policies and programs. It publishes a newsletter, *Work and Family Newsbrief,* a monthly "snapshot of the most important news from 11,000 publications around the U.S. and Canada"; *The Trend Report;* and a community report on work-life issues. Recently published is *Work and Family: A Retrospective,* a 340-page resource subtitled "Research and Results from 1990–1996." The WFC will help companies conduct a comprehensive needs assessment, develop a plan, and implement programs. The Newsbrief office also acts as a database, and included in the subscription price is the service of getting answers by telephone about, for example, what other companies are doing or what legislation is being considered. WFC also offers a unique training program in which managers, supervisors, and employees participate jointly.

## Work and Family Resource Center
Community College of Denver
P. O. Box 173363
Campus Box 750
Denver, CO 80217-3363
Tel.: (303) 620-4460
"4 Parents HelpLine": (303) 620-4444
Community R & R: (303) 534-2625

Started in 1986 as a program of the Community College of Denver, this has evolved into a comprehensive slate of services to provide work/family options for parents, children, families, and employers, as well as training and resources for childcare providers. Childcare specialists serve as "informational advocates" who offer care options, information on the needs of children at different stages in their development, tips on helping children adjust to care, and practical suggestions on monitoring care over the long term. In a joint effort with Channel 4 KCNC-TV in Denver, the Center provides parenting education, nonmedical support, information, and resources for parents all over the Denver metro area.

• • •

The following materials are of interest to individual women affected by changing trends in the workplace as well as to corporate leaders and others seeking to play or playing an active role securing improvements in the areas of family leave and family-friendly policy.

# Pamphlets/Newsletters

*The National Report on Work and Family*
1350 Connecticut Avenue, NW
Suite 1000

Washington, D.C. 20036-1701
Tel.: (202) 862-0990

This bimonthly newsletter monitors work/family issues across the nation.

*Update on Women and Family Issues
in Congress (UPDATE)*
Congressional Caucus for Women's
Issues
Available through Caucus members

*Update* is published by the bipartisan Congressional Caucus for Women's Issues on a monthly basis during congressional sessions. This informational bulletin can help you keep up with the status of current is-

sues and legislation, and is available through members of the Caucus.

*Work and Family Life: Balancing Job
and Personal Responsibilities*
Tel.: (800) 676-2838

Begun in 1987, this monthly newsletter covers issues of interest to families, including returning to work after having a baby; toddlers; school-aged kids; adolescence; elder care; health; and nutrition. Available by individual subscription, as well as for purchase by corporations, institutions, and family support programs for distribution to employees or clients.

# 7.

# STAYING AT HOME

*The Hardest Place to Network—Or Is It?*

••••••

*I think it's very important to keep in touch with other women just for the support. It's so easy to go for days without talking to anybody. It happens to me all the time. You get so caught up in what you're doing and running around and taking care of the house and kid or kids, that you just don't do anything for yourself or talk to anybody except the grocery clerk, and I think it's very important to somehow keep in touch with other women, particularly because they're doing it, too. They understand and they need it from you as much as you need it from them.*

        —Betsy, a first-time at-home mother

*My support group was my doorman.*

        —a first-time at-home mother

## Motherwork: The Job Begins . . .

When you're at home with a newborn, you may not feel as if you can network any farther than the local drugstore, pediatrician's office, or take-out pizza parlor. During those intense early weeks, you may have found the perfect doula, or you may be going it alone. You may be singing every romantic ballad ever written to your baby, or you may be crying your eyes out. You may be sick of reading books on parenting, or finding out "how to" anything. You may be in love, or you may be in terror of your new obligations. You may have left a job you loved, or you may have left a job you find you do not miss at all. That terminal and modem that you set up so carefully during the third trimester to tie into your office may be beckoning less and less. Or you may be secretly hoping the phone will ring with the voice of a former colleague at the other end, begging you to come back, the workplace is falling apart without you. . . .

You may feel giddy or grumpy. Mellow or miserable. Love or loss. You may feel all of the above.

For many new mothers, the following is a familiar scenario: One day, about five or six weeks postpartum, Grandma, aunt, sister, friend, or doula, if you've had one, is suddenly gone. Even your midwife has given you her blessing, and your mate is back at work with "professionals"—a term you now loosely use to refer to any grown-ups who actually do sleep through the night. All of a sudden, there you are, one-on-one with baby. Solo flight. "High from parenting," as one mother put it. Hooked on motherhood.

Or all may not be so placid. The attention you've gotten as a brand-new mother (if you got any) may be starting to dissipate. As the novelty wears off and the longing for routine and daily connections begins, the sense of invisibility described by so many moms at home with young babies may be starting to sink in. The solitude may be too much if you have no extended family and don't know any neighbors. By 10:00 A.M. on a typical morning, you've already been up six hours, and you see the endless, sleepless days stretching ahead of you forever. You're far too tired to get dressed, muster up your social skills, and go out and comb the parks and malls in search of other mothers, and you consider yourself triumphant if you can make it into the shower by dinnertime. June Cleaver flashes through your mind. How did she do it? (Or did she?) How can you do it, as you project the weeks turning into months, months into years? Where will you find companionship and nurturing connections to support you in an ongoing way? How will you address your at-home role and your own individual needs as an adult mother/woman trying to reconcile talents, needs, drives, and family obligations over the next nine or ten months and even beyond?

"I think it was easier in my mother's generation," admits Mary-Ellen, an at-home mom of two children ages seven months and three years. In her mother's day "everyone [in her community] was home with their baby . . . very few women worked when they had infants." Sisters, sisters-in-law, mothers, and aunts formed informal support networks; siblings and cousins made up ongoing playgroups. Less isolation went with the territory. But so did fewer choices. For Mary-Ellen, and many other new mothers today, there is an added dimension to being at home. Not only has she made the conscious choice to be at home full-time, but in doing so, also decided to leave a job she loved. "People look at me and say, 'You had a good job, why did you give it up?' I couldn't have done [my old job] part-time, and to me, this job is more important."

And yet, mothering is one of the few jobs that women describe in absolute and simultaneous polarities. They use terms such as "absolutely terrible" and "totally miraculous" in mercurial succession; women say that as they do it, they regress, lose their adult selves, feel incapable of carrying on a coherent conversation, give up everything; and yet they call it—the play, the nurturing, the intimacy, the sharing, the caregiving—the most important work in the world; their moments leap from drudgery to bliss and back. The quality of at-home time is crystallized into those fleeting, perfect moments walking in the park with your children—moments that shine like diamonds against a background cluttered with laundry, half-eaten sandwiches, and random piles of unopened mail.

According to many mothers at home, the isolation, loss of self-esteem, relative loss of mobility, end-of-winter cabin fever in the colder climates, and lack of value on the work of mothering and parenting itself that goes along with the territory as it exists today all make the job more difficult. In addition, brand-new mothers may underestimate the intensity of constant interaction with a baby over time.

JoAnne Brundage, founder of FEMALE, recalls not leaving her suburban house for nine months after the birth of her second child, and suffering "incredible isolation." Pam Goresh, editor in chief of *Welcome Home*, the publication of Mothers at Home, also recalls isolation as being the most difficult aspect of at-home mothering, despite her total commitment to being at home, when her children were born more than ten years ago. "There weren't nearly as many support groups as there are now," she says. "But I think no matter what, even though the mom has those support groups, it's up to the mother to get out. The challenge is within her to recognize that you can't go this alone."

During those moments when you are not in love and riveted on your baby, you may be thinking: Who am I? Where am I? Who are my friends now? Who is here to see me, encourage me, talk to me? What do I do next? What do I do in winter? What do I do if it rains? As you recall the women in the African tale of birth who welcomed the brand-new mother as she crossed the river of delivery, you may be wondering who is there to greet you with open arms a little farther down the path of new motherhood. You may be seeking structures that will support your at-home life, and finding them very hard to come by. "That's very sorely missing for women at home," says Carol Lees, at-home mother of three teenagers and founder of a Canadian group called Canadian Alliance for Home Managers (CAHM), which supports both women and men who have chosen "home management as part of their lifestyle or career development."

If you are staying at home over this first year or longer, you may be wrestling with a new definition of yourself as an "at-home mom," or "formerly employed mom." You may be testing your new role, evaluating the trade-offs, comparing it with how the society at large sees you, and feeling some discrepancy. You may be surprised at how the media portray you. You may be seeking validation (or constantly providing it for yourself), and you may be feeling disappointed and angry at the gap between what you'd like your options and power to be and what they actually are. Or, if you're just too tired for all of that, you may be searching for the nearest movie theater with a "cry room," that wonderful, mother-friendly institution of the 1930s that gave mothers a separate room where they could sit with their babies and watch the feature. (But who has time for a movie anymore, anyway?)

In recent years, mothers who are at home full-time have created support networks and publications to support mothers who have chosen or would like to choose to stay at home to raise their children. They have provided a forum in which mothers support and validate each other, celebrate the rewards and acknowledge the challenges of being at home full-time, reaffirm what one mother called the "empowering dimensions of our experiences at home," openly value and define the work they do, and establish a context for at-home mothers that does not exist in the culture at large. They also provide reassurance that your efforts are not invisible on a landscape where much of the work of nurturing and caregiving is generally perceived by the mother as very invisible, largely because the nurturing and play you share with your baby are frequently done in solitude, away from other adults. Despite its importance, few really value the emotional, psychological, and physical caregiving and maintenance in a formal way.

Groups and individual members range ideologically from feminist to conservative, itself an interesting comment on the variety of women who are choosing an at-home path today, compared to the stereotypical view still held by some of the "typical" or "traditional" homemaker and mother who stays at home because it is her "place."

Whether you plan to be home for three months, six months, twelve months, or longer, or are undecided, these networks may help you to connect early with other women (and men) who have chosen to be at home full-time, to learn from their experiences, make your own decision, get through the difficult moments, and develop a definition and sense of importance (and humor) about the motherwork you are doing. They can also help to eliminate that sense of "either/or" that so many mothers feel they have to choose between, particularly as media headlines escalate the "mommy wars" and make women feel as if they must not only choose, but also uphold, one path or the other.

While members of such organizations as FEMALE, Mothers at Home, or the Canadian group Mothers Are Women have children of all ages, many members are new mothers who have found the contact and the context helpful whenever they became ready to reach out, either as they contemplated their decision about whether to stay home full-time or during their first year of at-home motherhood.

## Making the Decision

*To say, 'I need to be with my children' doesn't command the respect that it used to. . . . So it is a difficult decision to make.*

—Gae Bomier, former PR director, Mothers at Home

*How many of us are strong enough, or determined enough, to choose a position in society that is given no payment (thereby ensuring that we and our families will have fewer material benefits), virtually no recognition (ensuring that our labor is seen to be of little value and of absolutely no interest), and that requires a high level of social isolation?*

—Carol Lees

Mothers who stay at home with their babies during the first post-partum year arrive at that decision through a variety of routes and backgrounds. Some have long leave options—a year or more—and take them. Others face an either/or work choice, and quit their paying jobs to be at home. Some enter into it for a shorter term—a year or two or until their children start school; others say they discover later that older children still need them equally if not more after school hours, so extend their at-home stays.

Sometimes moms are clear long before their baby arrives that they want to be at home; others don't realize until after the baby comes that they would really rather be at home. For some women, staying home is not an option. Others are able to trade off income for at-home motherhood, opting to cut corners in order to make it possible.

Many factors play a role in shaping each individual mother's decision: Personal beliefs about what is best for her baby. Work options. Family or social pressure. Stereotypes and images of the at-home mother and the threat of losing one's self entirely. And, there is, too, that amorphous, abstract, riveting component—"the personal connection with your baby," says Carol Lees. "That's something you cannot explain to anyone else."

Similarly, each mother experiences staying at home differently, depending on her own personality, social needs, networking skills, available resources or outlets, previous life experience, and support she feels for her choice.

Marla Waltman-Daschko is a member of Mothers Are Women (MAW), a Canadian group that supports mothers who are at home or who would like to be at home. "There are women who have told me that they're made to feel like nothing when they're at home," she says, "and that's why they went back to work, because they had no sense that they were anything when they didn't receive a paycheck. I don't feel that, because I feel like I've accomplished something, and I feel like MAW has helped me maintain that."

Tanya, a new mom of twins, left work and did not join a group for at-home moms, but did go for counseling for PPD. She found that "the hardest thing was trying not to get depressed thinking that this is my life—no me—just a mom and wife."

For Stephanie, a public health nurse in Canada and mother of a nine-month-old, MAW provided a way for her to actualize her skills and talents and also follow through on her politics and family philosophy once she was ready to do so, at about four or five months into new motherhood.

Here is how some mothers explained how, why, and when they made the choice to stay at home (the great majority of them left jobs), as well as how they felt about the transition to being an at-home mother.

**Robin** (two children, ages five-and-a-half and three): Robin worked full-time in hospital administration, and at the end of a nine-month leave, after her first child was born, faced an either/or choice. She chose to stay home, and worked out a part-time consulting arrangement for hourly work that she did for her old employer at home during her daughter's nap time, without benefits.

*"I really considered myself an at-home mother with an ability to earn some income. . . . . I had always felt that I wanted to be home and enjoy my kids while they were really little, and after experiencing infertility for three years, it made it much clearer to me that I really didn't want someone else to have that time with [them]. The other piece of it was that after paying baby-sitting costs it didn't seem like I would be making enough to make it worth it to me. But [my leave policy gave me] the luxury of having nine months to think about it."*

*The experience of defining herself as an at-home mother, she says, was "very mixed," but her conviction about why she was home was very clear. "It was very important to me to be with Alison and I really enjoyed it. I think that for a long time I kind of lost my sense of self as anything other than a mother, in a way. There was a certain amount that I felt I really had to proselytize about . . . how important it was to be home in order to justify my being home. To make it seem like a valid choice for an intelligent adult."*

**Marla** (one child, age four): Marla had a high-profile job in the Canadian government when her son was born in 1988. She knew she would take off at least the first year, and was able to get a six-month leave with pay, plus another six months, and then had the option to extend that to five years without pay. Her son is now four and she still has not gone back to work. She recalls the early months at home.

*"All of a sudden I found myself at home with a young child and didn't really know where to turn. I knew that I didn't want to go back*

*to work full-time. It was a fascinating area, I had traveled a lot, usually got to Europe once a year, cross Canada, to the United States, reasonably high profile, wardrobe, I even wore heels all the time, and all of a sudden there I was at home. I haven't been in the office in four years, and if I meet people I haven't met before, although I do quite proudly say, 'I'm a mother-at-home,' I also probably fit in the fact that I used to be . . . or whatever, because I do still feel that helps validate me."*

**Betsy** (one child, age fifteen months, and pregnant with her second): When Betsy's son was born in 1991 in northern California, she stayed home for three months and then returned to her job at a mail-order catalog. There were a number of other working mothers there, and the company used a small apartment they owned across the street from the office as a nursery, so Betsy had easy and ready access to her son throughout the workday. When her son was nine months old, her husband got a new job in Portland, Oregon, and the family moved.

*"Since I didn't have to work, I didn't want to, because it would break my heart to drop him off at seven o'clock in the morning and then pick him up at night. It was hard. It's a constant struggle because on the one hand I really enjoy being with Casey and I think it's good for him, he's very happy and secure and a loving child, so I don't feel like I did the wrong thing. But it's difficult going from having a job and feeling like you're doing something, you're bringing in money, and in some small way contributing to this company and doing a task that has a certain amount of ego involved, to not having that, and your biggest accomplishment is getting the dishwasher unloaded and maybe sweeping the floor or vacuuming. Going from a professional job to basically manual labor, it's a big mental adjustment. There's that constant fear that I'm going to lose my mind, I'm never going to get a job again because I can't compete, I'm not going to be able to catch up again. It's always there. Basically every day I think maybe I should go back to work now, or maybe I should work part-time. The other part [of me says], 'You should take advantage of this opportunity, because nowadays there aren't very many people who can do what you're doing. It's a privilege.' [Since] I'm pregnant again there's no point in going back to work now, and I can always work. I keep telling myself when I get wigged out, I can always work, but you can't always have your child be a year old. For the most part I don't mind changing diapers all the time, and pick-*

ing up after him. That's just the way it is. I think it's worth it. But there is definitely that guilty feeling like maybe I should be working or something. But I think if I were working and not taking care of Casey, I'd feel much worse. I should be there with him. . . . It's such an awful double bind that women are put in. It really makes me angry."

**Ruth** (two children, ages six and three): "[When my children were born] I was a full-time working parent. . . . I chose to go back to work. . . . I was always interested in being at home full-time, but I didn't feel like I could give up my job. . . . I've been at home with my children for about eighteen months now. I finally made the decision to make the break, to stop working full-time and stay at home with them. . . . I wanted to be with them more, and I found working full-time and trying to raise two young children not worth it spiritually, emotionally, financially. But it was a real struggle. I agonized over that decision for about two years before I actually did it, because I was really insecure about giving up my place in the workforce. But finally after my second child [was born]—she was an infant, and you know how hooked you are into your infant—I made the decision, and I haven't really looked back.

"I'm finding it hard to be at home after being mostly a working person. . . . You have the camaraderie of your colleagues—depending on where you've been working it can become like family, too. So I find being at home full-time can be very isolating unless you make a real effort. Luckily I live in a big city. Even there you have to make a real effort to get out and meet people and be very proactive, otherwise you can end up feeling very isolated. For me, the feelings of isolation are not conducive to positive mothering. You have to make a whole new set of friends and support, and there are fewer women staying at home so it's that much more difficult.

"But it's better for our family life in general, and the financial part of it hasn't been as much of a worry as we thought it would be. Largely because most of my salary was going for day care. I worked for the federal government. It was a very interesting but very stressful position, and I was wasted at the end of the day. The big thing about that work is that I believe that in five years it will all still be there, but my children will have grown, and I didn't want to miss the wonder years."

**Mary-Ellen** (two children, ages three-and-a-half and seven months): Mary-Ellen worked for ten years before her first child was born, in 1989.

*"I thought I was going to go back to work part-time, and I couldn't when she was born. I just decided that it was more important for me to stay home. And also the money part of it—when I figured out how much money I would be bringing in, and how much I would be spending on baby-sitters or whatever and transportation costs—I would have been working just to work, not to be bringing any money into the household. And I decided that I had a very good job, but it wasn't as important to me as being home when she was little. So that was it. I stayed home.*

*"The first year was terrible. I didn't know anyone else who was at home with young children. Everyone else I knew at that point didn't have kids. I only had a few friends with children, and most of them were working part-time, so it was very rough. I didn't know what to do with my days. And then when Dana was about four months old I did Playarena, and that's when I first started to meet some other people who were at home. I hung out in the playground, and I would talk to people, and I made a few friends. . . . [It was still] very hard because all of these other people had worked, too, and I found all anyone ever spoke about was their babies. Conversations rarely went past that and that's what I found very hard and very depressing, that we all had these other lives, and everything else going on around us, and yet everybody just talked about their infant. That was hard for me.*

*"I didn't have a car, so I couldn't get around. I did, anyway—I walked everywhere, and I took buses—but it's not easy with all the paraphernalia you carry around. Those first six months are very hard. The first four months in particular.*

*"I'm very glad I did it. Dana's three-and-a-half now, and I look at her and she's this whole little person, and I'm glad I saw it happen. I feel quite fortunate that I was able to make this choice and not be forced to work if I didn't want to."*

**Caroline** (four children, ages ten, eight [twins], and four): Caroline came to the United States from England in 1980, when her company transferred her to New York to set up a U.S. division. When her first child was born, in 1984, she left work to be at home because she faced an all-or-nothing work option. Caroline eventually took matters into her own hands and founded the newsletter *ConneXions,* for moms working out of their homes, and later MATCH (Mothers' Access to Careers at Home), a District of Columbia–based support group.

"*There was this black-or-white divide between did you stay home or did you go back to work, and that was a real problem for me, because I wanted to do it both ways. I wanted to retain professional career connections, but I wanted to do it on my terms, which maybe sounds idealistic and naive and stupid, but I didn't see why I couldn't. I didn't see why just because I wanted to spend time with my child I had to be branded a mushhead that was only capable of stuffing envelopes. Whether it was my perception of it happening [or whether it really was], I found that there wasn't a means for me to continue using my skills and experience in a different context than the only one that corporate America wanted to offer me, which was nine to five, five days a week, or you stuff envelopes for a meager sum. I wanted to feel like I was being compensated pro rata and commensurate with what I was capable of providing. That was a major problem for me. I think for mothers now, if you can decide ahead of time that what you want is a mix and a blend and a balance, and talk to other people about how to achieve that, then that gives you a step ahead of the game. Or talk to your employer. That's not always an issue. Some women are very happy to have a baby and then go straight back to work. What I find in the eight years that I've been a mom now, in the women I speak to, most women would like a better balance. Most working moms would like to be able to be home for the school bus, or not have to rush and pick kids up from day care and do all that. Many stay-at-home moms that I speak to would like a means of keeping up some career connections, unless they're very well off financially. And that makes a separate situation. Most of them would like to be doing something other than just diapers and childrearing, something just for them. Something that connects them to their past, and hopefully to their future.*"

**Susan** (two children, ages thirteen and nine): As an artist, Susan had worked at home even before she had her children. But her decision to stay at home was based on a number of other factors as well.

"*Partly my mother's influence. She was a teacher and taught out of the home. She was a very strong advocate for staying at home when your kids are really little. It was just an intuitive thing, and my husband and*

I both felt very strongly about that—this was our child and our decision and we wanted to be there. I think it was a gut reaction. I just couldn't stand the idea of all that emotion and love and caring going to someone else. It was quite selfish of me as well, in some ways. . . .

"The first year when I had my first child is the only time in my life my house has ever been really clean. I realize that we are our mother's daughters. . . . I had no idea that this was the image that I always had, because I had been an artist and had that lifestyle . . . [but after having my baby,] I vacuumed every day, I had everything perfect. I was in fear of germs attacking my daughter or something. It was a combination of all those things, that there were these BIG germs out there, and at the same time if I kept everything really clean, nothing bad would happen. It was also because I was bored stiff, but I felt guilty because I wasn't supposed to be bored with this little wonderful human being that all the books said you could watch them all day doing their cute little things. . . .

"I was so careful to tell everybody that I was an artist and I was staying home with my child but I was an artist so I stayed home anyway. That is just ridiculous! I realize now how hard it is to bring up children. It's got to be one of the toughest jobs and one of the most important jobs around. . . . What saved me was a playgroup, I think, which again is reaching out to a different group, but it was finding someone else to talk to."

**Gae** (two children, ages seven and twelve): "Going through it isn't always the easiest. There's an isolation from people who were your colleagues and peers who now look at you like someone who has given up. 'You don't do as much as I do because you quit working.' It's as if your brain has atrophied, and they no longer want to get together to talk about ideas, because they can't relate. What I find interesting is, when I was a working mom, I couldn't relate to moms who'd always been at home either, that was something so foreign to me, even though my mom had been at home. People in my age bracket didn't do that. But after being at home, I find that I can relate to both segments. . . . I find those very stressful. The assumption that you've got more time because you're at home. You really don't. In fact, when I went back to work when my first child was born, and she was eight weeks old, and I was in process of a separation and divorce, and I was nursing her, and was pumping, I honestly found that going into the classroom provided me a *sense of relief, because it was predictable . . . that brief time in the classroom offered me time to regroup before going home to unpredictable stresses. But everyone assumes that what is there to caring for an infant, you feed them and wash them and put them in bed, and it's not true."*

# Who Am I? Where Am I?

For many women who grew up in the baby boom generation of the late 1940s and 1950s, the images are vivid: the glossy pages of popular magazines, with their advertisements showing Mom in the kitchen, dressed to the nines (but wearing an apron), some miracle cleaning product in her hand, happy children at her feet. Donna Reed and June Cleaver on our TV screens. These were some of the predominant images that shaped our vision, regardless of what our mothers did, where they worked or didn't work, in or outside the home, whether our own real lives resembled those monodimensional media creations that so many young girls and adolescents were led to believe should become their reality. These images touched women across class lines, across cultures, and across national borders.

Susan Rennick Jolliffe, an artist and mother of two, was born in Canada in 1949. She recalls the images she saw in magazines and on television during her childhood years. "In some of my art I collect it and I use it—the kind of woman who's living better electrically, who's standing in front of her fridge, and she opens it up and it's all very clean, and she opens her oven, and the children are always perfect, and dinner's always done on time, and then she has a bridge club. Basically *Leave It to Beaver*, which in Canada was as big as it was in the States. We grew up with that image as the perfect mother."

Naima Major is an African-American writer who worked for six years for the National Black Women's Health Project and is currently working with an African-American filmmaker to "reimagine the lives and stories of black women and other people." The mother of three grown children, she was born in 1950 and grew up in a working-class, single-parent family on the South Side of Chicago. Her mother worked nights at the post office full-time, and Naima grew up with a strong sense of extended family—both from her aunt, grandmother, and cousins, as well as from women in the neighborhood. But ironically, she recalls that in the African-American publications of the day, the images of motherhood were similar to those in their white mainstream counterparts.

"One in particular that I know is out of print was called *Sepia*. It was like *Ebony* and *Jet*. It was a black publication, and since I was probably looking more at the pictures than anything else, I do remember the images and there were the standard images of a happy mom who generally had on—I started to say curtains—had on an apron that looked like curtains! And smiling, usually if not with a babe in arms and one toddling around underfoot, definitely children in the picture with her. They were very ideal positive images, because for us growing up on the South Side of Chicago, those were the magazines that our folks, people like my mother, working-class people who wanted to do the best for their children, those were the kinds of magazines that they had for us to see positive images of [ourselves]. I know that sounds anachronistic because nobody said that in the fifties, but this was what you had in your home. But I do remember noticing or feeling that these women were not like my mother, who did work outside the home, and although she did housework and those kinds of things, she didn't do it happily. She did it because it needed to be done. But it wasn't this ideal version of the happy housewife humming as she worked. These were things that needed to be done generally as quickly and efficiently as possible so that more important work like getting to work on time or doing something with my brother and me could be done. You just weren't mopping the floor and smiling with the kids sitting around, playing with their dolls."

These images, she says, "basically did not validate the women in my family and community that I did admire—my mother, and my aunt, and my grandmother, all working-class women who worked very hard in and out of the home," and yet "girls and children would see those images and elevate them as the idealized image of womanhood."

By the 1960s, for Major, these glossy media images of idealized domestic motherhood were juxtaposed with the images of violent segregation and the civil rights struggle. "Women were certainly raising their families, staying at home, or whatever, but the issues of the day had to do with civil rights and segregation and equal opportunity, fair housing, particularly in Chicago, which is very much a working-class city where issues like that are very close to the heart and the home."

Thirty years later, says Major, Julie Dash's film *Daughters of the Dust*, about the women in a Gullah family in the Sea Islands off Georgia at the turn of the century, further validated the image of "the black woman as an individual" who takes a traditional role of nurturer and parent, as well as a larger role in the society. In the film, she says, "the central role of the women was not only keeping the family together but holding on to that culture. I remember the images of the women talking and cooking and working and thinking and working out issues, and some of them carrying infants and children, and older children and teenage girls close to the older women. You could carry and nurse this baby and yet have an adult conversation with somebody about moving to the new world, going North for a better life for your children. Nursing this baby, taking care of these children, didn't mean that you had nothing to say about the future of this family and by extension the future of the race."

In contrast to this image of strong women assuming multiple important roles, including the traditional role of mother and nurturer, being an at-home mom today is sometimes misrepresented as a lifestyle rich in free time. "That's usually the misconception," says Gae Bomier, former PR director of Mothers at Home. "'What do you do all day?' Because you've made this difficult choice to be at home [and are not bringing in any income] you'd better smile and put forth this glowing image of children that are well kept, your house is neat as a pin, and everybody's happy. When kids are in arguments, you break it up by problem-solving rather than yelling at them. It didn't work that way for me. My house is a continual wreck because there's so much activity, I don't look that great in my blue jeans all the time, and I hit my limit and I scream. So it's hard to maintain that kind of media image.

"Those who really get into nurturing and being with their families realize that it takes every ounce of energy, every skill, every talent that they had before and that they can glean as they go along, to produce a family environment that's healthy and stimulating and challenging and good for growing children. [But] the stereotypes I think are what people believe mothering is all about."

Carol Lees recalls that when she was born in Canada in 1944, her mother, who stayed at home, had a very strong support system, as most women—including women who worked outside the home—did at that time, when neighborhoods were tighter and families closer by. Mothers at home still need it, she says. But as one of the voices—or what she calls a "voice in the wilderness"—that is working to break down the old stereotypes, she is quick to add that she is not advocating a return to those times—something that is apparent from the fact that her organization also supports men who choose to take on the role of full-time at-home caregivers and home managers.

## Motherwork: Revising the Job Description

*I knew nothing about what childrearing would entail, and I think I had a lot of very romantic images of what it would mean to take care of a baby and how I would feel, and so on. When I had my first child in 1988, I was very thrilled, of course, but it also struck me in a very very intense way that although I was thirty-two years old, I had gone through most of my life not really seeing the work that women do. And it was only when I had my child I realized what all that caring work meant. How important it was to a person's development, how important it was to keeping the society going. And I think for many women it's only when you start doing that work yourself, when you become responsible for caring, feeding, clothing, nurturing someone else, that you realize how much that work is taken for granted.*

—Helene Klodawsky, mother and filmmaker, Toronto

*It would have been nice just to have someone there just to let me know what I was getting into.*
—Jessica, new adoptive at-home mother

Child-centered feminists. Seed-planting. Sequencing. Home managers. The language central to the motherwork experience is beginning to change because those who are doing the work are talking about it themselves. More women-centered definitions of the job they do are coming into the vocabulary. The options, strengths, challenges, job descriptions, the multiple talents and roles of at-home mothers are slowly coming to be reflected more accurately in places and publications where women talk and share and gather with each other.

In Canada, Mothers Are Women members describe themselves as "child-centered feminists." Marla Waltman-Daschko believes that "just because you're a woman at home with children does not mean that you're not feminist. In some ways it helps define what a true feminist is. It's not just looking for equality in the work. There's a lot more to being equal and being a positive force than working in a man's world, in a workforce that is oriented toward men in full-time positions." In their view, a woman's productive and reproductive work no longer tips the scales.

Gae Bomier, former PR director of Mothers at Home, describes the valuable nature of the work itself, so often felt to be invisible by those doing it. "It's hard to observe it because it's a seed-planting process. You don't know when it will grow. It's a long-term project. It's something that grows very slowly sometimes, and then there are spurts. It's hard to observe it, and there is little value because our society seems to equate value with how much income you make, so people who are at home struggling with income are viewed as valueless."

Carol Lees expanded the language further when she founded a group she calls the Canadian Alliance for Home Managers to describe the choice of men and women who choose that path, even though it is unpaid labor. Lees has also brought the lack of value placed on the work of at-home mothers and fathers to the fore by refusing to complete the 1991 Canadian census form because one question asked how many hours she worked in the previous week, but instructed her not to include volunteer work, housework, maintenance, or repairs on her own home. A second question requires a woman who has worked all her life at home and as a volunteer to fill in a box marked "never worked in lifetime." Lees refused.

Members of Formerly Employed Mothers At the Leading Edge (FE-MALE) are reminded of Arlene Rossen Cardozo's theory of sequencing, and reassured that it is all right to postpone by choice some aspects of your life until your children are older; that it can be done with a deliberate purpose in mind; and, perhaps more importantly, with a support group also reminding you that it's all right to take pieces of your own life back, nurture yourself, and find other outlets for talents, drives, and ambitions.

New mothers making these changes and defining themselves and their work today have learned important lessons from women who have gone before them in this process. Helen Levine, feminist counselor, adjunct professor of women's studies at Ottawa's Carleton University, and mother of two grown daughters, articulates what she believes to be one possible long-term effect of postponing aspects of one's own life:

"If we're located full-time within the home, or even part-time, if this is our primary task over a significant number of years, what it means is that we put our talents, aspirations, our contributions to the world on hold. This is not to say it's good or bad. But something happens to any person whose central task is related to ensuring that others grow and develop and thrive. The clear message to wives and mothers is that our own lives, as separate adults, are on hold, that our own drives, needs, or talents are and should be secondary or nonexistent. I don't think anybody survives over time that way, really survives. There's a kind of dying, a loss of self in the process. That's what depression is often about."

Levine herself left the paid workplace for seven years after her children were born in the mid-1950s. She went back to work on a part-time basis, trying still to hold on to her "very romanticized notion of motherhood that lasted a long time." By the late 1970s, she recalls, she and others involved in the early feminist movement "began to realize that we had tackled all kinds of issues in women's lives, and somehow had left motherhood and motherwork out. Partly because so many women felt and were suffocated in the nuclear family, in the role of wife, mother, keeper of the home and keeper of the peace." Levine herself endured a breakdown and long, painful struggles as she "began to search for my own life and my own sense of significance" by the time her children were in their teens.

It was with this growing consciousness that she and a student, Alma Estable, began to work collaboratively on a paper titled "The Power Politics of Motherhood: A Feminist Critique of Theory and Practice." In their paper, Levine and Estable offer the following definition of the unpaid work that women do:

*Women do the unpaid work of family and community. This includes the bearing of children, and the physical maintenance and emotional work women do in the home. There are no wages for this work. It is the only labour assumed to be undertaken for love and by one sex exclusively. Motherworkers sign on indefinitely. There are no fixed hours, sick leave, vacation, pension, job security, collective bargaining, or unionization. Training is considered unnecessary and it is assumed there are instinctual blueprints for productivity. When instinct fails or when the "plant" is in trouble, mothers do not enjoy leaves of absence, unemployment insurance, or workmen's compensation. Instead, we are labelled inadequate or unfit.*[1]

Betsy, who became a first-time mother in 1992, is also a member of FEMALE. She believes that it is still very common for mothers—particularly those staying at home to raise children—to lose and submerge their own identities during childbearing/childrearing years. "I hope that I can be self-aware enough that I can keep on top of it, and do other things besides raising kids, and take classes, have friendships, socialize, keep reading and doing things and keeping my brain alive. If I feel like I'm getting to the point where I'm really stuck, I'll do something about it, get a job part-time, or whatever I need to do to fix it. I just hope that I can. Because it still happens. It happens all the time."

Today Helen Levine works with women individually in small groups and in workshops which address women and anger, housework, stress—"stress at home is real; housework is frustrating," she writes, "someone always comes and messes it up." Other issues emerge in the lives of mothers, according to Levine, regardless of whether they return to the workplace for pay, do unpaid motherwork at home, or, most commonly, do both. A session on women and anger was given as part of a series of workshops offered by the organization Mothers Are Women. In bringing together full-time mothers at home, the 1992 Childcare Policy Statement of Mothers Are Women offers the following definition:

> *The contemporary "mother at home" embraces a variety of women who are the primary caregivers of their children. This includes mothers who work in the home full-time and are partners in a single-income "family," mothers who are single, mothers who are self-employed and work from home, mothers who work seasonally or on a contract basis, mothers who are on welfare, mothers on maternity leave, mothers who are students, and mothers who work part-time.*[2]

The group's focus is on issues of interest to women not only as mothers but also as women who happen to be mothers. "We are brought closer together by the fact that we are also mothers," says member and mother of two, Ruth Znotins.

Filmmaker Helene Klodawsky, mother of two daughters, ages three and five, was at the Women and Anger workshop gathering footage for *Motherland: Tales of Wonder?*, her 1994 full-length documentary film on motherhood and the invisible nature of the work that women do that is so taken for granted. "I think a lot of women spoke to that sense of invisibility. A lot of it was in relationship to the men whom they lived with, or to the society in which they did their mothering work. Through all the research I've done—I did two years of research even before filming—I found that women were very passionate about the love that they felt for their kids; it was more I think the frustration that women felt with the society or with their partners. The anger didn't seem to be directed really at the children, although mothering work is often hard and frustrating, but at the conditions in which they did it. That's where people seem to be asking the questions and voicing concerns for change."

Betsy redefined herself in her own eyes as an at-home mom when she left her job in Portland. "I don't always feel particularly good about it, I feel like I'm at a disadvantage in some ways, like that's not really a very prestigious thing to be. But on the other hand, it makes me angry that I feel that way, that it's not prestigious, and that I'm a little ashamed of that or something."

Here, for example, is the way Betsy described a typical day when her son was just under a year: "We would get up and have breakfast, and then in the morning, read some stories or play in the house, then he would take a morning nap. After his nap we would get up and run errands, get out, and do grocery shopping or whatever. Come back, give him some lunch or snack, and then he'd have his afternoon nap. Then I'd cook dinner, do evening stuff, do another errand, then Dad would come home and Dad would play with Casey, and we'd have dinner, and he would go to bed."

Sound familiar?

Yet within this seemingly mundane description—which is how many moms at home might describe or experience their time—there is another level of challenge, texture, and accomplishment in terms of what goes on between mother and infant and later mother and toddler. Psychiatrist Daniel Stern describes the earliest phase of this interaction in his book *The First Relationship: Infant and Mother*. This dynamic is also the stuff of motherwork, though often not recognized or put into words by mothers or others. What Stern describes is a unique, nonverbal interaction between mother and infant; he likens it to a dance, with the caregiver as creative artist—"the choreographer-dancer or composer-musician."

Stern has observed how caregivers—"mostly first-time mothers—really 'learn their trade.' It's not through any of the medical, paramedical, or educational institutions. If a woman does not live in an extended family—and most no longer do—she learns through informal groupings of caregivers. These small and transient yet powerful and ubiquitous floating 'institutions' are the vitally important disseminators of information. They are usually formed haphazardly by who lives on your block, or in your building or who your sister knows, or who you met in the playground and happens to have an infant roughly your infant's age, or a little older, if you are lucky, since she has been there already last month."

Even when such networks have been formed—itself a great challenge for many women—it is still, he further suggests, a role that is both creative and lonely. "At some point, then, most caregivers find or feel themselves to be out alone on a limb of improvised behavioral interactions of their own personal creation. To some this experience is exhilarating, to more it is often frightening."[3]

This is the deeper job of motherwork, which women may vaguely recognize in their daily lives but that more often than not may go unacknowledged and undervalued. As far as your newborn herself is concerned, despite your best cuddling and nurturing, your ability to provide bathwater akin to ambrosia or the softest towels ever to wrap a baby's bottom, she will not bestow any slaps on the back. There are no praises, no raises, few lunches out, and none of the measurable rewards the culture generally goes by. The most you're likely to get is a goo or a giggle—but this, say many mothers in the next breath, is worth far more than rubies.

While Betsy says that she and other moms value the work they do at home full-time with their infants or they wouldn't be doing it, for a host of reasons she believes it is viewed as a second-rate job, and children as a second-rate priority. This message is partly responsible for women's feeling that they're never doing it well enough.

"I think there's always a tendency," she says, "to feel like you're doing something wrong or you're not doing it well enough or you're not efficient enough. It's very difficult, especially if you've been working and then you go to not working, to shift modes from task-oriented, [where] you get certain things done and can accomplish things, to this nebulous take-every-day-as-you-can, if you can get something done great, but most of the time you won't because you're going to spend the whole day chasing the kid and making sure he doesn't kill himself, and changing diapers, and just maintaining. You don't accomplish much, you just sort of keep it going, and you have to learn that that's okay for a while. For me particularly, or for any woman who's been working and been used to checking things off the list, accomplishment-oriented, it's very difficult to come to the end of the day and say, 'What did I do? I didn't even get the bills paid, for God's sake!' It's very difficult."

So how do new mothers at home learn to measure and reward themselves for their efforts and accomplishments there? While an office job may give you feedback from colleagues, when you're at home with a baby, your evaluation system may need some revision. Honey Watts, executive director of the Calgary Post Partum Support Society, describes one way to change the standard and give yourself a break using the Rule of Quarters that the CPPSS outlines—get one thing done in every quarter of the day—and most importantly, do something for yourself as well. But this shift in reward systems is not easy to come by.

Ruth Znotins joined Mothers Are Women after having worked for the government for many years. "How you view a successful day when you're in an office and working, there are obviously frustrations there, but you have a certain sense of accomplishment, very tangible things. You've put in so many reports, or dealt with so many clients, or whatever. And you have the intellectual stimulation of the work that you're doing."

As far as holding on to aspects of your "old life" are concerned, mothers find their own definitions of this. Mary-Ellen takes two nights a month for herself for dinner or a movie with a friend. Susan Rennick Jolliffe, an artist, switched to exclusively nontoxic materials that could be left all over and freely shared with her toddlers, drew during nap times (when she should have been resting herself), and started doing illustrations for—what else?—children's books "to give myself some kind of discipline again, because I really felt there was a big part of my spiritual self in terms of doing artwork that was being denied." Some moms strive for fifteen minutes to themselves each day for a walk or bath—but realistically, if you have an older child as well, you'll know that, as in Jill Murphy's children's book Five Minutes Peace, your fifteen minutes will probably boil down to three minutes and forty-five nonconsecutive solo seconds total.

Robin says that she understood intellectually that this early time in her child's life "was a short time, and [because I understood that] I wound up basically giving everything up. Emotionally, I don't think it worked that way. I'd find myself a little depressed about what was missing. . . . I really had no sense of the future and a separate me for several years there. When the kids were between three and four, I started to feel more like a separate person."

One image Robin kept in mind to help her through the overwhelming times as an at-home mother was in the form of an anecdote about a mother who steps into the thick of the fray one day—her kids are in the middle of their most trying moments, her house is a disaster, everything is chaos. "She walked into the living room, threw up her hands, and said, 'I surrender.' Just 'I surrender,' and she just kind of sat there in the middle of it, and that's a little bit of an exaggerated model for me, you know when you surrender to it, and totally give in and immerse yourself in their world, you cope with it, and you learn it and you're a better mother for it, and they're happier kids for it."

# Mommy Wars/Mommy Myths

In recent years, women who are mothers have often been cast onto a playing field under the banner headline "Mommy Wars," calling up images of a vast battleground strewn with broken rattles and battered briefcases as women attack each other in harsh, judgmental combat. Is it really this bad? Or has this conflict been manufactured and overblown to keep at-home mothers and mothers in the paid workforce from discovering and sharing their common ground and goals?

Women acknowledge that some tensions and misconceptions may exist—from the playgroup that forms around caregiver category (either Mom or baby-sitter), to some organized support groups that openly pass judgment on the choices of other women. But according to many moms, the truth seems to be closer to a gray zone in which both sets of moms—those staying at home and those working outside—each deal with advantages and disadvantages; both have good days and bad days. Moms at home may feel isolated from the world of things adult and the kind of social outlets, concentration, productivity, and economic independence that go along with it. The mom back at work may feel isolated from or deprived of the small details of her infant's ever-changing daily world. Women working outside full-time and coming home to spend as much time as they can with their baby won't have as much time to forge friendships as other mothers who see each other during the day because they are at home. Mothers who are at home may mourn the loss of the mobility and economic power they may have traded off to be at home, while feeling that the work they do is underrespected, even by their counterparts in the outside workforce. And two women on the same schedule may define themselves differently: A mother working out of the home three days a week may consider herself primarily a working mother, while another mom doing the same thing may consider herself an at-home mom working part-time.

In truth, there are many areas where the concerns of mothers at home and mothers working outside the home overlap. Interestingly, while the majority of readers of *Welcome Home* are probably at home full-time, some readers are working from home for varying numbers of hours. Others are moms who work outside the home full-time but would love to opt to be at home more or full-time if they could. In fact, says editor in chief Pam Goresh, noting the common territory mothers share, one reader jokingly suggested changing the subtitle from *A Publication in Support of Mothers Who Choose to Stay at Home* to *A Publication for Mothers When They Are at Home*, because many of the issues addressed seem to be universal themes of mothering.

In the final analysis, many mothers—those who stay at home and those who go back to the paid workforce full-time—acknowledge trade-offs. Each, it seems, might like a little bit of what the other one has—more time at home with their children, or a way to have some interaction with and earn some money in the adult world. One thing most mothers agree on is that, so far, no solutions are perfect. But as many have noted, the more flexibility women have in choosing how they will combine motherwork and other work over those first twelve months, the more we may see divisions among women begin to melt away.

## The Public Policy Arena and Mothers at Home

If you choose to stay at home to care for your child, should your choice be accepted as a legitimate childcare choice within the system, or has "childcare" become synonymous with "day care"?

If you take on the work of nurturing and raising your children for no money, should you be paid for the motherwork you do at home? Should you, at the very least, be able to make the same contribution to an IRA as your working-for-pay partner?

These are some of the issues mothers at home are tackling in the public policy arena, both in the United States and Canada.

Public policy decisions on childcare policy, childcare credits, taxes and personal exemptions, and economic issues such as IRA contributions and other retirement vehicles are perhaps those of most importance to mothers at home and how supported or excluded they feel their interests are from the public arena.

Organizations supporting at-home mothers, or your own congressional representatives can update you on the progress and status of relevant legislation if you are at home full-time with a new baby, or are planning to be at home and want to evaluate the economic ramifications of your decision.

## Formerly Employed Mothers: The Feelings

*I didn't like being branded a mushhead. . . .*
—Caroline Hull, *ConneXions*

In 1986, JoAnne Brundage was a letter carrier outside Chicago, with a six-year-old and a three-month-old baby. Just weeks before she was supposed to return to her job at the post office, she and her husband came to the painful realization that her second-born, was, in fact, a more difficult baby than her first, and they just "didn't feel confident that anyone else would be able to cope with this child." So JoAnne quit work when he was four months old and became a full-time at-home mother.

"I went through a real emotional shock in quitting work, as I know a lot of women do. It's hard enough when you have a new baby—that's a huge adjustment. But when you then make another radical change such as quitting work, that just takes away the last underpinning of your identity. I literally did not leave the house the first nine months that he was with us, except to run to the grocery store or something. The isolation I suffered was just incredible."

When her son was six months old, she began looking for other women to talk to but found "no one. I was very specific in my needs," she recalls. "It went beyond postpartum depression. . . . I went to a lot of related organizations who were sympathetic and could speak to PPD, but when it came to having problems with leaving the workplace, not being delighted with being at home, I got blank stares. I got hostile reactions. It was very upsetting."

Brundage felt that, for her, there was clearly a conflict in the mixed messages her generation had received. "[As] baby boomers, we're betwixt and between, because when we were growing up as children we got one message given to us. Then when we were growing up as women, the rules entirely changed. We have this very deeply rooted image of at-home mothers and what it means to nurture and to give your all to your children, and how wonderful that it is to be able to stay home and bake cookies, or be there with lunch ready. On the other hand, we also have these messages that we got in high school or college, that you're to leave that behind, and that you deserve to have a life outside the home, that you can pursue a career like any man."

Brundage's point suggests that perhaps the "mommy wars" have more to do with each woman's internal conflict waged on her own inner landscape, than with any two groups of women. It also confirms many women's sense that the structures in which new mothers and mothers of young children live and work need to be more responsive to women's current choices and capabilities.

"You have this internal battle going on when it comes to staying at home. I find a lot of women still feel deeply conflicted about it, but how it comes out most of the time is with being very defensive, almost militant about it, and not being able to say, 'You know, I'm not comfortable about this.'"

Caroline Hull, who moved to New York City from her native England in 1981, left full-time work to stay at home with her first child in 1984. She experienced similar feelings: "I loved the baby, and I felt that I took very naturally and instantly to motherhood. But I was dealing with a host of feelings that I hadn't expected or anticipated. Guilt about not working, not bringing in an income. Living off somebody else's money. I hated it, I couldn't come to terms with that at all. I didn't like the structurelessness of my day. I felt as though I'd been forgotten. After the initial flurry of interest because you'd had a baby, everyone goes back to what they were doing, and I didn't have much in common with my single friends anymore because they didn't have children. Life went on the same for them, but life for me had taken a dramatic turn. My husband's life went on pretty much as it had before, he still took his business trips, and went to the office every day, and mixed with adults. I just felt like I'd been thrown out of my comfort zone into this strange new world that I couldn't relate to. . . . I very much remember the awkwardness I felt when I'd first had the baby, and I'd feel very jealous if I walked into town with the stroller and I'd see a couple of moms having coffee in a coffee shop together or something. For me it felt as awkward to try and strike up a conversation with another mother as it was to go and ask somebody for a date. I didn't know how to do it. I could call a company and get myself a sales appointment, or stand in front of a room of fifteen people and train them on a software product, but I felt very awkward about finding another mom to be friends with. It was absolutely horrible. . . . It was really a very difficult period of my life, because I didn't have family here.

"What saved me, ironically enough, was I happened into a playgroup just about the time I made the decision to go back to work. That really provided a tremendous help to me, just being with other moms who had babies in a similar age range, and moms who had older children as well. That kind of grounded me a little bit."

Although she felt "absolutely paranoid" about leaving her son with anyone else, Hull also felt that she had to reclaim some of her "old life." "My solution was to go back to work part-time, but as an independent consultant with the company that I had worked for, and work out with them a schedule that gave me ultimate control and flexibility. I was paid by the hour, there weren't any other benefits particularly. It was really a question of me keeping my hand in, keeping contacts up, doing something interesting, having two or three days a week in the adult world, and feeling a bit more like my old self again."

Many women who have left work to stay home full-time talk about their overpowering priority to be there with and for their babies. But they also acknowledge some of the losses they feel: loss of identity, economic freedom, money, financial and other independence, self-esteem, "brain food," spontaneity, friends. Even conversations change. "People were certain that the only thing I wanted to talk about was kids, which was not true," says JoAnne Brundage. "I think that's an assumption that a lot of people make about women who have children and who are at home. . . . It was very upsetting to realize that this is how people think of you, and a lot of times I think you begin to internalize it. . . . The feeling is that this is the totality of who you are, and this is all you are allowed to think about, talk about, work on. We don't feel we have any right to talk about our needs anymore, that we have any right to a life that doesn't include our children. We feel this overwhelming guilt that we're not making money, therefore we don't deserve our own lives. In no other situation are you not allowed to continue your own life, but this is the attitude that women internalize: My life's on hold now."

Finances are another big consideration. Many women, says Gae Bomier, former PR director of Mothers at Home, are making economic sacrifices and cutting corners constantly to remain at home, despite the assumption that all women who stay home must have husbands or partners who earn enough money to make it not only possible but also easy. "It's very strange, the financial part," says JoAnne Brundage. "The whole dynamic in your marriage changes. For me, it turned out to strengthen it. My husband and I had been together for eight years at that point. As long as I was working, I had a sense of mine, yours, and ours. And I always held out a little bit of mine, and I don't think that's so bad. I still grapple with this, but my husband switched gears immediately. 'This is our salary, this is our life together.' He would say things like 'We got a raise!' But it forged a stronger union. Now we are actually a working unit, and it strengthened our marriage and our commitment to our family. Having said that, there's still that other terror somewhere in my head about being totally financially dependent. . . . That's a scary thing that I don't think any woman dare dismiss. That's an ongoing issue for me."

Eventually, says Brundage, "I thought, well, maybe I'm just a drudge now, just a housewife, and I have nothing to contribute to society. Overall, that angered me terribly." This anger served as a motivating force in helping her create a support network and a solution. "I hung on to my anger, really. And there were days when I wasn't very strong. There were days when I was really in the depths of depression, and that was very hard. When Zack was six months old, it was right around the holidays, I made a New Year's resolution that I was going to drag myself out of this, because it was getting old—for everybody. I was lying around moping and tearful. I wasn't going to let this hold me down, but I was going to do something about it."

She started with a trip to the local library to seek out an organization that might address her situation. She found none. But she did come across a section in one book about how to start a women's support group. After coming up with a name that she felt precisely conveyed her predicament—Formerly Employed Mothers At Loose Ends (FEMALE)—she put an ad in the local paper, and four women responded. All of them were second-time mothers, and even they, she recalls, had difficulty talking about issues other than their children, breastfeeding, sleep patterns, and other child-related matters. "For a first-time mother," she says, "that's very important talking about that stuff, but I wasn't a first-time mother. The other four were also on second children, but we all talked about it, because that's what women do when they don't have their jobs to talk about."

JoAnne's group took shape, and within one year had "all of about fifteen women." But "what was fascinating," she says, "was that when we got a group of women together, it was very akin to the women's movement, where the personal was political. And as soon as we got together we realized that, wait a minute, we don't all have the same problems coincidentally. Maybe it speaks to a larger issue, which is society's attitude toward nurturing and women's need to do both—have a public life and a personal life. We began to evolve into something that was sort of a mixed bag.

"Just because you're at home does not mean your life's on hold now. That's one of the most valuable things that FEMALE offers as a message: You do still have a life. You can pursue your own interests, you can go back to school, you can look into some sort of flexible work arrangement that allows you to put your family first and still pursue your own needs and interests. And that's okay, and it's all right to hire childcare occasionally just for you. Not because you have to go to the doctor, but because you deserve some time off for yourself. You're allowed to have discussions. . . . But it's very difficult."

Early in 1988, a small story about FEMALE appeared in the *Chicago Tribune*. "We got sixty calls in twenty-four hours," Brundage recalls, "and it just snowballed from there." Clearly, her instincts had been right, and she had hit squarely on the feelings and struggles of so many new mothers. In March FEMALE had a letter to the editor printed in *Ms.* magazine, and soon they heard from hundreds and hundreds of women throughout the country and even outside the country.

"You can read all the books in the world, you can read magazines, you can read newsletters. But having a friend who's been through it and can tell you, 'Don't worry about it, you're okay. Be okay with being a mess for a while, it's expected, it's part of the job.' That's really good to know.

"You need time off where you don't have any other expectations on you. It's helpful to have a mentor, if you will, to say, 'Okay, things are getting better, you're getting more sleep, now it's time to make time for yourself.' And not only give the new mother time to go to the library by herself, but to say to her, 'I'll take the baby for a couple of hours, go out and relax, or go home and take a nap—now it's okay to begin taking little pieces of your life back.'"

# Doing Your Homework: Home-Based Work for Pay

If you are an at-home mom of an infant or are considering staying at home full-time after your baby is born, you may believe, hope, or fantasize that working at home for pay may be a way to strike a balance in your life as a new mother, whenever you need to or feel ready to take on paying work.

Some new mothers have considered themselves at-home moms with an ability to earn some income; others open an office on a third floor or in a back room, and take on considerable commitments, striking out on their own, or taking on projects or freelance work from a previous employer, usually forgoing the benefits of the workplace. Some have been successful; others have found it too difficult to manage. It is rarely a panacea, but for some women it can be an alternative, or even a very effective way to keep skills and profiles alive or explore an entirely new avenue, provided they have a realistic sense of what to expect when they combine new motherhood with a new business venture or an old business in a new setting.

While JoAnne Brundage bridged the gap from work to home by rallying and joining with other mothers who were staying home full-time and devoting her time to a vital but unpaid project, Caroline Hull took an alternative route, in creating supports for mothers who wanted to choose the option of home-based work for pay. Mothers who communicate with *ConneXions*, Caroline Hull's newsletter for mothers doing home-based work, do a wide variety of things, from handicrafts to consulting work, and have hit upon businesses that can grow as their children grow, or are otherwise realistic in scope and expectation.

It is worth looking at the lessons other women have learned in doing this (as well as at some of the pitfalls) and at some of the support networks now available to help you if you are contemplating starting or are already doing this yourself.

In 1984, Caroline Hull left a full-time job when her first child was born. Before her son was a year old, she started thinking of paid work she could do from home. Before she came up with an answer, however, she found herself pregnant with twins, who were born in 1985. More determined than ever to work from home around the hours of her children, upon further exploration she found that the options she faced were "exploitative of a very vulnerable segment of the market, that is, women who wanted to or needed to be at home for some reason." In 1987 her family moved to Virginia from New York City. Still finding few satisfactory alternatives, she started looking for other women who felt as she did about the issues. "I felt that by combining efforts with like-minded women who had professional backgrounds, and were frustrated in their ability to combine family and career in what was for them a satisfactory way, I had this vision of a sisterhood of powerful women who would join forces and start maybe affecting how corporations viewed family responsibilities and conflict-with-work commitments."

Hull did not find exactly the sort of group she was looking for, and in the meantime had a fourth child, in 1989. At this point she decided to create the very thing that would have helped her five years earlier: "I decided it was time for me to start thinking about doing something specific. . . . It seemed to me the best thing to get myself going was to start publishing a newsletter that would provide the type of information that I really wanted when I was first looking for ideas about working at home." Thus *ConneXions* was born.

In New York City, at about the same time that Caroline Hull's first child was born, Dr. Kathleen Christensen, a professor of environmental psychology at the CUNY Graduate School and director of the National Project on Home-Based Work, was thinking about the very same subject: women and home-based work.

"There was a fair degree of public attention to this issue of work at home," recalls Dr. Christensen, "and a lot of the attention was focusing on the supposedly ideal arrangement of working at home for mothers of infants and toddlers."

Reminiscent of the 1950s, advertising campaigns again showed us images of idealized motherhood—this time, not Mom standing in her sparkling kitchen with sponge and mop in hand, but instead sitting in her converted kitchen "office," with her fingers flying over the keys of a computer keyboard. (Indeed, mothers of small children have often done their best thinking, talking, writing, working, and sharing at these kitchen tables, and have created what Naima Major recalled as the vibrant "kitchen table society" of her youth, but depictions of these images of kitchen life are the ones we see less often.)

Forty years after classic 1950s advertising aimed at home-based moms, says Dr. Christensen, here were "advertising programs which showed the woman at the kitchen computer with the toddler and the puppy playing quietly behind her as she was typing away at her word processor. It just struck me that there was this public and political push toward promoting work at home for mothers of young children, and there yet was no research available as to how well it actually suited the needs of mothers and under what conditions it suited their needs. I wanted to examine how well it fit, and for whom and when and under what conditions."

Dr. Christensen found out by surveying fourteen thousand women who were readers of *Family Circle* magazine. Her survey showed that seven thousand worked at home, and that more were doing management or were self-employed, and doing clerical and technical work rather than sewing or crafts-type work. Not surprisingly, most felt that no one had ever asked about their stories, or had shown much interest in the quality and texture of their lives.

The survey also showed, says Dr. Christensen, that often women had romanticized, dreamy notions about working at home when their children were young. "First of all it's been promoted in the media as this great panacea that will solve all your problems—look, you can have work and family in one place, you can be with your baby and at work at the same time." The forces that encourage women to try to create and manage a work-at-home option are powerful. "If a woman has young children," she says, "there is such a desire to have a life in which work and family are integrated, that I think oftentimes there is the hope or the desire that this will really allow that kind of integration."

While many women have been successful at combining otherwork and motherwork at home, they admit that there are pitfalls new moms should be aware of so they are not shocked when things do not run as smoothly as they had hoped. For example:

• Sleeping infants wake up—your stretches of concentrated work-time might be unpredictable or interrupted frequently.

• If it's a new business, you may have underestimated the time involved—a new business, in fact, can be very much like a new baby in its constant demand on your time.

• Your image and credibility may be perceived differently. Even though you know you're working, friends and relatives don't really understand that you're not free to chat on the telephone or have company. Some moms report that their work wasn't taken as seriously when they worked at home.

• Domestic boundaries may melt away as laundry spills over into your office space and dirty dishes pile up in the kitchen.

• In addition to the isolation of new motherhood, there is the isolation of the discipline required to keep your work schedule on track. (Unions criticize it for this reason, because they fear it will lead to abuses if women are not in a common workplace and are cut off from sources of information about equitable salaries for the work they are doing. In addition, if you switch your status from employee to independent contractor, your compensation package may change.)

• Don't forget that separation issues come up as the baby moves into toddlerhood. "Young children going through separation," says Dr. Christensen, "have a difficult time having the door closed in their faces. They don't understand that. They don't have this notion of multiple-role theory, that Mom is Mom, and Mom is also a writer, or a computer operator, or whatever."

• Working at home is not necessarily a solution to childcare. Based on her research for the Office of Technology Assessment, says Dr. Christensen, "If a woman didn't have any solution to childcare, what she ended up doing was working through naps and after children went to sleep or before they got up, and it was, as we well know, a difficult balancing act."

• If you do secure additional childcare, either inside or outside your home, first-time new moms, says Dr. Christensen, found this third-party involvement especially difficult. "There's such a falling in love in most cases with your firstborn, that it's hard knowing someone else is there taking care of the baby, and sometimes you'd much rather be with the baby than working. When you leave the house it almost makes it easier."

Caroline Hull offers the following advice to mothers who are thinking of working at home with an infant or baby:

• Be realistic about the time you can put in, especially if you don't have on-site childcare.

When Hull started *ConneXions*, she knew her worktime would not be more than nine or ten hours a week, or the total nap time of her youngest. "That's what I budgeted for in terms of the type of business that I started. You cannot expect to put in sixty hours a week if you have a newborn and you want to spend time with the baby. 'Cause the babies don't just sit there and occupy themselves while you get on with your business."

• Learn to work in small snatches of time.

"Learning to be realistic about the time, and learning to work in small snatches of time is a real challenge," says Hull. "If you're used to having scheduled or uninterrupted blocks of time, one of the most frustrating things for many women I speak to—not just working mothers at home, but women with a hobby or anything—you have to rely on getting fifteen minutes here, and twenty minutes there, and it's fragmented. That's hard. Incredibly frustrating. You never feel as though your fulfilling. Everything's always half finished. In fact, that's why I turned to bread-baking. It was a great way of relieving the frustration. I'd smack that dough on the counter, and it's ideal for a fifteen-minute burst, because you just mix it and you knead it and you leave it for three hours while the baby's up, and then put her to bed, and thwack the dough again; it's great. And you get a nice product at the end!"

• Assess your self-discipline honestly.

"Instead of putting on TV, getting to the computer if you have an hour can be difficult. You have to be motivated and self-propelled," Hull advises.

According to Dr. Christensen, those women who started their businesses before their babies were born seemed to have a better sense of the rhythm and of their own confidence in controlling the flow of the work.

For all of those women who did work out a successful home-based work situation, "It seemed that the critical factor was how well the woman was able to conceive of herself in whatever her occupation was, and how well she understood her own needs and was able to develop systems or supports to meet those needs. And there were some women who were really very successful. For example, there were a number of women [in Manhattan] who started a word processing service in the mid-1980s. Because there was a sufficient demand for their skills, instead of trying to cut each other out they decided to develop a guild where they would support each other. They met on a regular basis. They shared information. They backed each other up if there was overflow or if someone was sick or on vacation. And they had very clear ground rules about not taking each other's clients, and things like that. That was a case where the women really initiated and supported a group that provided them with information as well as personal and professional support for their work. And then other women [were successful when they] were able to negotiate within the family the kinds of needs that they had. . . . I think the major lesson was that while it solved some problems for everyone, it created other kinds of problems that weren't necessarily insoluble but that required thought."

Dr. Christensen says that she has observed that the focus is shifting from entrepreneurship to working for employers out of your own home. But even as the status of women in the workplace very slowly becomes more fluid and time-appropriate for their lifestyles, inequities remain. The women she speaks to, says Caroline Hull, are well aware of the trade-offs of benefits, compensation, seniority, and status, but are willing to accept them in order to have the flexibility and to work at least partially on their own terms, until such time as there are better options available to them.

## Beyond Your Own Four Walls: Staying Connected

*When you get that glimpse into another mom's life, and you realize how similar it is to yours, you really feel a sense of camaraderie. I think that's the nicest thing [about the journal* Welcome Home]. *It's like a chat over the backyard fence when you don't really get that anymore.*

—Elizabeth Foss, Mothers at Home

As with so many aspects of motherhood, women have themselves created the journals and networks and books to address their own needs as at-home mothers, in a context that suits their schedules and the demands on their time. Both Mothers Are Women (MAW) and Mothers at Home (MAH), for example, consider their publications significant because without nationwide chapters, these are the forums through which mothers around the country are able to speak to each other on a regular basis. Indeed, some of the issues they address touch the lives of all mothers; others are specific to the daily texture of life for at-home moms, providing the voices and inspiration to help them through the sick days, winter days, cluttered days, days when walls are closing in and a sense of humor fails. Others celebrate the rewards of being present with and for their children. Others target the larger public policies that either further or impede their efforts. Articles, artwork, and other contributions all come from women who are members.

JoAnne Brundage's group FEMALE grew from five women in a living room to more than fifty chapters nationwide, and includes many new first-time mothers. FEMALE, says Brundage, also works on the local level to increase sensitivity to family and mother-friendly environments—for example, by advocating at the local supermarket for a candy-free checkout aisle. In Canada, in addition to her efforts to reform the census, Carol Lees's Canadian Alliance for Home Managers has also worked on increasing local sensitivity to families and at-home mothers. Its restaurant survey evaluated local restaurants to determine how well they met the needs of families, and a "Best Family Restaurant" listing was published, along with an information sheet of recommendations to restaurants; and when International Women's Day was celebrated at the Saskatoon YWCA, CAHM commended them for their decision to charge two different admission rates to the celebration: The prices were assessed according to whether attendees were waged or unwaged.

In Ottawa, Susan Rennick Jolliffe and MAW organized an art show with works by thirty female artists, all of whom worked out of home-based studios and had children of various ages. The name of the exhibition was: "Wait Until I Scrape the Jam Off"—an image any mother can relate to.

Below, a group of at-home moms talks about the empowering effects of the work they do, both as at-home moms with their children, or through their various groups and organizations:

*Marla: During the early time that Marla was at home with her new son, one of her friends who'd just had a baby also had to walk away from her job entirely.* "We relied on each other a lot. I started to meet other women in parks, and I went to [a] postnatal care group once a week. . . . When I realized I wasn't going back to work and would have to give in my request for an extended leave, I was starting to feel very frustrated. We had moved to a new neighborhood, we'd bought a house, and I didn't know anyone, and felt very isolated and really quite unsure about what I was doing. I had read months before in a publication called Today's Parent that there was a group called MAW that was located in Ottawa, and on one particularly bad day, when my son threw his food on the floor one time too many, I just thought, 'I'm going to kill him or kill myself,' whatever, I remembered this number. It sounds so clichéd, but the lightbulb went off, and I phoned, and lo and behold, somebody answered. She was actually there, rather than getting a message. It was July. And they were still holding workshops in the summer. . . . [I took my friend] and I was just so thrilled to find that there were other women there who were older, were intelligent, who weren't babbling, who could talk about something other than children. They had shown a couple of national film board films from the women's program, and it was so great that I went again, and slowly became more involved, knowing that I needed an outlet other than just being a mother and going to playgroups. . . . It's become a very important outlet for me. It mirrors what I was doing at work, but now instead of reviewing applications for government grants, I'm writing them.

"I think some of [motherwork] can only be done through example. It [helps to know that you're not alone and other women are struggling with the same things]. . . . Although our meetings tend to be more issue-oriented, and we don't sit around and talk about what it means to be a so-called modern woman at home with children, although we probably need to do more of that, there is this feeling sometimes that it's almost like a revival meeting—'Yes!' That you're reaffirming each other's worth, that you're going through the same things, that you're not alone, we don't have to justify ourselves to each other like we might to friends who are back in the workforce. It does give you a feeling of strength, that you can go home and say, 'Yes, I can do this, tomorrow is a new day!'"

**Ruth:** "This is going to sound like a TV commercial—dial long distance—[but for me the greatest reward was] being around to [share] all those quiet moments with my children. There's a lot of drudgery in-

*volved in staying at home, but what I really enjoy is being there for when my daughter woke up from her nap, or putting her to sleep by myself, seeing expressions on their faces and different things that happened to them during the day—happy things or sad things—being there to be the one to comfort them, or seeing them discover something delightful and seeing it in their faces. That would probably be the most rewarding thing. After that, it would be our family lifestyle; when I was working, we had to be up and have our kids dressed and in their snowsuits in the wintertime and be out of the house by seven-thirty in the morning, and it went okay, but I think it's a lot better for our family life to not have to do that."*

**Robin:** *"There are just these blissful moments . . . the most intimate connection with another person, just watching [my daughter] respond to the world. We'd have these days that were just gorgeous, and we'd be able to be outside and enjoy it, which most of us as adults don't get to do. . . . So there I was being able to be outside, and enjoy life and enjoy the world and share it with her, and have her respond to me at that age, that six to nine months when they really become little people, interactive, when they giggle and smile. Alison's first real belly laugh was around that age. . . . We were doing something stupid—buzzing like a bee—and she just giggled, and it's the same giggle! Part of the wonderful thing that first year, you wonder who your child is going to be, and around that age, who she is is becoming evident . . . it's really the same personality now, just fuller. And I have these memories of walking in the park with her when she was fourteen months old, and being outside with her on this gorgeous fall day, and her handing me leaves. Everything she saw was amazing and she wanted to share it with me. You are also being given this privilege of seeing the world again through a child's eyes, sort of getting to start over again yourself. It's a real renewal when you have those moments, when you really share your child's vision."*

**Elizabeth:** *"Welcome Home [offers] monthly doses of, 'You're doing the right thing, you're making a difference!' We need that because I don't think society does that for you. I don't think that mothers, especially mothers at home, are regularly given a little boost of appreciation, a pat on the back, applause, or anything. A lot of times we hear,*

'Isn't so-and-so incredible, she's managing to hold down a job, and her kids are doing so well,' and that's all well and good. But what about the mom who's sacrificing and not having a job and staying home, and really dedicating herself to her kids? Welcome Home does that. It's a nice shot in the arm."

**JoAnne Brundage:** "The whole situation of starting this group [FE-MALE] has been a huge turning point in my life. It's amazing to me that only when I quit work did I begin to really find the direction I wanted my life to go in. I think oftentimes when you let go of that handy image you have, you're forced to evaluate your life and it is an opportunity. It's difficult, it's frightening, it's terrifying, but it does afford you an opportunity that many people will never get."

**Carol Lees:** "In making the choice to stay at home, women need to know that if they give up certain commitments while their children are growing up, they really need to be reassured that they will be able to regain that, or discover something else and encounter new vistas that did not exist for them before. I think young women need to be assured that will happen for them, and it's okay for a while to be taken up with your children. That's a legitimate thing to have happen. It's not a wrong thing. It's not enough for every woman, and for those women for whom it is not enough, then I think it is right for them to find alternative care for them when they need to do that and develop other interests of their own. I think that we need to legitimize women's choices."

# Notes

1. Helen Levine and Alma Estable, "The Power Politics of Motherhood: A Feminist Critique of Theory and Practice," occasional paper (Centre for Social Welfare Studies, Carleton University, Ottawa, 1984), p. 6.

2. "Mothers Are Women," Childcare Policy Statement (Ottawa: Mothers Are Women, 1992), p. 3.

3. Daniel Stern, *The First Relationship: Infant and Mother* (Massachusetts: Harvard University Press, 1977), p. 132.

# Resources

The resources listed here are described in further detail in the following section:

**Support and Advocacy Organizations for Full-Time At-Home Mothers**

UNITED STATES
FEMALE (Formerly Employed Mothers At the Leading Edge)
Mothers at Home
Welfare Warriors
CANADA
Mothers Are Women

**Books**

*Discovering Motherhood*
*The Family Manager's Guide for Working Mothers*
*Going Part-Time: The Insider's Guide*
*for Professional Women Who Want a Career and a Life*
*Staying Home: From Full-Time Professional to Full-Time Parent*
*What's a Smart Woman Like You Doing at Home?*
*Women and Homebased Work: The Unspoken Contract*
*The Working Mom's Hints and Tips and Everyday Wisdom*
*You Can't Do It All: Ideas That Work for Mothers Who Work*

**Newsletters/Journals**

*Homebase: A Forum for Women at Home*
*Welcome Home: A Publication in Support of Mothers Who Choose to Stay at Home*

## Support and Advocacy Organizations for Full-Time At-Home Mothers

UNITED STATES
**FEMALE (Formerly Employed Mothers At the Leading Edge)**
P.O. Box 31
Elmhurst, IL 60126
Tel.: (630) 941-3553
www.femalehome.org

FEMALE, founded in 1987 by JoAnne Brundage, is a support and advocacy group for women taking time out from paid employment to raise their children at home. A national at-home mothers' organization with over 170 chapters, activities include regular meetings (featuring topical discussion groups, book discussions, or guest speakers), playgroups, a membership directory, a community resources guide, Mom's-Night-Out activities, and a support system in times of personal need. Membership also includes *FEMALE Forum*, a newsletter that covers current legislation and business issues regarding working families, personal accounts of life at home, survival techniques, book reviews, political and environmental issues, and columns providing networking among FE-MALE members across the country. Local chapter start-up materials and ongoing assistance are available.

**Mothers at Home**
8310A Old Courthouse Road
Vienna, VA 22182
Tel.: (703) 827-5903
Info/Order Line:
  (800) 783-4MOM (666)
www.mah.org

This is a Virginia-based nonprofit organization that supports moms who choose (or would like to choose) to stay at home to raise their families. Its goals are to affirm the choice to be home throughout the many stages of motherhood; to provide mother-to-mother support, education, and networking; to correct society's misconceptions and refute stereotypes about at-home mothers; and to serve as advocates for children concerning their needs for generous amounts of their parents' time. They publish *Welcome Home*, a monthly journal that supports mothers through essays, informative articles, poetry, and more. Also published by MAH are three books: *What's a Smart Woman Like You Doing at Home?*, written by the founders of Mothers at Home; *Discovering Motherhood*, an anthology; and *Motherhood: A Journey Into Love*.

**Welfare Warriors (WW)**
2711 W. Michigan
Milwaukee, WI 53208
Tel.: (414) 342-6662
Moms' Helpline:
  (414) 873-Moms (6667)
Fax: (414) 342-6667

Founded in 1986, WW is a multiracial group of mothers who have had to receive public child support (welfare) to raise their children. Its headquarters are in Milwaukee, with chapters around the U.S., and its mission is to create policy and media attention responsive to the needs and concerns of mothers, especially single moms and those in poverty. The MOMS Line offers new moms emotional support, and lessons in self-advocacy and bureaucratic self-defense. WW validates women in their choices and lack of choices, and encourages mothers to create their own support systems. The organization also seeks to make the voices of low-income mothers heard so that decisions affecting "our lives will be made by those of us with actual knowledge of the problems, rather than by people with theories and privilege but little life experience." Subscriptions are available to *Welfare Mother's Voice*, a quarterly, national, bilingual newspaper; and members have also written a 180-page book, the *Mothers' Survival Self-Help Manual*. Start-up materials and mentoring are available for mothers who want to start "fighting for the lives of mothers and children."

CANADA
**Mothers Are Women (MAW)**
P.O. Box 4104, Station E
Ottawa, Ont. K1S 5B1 Canada
Tel.: (613) 722-7851
E-mail: maw@cyberus.ca
www.cyberus.ca/-maw

Mothers Are Women (founded in 1984) is an independent, volunteer-run, feminist support and advocacy organization for mothers who have chosen to be the primary caregivers of their children for some period of time.

MAW respects and supports other childcare choices. It believes, however, that the ability to exercise the choice to care for one's own children at home without threat of social or economic penalties is part of the struggle for equality for women. *Homebase: A Forum for Mothers* is a quarterly magazine nationally distributed by MAW in which members are encouraged to voice the love and humor, isolation, and politics of their experiences as mothers and women. MAW also offers educational and experiential workshops on various topics, as well as a monthly book group and biweekly discussion groups. The organization compiles resources, provides information, and advocates on social, economic, and political issues concerning mothers from a feminist perspective. It seeks to make the contribution of mothers visible and valued by policy makers and the public at large, and participates actively in the women's movement. Membership is through subscription to *Homebase*, and MAW encourages the formation of local community MAW discussion groups.

## Books

*Discovering Motherhood*
Mothers at Home

This anthology from Mothers at Home brings together articles, poetry, essays, and artwork that offer support and a sense of community to moms in their first years of at-home motherhood. Its focus is on the "transitions, realities, and rewards of motherhood."

*The Family Manager's Guide for Working Mothers*
Kathy Peel
Ballantine

This book teaches working mothers how to make more time to enjoy their families, organize their home, and simplify their lives.

*Going Part-Time: The Insider's Guide for Professional Women Who Want a Career and a Life*
Cindy Tolliver and Nancy Chambers
Avon

From the author of *At Home Motherhood: Making It Work for You*, this is a step-by-step guide that helps professional women find and thrive in part-time positions. It offers practical advice on how to find creative compromises that will keep them professionally active while allowing them the time to participate in the lives of their partners and children.

*Staying Home: From Full-Time Professional to Full-Time Parent*
Darcie Sanders and Martha M. Bullin
Little, Brown and Company

Based on surveys of 600 at-home mothers, this book helps women make the sometimes difficult transition from office to home. Written by a member of the board of directors of FEMALE and an instructor at the University of Chicago, it addresses such issues as changing relationships with spouse and family, coping with isolation and twenty-four-hour workdays, managing loss of income and professional identity, and home-based employment opportunities.

*What's a Smart Woman Like You
Doing at Home?*
Mothers at Home

Written in 1986, three years after they began publishing the national newsletter *Welcome Home*, the Mothers at Home founders wrote this book to help define the "new mother" who is emerging, "neither the housewife of the '50s, nor the working mother of the '70s; a mother who has decided to put her family first without putting herself last." Combining essays and many excerpts from readers' letters, the book addresses such topics as discrepancies between media perceptions and moms' perceptions of their choices, revelations about "feeling guilty no matter what we do," "Startling Realizations and Gentle Discoveries" ("Am I the Manager or the Maid?"), "Mothers and Society: Perceptions and Possibilities," and others.

*Women and Homebased Work: The
Unspoken Contract*
Kathleen Christensen
Henry Holt

This book looks "behind the public images of homebased work" to explore the "unspoken contracts" women have "about who they are and what they are supposed to do." Dr. Christensen is head of the National Project on Women and Home-Based work. Her book incorporates the results of her survey of 14,000 readers of Family Circle magazine.

*The Working Mom's Hints and Tips
and Everyday Wisdom*
Louise Lague
Peterson's

A witty and practical guide with good advice on how to deal with guilt, housekeepers, and day care; organizing quality time; couples after parenthood; and building support systems.

*You Can't Do It All: Ideas That Work
for Mothers Who Work*
Irvina Siegel Lew
MacMillan Publishing Company

Puts work and family into perspective, and offers advice on how working mothers can do it a little more easily.

# Newsletters/Journals

*Homebase: A Forum for Women at Home* (see Mothers Are Women, p. 309)

*Welcome Home: A Publication in Support of Mothers Who Choose to Stay at Home* (see Mothers at Home, p. 309)

# 8.
# THE SECOND
# (THIRD . . . FOURTH . . .)
# TIME AROUND

*Old Pro/New Feelings*

• • • • • •

*Giving birth is a transformation and it doesn't matter whether you've had eight babies before. It's still a transformation the next time you have another baby, because you are no longer the same woman you were before you had that baby. We have to acknowledge that.*

—Penny Handford, PPPSS

## What Have We Learned from This Experience?

As second children enter a family, there is enormous joy and pleasure that women feel at seeing their families grow. The arrival of each new child, Penny Handford reminds us, brings a transition in which mother and new baby still play a central role. In Uganda, Sara Kunsa points out, there is a special word, *nakawere,* meaning "mother of a newborn." This word and the special treatment that goes with it apply to a woman following every birth, not only the first one. The massages, the foods, the care—"they have to take care of you in a special way for about a month."

In Korea as well, In Lee explains, the term *san mo* means "mother of a newborn child" and is used to describe a woman every time she has had a baby. Extended family and neighbors who act as family care for older children and for the new mother. "This lasts for about twenty-one days," she says. "They take special care of you."

When her third child was born, recalls Liz Koch, founder of the California-based magazine *The Doula,* she understood her own needs as well as those of her family members, and created a large support network to help them all get off to a better start. Indeed, if you have older children, you may already have a larger support base, through parents of your older children's playmates and schoolmates.

Often the arrival of a second brings with it a strong, satisfying sense of physical and practical confidence. The basics are "under your fingers," says Koch. You can change a diaper anywhere with grace and speed, standing in a moving elevator, or sitting on a crowded bus . . . hold the new baby without fear that he or she will break, and you can even give it a bath calmly and serenely, without rushing it to the waiting towel football fashion, for fear that cold air might touch its tiny body. And, seasoned pro that you are, your metabolism may already be used to less sleep compared to the first time around. This is probably a good thing, since parents seem to agree that while numbers of children increase numerically, workloads seem to increase exponentially: Having one child is having one child; having two is like having ten, and so on (or so it feels). The scope of the practical this time includes not just a house, a partner, and perhaps a pet and plants, but also the needs of your older children—school pickups and drop-offs, outings, park time, food, laundry, special time, and other logistics.

In addition, your own situation may have changed in any number of ways: You're older—maybe one year, maybe two years, maybe ten or more years; your employment and childcare situation may have changed or may be making different demands on you. Your helpers and support system may be different: Relatives who were available last time may not be able to help; on the other hand, through your older child's friends, you may already have an expanded support network of friends who are also parents and are only too happy to help, especially with care and attention for your older children.

As for mates and partners, while some feel very comfortable diving into the daily fray of feedings and shampoo as soon as they're in the door, others may feel totally intimidated and even more displaced by two children, and suddenly forget where the linen closet and bathroom are altogether. In addition, Luz García points out, relationships may have changed and perhaps partners may be out of town more often, away in the armed services, or out of the picture for some other reason. "Moms need a focus for moral support," she says, "especially as a single parent. She may connect to a second child faster, because she already knows what the love of a child is, but the surroundings make a difference in the way that we connect."

With second and subsequent children, many women feel that they are well prepared and able to plan for the practical. Some women have altered views about entitlement and self-expression when it comes to maternal matters. They have learned from the first time what kind of help and support they need, and have actively sought it out a second time. Many still struggle to maintain additional responsibilities with little help and even less debriefing time. They still hold on to images of what they think they "should" be feeling about new motherhood. You may have clear recollections of emotions you experienced the first time and feel totally prepared for melancholia, baby blues, exhaustion, elation. But—and this is often unexpected—the unpredictable terrain of maternal emotions still has the power to take you by surprise. Totally new feelings may jump out from left field: elation that your older child will have a companion; sadness over the loss of your exclusive relationship with a firstborn, the one who taught you all the ropes in your novice days, when you burped him wrong, diapered wrong, and put the tiny tees on backward ("I think that's one of the most common things that never gets talked about," said one mom, "that feeling of loss of exclusivity with your first child"); guilt over putting the firstborn in second place; intense memories of your own experiences as a sibling or an only child; and a strong, sometimes overwhelming desire to handle your firstborn's transition with smoothness and sensitivity, especially if your own, as a child, was not handled that way.

These are among the common feelings that women talk about having experienced to one degree or another when second or subsequent children entered or were about to enter a family. If there is little extended family to give special time to older children, and all the attention generally comes from the supposedly bottomless wellspring of Mom and Dad, the challenge to Mom to be "available" to everyone can be even greater.

"There's a lot of complex emotional shifting that goes on," says Dr. Bernice R. Berk, clinical psychologist at the Bank Street School for Children in New York City. Mom has progressed from a one-to-one relationship with partner, to one-to-one with firstborn, and now finds herself suddenly thrust at the helm of a rocking and reeling group dynamic. If women are generally geared to putting their own needs last and caring for everyone else first, those instincts may really intensify at this emotionally demanding time in a family's life and growth.

"Mothers at the time [of a second child's birth]," says Berk, "feel they have to be available to everyone, and the rewards of being emotionally available to everyone certainly begin to diminish as compared to the rewards of being engaged more equally in a one-to-one relationship with another caring person, whether that person be an infant or a spouse, or preceding that, a parent."

When a second child arrives, "the whole dimension is one of how do you balance; how do you change and alter the time you spend with each one; and the competition between children for your attention, with yourself in terms of who do you want to spend time with. . . . . It's very hard."

Dr. Berk also validates the sometimes unarticulated feelings of loss that women experience, particularly with regard to the exclusive relationships in their lives. Some women perceive it as a longing for even just a few hours of their prebaby life to take a walk or have a quiet afternoon alone with their husbands. If they have never felt comfortable putting it into words, and have not been able to arrange for it often during their first child's babyhood, their feelings may be even more intense by the time a second child arrives.

"There is a very real loss," says Dr. Berk. "A lot of mothers have never really dealt with [it] because they don't feel entitled to grieve for that. You're supposed to be only happy when you have a child. But then when you have a second or a third child, all of the losses of the one-to-one second relationships become cumulative. And I think in many ways, for the second child even more so. Sometimes it's compensated for when the second child is of a different sex than the first child, so then it becomes special in that way—'I have a special relationship with my daughter now, instead of just with my son.' But ultimately it's children, and [unless it's a single parent] it's children and a husband or partner."

However many children a woman has, each birth is individual. It is important to acknowledge and respect the possibly changed and different vulnerability and needs of a new mother after every birth. Just because you've already had one child doesn't mean that a second is "no big deal." "You have to be able to take care of yourself and feel entitled to do that in order to function effectively as a parent," explains Dr.

Berk. Whether it is a first, second, or fifth child, it is important to remember that your needs still enter into the mix.

Several women compared their first and subsequent postpartum experiences, and some suggested how and where they did or would make changes. In reading their comments, consider that you are your own best teacher as you approach a second or subsequent postpartum experience, because you can evaluate what worked well and what didn't work well for you the first time around, and possibly find ways to improve or be aware of it the next time out.

**Evelyn:** *"The second time has been easier all around. The only thing that's different is that you have to spread your time out in a different kind of way. If one is up, the other one may be sleeping, and you have to divide your time differently. That, I think, is harder. But in terms of my level of anxiety, I just feel more equipped this time. Things don't throw me as much. I don't run to the crib every time he makes a sound, which I think probably drove me and my daughter crazy when she was born. I don't use that monitor. . . . I'm tired, but I guess I feel like this time around is easier. In terms of getting out of the house and all of that, that's harder, but I guess I'm feeling calmer in general."*

**Wesley:** *"With the first one I was a total wreck. With this one I'm a lot more relaxed. [The first time] I didn't think I was doing anything right. The whole pregnancy I cried, when I had her I cried. I was so scared that I wasn't doing something right. You sterilize everything, you don't want anybody to touch her, I remember when people used to come over I used to have them wear the robes to hold her. . . . I used to call my pediatrician for everything. . . . Now I'm a pro, you could say, because I really feel very comfortable with the second one."*

**Robin:** *"The second time is easier in terms of physical caretaking. But depending on age differences of your kids, second times out send you reeling for longer, because it's ongoing rivalries and ongoing conflicts. Your job as a parent changes so completely. You're always negotiating their conflicts and their conflicting needs for you.*

*"The second one doesn't get to have a real schedule, the second one's schedule is totally conforming with the first child's schedule that already exists. Alison was in nursery school and we had to go pick her up*

*at eleven-thirty every day. . . . With the first baby, you sit and read all the baby books, and you watch for all the stages. The second kid, you just go through them, and you don't remember which stage you're in. . . . It also brings up any unresolved sibling rivalry of your own."*

*Robin's children are two-and-a-half years apart in age. "I felt like I didn't get to relish them each enough. You lose that intimacy—but if you're lucky, you get a three-way intimacy."*

**Suzanne,** *adoptive mother: "We had a year's notice of the possibility of our first adoption, and we had six weeks for our second. We had a tremendous amount of paperwork to go through in a short amount of time. The ways that it was made easier the second time around with adoption was that we didn't have to go through a whole home study, and some things took less time. We were more familiar with the application process, and our autobiographies could just be updated. So there were some things about it that were easier. It was harder to prepare Scott, because he only had a very short time. We told him about three weeks beforehand when it really seemed like it was definitely going to happen. We didn't play it up as much because at the last minute if things fell through, we didn't want a lot of people to talk to him about it.*

*"We brought her home, and there's always a couple of days after placement before the final papers are signed so that's kind of an uptight time, because there's always the possibility of second thoughts. It happened during a major hurricane so my sister was actually very supportive because we had to move in with her for a week because we had no water or electricity.*

*"It changed a lot for me just because it's so much different with two than with one. I felt kind of pulled in two different directions. It depends how much support you get from your spouse. At the time Jack was working eighty hours a week so it was basically me and the kids. I think people think that you're so busy that they tend to stay away, when I was like, 'No, come over! Come over! Don't stay away!' It was just very hard to divide myself and not make Scott feel slighted, especially at night, because she was very colicky and she would scream for three hours straight every night just when he really needed me to get him settled down. I think the more kids you have the more [people] tend to think you're too busy, when actually, I made it clear that I wanted people to come over, please, come over and give me a hand! My mother*

*would bring food over to the house. The first time it was more like show and tell. The second time it wasn't as big of a deal, [but] even though it was a big deal, it wasn't the same."*

**Anna:** *"The first time was absolutely an awful process. My husband went back to work two days after I came home, which was five days after the baby was born. My mother wasn't sure what she wanted to do and what I wanted her to do and wasn't able to be that present, and I didn't have any extended family and I didn't know anybody that had ever had a child, so I had nobody to draw on. The few friends that did come by really came by to be entertained and to play with my baby, not to give me any assistance, and it only ended up being burdensome to me. I had a very high-need baby, and I ended up being very unsuccessful at breastfeeding. . . . I had a lot of pain, nursing was excruciating for the first ten weeks, my baby wasn't gaining well for the first seven weeks. It was awful. . . . It was very hard and I felt very alone and I felt betrayed by everyone and everything about what I had expected was going to happen when I had a baby.*

*"Between the seventh and tenth weeks lots started to turn around for me. The breastfeeding started to go better, it became much less painful. She began to sleep a little bit more, she became a little bit more predictable, and I began to understand what the cries were all about. By the time she was four months old, she was fat and juicy and was sleeping more, and wasn't crying all the time, and it was fine. But it really took me until she was four months old to be able to take a deep breath and say, 'Okay, I'm all right.'*

*"So when I thought about having the next one I just assumed I was going to have the same kind of experience. And I just knew that I couldn't take care of a high-need two-and-a-half-year-old and have that same event happen again. And [instead] I got this incredibly placid baby! She'd nurse for twenty minutes and then sleep for three hours! [The support network I'd set up] was so much better and because it was so much better, the passage for my first child and for me through all the turmoil of a second child was relatively smooth. My husband took off a full week of work after the birth, not including labor. With the first child he had arranged to take off one week of work, but he ended up using three of those days with my labor, so he only had two days left. We hadn't thought of that! And then my mom came every other day for*

two weeks after he went back to work. She cooked, she cleaned, she picked my daughter up from school. It would have been great if she could have come every day but she couldn't afford to take off that much time from work, so we kind of eked it out on the days she wasn't here, and the next day it was glory!"

**Tanya:** "I learned from the first time not to have any expectations. I felt [my firstborn and I] were just getting to know one another and that the second one would put the new relationship on hold. . . . My second postpartum period did not seem nor was it as severe as the first. However, I expected to cry all day on the third day and I shared my concern with my husband. It never happened, but talking about it and asking for support from him gave me a sense of security."

# Helping Your Older Child Prepare Can Also Help Ease Your Own Transition

*Mommy, when baby Emma grows up, I'll teach her how to play with blocks and clean up her room, and play with my toys. . . . Mommy, can we put baby Emma in the pot and cook her?*
—a new two-and-a-half-year-old big brother

*She loves the new baby—she's just furious at me!*
—mother of a three-week-old and a three-year-old

*A few weeks before my second child was born, my first asked me if she was going to be thrown out like the old refrigerator was after we got the "new" one! We'd talked so much about the "new baby," but she didn't know there was a difference between objects and people—that just because a new baby came didn't mean she was the "old baby" to be discarded like a broken appliance! You have to be really sensitive with the language you choose!*
—Anna

While the primary focus of this book is on caring for the new mother, most moms agree that having some tools and being prepared to give some time and sensitivity to help your older children adjust can help make the overall postpartum transition easier for everyone. This also includes Mom herself, who, unless she is very much surrounded by friends and family who can provide outings and distractions for older sibs, is usually the chief mediator in the new sibling relations. (Even the busiest older siblings still want her attention, her eyes open, looking at them and all their cute little things, no matter how tired she may be.)

After your new baby is born, in your vulnerable, highly protective postpartum state it may seem hard and even unfair to have to incur the wrath of a raging three-year-old, and even harder to fathom the notion of a pot of simmering hot "baby" soup. But, say the experts, an older sibling speaking of such things, drawing them, doing them in play to clay or a doll while Mom watches and acknowledges nonjudgmentally is actually a very healthy sibling reaction. As you allow your children space and recognition of their frustration and anger, it is, of course, also necessary to make it absolutely clear, perhaps many times over, that they cannot act on their feelings with the real baby. (Some pediatricians advise new parents not to leave older siblings alone with a newborn "even for a second"; those heavy wooden blocks your four-year-old loves so much may be dangerous when he tries to "share" them with his brother by tossing them into his bassinet from across the room.) Along with these ventings may come the more tender moments as well, as in *Billy and the Baby*, where the new big brother brings a box of his own baby treasures to the newcomer.

In addition to shoring up yourself and your family with enough of a support network to allow you to pull yourself, your newborn, and at times, your older child as well into the necessary settling-in postpartum orbit, other suggestions for helping smooth the way for an older child or children might include:

• Talking with your older child and including him or her in the process to the degree he or she is comfortable, taking your cues from your child's level of interest: One child might want to know everything, and be present every moment; another child might prefer to go to the zoo. Your child will let you know which kinds of involvement are appropriate for him or her and which are not. One three-year-old was happy to be the "diaper man," bringing diapers to the changing table when needed, but announced to his mom some weeks before the arrival of a sibling, "I don't want to dress the new baby. Its mother can do that," reminding her that he was still, himself, a child, lest she forget that after the new one got there.

• Both before and after the birth of a sibling, many children love to see pictures about their own births and infanthood. They love to hear stories about their trip home from the hospital, or who was there with them during a home birth. Some wonder why the new baby is getting so many presents and like to have a list of the gifts they got when they were babies to carry in their pockets. They love to see their own first blankets and baby hats and toys. Sharing this with them involves them in the birth but also keeps some attention focused on them. After the new baby has arrived, they still like to hear about themselves: "You loved being held this way," "You always fell asleep like this," "You were different from your sister, you liked to be carried in your Snugli right away." They may be glad to know that you still remember their babyhood and that it is important to you, but it is also important for them to know that you recognize the ways in which they are unique, older now, and different from their new sibling.

Suzanne, an adoptive mom, spent time sharing her older son's adoption book with him. This told the story of how he came into the family and was written by Suzanne and her husband. "We talked a lot about his adoption. We have a book called *The Day We Met You*, which specifically deals with the day we met him, got in the car, went to the hospital. We said we're going to pick up another baby. It wasn't until the day before we were going to pick her up that they told us where we were picking her up. I told him, 'We picked you up at the hospital, but we're not sure where we're going to be picking this baby up.' (Every time we pass a Jordan Marsh he thinks that's where we picked up the baby because it looked like that. Recently we were driving past and he said, 'Can we take her back there?')

"Telling him about his own adoption reinforced him. We took him with us. Jack and I stayed in one room and he went with the social worker and the birth mother and birth grandparents in to another office to get the baby and then the whole group of them brought the baby in to us. And they were very nice, they had bought a toy truck for Scott, so that made him feel happy about that. And he was the one that brought the baby to us, so that made him feel like a big deal. We tried to include him that way. I think it helped, too, because after that it was 'my' baby, so he really claimed her for his own, although now he'd probably say, 'Oh forget it, give her back'—typical sibling rivalry! What we mainly did was reinforce his own adoption story, say this is what we're doing again, and show him the picture book of all of us that we put together for the birth mother. He had helped pick out the pictures he wanted to put in the book, and we just tried to include him in the whole thing."

• If possible, schedule some time for one or each parent to have alone with the older child after the birth of a sibling. "Perhaps either the father or the mother can take turns so that [an older child] still has the benefit of having undivided time with the parents occasionally," says Dr. Martha Lequerica. Some children might enjoy planning some simple special time or event with Mom after the baby is born, even something like watching Sesame Street with her on her bed or the living-room couch, so she can be resting at the same time. It can be a special time of day together, a favorite or new book read together, snack time, a videotape, a card game, eventually a walk to the library, or anything that will be reserved for Mom and the older child and that your older child can have a say in shaping. Some children might enjoy making a list with their parents of things they want to include—books, games, activities—and then hanging it on the wall or refrigerator. Writing, helping to write, and then seeing that list posted as a reminder of an exclusive link to Mom or Dad can be very empowering for a child who feels that control is going out of his or her world with the chaos of a new arrival. Of course, if you have several older children, time with each parent may decrease, but a good image to hold on to as you progress is the three-way or multiple intimacy that Robin talked about.

• Try not to make promises that you probably won't or know you won't be able to keep, just to make your older child feel better or special at the moment you make the promise.

• It is important, stresses Dr. Berk, to be accepting of a child's resentment. "After all, this is a parental decision to have a second child, not a child's decision, and [it's important] to be clear that you're not going to let him or her hurt the second child. The second child is a decision that you've made and care about and is part of the family. Be inclusive where you can. Include the second child, but also be able to recognize that there are differences. Those differences are related to the fact that they are different people. And really try not to make it so that one position, either the older or younger, is clearly the best. Be open to looking at intrinsic advantages and changing advantages." Dr. Berk notes that as the children grow older, "if parents can recognize that conflicts between the young will resolve spontaneously, do not put pressure on an older child to love and enjoy the younger."

• Once the baby arrives, be prepared for an older child possibly acting out a range of feelings toward the new sibling. Just as Mom may be experiencing some mixed or downright negative feelings, so might an older child.

"If the sibling doesn't love the new baby instantly or does not express positive feelings, she may just be looking on and thinking about it," says Dr. Lequerica. "But just as we're beginning to say that women don't have to be obliged to bond to their infants right away, also the siblings don't have to be under the pressure of showing or feeling how much they must love this creature, or that they must hate it. They have to own their own responses, be they what they may. They may just feel indifferent for a while. That's not going to last forever necessarily. The best thing is to acknowledge them honestly, and say, 'Yes, sometimes we do feel that way.' That, in a sense, is legitimizing them, rather than making the kid feel guilty about it. Say, 'Yes, sometimes you get angry that he is taking time away from you, or you want to get rid of him.'" It is also necessary, she adds, that while Mom listens nonjudgmentally to these feelings, she must also make it clear that "we are not going to act on it. We're going to talk about it, but we're not going to act on it. We can play it out with dolls. Let's put the baby here," putting the newborn in a safe haven, while the older sibling shows her with a doll how she feels.

• If you can, and if your child is interested, let him or her spend some time with friends who have a newborn baby. Prepare them for the kinds of care you will have to give the new baby, and what babies are like. Let your own child know that your new baby is a child who will live with you, and you will welcome it into the family. "Pass on to each one," says Luz García, "the message that they are special and precious no matter how old or young they are. 'The new baby is precious, just as you are precious. You just got here first!'"

• Finally, don't put too much pressure on yourself or on your children to have a perfect relationship when they're young. "[It helps]," says Dr. Berk, "if you're tolerant and able to accept the conflict that may occur when they're young with some recognition that conflicts that occur when they're young can be resolved when they're young, and need not be carried through to adulthood, where they fester into feuds. Where there's too much pressure on young siblings to get along and love each other there's a host of resentments that get carried through into adulthood, and then are often no longer really resolvable."

## Sibling Classes

Some parents have found sibling classes in hospitals or birthing centers useful in preparing and including older children. If your hospital does not offer formal classes, you might inquire about taking an informal tour of the nursery and maternity floor so your older child or children can see where you and the new baby will be.

---

### LOCAL SIBLING CLASS OR PROGRAM INFORMATION

Location_____

Instructor_____

Telephone number_____

Days/hours_____

---

## A GOOD SIBLING CLASS OR PROGRAM MIGHT ACCOMPLISH SEVERAL GOALS

• Let your older child see where you will be
• Provide clear, simple information about birth and babies
• Touch on your child's emotional responses to the baby
• Offer hands-on experience with birth or newborn dolls if your older child is interested
• Offer some constructive options for how to express negative feelings

## TWO MODEL SIBLING CLASSES

Salvation Army Grace Hospital in Calgary, Alberta, Canada, offers a class for children from three to ten years of age. It is staffed by a child-birth educator and junior volunteers, boys and girls age twelve and thirteen, who can sit with younger children who may prefer playing with newborn or birth dolls over watching the puppet show about a little girl who has a new baby in her family.

The children then create the agenda with their own questions and comments, says Donna Wallace, manager of the Childbirth Education Program at the hospital. "Sometimes [they] use the puppets, sometimes they don't need to use the puppets to talk about Mom being pregnant and the baby coming. [They] talk about after the baby comes, the feelings and emotions. 'Is it okay to be angry? What do you do when you're angry? What kinds of things do you do for your baby? How can you play with them?' We do go over a little bit about the labor and the birth and how a baby is born, and the correct terminology. They all seem to know that anyway. They talk about the new baby, and practice diapering and holding a baby. It depends on what the children bring up as well."

The class also includes a tour of the unit just for the children, as well as a slide show to reinforce the program that they've just done. For the very young children, stresses Wallace, the most important aspect of

326 • Mothering the New Mother

their visit is to see the physical surroundings where their mother will be so they have some images to remember if they are not present for the birth. One mom whose child attended a sibling class at another hospital reported that knowing the color of her room and the pictures on the wall gave her older daughter a very important and concrete image to hold during their separation.

At North Central Bronx Hospital in New York City, says Luz García, the sibling class includes a tape of other children talking about how it feels to have a newborn in the house, along with a talk about behavior of newborns, why they sleep, why they cry. There is also a talk about the birth process, a tour of the labor and delivery area, and a chance to see the newborns and meet the nurses, as well as a discussion about the children's feelings.

Older children eleven or twelve years old, she says, are sometimes "very upset that Mom is having another baby. The class is a place to talk about the issues, how they feel about their plans being disrupted possibly. We talk about their interests in their day, and how they can help when Mom comes home. [We have them] make drawings about how they feel the baby will be in their life. Grandmothers are also welcome." When they return, some children are prepared to be in the labor room during the birth if they wish to be. They need to have an adult with them who can be responsible for taking them out if they want to leave, or if there are any complications with the birth itself. The class at North Central Bronx Hospital meets once a month after school hours, so children can come.

Because classes sometimes meet once a month or less frequently, it's a good idea to call your hospital or birthing center well in advance so you can be sure not to miss the date.

# Resources

The resources listed here are described in further detail in the following section:

## Videotapes

*Kidvidz: Hey, What About Me?*
*Lizzie and the Baby: The Childbirth for Children Video*

## Books

*Arthur's New Baby Book: A Lift the Flap Guide to Being a Great Big Brother or Sister (A Great Big Flap Book)*
*Baby Comes Home*
*A Baby for Max*
*A Baby Sister for Frances*
*Big Brother Dustin*
*Big Like Me*
*I'm a Big Sister*
*I'm a Big Brother*
*Julius: The Baby of the World*

*Mommy's in the Hospital Having a Baby*
*The New Baby*
*The New Baby (Usborne First Experiences Series)*
*The New Baby at Your House*
*101 Things to Do with a Baby*
*On Mother's Lap*
*Our New Baby (All Aboard Book)*
*A Place for Ben*
*She Come Bringing Me That Little Baby Girl*
*Something Special*
*That New Baby*
*We Have a Baby*
*When I Am a Sister*
*Will There Be a Lap for Me?*
*You Were Born on Your Very First Birthday (An Albert Whitman Prairie Book)*

**A Note for Adoptive Families**

## Videotapes

*Kidvidz: Hey, What About Me?*
Kidvidz

Designed by professionals to help children (ages 2–6) adjust to a new baby in the family, this video shows real kids and their new brothers and sisters interacting in good and bad times. Included is an activity pamphlet that contains rhymes, games, and fun facts.

*Lizzie and the Baby: The Childbirth for Children Video*
Distributed by Injoy Productions
Tel.: (800) 326-2082 or fax: (303) 449-8788 (for Visa and MasterCard orders only)

This video presents a unique view of pregnancy and the birth of a sibling. It also covers how a fetus develops, what pregnancy is like, what happens during a birth, and why it is a time of both joy and adjustment for the family.

# Books

The selected sampling of books that follows helps children see and feel some of what other young ones—human, monster, and anthropomorphic animal—experience with the arrival of a new sibling. Using colorful illustrations, or color and black-and-white photos, these works help demonstrate and articulate what may be the older sib's fears, anger, frustration, sadness, excitement, curiosity, happiness, and even resolution as he or she slips into the new role of older kid in the family.

*Arthur's New Baby Book: A Lift the Flap Guide to Being a Great Big Brother or Sister (A Great Big Flap Book)*
Marc Tolon Brown
Bullseye Books

In this lighthearted and sensitive book with more than forty flaps to lift (plus holes for little fingers to make wiggling rabbit ears), Marc Brown, the creator of everyone's favorite aardvark, Arthur, offers youngsters a reassuring look at what they can expect when a new baby arrives in the house. Arthur, himself a big brother, helps his younger sister, D. W., get used to the idea of another new baby in the house, as they reminisce about peek-a-boo, learning the alphabet, and reciting nursery rhymes. The book also reminds older sibs that they are still loved, even though the newcomer demands lots of attention.

*Baby Comes Home*
Debbie Driscoll
Illustrated by Barbara Samuels
Simon & Schuster

This book shows the arrival of a new baby as seen by the toddler in the family—who is suddenly a new big sister. Children will probably recognize her uncertainty and curiosity, as well as the relief of the moment when a smile is shared with the baby in the end.

*A Baby for Max*
Maxwell B. Knight
Text by Kathryn Lasky
Photographs by Christopher Knight
Macmillan

In this book illustrated with black-and-white photos, Max, a real five-year-old boy, tells in his own words the story of having a new baby in the family.

*A Baby Sister for Frances*
Russell Hoban
Pictures by Lillian Hoban
Harper & Row, Publishers

When Frances's baby sister arrives, things just aren't the same: No one's had time to iron her blue school dress, and bananas have to substitute for raisins in the morning because Mother hasn't had time to get to the store. Frances takes matters into her own hands and, while carrying out her plan, learns how necessary and loved big sisters really are.

*Big Brother Dustin*
Alden R. Carter
Illustrated by Dan Young and Carol Carter
Albert Whitman & Co.

Dustin, a young boy with Down's syndrome, is excited about the arrival of a new baby in the family. Bright color photographs show him attending a sibling class, visiting with his grandparents, thinking of the perfect name for the baby (Mary Ann), preparing the new baby's room, and visiting his mom and new baby sister in the hospital. The book closes with a selection of photos featuring Dustin and his new baby sister.

*Big Like Me*
Anna Grossnickle Hines
Greenwillow Books

A big brother greets his new sibling in January and then, month by month, shows the newcomer "everything" from snow and stories in February to "splashing and pouring" in July to having races ("I'll let you win") and blowing out birthday candles in January again, when baby is growing "big like me!"

*I'm a Big Sister*
and
*I'm a Big Brother*
Joanna Cole
Illustrated by Maxie Chambliss
William Morrow & Co.

These books tell in simple straightforward language what babies are like, why they cry, what they can't do that older sibs can, and how much parents love their older children. The line and watercolor drawings celebrate family life from a child's point of view and present older sibs who recognize the difficulties, but who are confident and curious about the experience of older sister- or brotherhood. On the last page, Cole offers advice to parents on how to guide and reassure children with a new baby in the family.

*Julius: The Baby of the World*
Kevin Henkes
Greenwillow

Lilly, a little mouse, thinks it might be fun to have a new baby in the family—until her brother Julius arrives and her parents repeatedly declare him to be "the baby of the world." Suddenly jealous, Lilly expresses her resentment in lots of wickedly creative ways: when she paints a family portrait, she leaves Julius out; when she invites her stuffed animals to tea, baby Julius doesn't get an invitation. But when a cousin starts insulting Julius, Lilly's love and loyalty are suddenly awakened. Illustrated with bright watercolors and written in handwritten, cartoon-style dialogue, this is a funny and comforting book for new older siblings, who may recognize in themselves some of Lilly's mixed emotions.

*Mommy's in the Hospital Having a Baby*
Maxine B. Rosenberg
Photographs by Robert Maass
Clarion Books

This book, which depicts a traditional hospital birth, describes from a child's perspective the experience that Mom and the new baby will have in the hospital. It pictures several different families, and covers the time from Mom's leaving the house to Mom's leaving the hospital.

*The New Baby*
Fred Rogers (Mr. Rogers)
Putnam

A familiar television friend reassures older siblings that despite the disruptions in their lives when a new baby arrives, they still hold a special place in the family.

### The New Baby (Usborne First Experiences Series)
Anne Civardi and Stephen Cartwright (illustrator)
EDC Publications

Part of a series that introduces young children to experiences they might be having for the first time, this friendly and amusing book is full of colorful illustrations and interesting, informative insights on the experience of welcoming a new baby into the house.

### The New Baby at Your House
Joanna Cole
Photographs by Hella Hammid
Mulberry Publishing

In this book by science writer Joanna Coles, over fifty black-and-white photos show a number of real children interacting with the new babies in their families. Young readers get a look at a baby's body and how it works, as well as a taste of the curiosity, envy, anger, fear, and finally, reassurance that may all be part of becoming an older sibling. Also includes "A Note to Parents" on how to help children prepare for the new arrival.

### 101 Things to Do with a Baby
Jan Ormerod
Puffin Books

A big sister shows readers 101 things (each one numbered!) that she can do to play with, entertain, and help take care of her new sibling.

### On Mother's Lap
Ann Herbert Scott

Illustrated by Glo Coalson
Clarion Books

Michael's favorite place to be is snuggled on his mother's lap, along with favorite toys and a warm reindeer blanket. When his baby sister starts to cry, he learns that, despite his fears, there is always enough room on Mother's lap. The story is set in an Inuit fishing village, not unlike Kotzabue, Alaska, where the illustrator did the original sketches that were the basis for the book's full-color illustrations.

### Our New Baby (All Aboard Book)
Wendy Cheyette Lewison
Photographs by Nancy Sheehan
Grosset & Dunlap

This book, filled with color photographs, helps reassure older siblings that they are still very special to their parents, even though a new baby can take some getting used to.

### A Place for Ben
Jeanne Titherington
Greenwillow Books

When Ben's brother, Ezra, is born, there seems to be no place in the house where Ben can be alone. He finally finds a private corner, and sets it up with all his favorite things. Only one thing is missing: somebody to share it with. Finally, some interesting company comes along.

### She Come Bringing Me That Little Baby Girl
Elouise Greenfield
Illustrated by John Steptoe
J.B. Lippincott Company

Kevin asked for a little brother, but Mama brings home a girl instead. She cries too much, shows no promise for football, and her face looks old, not new. But as Daddy, Mama, and Uncle Roy—Mama's big brother—put the baby in Kevin's arms and lovingly explain how important big brothers are, and how much Kevin is needed, the baby begins to look a little cuter. In the end, Kevin is even ready to let the baby have one of Mama's arms, as long as the other one is holding on to him.

*Something Special*
Nicola Moon
Illustrated by Alex Ayliffe
Peachtree Publishers

Friday is "Special Day" in Charlie's classroom, when kids bring in special things to share at show-and-tell. Charlie can't think of anything special enough to bring in. His mom is busy taking care of Sally, his six-week-old sister, but tries to help him come up with something, as do his classmates. It isn't until Sally smiles at him for the first time that he thinks of what to bring in to share with the class: his baby sister. The story is illustrated with cheerful cut-and-torn-paper collages.

*That New Baby*
An Open Family Book for Parents
    and Children Together
Sara Bonnett Stein
Photography by Dick Frank
Walker and Company

Presented with separate texts for adult and child together, and illustrated with black-and-white photographs, this book tells the story of the arrival of a new baby into one family. It shows readers some of the things the older siblings (in this case, two) may be doing, and demonstrates appropriate responses from Mom, also demonstrating simply the different needs and abilities of babies and older children. The book is written in conjunction with the Center for Preventive Psychiatry in White Plains, New York.

*We Have a Baby*
Cathryn Falwell
Clarion Books

Illustrated with full-color cut-paper illustrations, this book shows with vivid illustrations and simple text the things a family gives to a new baby and the love the baby gives in return.

*When I Am a Sister*
Robin Ballard
Greenwillow Books

This book is about a little girl visiting her father and pregnant stepmom, Kate, for the summer. As the summer comes to an end, she wonders what will be different on her next visit, after the baby arrives. Her father gives her reassuring but realistic answers to her many questions: small gray-toned illustrations show us what Kate fears in each situation, and large ink-and-watercolor paintings show the more positive picture described by her father.

*Will There Be a Lap for Me?*
Dorothy Corey
Illustrations by Nancy Poydar
Albert Whitman & Co.

Kyle's favorite place is on his mother's lap. He likes to sit with her and rest, talk, read, and watch the birds on his porch. As Mother's lap gets smaller and the new baby grows bigger, no other lap seems to feel just right. And after Baby Matt is born, his mom is almost too busy to sit down anyway. He misses his favorite place, until one day, Mom is ready for some special time for just the two of them. Kyle's excitement, sadness, frustration, and realization that there is still a special place for him will mirror the experience of many children.

*You Were Born on Your Very First Birthday (An Albert Whitman Prairie Book)*
Linda W. Girard
Illustrated by Christa Kieffer

Edited by Kathy Tucker
Albert Whitman & Co.

This book describes in lyrical and poetic language the life of a tiny baby before it is born. The book can help older sibs understand their own journey to birth, as well as give them an idea of what's happening to their yet-unborn younger sib.

## A Note for Adoptive Families

Adoptive Families of America (page 43) can provide titles of books that can be shared with older siblings in adoptive families.

# 9.

# PUTTING IT ALL TOGETHER WHEN YOU'RE THE NEW MOTHER

*Creating a Postpartum Plan*

• • • • • •

## From the Page to the People . . . Making a List

........................................................................................................................

While there are many books to help us learn how to mother and care for our babies, many women say they feel the lack of female companionship, mentors, and role models as they move through the transition to new motherhood. They feel overwhelmed by the need to orchestrate the practical aspects of life postpartum; hungry for know-how and nurturing, yet easily crushed by overeager helpers, each with a new philosophy or thought on motherhood to impart; undernourished on the spiritual and emotional fronts.

This section is meant to serve as a bridge to help you get from the page to some of the people who can help you after your baby is born. In some ways, creating a postpartum plan is very much a case of organizing the obvious. It is a way of validating your own needs and instincts. It is also a way of taking a proactive role in making new connections to people with whom you feel comfortable, and a way of writing, as much as possible, your own postpartum scenario.

The lists are divided roughly into two categories:

1. Those people who and services that can take on practical chores to free you to be with your baby, and

333

2. Those people who may become your chosen doula, mentor, or role model and who can specifically help by sharing their time and wisdom with you, which in turn will nurture and build your own confidence as a new mother.

If you have many candidates to fill these roles, these pages will give you a chance to prioritize, do some weeding out, and establish as much of a sense of control as possible about what will happen in your life postpartum. On the other hand, if, like many women, you feel that you're on the scant side when it comes to role models, helpers, and doulas, these pages, and the words and resources shared in this book may provide inspiration and direction for you to make a few new contacts and start building some relationships prenatally that can continue after your baby is born. Some new moms, says Luz García, feel unentitled to seek help and believe that these needs make them a bother, rather than recognizing them as a right of the parenting transition. Those moms need to know, she says, that "they have done a valuable service. The human race will continue because they put this effort into childbirth!"

If you haven't had your baby yet, the items on these lists may feel as alien as a shopping list for Mars. You may not even be able to look at or relate to them. Or you may be able to scratch in an obvious name or two, and put it in a drawer for later. Depending on your nesting instincts and your penchant for research, you may leap at the chance to undertake a few more prenatal projects, and enjoy making some phone calls and identifying concerned people you can check back with after your baby is born.

If you have already had your baby, you may have a strong sense about which sections of this book and list will meet your most pressing needs, or you may be so overwhelmed that you can't sort any of it out. Some moms have also used the questionnaire (Appendix B) to help define and validate their priorities and feelings postpartum.

If you have specific issues of concern—breastfeeding questions, or being at high risk for PPD, for example—you might follow the example of mothers who have sought the advice and input of doulas, support group leaders, lactation consultants, or others in formulating plans and contingency plans.

## PEOPLE WHO HAVE PLAYED A SIGNIFICANT ROLE IN MY PREGNANCY AND BIRTHING PROCESS

Obstetrician/gynecologist _____

Midwife _____

Childbirth assistant, labor doula, or birth companion _____
_____

Childbirth educator _____

Pediatrician _____

## PEOPLE/SUPPORTS I MAY NEED AFTER THE BABY IS BORN

Breastfeeding supports:

In-hospital support person _____

(This can be someone on staff or someone you have a private relationship with.)

Local support group _____

(e.g., La Leche, NMA, local hospital group)

Lactation consultant _____

Lactation clinic warmline _____

New mothers support group _____

Depression after delivery

National _____

Local _____

Four friends or relatives who can rotate coming into the home to help—watching older siblings, holding or watching the baby so Mom can sleep or shower, doing the laundry, changing sheets, preparing food, etc.

1. _____

2. _____

3. _____

4. _____

These friends, local shops, and service providers may make my life easier at some point during the postpartum weeks:

Grocery that delivers* _____

_____

Pharmacy or drugstore that delivers (preferably late-night or all-night)

_____

Local baby supply store _____

Restaurant that delivers _____

Laundry helper _____

Shopping helper _____

Meal helper (especially a casserole expert; casseroles are easy to prepare, can be frozen, and are cheap to make; they are, says Luz García, "the new mother's best friend") _____

_____

Neighbor with car for emergencies _____

Local cab service _____

*If there is a grocery store that you feel comfortable with, some moms leave cash on deposit with the store so they can call in orders, and older children or neighbors can pick up small orders without having to carry money or make an extra trip to collect the cash.

These people may be helpful to me with emotional support, baby basics information, experience, commiseration, note-comparing, outside-world contacts, nurturing:

Doula _____

Childbirth classmates _____

"Baby basics" friend _____

Special relative _____

Workplace contacts: _____

    Official (human resources, benefits, etc.) _____

    Unofficial (friend) _____

Shopping help for my needs (some of these items may be welcome as shower gifts) _____

Neighbor _____

Church, synagogue, community center, YM/YWCA, or YM/YWHA

_____

# Creating My Postpartum Support Network

Not all categories will apply to all new mothers. If you have two or three reliable, supportive people to include on these lists, you may feel way ahead of the game. And if this all seems too hard to research, perhaps someone else—doula, labor support person, godmother, or close friend—can compile this kind of information for or with you.

## Visitors on Parade . . .

Depending on your visitors' expectations of you, a steady stream of guests to meet and greet the baby can be either helpful or depleting. Putting a cap on visiting sessions or excusing yourself after a short while, though, can be tricky because friends and relatives may be offended, particularly if there are strong family or cultural traditions about visits to new mothers and babies.

However, if you have strong feelings about your need for privacy and rest at this time, or about whose input will be most valuable and calming to you, you might give some thought to structuring a schedule you feel comfortable with and then gently convey the parameters to family and friends, or have someone else convey it. If it is expected that you and the baby be available to certain friends and family members, you might enlist the aid of those same people as a shield in limiting the visits of others. (One mom sent out prenatal notes saying that although she would love to see everyone, her doctor said she'd need her rest, and asked people to return a card saying when they'd like to come so she could make up a reasonable visiting schedule.)

Doula and lactation consultant Anna Werner suggests that even a fifteen-minute cap on visits is not too short if that's what you need. She also suggests thinking about your list of people and visits as follows:

1. People who will be called immediately on birth
2. People who will be coming to help
3. Time limit you feel comfortable with for guests

## SOME MOTHERING-THE-NEW-MOTHER GIFTS

When friends ask you what you need for the baby, also tell them what you need for yourself or the family:

- Relaxation tapes (tastes vary on these, from lullabies for baby to the sounds of rain forests or waves crashing on Cape Cod)
- A selection of herbal teas
- Casseroles or other cooked meals
- Nursing gowns
- Body lotions
- Sleep bonus: two hours of time from a friend who comes to watch the baby while you sleep (this becomes especially important around the second week, as the baby wakes up and your helpers simultaneously ride off into the sunset)
- A mom's journal (blank, of course)
- A gift certificate or a contribution toward a "doula fund" or breastfeeding class for you
- An hour or two of help with your house and laundry or shopping
- A massage

4. People who will come to visit after you're settled in (say, after two or three weeks)

5. People who may be invited to an open house to meet the baby when you're really ready

Jeanne Driscoll suggests in her tape *Diapers and Delirium* that the new mom should come to the door in her worst housecoat and looking dreadful as a way of conveying the message that she must get straight back to her bed. Another new mom suggests not letting anyone in who isn't bearing food, and not letting anyone out unless they are carrying a bag of garbage to throw out on the way. Still another mom allowed people to come freely as long as it was understood that she and the baby would for the most part remain in the privacy of her bedroom. You can set the criteria depending on your own feelings and needs.

## Some Ways to Make Connections Prenatally

• Get to know and help your neighbors when you are pregnant, so they will be more likely to be available to you after your baby is born. This can be especially helpful if you are new to the area where you are living or don't feel that you have a large support network to call on.

• During prenatal care, single moms especially have an opportunity to connect with other expectant mothers. "Be willing to share your experience," says Luz García, "and other moms will feel the same way. It just takes one mom to make the first step to exchange numbers. Especially in the inner cities, prenatal care providers can be very helpful in making good recommendations, and leading you to a good match to set up a buddy system."

• Setting up a buddy system: After your baby is born, it is likely that you will not have the time or energy to set up a network. You might consider prenatally setting up a buddy or barter situation with a friend who will call you two days, four days, six days, and so on, postpartum. In this way the calls will automatically come in without your having to solicit them after the birth. You may also want to set up some arrangement with another friend who is not also pregnant herself and who will be available to come over and help if you need something suddenly.

## Helping Your Friends Help You: Orchestrating a Mothering-the-New-Mother Circle

If you're uncomfortable pinning down helpers, or are just too busy or preoccupied to think about postpartum help, you might like the idea of having one good friend or relative coordinate a network for you. After assessing what your own postpartum needs might be, you or your coordinator might want to compose a letter, using the one on page 340 as a guide, and pass it around to designated friends, colleagues, neighbors, church or synagogue groups, and elsewhere as

## SAMPLE LETTER ORGANIZING HELP FOR THE NEW MOM-TO-BE

Dear friend [or name],

Thanks for your offer of help after [name]'s baby is born. As you know, it's sometimes overwhelming for new moms to sort out or anticipate all of their needs, and many well-meaning and eager friends who want to help may not know exactly what to do. We are trying to help [mom's name] prepare for and honor her early weeks at home with baby by setting up a mothering-the-new-mother circle to help in a variety of ways. If you'd like to be part of it, we would appreciate having an idea of when and how you'd feel most comfortable lending a hand. For instance:

*Can you bring a soup, salad, casserole, or other dish?*
*Can you do an activity or play date with her older child?*
*Can you be called on for grocery or other shopping?*
*Can you come over for a few hours to sit with the baby or answer the telephone while [new mom's name] naps?*
*Do you have any special skills or interests you can share? (Massage, expertise in baby basics, driving a car, etc.?)*

If you'd like suggestions about what kind of help to offer, call [name of friend or relative] so [he or she] can let you know what's most needed and which times are best.

Thank you for being a special part of [new mom's name]'s mothering-the-new-mother circle.

you create your support team and fill in specific roles and time slots. (Remember, flexibility is mandatory, as babies do not always arrive on time.)

For moms who really want to show their appreciation and share some time with their helpers, offer a contemporary version of the Colonial groaning party when the baby is eight or ten weeks old!

# From Three to Four and Beyond: Expanding the Postpartum Plan

As always, you are the best judge of what else you need to factor into your plan for each new arrival into your family. While some women feel more entitled to seek help with second and subsequent children, some moms still feel that they have to do it all themselves, and indeed may have no choice. Economics may be the ultimate decision-maker, and financial resources may be stretched thinner with each additional child. Sources of help among close family may be fewer. On the other hand, additional sources of help may be available for the thinking, asking, and organizing, since families with small children tend to make new ties rather quickly once their older children begin going to the park, preschool and elementary school, local community centers, or Sunday school.

In planning for subsequent postpartum periods every woman takes an individual course. Some don't plan at all. "I didn't plan differently," says Gay, mother of three. "In fact, I had a hard time planning, even though I knew the baby would be coming." But Gay had warnings about PPD during her second postpartum period, and so was armed with information and referrals the third time. When the symptoms surfaced, she recalls, she knew where to go for help at once.

Even though each birth and postpartum experience is to some degree unpredictable, some women consciously decide to reverse the circumstances of a first postpartum experience—for example, changing from a hospital to a home birth; some women who turned down offers of help from family and friends the first time, painstakingly orchestrate a network of helpers who will be available over a period of weeks or months for the second time. Some moms are ever hard-pressed to find a few minutes for themselves in the midst of the whirlwind.

Sometimes circumstances themselves are entirely different: One birth may have been a cesarean section and the other not; someone might have experienced PPD one time and not the other. Nevertheless, a good starting place in contemplating the arrival of a second baby and your needs as a new mom may be to spend some time recalling your first postpartum experience (if you can remember it!):

• What worked well the first time around?
• What didn't work so well?
• What kind of help or support do I wish I had had?
• What supports can I call on this next time?
• Where would I make some changes or improvements if I could?

## BEYOND THE FIRST BABY: A NEW KIND OF PLAN

A new plan will also embrace the needs and obligations of your first child or older children. While some moms have found it overwhelming and have not made any plans at all, other moms have found it helpful—indeed, necessary (depending on age differences, numbers of schools involved, and after-school activities)—to line up some support to help with older sibs or to assign that responsibility to a mate, relative, or good friend. This layer of planning may include:

• Friends/relatives to handle school drop-offs and pickups or other logistics:

_____

• Relatives or friends for play dates, walks, park trips, etc.:

_____

• After some weeks have passed, friends/relatives to watch the newborn for a few hours so Mom can do something special with an older child or take him or her to school, etc.:

_____

• Some families have also found it a good idea to make note of any special events coming up in the life of an older child during early postpartum weeks (birthday, school event, sports event, outing) and to focus some special attention on that:

_____

• Assign several friends to bring in gifts for your older child and celebrate him or her as well, since everyone generally tends to focus on the new baby to the exclusion of the new mother and the siblings. This will also provide extra outside attention for the older children and alleviate some of the pressure on mom to provide it all:

_____

_____

# *Appendix A*

## *Prenatal Questionnaire*

••••••

This questionnaire, created by the author, was distributed to women who participated in research for *Mothering the New Mother*.

1. Often when we're pregnant, we don't really know what to expect after the baby comes. How long do you expect it will take you to feel comfortable with your new role as mother? Please circle one:

    two weeks
    six weeks
    three months
    six months
    twelve months
    don't know

2. When we're pregnant we often don't think about what we might need after the baby is born, whether it is help with shopping and cooking, or just a good, encouraging friend who's already been through it and is happy to listen and talk to us. Do you think you will need help after your baby is born? If so, what kind? (Practical help, help with baby, help with breastfeeding, emotional support, etc.)

3. Do you and other pregnant women you know feel that it's all right to ask for help adjusting to the role of new mother in this society? Why or why not?

4. As one postpartum support group leader said, "No one ever really feels prepared for a new baby." Do you feel prepared for motherhood? Why or why not?

5. New mothers love to talk about the birth, the baby, and their feelings about it all. But they don't always get the chance to talk. Is there

someone you would feel comfortable talking to about your feelings, questions, and doubts after the baby is born? If so, who is it? (It may be the same person or support group helping you through the prenatal period.)

6. Is there a support center or group in your community that you joined or visited during your third trimester to talk or learn about life with baby? What group was it, and how did it help?

7. Is there a support group—e.g., mother's support group, La Leche League, etc.—you know of and/or plan to join or contact after your baby is born? What is it, and what does it do?

8. Who do you think will be your greatest source of support and help after your baby is born (e.g., mate or partner; mother; sister; mother-in-law; friend; support group; don't know; don't have any help)?

9. Many diverse cultures have postpartum traditions that support and honor the new mother. Are there any traditions or customs in your own cultural heritage that will occur after your baby is born (e.g., special foods that will be cooked for you, relatives coming to help, older women in the community offering advice and support, special baths or massages for the new mom, or other rituals)?

# Appendix B

*Postpartum Questionnaire*

......

This questionnaire, created by the author, was distributed to women who participated in research for *Mothering the New Mother*.

## PART I. OUR FEELINGS—ALL OF THEM!

1. Often when we're pregnant, we don't really know what to expect when the baby finally arrives, and we all have our own individual responses. In the first days and weeks after your baby was born, what do you most remember feeling about your new infant and your new role? (New moms have noted every feeling from passivity to joy to euphoria, from melancholia to panic to out-of-control, and more . . . so please feel free to be as open as you can.)

2. What felt most comfortable about being a new mother?

3. What felt most stressful about being a new mother?

4. Did any of your feelings surprise you? Which ones?

5. What was your greatest fear as a new mother?

6. As we know, the arrival of a baby can have a powerful effect on marriage and partner relationships. If you shared new parenting with a husband or partner, how did the new baby affect that relationship?

7. Often, as new mothers, we feel afraid that something's wrong with us if we feel anything other than happiness and joy. Our own negative or ambivalent feelings about the baby and about our new responsibility frighten us. No one has ever told us that other women also have those feelings and that it's all right, even normal. Do you (or did you) feel that it's all right to admit or talk about any negative or ambivalent feelings you have as a new mother? Why or why not?

8. Although we're often not encouraged to talk about our deepest feelings as new moms, the truth is that simply sharing our feelings with other women can help alleviate some of the anxiety and stress we feel

345

postpartum. Is there another person with whom you can speak honestly, one-on-one, and feel that you are heard, understood, and encouraged? Who is this person, and what kind of feelings did you talk about? How often was he or she available? How did he or she respond?

9. Society tells us that just because we're women, we should be able to adjust to motherhood from day one. No one tells us that the transition to motherhood is a gradual and major life change requiring support, encouragement, and education. Did you feel it was all right to ask for help after your baby was born? If so, what did that help consist of, and who provided it (e.g., a neighbor shopping, a family member coming to cook or clean, a baby nurse or postpartum care service, professional help of any sort, a friend coming to talk about the birth)?

10. If you did not feel comfortable asking for or admitting that you needed help—whether it was laundry and shopping, companionship, instruction, or just general moral support—what made you feel uncomfortable about it (e.g., pressure to live up to an ideal image of the perfect mother, messages from society that mothering was natural and "instinctive" and should require little moral support, other feelings)?

11. Why do you think it's hard for many postpartum women to ask for or admit to a need for help, companionship, moral support, etc.?

12. In retrospect, what kind of help do you wish you had had that you didn't have?

13. Were you aware of the full range of feelings other new mothers experience, or did you feel that you were the only new mom who ever felt that way? If you did know that other women experienced similar feelings, how did you gain that awareness (e.g., mothers' group, counselor, shared stories with family members or friends, read it in books)? Please be specific in your answers.

14. Although awareness of postpartum depression and its various stages of severity is growing, postpartum mental health still has a long way to go in gaining recognition and consistent definition by the medical and psychiatric community. Many of us experience some less severe stage of PPD and don't even know that's what we're going through, or that it's very common. Did you experience the "baby blues" or any form of PPD? Please describe how you felt, how old your baby was when it occurred, and whether and how you got help for it.

15. Did you feel that any person, experience, or class really prepared you for the range of feelings you had as a new mother? If yes, please identify the source of your preparedness, and describe.

16. Were you able to do anything to help yourself with any of the more difficult issues or feelings you experienced postpartum (e.g., join a support group, start your own support program where nothing else existed, get individual help, talk to friends)? How did this help you both short- and long-term?

17. For the dreamers among you—sleep-deprived as we are during those early weeks and months, often our dreams tell a lot about our exhaustion, anxiety, endurance, euphoria—please recount any outstanding dream or dreams from your postpartum period. If possible, give the age of your child at the time you had the dream or dreams.

## PART 2. FEEDING YOUR BABY

1. Did you breastfeed or bottle-feed?

2. How did you make your decision about how to feed your baby?

3. If you breastfed, how did you learn how to do it (e.g., just did it by yourself because everyone told you it was "natural," or learned from a family member, lactation consultant, class, nursing staff)?

4. If you delivered in the hospital, were the hospital staff consistent in their instruction? Was the routine supportive or sabotaging? (E.g., did you have rooming-in? Was your baby fed bottles in the nursery?) Does your state have guidelines regarding the hospital policy and breastfeeding support?

5. Did you have any special problems with breastfeeding? If so, who helped you to solve them (e.g., hospital or breastfeeding clinic warmline, individual visit to lactation clinic, La Leche League or other support group)? Please identify fully.

6. How long did you breastfeed? (If you still are, please indicate how long you have been nursing and how long you will continue.)

7. Did you breastfeed in public? Did you ever feel other people had a problem with this? Please be specific.

## PART 3. WORKING: NEW MOTHERS WORKING OUTSIDE THE HOME

1. Sometimes we don't have a choice about whether we stay at home or go back to work. Did you return to work because you:

a. had to in order to keep your job?

b. had to for economic reasons?

c. chose to?

d. other (Please explain.)

2. How old was your baby when you returned to work?

3. What is your job, and how many hours a week do you work?

4. In what state of the country do you work? Are there any state laws governing maternity or parental leave policy? (Please be specific if you can in outlining the laws.)

5. What were the terms of your maternity or parental leave (e.g., how much time off, with or without pay, job security)? Did you feel they were adequate?

6. What would be your ideal terms for maternity or parental leave?

7. Were there any particular arrangements that helped you or made it easier for you to return to work (e.g., flextime, job-sharing, part-time employment agencies)?

8. What arrangements were you able to make for your childcare? Did your place of employment help with this (e.g., subsidizing cost of care, on-site day care)?

9. How did you feel about leaving your baby to return to work? Was the workplace supportive in helping you deal with these often powerful feelings? (E.g., Did they offer noontime parenting classes? Support groups?) Please describe in detail.

10. Were you breastfeeding, and did you continue after you returned to work? Did the workplace support your breastfeeding routine? If yes, please explain in detail how it did.

## PART 4. WORKING: NEW MOTHERS WORKING FOR PAY INSIDE THE HOME

1. If you work at home for pay, how old was your baby when you resumed work?

2. What is your work, and how many hours a week do you work at home?

3. Did you go back to work because you:

a. had to for economic reasons?

b. chose to for other reasons (e.g., missed professional

identity, felt the walls closing in, loved your work)? Please don't hesitate to be specific.

c. other (Please explain.)

4. What arrangements, if any, did you make for childcare?

5. What was the hardest thing about working at home as a new mom?

6. What was the best thing about working at home as a new mom?

## PART 5. NEW MOTHERS AT HOME NOT WORKING FOR PAY

1. Did you work for pay before your baby was born? If yes, what was your job, and was it inside or outside the home?

2. Sometimes the cost of childcare makes return to work prohibitive. Are you not working now because:

a. you could not afford to go back to work given childcare costs?

b. you chose not to and preferred to be at home with your baby?

c. other (Please describe.)

3. If you did work for pay before your baby was born, what if anything do you miss about your worklife now that you are at home as a full-time mother (e.g., friends, professional identity, economic independence)?

4. Even though you are not working for pay, do you have baby-sitting or child-care help? Please describe (e.g., number of hours a week: hired baby-sitter, relative, baby-sitting co-op).

5. What are the greatest rewards about being home with your baby full-time?

6. What are the greatest challenges about being at home with your baby full-time?

## PART 6. THE ONE-YEAR MILESTONE

1. For moms of one-year-olds or older: Some mothers consider the twelve-month mark a turning point. Did you have any special feelings at your child's first birthday? Please describe them if you did.

## Part 7. Second Time Around

1. How old was your first child when your second was born?

2. How did you feel during your second pregnancy about your relationship with your firstborn and the impending change?

3. Second-time moms may feel more prepared for motherhood in some of the practical aspects (diapering, bathing, etc.), but also more exhausted and overwhelmed by logistics and new emotional challenges. Did you plan for or handle your second postpartum period differently from the first? How (e.g., more help)?

4. Was there anything that especially helped you to prepare your firstborn for the arrival of a sibling (e.g., books, videos)? Please be specific.

## Part 8. Finally . . .

1. Now that you are a new mother, how long would you say the postpartum period lasts? Please circle one:

> two weeks
> six weeks
> three months
> six months
> twelve months
> more than twelve months

2. Are there any special resources or programs in your area that you think other women should know about? Please give their names, addresses, telephone numbers, and a short description of what they do.

# Index

••••••

351

# About the Author

••••••

    Sally Placksin is an award-winning nonfiction writer and writer-producer of many programs heard over public radio. She writes, hosts, and produces the highly acclaimed weekly public radio series *What's the Word?* and has produced programs for National Public Radio's *Jazz Profiles* and its *Horizon* series, including the program *Mothering the New Mother.* Her book *American Women in Jazz* is winner of an Ascap Deems Taylor Award. Ms. Placksin lives in New York City and has two children.

# CHILDCARE/PARENTING BOOKS

**Amelia D. Auckett**
*Baby Massage*
$12.95 pb (978-1-55704-022-0)

**Elissa P. Benedek, M.D., and Catherine F. Brown, M.Ed.**
*How to Help Your Child Overcome Your Divorce*
$16.95 pb (978-1-55704-461-7)

**Lucy Burney**
*Boost Your Child's Immune System*
$14.95 pb (978-1-55704-642-0)

**Sarah Cheyette, M.D.**
*Mommy, My Head Hurts: A Doctor's Guide to Your Child's Headaches*
$22.95 hc (978-1-55704-471-6)
$12.95 pb (978-1-55704-535-5)

**Anne Ford**
*Laughing Allegra*
$24.95 hc (978-1-55704-564-5)
$16.95 pb (978-1-55704-622-2)
*On Their Own*
$24.95 hc (978-1-55704-759-5)
$16.95 pb (978-1-55704-725-0)

**Lee F. Gruzen**
*Raising Your Jewish/Christian Child*
$16.95 pb (978-1-55704-414-3)

**Debra W. Haffner**
*Beyond The Big Talk: A Parent's Guide to Raising Sexually Healthy Teens*
$16.95 pb (978-1-55704-811-0)
*From Diapers to Dating: A Parent's Guide to Raising Sexually Healthy Children*
$16.95 pb (978-1-55704-810-3)

*What Every 21st-Century Parent Needs to Know: Facing Today's Challenges with Wisdom and Heart*
$24.95 hc (978-1-55704-787-8)
$16.95 pb (978-1-55704-726-7)

**Frederick Leboyer, M.D.**
*Inner Beauty, Inner Light: Yoga for Pregnant Women*
$19.95 pb (978-1-55704-315-3)

**Lynda Madaras & Area Madaras**
*The "What's Happening to My Body?" Book for Girls*
$24.95 hc (978-1-55704-768-7)
$14.99 pb (978-1-55704-764-9)
*The "What's Happening to My Body?" Book for Boys*
$24.95 hc (978-1-55704-769-4)
$14.99 pb (978-1-55704-765-6)
*My Body, My Self for Girls*
$12.99 pb (978-1-55704-766-3)
*My Body, My Self for Boys*
$12.99 pb (978-1-55704-767-0)
*Ready, Set, Grow!*
$22.00 hc (978-1-55704-587-4)
$12.99 pb (978-1-55704-565-2)
*On Your Mark, Get Set, Grow!*
$22.00 hc (978-1-55704-780-9)
$12.99 pb (978-1-55704-781-6)
*My Feelings, My Self*
$12.95 pb (978-1-55704-442-6)

**Sally Placksin**
*Mothering the New Mother, Rev. Ed.*
$19.95 pb (978-1-55704-317-7)

**Teresa Savage**
*The Ready-to-Read, Ready-to-Count Handbook*
$16.95 pb (978-1-55704-413-6)

**Dan Schaefer & Christine Lyons**
*How Do We Tell the Children?*
$14.95 pb (978-1-55704-425-9)

**Robert Schwebel, Ph.D.**
*Keep Your Kids Tobacco-Free*
$14.95 pb (978-1-55704-369-6)
*Saying No Is Not Enough, Rev. Ed.*
$16.95 pb (978-1-55704-318-4)

**Marilyn Segal, Ph.D.**
*In Time and With Love, 2nd Ed.*
$18.95 pb (978-1-55704-445-7)
*Your Child at Play: Birth to One Year, 2nd Ed.*
$18.95 pb (978-1-55704-330-6)
*Your Child at Play: One to Two Years, 2nd Ed.*
$27.95 hc (978-1-55704-335-1)
$18.95 pb (978-1-55704-331-3)
*Your Child at Play: Two to Three Years, 2nd Ed.*
$27.95 hc (978-1-55704-336-8)
$18.95 pb (978-1-55704-332-0)
*Your Child at Play: Three to Five Years, 2nd Ed.*
$27.95 hc (978-1-55704-337-5)
$16.95 pb (978-1-55704-333-7)
*Your Child at Play: Five to Eight Years*
$29.95 hc (978-1-55704-402-0)
$17.95 pb (978-1-55704-401-3)

**Eric Small**
*Kids & Sports*
$14.95 pb (978-1-55704-532-4)